The Elizabethan Club Series 7

THE LIGHT IN TROY

Imitation and Discovery in Renaissance Poetry

THOMAS M. GREENE

Yale University Press

New Haven and London

Published with assistance from the foundation established in memory of
Oliver Baty Cunningham of the Class of 1917, Yale College.

Designed by Nancy Ovedovitz and set in Baskerville type. Printed in the
United States of America by Vail-Ballou Press, Binghamton, N. Y.

Library of Congress Cataloging in Publication Data
Greene, Thomas M.
   The light in Troy.
   (Elizabethan Club series; 7)
   Includes index.
   1. Imitation (in literature)   2. European
poetry—Renaissance, 1450-1600—History and
criticism.   3. Literature, Comparative—Classical
and modern.   4. Literature, Comparative—Modern
and classical.   I. Title.   II. Series.
PN223.G7   809.1′024   81-21816
ISBN 0-300-02765-6   AACR2

10 9 8 7 6 5 4 3 2 1

For Liliane—after thirty years

Hector is dead and there's a light in Troy.
                    —*Yeats, "The Gyres"*

Contents

Acknowledgments

It is a pleasure to express my gratitude for assistance received during the writing of this book. I am indebted to Daniel Kinney for his valuable help in the preparation of chapter 9, and to George W. Pigman III, an authority on Renaissance theory of imitation, both for his published essays and for a transcript of an unpublished manuscript by Barzizza. My debt to Pigman can be traced on many pages of this study. It has also profited considerably from a judicious and attentive reading by James Mirollo. A research grant from the National Endowment for the Humanities accelerated the slow approach to conclusion. Without the support of my wife, Liliane, that conclusion might never have been reached at all.

Most of chapter 5 first appeared in *Italian Literature: Roots and Branches*, ed. G. Rimanelli and K. Atchity, and is reprinted by permission of the Yale University Press. A section of chapter 11 appeared in *Rome in the Renaissance: The City and the Myth*, ed. Paul Ramsey (Binghamton, New York: Medieval and Renaissance Texts and Studies, 1982). (Copyright 1982: Center for Medieval and Early Renaissance Studies.) In both cases I am thankful for the right to republish.

One • Introduction

This is a book about the literary uses of *imitatio* during the Renaissance era in Italy, France, and England. The imitation of models was a precept and an activity which during that era embraced not only literature but pedagogy, grammar, rhetoric, esthetics, the visual arts, music, historiography, politics, and philosophy. It was central and pervasive. The period when it flourished might be described as an era of imitation, but this description would have value only if the concept and praxis were understood to be repeatedly shifting, repeatedly redefined by the writers and artists who believed themselves to be "imitating." This is true even when the imitation of models is distinguished from the imitation of so-called nature, a distinction that could not always be maintained since some theorists, from Lodovico Dolce to Alexander Pope, held that to imitate the greatest masters was only another way of imitating nature at its highest and most characteristic. But despite all redefinitions and variations, enough remained constant to constitute a real subject, whose literary applications lead deep into the imagination of a civilization. From one perspective a good deal is known about imitations in the literature of these three countries: who modeled himself upon whom, who made certain pronouncements, who debated over which issues, even which children were taught the technique in school. But from another perspective we know very little. We cannot say with assurance why imitation flowered so brilliantly for a period and then lost its vigor; we cannot say what profound needs of the era it answered or was intended to answer; in analytic terms, we are not skilled in discussing imitative works *as* imitations. Once we have noted a so-called model or source, we are only beginning to understand the model as a constitutive element of the literary structure, an element whose dynamic presence has to be accounted for. We have not been adept as literary critics at accounting for imitative successes as against the many failures, or at recognizing the variety of strategies imitative writers pursued. The present study sets out to sketch suggestions which might solidify a little these areas of insecurity.

For these methodological suggestions to carry any authority, even for the terms used to be clear, a certain grounding in theory has seemed to me desirable. For once the positivist stage of investigation is passed, then the structures of imitative texts confront one with the enigmas of literary history, enigmas that transcend the praxis of any era and call into question the meaning of periodization, the nature of historical understanding, the precise operations of change, the diachronic dimension of language. To reflect upon one large but more or less localized phenomenon of literary history, I have discovered, is to stumble upon the central riddles of all

1

such history and to look for the bases of a future historiography. Thus chapter 2 of this study is devoted to a theoretical prolegomenon which then leads in chapter 3 to a tentative theory of imitation and its methodological correlatives. After this, theory tends to give way to history and analysis proper, but the shift is only relative since history includes the development of Renaissance imitative theory. After a glance at several ancient and a few medieval discussions of *imitatio*, there follows an extended section on Petrarch, whose written opinions on this subject and whose poetic practice on the eve of Renaissance humanism are both rich and crucial. Petrarch is and deserves to be the central figure of this book. It has occurred to me that some of my remarks might be taken to express hostility toward this infinitely complex, volatile, and egoistic genius. Let me state at the beginning my belief that he was the greatest of those who receive major treatment here. The section on Petrarch is followed by shorter chapters dealing with five later imitative poets. The texts in each instance are so rich that they could furnish, and in some cases have furnished, material for one or more books. The intent here is again to suggest orientations and to offer methodological illustrations rather than to exhaust the inexhaustible. In the case of each poet the reading of poems as imitations has been inextricable from their reading as poems. It is precisely my argument that this is inevitable, just as theory, history, methodology, and exegesis seem to me equally inextricable.

Imitatio was a literary technique that was also a pedagogic method and a critical battleground; it contained implications for the theory of style, the philosophy of history, and for conceptions of the self. In practice it led not infrequently to sterility. It led also, if less frequently, to a series of masterpieces. Situated at the core of Renaissance civilization, it can be traced through manifold forms and influences, extraordinarily complex and multifarious, which no single book could trace. What is perhaps more feasible is an attempt to discern whatever a twentieth-century scholar can make out of the uses of *imitatio* for those cultures touched by humanism, as well as its structural function in representative texts. *Imitatio* produced a vast effort to deal with the newly perceived problem of anachronism; it determined for two or three centuries the character of most poetic intertextuality; it assigned the Renaissance creator a convenient and flexible stance toward a past that threatened to overwhelm him. For these reasons and others, it deserves our interest. It can never of course be isolated in its pure workings as an ideal force, but only as it was colored by local embodiments. It needs to be seen as a European phenomenon making a markedly different imprint on each particular nation and vernacular it touched. The goal in this book will be some sort of holistic view of that phenomenon refracted by three sharply individual national traditions. No attempt has been made to be truly inclusive or conclusive. In defense of the neglect of other literatures, most notably Hispanic, I can only say that my incompetence to deal with them has saved a long book from growing longer. The decision to focus mainly on lyric poetry was made in part to facilitate exposition and provide continuity. Other studies of the same problems clearly could be written with different foci and limits.

It is true that my own reflection has been heavily influenced by the thought of the Renaissance itself. It is also true that this study is intended to give comfort to those who believe in the unity of so messy and shifty a block in time. The most acerbic polemics over the relation of a so-called Renaissance to a so-called Middle Ages are behind us, although the question in some form will doubtless prove to be long-lived. No informed scholar today can blind himself or herself to the powerful lines of continuity binding the two eras; if many of these lie outside the boundaries of this study, the omission corresponds to no desire to deny them. Still, my work began and ended with the belief that to speak of a civilization nameable as "the Renaissance" is a reasonable act. Indeed this study aims to enlarge the grounds of this rationality.

One obvious point of reference, particularly on the Continent, is the will of Renaissance cultures to distinguish themselves diacritically from their immediate past. The Renaissance, if it did nothing else that was new, chose to open a polemic against what it called the Dark Ages. The ubiquitous imagery of disinterment, resurrection, and renascence needed a death and burial to justify itself; without the myth of medieval entombment, its imagery, which is to say its self-understanding, had no force. The creation of this myth was not a superficial occurrence. It expressed a belief in change and loss, change from the immediate past and loss of a remote, prestigious past that might nonetheless be resuscitated. "The men of the Renaissance," wrote Franco Simone, "saw a rupture where earlier there had been a belief in a smooth development, and from this rupture they took the origins of their enthusiasm and the certitude of their originality."[1] A civilization discovered its cultural paths by the light behind it of a vast holocaust, and it used this mythical light as the principle of its own energy. It made its way through ruins by the effulgence cast in their destruction, finding in privation the secret of renewal, just as Aeneas, sailing westward from the ashes of his city, carried with him the flame that had consumed it burning before his Penates.

Two • *Historical Solitude*

The specific imitative structures found in literary texts of the Renaissance serve both to distinguish it as a period and to align it in a long, disorderly history of western intertextuality. If the Renaissance era (very roughly: in Italy, Petrarch to Tasso; in France, Lemaire de Belges to d'Aubigné; in England, Wyatt to Milton) produced structures that for all their diversity reveal certain common patterns, the cultural pressures and impulses behind them need first to be considered. If some of these pressures appear to be, in our tradition, pervasive and continuous, this continuity is itself an important context for the understanding of a specific, finite phenomenon. The chapter that follows attempts to sketch both a historical and theoretical prolegomenon to the study of *imitatio*, attributing to the Renaissance text a privileged but circumscribed role in a vaster story. It takes as its point of departure a world artist writing a little before the decisive changes occurred which would determine the subject of this study.

1

In the twenty-sixth canto of the *Paradiso*, Dante meets the soul of Adam. The poet is full of questions for the patriarch, who is aware of them without needing to hear them expressed and who goes on to answer four. The longest of his replies concerns the language first spoken in Eden. It was a language, Adam says, that quickly disappeared, well before the building of the tower of Babel.

> La lingua ch'io parlai fu tutta spenta
>   innanzi che all'ovra inconsummabile
>   fosse la gente di Nembròt attenta.   [*Par.* 26.124–26][1]
> [The tongue I spoke was all extinct before Nimrod's race gave their mind to the unaccomplished task.]

Adam's denial of authority and permanence to the first of all languages, his own first language, reverses an affirmation made in Dante's earlier work, the *De vulgari eloquentia*, where it had expressly been stated that the Adamite language remained current until Babel, and even after Babel, among the Hebrews. This denial also omits reference to that language, Latin, which the same treatise had excluded from linguistic mutability and praised for its enduring continuity. The reversal of the *Paradiso* seems to stem from a deeper sense that all human things are capricious and unstable, subject as they are to the alterations of astral influence and historical vogue.

4

ché nullo effetto mai razionabile,
  per lo piacere uman che rinovella
  seguendo il cielo, sempre fu durabile.
Opera naturale è ch'uom favella;
  ma cosí o cosí, natura lascia
  poi fare a voi secondo che v'abbella.   [*Par.* 26.127–32]
[For no product whatever of reason—since human choice is renewed with the course of
heaven—can last forever. It is a work of nature that man should speak, but whether in
this way or that nature then leaves you to follow your own pleasure.]

To attempt to create a language free of caprice and free of the interference of the
stars ("il cielo") would approximate the folly of a Nimrod; it would involve an
"ovra inconsummabile." Nature, the source of language, leaves man free to make
an endless series of linguistic choices too unpredictable to be called judgments and
perhaps too determined to be called art. Nature dissociates herself from the
aimlessness of human whim, and yet as Adam goes on to recall his own experience
of linguistic transience, he finds a natural analogy to carry its instability:

Pria ch'i' scendessi all' infernale ambascia,
  I s'appellava in terra il sommo bene
  onde vien la letizia che mi fascia;
e *El* si chiamò poi; e ciò convene,
  ché l'uso de' mortali è come fronda
  in ramo, che sen va e altra vene.   [*Par.* 26.133–38]
[Before I descended to the anguish of Hell the Supreme Good from whom comes the
joy that swathes me was named *I* on earth, and later He was called *El*; and that is fitting,
for the usage of mortals is like a leaf on a branch, which goes and another comes.]

This image of the transient leaf that issues from a soul bound in ecstasy
("letizia") would sound in any other context with a note of sorrow, intensifying the
accent of regret that would normally be present in the participle "spenta" at the
opening of Adam's little disquisition. That first Adamite language had been
extinguished or had burnt itself out with a loss of ardor and energy that from a less
celestial perspective might emerge as momentarily tragic. So the loss of the leaf on
the branch might appear tragic, the loss of a beauty that is perhaps hinted at
punningly in the adapted verb "abbella."[2] The entanglement of mere fashion,
astral determination, creative energy, and verbal loveliness, however, fails to
concern Adam; he is *bound* in joy, protected from an aimlessness that discovers,
makes, admires, and abandons. His joy, unlike the reader's, is unaffected by his
imagery.

Despite this joy, Adam's discourse remains a classic statement of a perception
that has troubled men since Plato: the scandal of the mutability, the ungrounded
contingency of language. Dante's image of the leaf that falls and is replaced echoes
a well-known meditation in Horace's *Ars poetica* (ll. 60–72) on the brief life span of
the word. There is something like an analogous recognition in Chaucer (*Troilus
and Criseyde* 2.22ff.; 5.1793ff.), a recognition that became a cliché in Tudor and

Stuart England.[3] To cite a particularly bleak example, Samuel Daniel closes his powerful "Defence of Ryme" with a warning against the coinage or importation into English of alien words, and then concludes with grim despair: "But this is but a Character of that perpetuall revolution which we see to be in all things that never remaine the same: and we must herein be content to submit our selves to the law of time, which in few yeeres will make al that for which we now contend *Nothing*."[4] We meet the same recognition in the first book of Castiglione's *Cortegiano*, which, echoing again the Horatian organic image, evokes the pathos of noble, forgotten words that wither and die, a loss felt as a special case of that larger fragility inherent in civilization which it is the work's deepest purpose to dramatize. A quieter formulation appears in Montaigne, who wrote quite simply: "Our language flows every day out of our hands."[5] The tone in Montaigne is characteristically serene, but for most medieval and Renaissance writers, the recognition of linguistic mutability was a source of authentic anxiety.

The fear of the premodern writer that his temporal dialect would become utterly indecipherable has not yet been confirmed. But we can discern in that particular and acute distress one form of a vaguer and deeper concern that appears to be permanently human. Plato in the *Cratylus* is tempted by a conception of uncentered linguistic flux, associating the etymology of *alêtheia* (truth) with *ále* (wandering) (421b) and the etymology of *onoma* (name) with words suggesting motion and flux (436e). But the *Cratylus*, deeply ambivalent as it is and perhaps ironic, also testifies to Plato's felt need for an extralinguistic grounding of the word. That need is manifest in Plato's effort to root the phonic structure of signifiers within what he apparently considered the natural associations of verbal sounds. The same need is manifest in the persistent Renaissance belief, lingering at least as late as Jean Bodin, that Hebrew was a "natural language" whose names for things corresponded to their true nature.[6] The need is still manifest in Noam Chomsky's universal grammar, which posits on somewhat shaky conceptual bases a deep mental structure common to all human beings. The pages of George Steiner's *After Babel* record the recurrent quest through western history for a fixed linguistic ground, a *Grund des Wortes*, which begins with Genesis and moves down through Paracelsus, Böhme, and Kepler, to end with Walter Benjamin and Chomsky. Saint Augustine, despite his unbridgeable division between our words and the Word, also belongs finally to this tradition. Its existence needs no elaborate explanation. The quest for a transcendental or universal authority for the word is so recurrent an impulse because without it we seem condemned to the mere accidents of usage, a pure linguistic contingency that divides us from each other and from our forefathers.

But fully to confront the anxiety of linguistic mutability, I think that first one has to see it as synecdochic. And fully to understand that synecdochic relationship, one is led back again to Dante and to the humanism of the quattrocento which in this area he can be said to have anticipated. In the *Paradiso*, the impermanence of language is associated with the greater impermanence of all human constructs: "nullo effetto mai razionabile . . . sempre fu durabile." In the *De vulgari eloquentia*, the same synecdochic conclusion is drawn; language is represented as that most visible element of a larger phenomenon embracing all culture:

> Cum igitur omnis nostra loquela, preter illam homini primo concreatum a Deo, sit a nostro beneplacito reparata post confusionem illam, que nil aliud fuit quam prioris oblivio, et homo sit instabilissimum atque variabilissimum animal, nec durabilis nec continua esse potest, sed sicut alia que nostra sunt, puta mores et habitus, per locorum temporumque distantias variari oportet. . . . Nam, si alia nostra opera perscrutemur, multo magis discrepare videmur a vetustissimis concivibus nostris quam a coetaneis perlonginquis.
> [Thus, since all of our dialects (with the exception of that one created by God along with the first man) were refashioned according to our pleasure after that confusion, which was nothing other than forgetfulness of the former language, and since man is the most unstable and variable animal, the language could not either endure or be uniform, but, like other of our characteristics, such as manners and fashions, it necessarily differs with the change of time or place. . . . For if we look closely at our other activities, we would seem to be more at variance from our fellow-countrymen of very ancient times than from our contemporaries at a great distance from us.][7]

This passage helps to define the nature of that mutability which the *Commedia* at once evokes and dismisses. The temporality of language is here linked with the temporality of human customs and styles—"mores et habitus"—and with that of other human works—"alia nostra opera" (translated above as "characteristics"). Aristide Marigo suggests that "opera" should be construed primarily, though not exclusively, as extant architectural structures dating from antiquity, since these would be the most visible products of ancient workmanship in the trecento and would have furnished strong contrasts with the style of medieval buildings.[8] If we follow this plausible suggestion, we must see in Dante one of the first medieval men to draw this contrast. The phrase "l'uso de' mortali" thereby gains a deeper resonance. Dante was evoking through Adam's voice the mutability not merely of specific words and dialects but of styles, the "mores et habitus" of culture, those styles by which civilizations in their temporality can be distinguished from one another.[9] It is doubtless significant that Dante could face the unqualified instability of this most variable animal's culture only at the end of his career. The earlier treatise does except the stable continuities of Latin and Hebrew. Only in the last poem, from the vantage of the eighth sphere, could he bear to acknowledge without exception the absolutely ungrounded historicity of the word, the element of style—we would say the historicity of the signifier. He saw this and he felt a disquiet which is a valid accompaniment to the perception. Both the perception and the feeling would become constituent experiences of the humanist Renaissance. In his exemplary anticipation of that movement, Dante was protohumanist.

2

The disquiet stemming from the historicity of the signifier adumbrates a pathos that is translinguistic, that embraces "mores et habitus," the historicity of culture. For Petrarch, a generation after Dante, the intuition of this pathos was no longer redeemable; it was tragic. It bespoke not only the impermanence but the solitude of history. This was a solitude which Petrarch lived out existentially, as estrangement from the ancients who were dearer to him—in the images he created of them—than all but a few of his contemporaries. The perception of cultural as well as linguistic distance, glimpsed briefly in the *De vulgari eloquentia*, became for Petrarch a certainty and an obsession; the discovery of antiquity and simultaneously the remoteness of antiquity made of Petrarch a double exile, neither Roman nor modern, so that he became in his own eyes a living anachronism. "I am happier," he wrote, "with the dead than with the living,"[10] but of course he was no more truly happy with his ghostly and imperfect intuitions of Virgil and Cicero than he was with his own Avignon and Milan. We have only to read his letters to his ghosts to feel the sorrow of his converse.

The humanists of the quattrocento did not suffer so intimately or so intensely from the knowledge of loss, partly because they devoted so much of their careers to the repossession of the lost. But the pathos is unmistakably there in Bruni, in Valla, in Alberti, in Poliziano, to speak only of the greatest.[11] Moreover it is in the work of the same humanists, most notably Valla and Poliziano, that the intuition of cultural historicity is definitively documented and codified. As the new science of philology, studying systematically the process of linguistic change, was firmly established, as this change was recognized to reflect the profound social and spiritual life of a people, as the concept of period style emerged from the new learning with growing clarity along with the corollary concept of anachronism, then the true problematic of historical knowledge—and literary knowledge—had to be faced. If a remote text is composed in a language for which the present supplies only a treacherous glossary, and if it is grounded in a lost concrete specificity never fully recoverable, then the tasks of reading, editing, commenting, translating, and imitating become intricately problematized—and these were the tasks that preoccupied the humanists. There was of course pride in the acquired learning and the skill that dealt with these problems: there is a magnificent and fierce arrogance in Valla's *Declamatio* on the Donation of Constantine as there is a more subdued arrogance in Pico's *De hominis dignitate*. But there is also an anger in the humanists' antimedieval polemic that is not purely perfunctory, since for them it was precisely the crime of the Middle Ages to have stood between the modern age and that which it hypostatized as lost.

There is a revealing remark by Poliziano in a letter to Pico about the honor due to philologists:

> Not only must they not be scorned who, however painstaking and scrupulous, fail to reconstruct that which fleeting oblivion—as Varro says—has taken from our forefath-

ers; but rather all the more worthy of eternal honors are those who in whatever degree have succeeded in understanding things so remote and forgotten ("assequi tam remota tamque oblivia").[12]

Poliziano's verb "assequi" could mean either "to pursue" or "to comprehend" or "to attain after great striving," and all three of these meanings seem to overlap and to challenge each other in his letter as in the entire humanist enterprise. Did one—does one?—attain the remote and the forgotten after great striving, or does one only pursue? Literally for a millennium before Poliziano, no one had achieved his philological precision, as no non-Greek had achieved the fluency of his written Greek; no one knew better than he the remoteness of the remote. His quiet remark to Pico registers his pride in an attainment that he and his fellow strivers understood to be honorable because threatened by impossibility. "There is no single book of Roman antiquity. . . , " he admitted, "which we professors fully understand."[13] The mingled courage and despair of that confession recall the calmly shattering comment of Valla: "Not only has no one been able to speak Latin for many centuries, but no one has even known how to read it."[14] Poliziano, considered not as a poet but as philologist, embodies with singular clarity that rage for contact with the past which remains unblinded by its partial success and recognizes any mitigation of its estrangement as an achievement.

Humanist pride and humanist despair emerge really as two faces of a single coin. The satisfaction of learning is repeatedly subverted by the confrontation with its tragic limits. Here is the architect and scholar Fra Giocondo writing to Lorenzo de' Medici.

> The ancient appearance of the city of Rome, most excellent Lorenzo, is changed to such an extent, and its place names so forgotten, that we can scarcely understand what we read in the books of the ancients, and often those very scholars who profess themselves to be best informed concerning antiquity, prove to know less than others, since the authors whose writings have transmitted learning to us are so faulty and corrupt ("mendosi et corrupti") that if they themselves were to be reborn through some Varronian palingenesis, they would not recoginze themselves. But even if these authors were not corrupt, *they would not sufficiently fill our need unless we could see the things which they saw.* (my italics)[15]

This text is characteristic in several respects: in the intimate relationship it postulates between the written work and the encompassing civilization (place names, the physical appearance of the city); in the hypothesis of rebirth, here played with only to be denied; in the sharp distinction between reading ("legimus") and understanding ("intelligere"); most significantly, in the awareness revealed at the end of the passage of inevitable hermeneutic anachronism. The physical transmission of correct texts is not enough; the final enemy of historical knowledge is not simply the carelessness of scribes and clerks but history itself. Not to have seen the place, not to possess the names, constitute fatal disqualifications for the belated interpreter. The transmission of knowledge, which was the humanist vocation, is perceived as inevitably blocked. Yet Fra Giocondo is not actually tempted to give up the effort.

It was the riddle of hermeneutic anachronism that possessed Valla. How is one to follow Aristotle if one cannot read him in his own language? And if in fact many things can be said elegantly in Greek for which no adequate Latin expressions exist? And if in any case the Latin versions we possess are wretched? And if, still worse, the modern audience is incapable of reading Latin properly? And if one reads Aristotle through the eyes of Avicenna and Averroës, who knew no Latin and insufficient Greek? The concrete knowable actuality of the text-in-itself fades away behind a series of distorting lenses so insidious that the firm possession of Aristotle's Greek becomes a quest requiring intellectual heroism. Some of those distorting lenses no longer baffle our modern eyes. But the advances of latter-day philology have not truly dispelled the radical problem of anachronistic reading Valla insisted on with all the energy of his formidable mind. We have not yet put to rest the problematic first lucidly and self-consciously exposed in the fifteenth century, neither as philologists nor as men and women living within a history. We have not conjured the riddle of historical knowledge, which must remain in some degree anachronistic.

The problem of historical understanding is doubtless even more complex than Valla and his contemporary humanists understood. As individuals and as communities, we learn who we are by means of private or collective memory. An amnesiac is considered sick and unfortunate because he doesn't know who he is. When he recovers his memory, he recovers his identity. Communities feel the same need. When they suffer from the unavailability of written history, they invent myths to define their origin, which is to say their identity, as tribe and nation, and belief in these myths persists of course even when writing becomes possible. Not to remember is intolerable because a past is formative: visibly or obscurely, it shapes us, filling our names with content and setting the conditions of our freedom. Yet neither as individuals nor as communities can we remember all of that past which has made us what we are and has bequeathed us those instruments, institutions, and languages which allow us the chance to survive. We cannot remember all as individuals because our memories are mercifully selective, because the critical years of infancy are somehow blocked from retrospection and because most of the formative past preceded our birth. We cannot remember all as communities because much that is formative has been written down inaccurately or not at all and because the language of past observers diverges to some degree from our own. Thus we are formed by a past that is slipping into indistinctness, playing roles whose rationales are fading, moving into a future with leaking signifiers. At the close of his essay "The Way to Language" (Der Weg zur Sprache) Heidegger quotes Wilhelm von Humboldt.

> Time will often introduce into language what it did not possess before. Then the old shell is filled with a new meaning, the old coinage conveys something different, the old laws of syntax are used to hint at a differently graduated sequence of ideas. All this is a

lasting fruit of a people's literature, and within literature especially of poetry and philosophy.[16]

One would want only to write "nearly always" in place of "often." The signifier is rooted in the activity of a society which alters, but the word in its apparent stability fails to respond sensitively to that alteration. Beneath the apparent constancy of the *verbum*, the *res* of experience is sliding into new conformations with the immense complexity of history.

3

The problem of linguistic drift has been radicalized by Jacques Derrida, whose philosophy of language extends still further the groundless instability of the word affirmed by Dante's Adam. Derrida may well extend it as far as it can be taken. In the representative essay "Signature évènement contexte," he describes the word as an orphan ("orpheline"), cut off necessarily and inevitably from its original progenitor, context, and intended meaning, and goes on to coin the term *itérabilité* for the incipient drift structurally inherent in all language, the drift not only from its original speaker and social context but also from its original referent and signified: "Cette dérive essentielle tenant à l'ecriture comme structure itérative, coupée de toute responsabilité absolue, de la *conscience* comme autorité de dernière instance, orpheline et séparée dès sa naissance de l'assistance de son père."[17] Derrida's coinage, *itérabilité*, depends on the derivation of the Latin verb *iterare*, "to repeat," from the Sanskrit *itara*, meaning "other": the repetition of a word or a text for Derrida involves its alteration, its wandering free from any home base, and its conceivable grafting on to a new text. Dante of course would have insisted on the writer's responsibility for his own work, but in his stress on the radical instability and variability of language, he could be said to anticipate the rupture Derrida sees between sign and context as structurally necessary to the sign, a rupture extending to the eventual loss of a determinate signified. "Cette unité de la forme signifiante ne se constitue que par son itérabilité, par la possibilité d'être répétée en l'absence non seulement de son 'référent,' ce qui va de soi, mais en l'absence d'un signifié déterminé ou de l'intention de signification actuelle."[18]

The implications of Derrida's thought lead in many directions, but it is worth lingering on this central problem and its consequences for the reading of literary works. We are faced with the historical frailty of the word and its slippages of signification stated in their most extreme form. There is no easy way to deny this errancy of word and text, but as we reflect on it we are obliged to ask ourselves, What are the properties of language that resist drift sufficiently to enable us to use it at all? Absolute and immediate iterability, after all, would make language into a nonlanguage; if each repetition involved a total transformation, a word as such could not exist. Communication would always fail. Even if the word survived for a generation, no tradition would be conceivable, certainly no imitation. Before examining the practice of imitation, we shall find it useful to consider how it is possible at all, to consider in other words what are the limits of historical solitude. What is it that permits cultures to communicate across time, even to survive, if in fact language is so radically unstable as Derrida argues?

In the search for a reply, one place to begin would be that twenty-sixth canto of the *Paradiso* already known to us. It is in fact a richer but also more problematic meditation on language than I have yet indicated. At the opening, Dante the pilgrim is subjected to a kind of oral examination on the nature and object of love. He begins his first answer with an elaborate reference to God as the ground of all his writing on this subject.

> Lo ben che fa contenta questa corte,
> Alfa ed O è di quanta scrittura
> mi legge Amore o lievemente o forte.   [*Par.* 26.16–18]
> [The good that satisfies this court is alpha and omega of all the scripture that love reads
> [dictates] to me in tones loud or low.]

This is a metaphor that praises the divine Source and End of inspired discourse while valorizing the poet's own writing—and by implication all writing of similar inspiration and similar obedience—as accessible to the intervention of the original Word on earth, in time.

But the metaphor also valorizes obliquely a third element of the linguistic act: not only the "Sommo Bene" and not only the writing directed toward it, but also the elemental signs, the actual letters that composed the record of the incarnate Word's appearance in history. The metaphorical equivalence between the godhead and the letters Alpha and Omega not only points to the supreme circularity of Source and End; it not only exalts human language in its rudimentary alphabetical constituent; it also dramatizes an enduring continuity of linguistic usage and communication through time. In endowing the mortal writer with the capacity to signify divine truths, God has permitted the survival of his very signifiers and their elements across the millennia, from well before the time of Christ up to the present. This implicit demonstration of continuity is strengthened by the appeal to ancient textual authority—*autorità*—made by Dante during his examination and later echoed approvingly by his questioner, Saint John (*authoritadi*, line 47). The prestige accorded these terms in medieval thought is reenforced by a cognate term applied in this same canto to the voice of God addressing Moses, as reported by scripture: "la voce del verace *autore*" (line 40). The author (*auctor, actor, autor*) at a medieval university was a writer whose work had commanded respect for so many centuries as to have become an authority (*autorità*), to be read as an *authentic* source of knowledge. The term *autorità* and its cognates imply that unflawed capacity for patriarchal communication and instruction through time which few if any medieval men perceived as problematized by history. The faith in authoritative continuity, both verbal and doctrinal, clearly rested on the belief in God as the ground and goal, alpha and omega, of human language.

Yet this divine grounding does not suffice to sustain the stability of any given word or any language, as we learn from Adam before the close of this same canto. Authority from one perspective may be absolute, but from another it is built on the drifting sand of the perishable *voce*. The reader is left with a tension that is close to an aporia. One way to resolve it would be to study not the linguistic theory but the poetic praxis of the poem and the canto. Adam's statement of the pure conventionality of the signifier has already been quoted.

> Opera naturale è ch'uom favella;
>   ma cosí o cosí, natura lascia
>   poi fare a voi secondo che v'abbella.   [*Par.* 26.130–32]
> [It is a work of nature that man should speak, but whether in this way or that nature then leaves you to follow your own pleasure.]

This doctrine of conventionality can be traced back to Aristotle through Aquinas (*Summa Theol.* II, II, q. 85, 1) and Boethius. But in Dante's formulation, one alien word draws attention: the verb *abbella*. This verb was unknown in any Italian dialect, and Dante evidently coined it from the Provençal. In fact the reader of the *Commedia* has already met its root form (*abellis*) in the speech of Arnaut Daniel in the *Purgatorio*:

> Tan m'abellis vostre cortes deman
>   qu' ieu no me puesc ni voill a vos cobrire.   [*Purg.* 26.140–41]
> [So much does your courteous question please me that I neither can]
> nor would conceal myself from you.

Abellis/abbella literally means "pleases," although there may be a punning secondary meaning in Adam's discourse: to become or to appear beautiful. This little example is worth pausing over because it fails to fit comfortably either of the two linguistic destinies we have already distinguished. It does not on the one hand conform to a doctrine of absolute semiotic continuity excluding all slippage and drift of significations from a millennial *traditio* grounded in the one Word. For here, in this half-punning adaptation and partial recasting of a foreign verb, that precise kind of slippage is occurring which undermines all fixity of signification, a slippage which, in Oderisi da Gubbio's phrase, "changes name because it changes place" ("muta nome perché muta lato"—*Purg.* 11.102). And yet on the other hand this slippage does not proceed from pure accident or astral influence or popular whim; it proceeds from the tasteful, perhaps playful, in any case carefully manipulated appropriation of a word whose earlier capacity for a certain noble courtesy has already been deftly established. The relation between *abellis/abbella* is not analogous to that between *I/El*. The leaf has not fallen from the branch to be replaced by an altogether new one. An errancy is taking place that is not purely random or destructive because it is observable within a specific cultural–historical situation and under the control of a self-conscious artistic intelligence.

This emergence of a linguistic *tertium quid* in our examination of a single word becomes more striking if we consider a slightly larger unit, that image of the leaf upon a branch, which seems to carry the ephemerality of the vocable. For this image is not of course in the conventional sense "original" with Dante; it depends on a subtext from a well-known passage of Horace's *Ars poetica*.

Ut silvae foliis pronos mutantur in annos,
prima cadunt; ita verborum vetus interit aetas,
et iuvenum ritu florent modo nata vigentque.
debemur morti nos nostraque: . . .
multa renascentur quae iam cecidere, cadentque
quae nunc sunt in honore vocabula, si volet usus,
quem penes arbitrium est et ius et norma loquendi.   [60–63, 70–72]
[As forests change their leaves with each year's decline, and the earliest drop off: so with words, the old race dies, and, like the young of human kind, the newborn bloom and thrive. We are doomed to death—we and all things ours. . . . Many terms that have fallen out of use shall be born again, and those shall fall that are now in repute, if Usage so will it, in whose hands lie the judgment, the right and rule of speech.][19]

These lines constitute one of the few surrenders to powerful feeling throughout Horace's epistle, and the eruption of this feeling is all the more remarkable because it is irrelevant to what immediately precedes and follows. Briefly the pathos overflows its argument, but by the end of the digression, the pathos gives way to the reassurance of the classical norm. Usage, "usus," the caprice of linguistic fashion, is first presented as the source of destruction but then is revalorized as the "norma loquendi," the source of propriety, judgment, and decorum. Dante interweaves the Horatian image into a fabric that transforms it, dropping the appeal to a norm, radicalizing the sense of transience, extending the loss of the word to the loss of an entire language, and setting the statement of transience in tension with a statement of divine grounding. Yet the image does undeniably call attention to its Horatian derivation: the Italian "uso de' mortali" corresponds to the Latin "usus," just as "fronda" corresponds to "foliis."[20] This very introduction of a historical passage, a cultural flow from one text and one civilization to another, qualifies the thematic argument: the human signifier may rise and fall with time, but its destiny is not totally aleatory. It finds a provisional ground in culture and cultural history. The ceaseless drift of the word, the utter instability of human artifacts asserted already in *De vulgari eloquentia*, proves, in the case of this little example, to have limits, boundaries that are not metaphysical but temporary and fabricated, not of theory but of praxis.

Dante's text thus allows us to discern not two but three incipient versions of linguistic history, and it is the third version, nonthematized but dramatized, that is the most helpful in dealing with the problem of Derrida's iterability, the question how linguistic alteration permits language to function at all. What is the structural element that informs the word and the text with whatever stability they succeed in achieving? The word for *drift* in Derrida's French is *dérive*. Taking our cue from his etymological play, we can note that the cognate French verb *dériver* possesses two meanings almost opposed to each other: on the one hand, "to float

aimlessly," but on the other hand "to take one's origin, to derive." Derrida himself
unwittingly points to this second meaning when he derives his coinage from a
Latin word derived in turn from a Sanskrit word, thus demonstrating a verbal
capacity for millennial continuity.[21] How are we to understand this continuity, in
view of his theory? I submit that it results from the progressive, concrete, and
incomplete experience through which the word installs itself in a culture as in an
individual mind. Time may be the element in which words are eroded but it is also
the element in which, for each of us, they acquire accumulatively their being and
their wealth. We understand any usage of a word as the last in a series which
possesses coherence; the word's relative stability *now* derives from the stability of
that series, just as our feeling of its gathering potency grows out of that series'
provocative complexity. The origin of the series, our first encounter with the word,
is likely to be lost to us. But the word contains its problematic power because it
derives from a flexible but continuous chain of concrete occasions that we organize
automatically as we speak and listen.

Benveniste has argued in a well-known essay that language is the source of
human subjectivity because "it permits each speaker to appropriate the entire
language in designating himself as *I*."[22] He goes on to show how much of a
language—deictic pronouns, adverbs, adjectives, verb tenses, and so on—is defined
only in reference to the specific utterance in which these elements appear and to the
speaker of that utterance. But in an ulterior sense all words, whether or not they are
ostensibly deictic, are understood in any given utterance as positing a present
moment, as *emergent* from a past without a beginning which the speaker and
listener separately construct at the moment of utterance. Whatever the problematic
relation between signifier and signified, that relation is carried along in a linear
progression which has a history, a history both for the individual and for his
language group. At either level, the full history cannot be known and remains a
construct; even the linguist, Benveniste admits in another paper, is reduced to
using his intuition in reconstructing derivations. The derivation at both levels is
ultimately a kind of etiological myth, an explanation of how the given word has
come to be what for us it is, but it is a myth which provides that measure of stability
enabling language to function.

It was one of Wilhelm von Humboldt's profoundest insights that linguistic
study must necessarily deal with a "midpoint," an insight that rendered obsolete
the eighteenth-century quest for linguistic origins.

> Neither a nation nor a language among those known to us may be termed original.
> Since each has received material transmitted by earlier generations from a prehistoric
> antiquity unknown to us, . . . intellectual activity . . . is constantly directed toward
> something already given; this activity is not purely creative but rather modifies the
> heritage.[23]

We always write and speak "in the middest," and we are able to tolerate this
fundamental linguistic ignorance because we habitually build up significations in

time that carry so to speak their causal structures with them. The word carries with it a story of its development, its evolution. I shall refer to this process of creating signifying constructs as "etiology" and instances of the process as "etiologies." To point to this etiological basis of language is not to challenge its ultimate ground-lessness and historicity. These are reaffirmed. But the contingency is perceived as one element within the word, a force for alteration playing against a stabilizing, retrospective fabrication that can be studied and described. Out of that interplay between drift and evolution, between *dérive* and *dérivation*, each word acquires its unique itinerary.

Just as an amnesiac recovers his identity with his memory, so it is with words; we learn them as they acquire a past for us. This is true even though a future experience of a word may prove to be in certain respects novel, just as a person's identity may be altered tomorrow by an exercise of freedom. Even a nonce word, a coinage by Rabelais or Lewis Carroll or Joyce, depends on our recognition of familiar fragments freshly combined. Orphaned the word may be, but its progress through space and time doesn't really resemble the helpless errancy of some Dickensian child-hero; it acquires a kind of ubiquitous foster parent in the presence of the maternal culture that has adopted it. Without our cultural and personal derivation, our etiology, the sound of the word has no meaning. Given the etiology, the word acquires a kind of ballast and tendency in its drift.

4

The description of the itinerary of the single word is the province of the linguist and the lexicographer. We as students of literature are interested in chains of words—images, sentences, passages, texts. In our province, the interplay between change and stability can be located most clearly in a work's intertextuality—the structural presence within it of elements from earlier works. Since a literary text that draws nothing from its predecessors is inconceivable, intertextuality is a universal literary constant. Tynjanov and Jakobson pointed out in the twenties that "Pure synchronism is an illusion, since every synchronic system has a past and a future as inseparable structural elements of the system."[24] This is clearly true, but it must be added that some systems, some texts, make greater structural use of these elements than others; some insist on their own intertextual composition, but not all. The *Aeneid* does but not the *Iliad*; the *Orlando Furioso* does but not the *Chanson de Roland*. When a literary work does this, when it calls to the reader's attention its own deliberate allusiveness, it can be said to be affirming its own historicity, its own involvement in disorderly historical process. Allusions in these cases might be regarded as secondary etiologies, constructions of meaning connecting the past to the present. The healthy interplay of linguistic change and stability requires these shared constructions.[25]

Something like this interplay occurs in all texts that can be said to possess historical self-consciousness, texts that manipulate or dramatize or incorporate their intertextual makeup as a constitutive structural element, texts that reflect an awareness of their historicity and build upon it. The *Commedia* was perhaps the first text in our millennium to possess something like a genuine historical self-consciousness. If we examine the intertextuality of medieval poems before Dante, if we consider particularly the estrangement from antiquity they reflect, then we do not find any historical construct because the awareness of estrangement was very restricted. No one before Dante could have described Virgil as hoarse from long silence because no one was capable of measuring his own anachronistic distance from Virgil. No one, so far as I can judge, neither Abelard nor Bernard of Chartres nor John of Salisbury, was fully sensitive to the fact of radical cultural change that would be glimpsed by Dante and then faced in all its overwhelming force by Renaissance humanism. Thus the use of elements from Virgil and Ovid found in the *Roman de Thebes* or the *Roman d'Eneas* does not provide an etiological construct to deal with cultural discontinuity, to connect subtext with surface text; they fail to provide this because they fail to register the discontinuity. They lack historical self-consciousness just as the *Iliad* lacks it.

We know from many of Dante's writings the construct by means of which he dealt with his historical estrangement from the Augustan Age: the universalist myth which assigned a parity to empire and church, which saw imperial Rome as completed by Christian Rome, which saw in ancient poetry a set of norms for all poetry, and which saw in modern Italian only an extension of Latin. Dante refused to see his historical estrangement as inevitable or providential or accidental; he saw it as shameful, as a token of moral decline, and he represented the character Virgil as hoarse from long silence because he thought that Christendom had unforgivably neglected its sources of wisdom. For him the failure to repeat ancient history was a tragedy of sin, and his own poem, his own language were calculated to reverse this tragedy and to repair the gap. Thus the imitations of Virgil and Horace and other Latin poets in the *Commedia* must be read as fulfillments of a superior historical necessity that actual history has disgracefully betrayed. For Dante, all of that history was played out within a single cultural and linguistic unity—*Latinitas*.

Dante's imitations then are justified in context by a theory of history; they depend not so much on a primary etiology of the word as on a secondary etiology of the image, a visible construct that sketches a certain itinerary through time. We are made aware of an emergence out of a past, and the itinerary concluding with this emergence is a myth that imposes a kind of order on the passage of centuries. The historically self-conscious text is that temporary shelter where the word finds a kind of lodging in its errancy through time, because the text assigns it a history, an identity, that solace its orphanhood. This history can never be complete and it can never be in any verifiable sense accurate, but it will provide that fabrication of a provisional source which the word needs to function. When an allusion is organic rather than ornamental, when it is structurally necessary, then it begins to sketch a miniature myth about its own past, or rather about its emergence from that past.

When in other words intertextuality becomes self-conscious, it tends to become etiological, and we are able to analyze the function of the subtext in terms of a specific retrospective vision.

Most texts since Dante do in varying degrees construct implicit versions of history. We need to consider further the structure of these versions. The *word* as an etiological construct has a dual structure. There will always be a prehistory, whose origins fray out into the unknown, and there will be a more or less dramatic emergence out of the prehistory. The intertextual *allusion* has a comparable duality; it contains an emergence out of a history which, in the cases of many topoi, can be extremely long and complex, but which in certain echoes of a specific text can be short and apparently simple. It could be argued that the structure of the allusion is fundamentally different from the word's because the source of the subtext can be known. The allusion after all qua allusion does specify some concrete, knowable origin in the form of the so-called source to which it points. Whatever the iterability of the passage, whatever the wound inflicted by the signature, the signed anterior text remains a public fact unlike the unknowable origins of the single word. This distinction has to be granted. But the allusion that concerns us is one that has already a historical itinerary behind it, one already subject to an estranging iterability, one which has to be felt as other because it reaches us from a remote culture. The etiology of the allusion, like the etiology of the word, originates in ignorance, in the inevitable slippage of understanding that divides us from our past, and not least the past we revere and use. The past from which writer and reader derive an etiology will remain in some measure anachronized; the projection of a prehistory stretching out behind the allusion cannot escape the vulnerability of a construct. The security of the emergent usage depends on a fabrication that is always open to question, as for example Dante's vision of a universal *Latinitas* is preeminently open to question.

Derrida insists on the absence in all writing of the original context, which includes the intention of the supposed author. "Pour qu'un contexte soit exhaustivement déterminable . . . , il faudrait au moins que l'intention consciente soit totalement présente et actuellement transparente à elle-meme et aux êtres."[26] Since the full intention behind any given text is unknowable, the original context is necessarily subject to loss: "Il n'y a que des contextes sans aucun centre d'ancrage absolu."[27] The force of history is a force that deracinates, a "force of rupture" that privileges no context and blurs all intention. The utterance, like the breath of fame in Dante, changes its resonance as it changes place and time: "muta nome perché muta lato." From this perspective, an etiological allusion fabricates a context that is itself of course subject to alteration, distortion, anachronism; it provides only a semblance of rootedness, an artifice of eternity. Still, I submit that it represents a limited means, a human means, for dealing with the force of rupture. It fails to satisfy the demands of exhaustive and endless knowledge, but it qualifies that basic ignorance of origins, "cette inconscience structurelle," which Derrida sees as essential to all utterances. The allusion pretends to knowledge; that pretense may some day come to be forgotten, but for a century or a millennium the text will not look altogether unconscious; it will carry with it the simulacrum of a context.

It is true that the ostensible allusion, the "official" allusion, may point to only one of many genealogical lines. Virgil may allude most visibly to Homer, Shakespeare may allude, say, to Plutarch, Racine to Euripides, Joyce again to Homer, yet the intertextual roots of each masterpiece are infinitely more entangled than the official advertisement would indicate. The unconfessed genealogical line may prove to be as nourishing as the visible, once revealed by a deconstructing analysis. All major works grow from a complex set of origins. But this proliferation must not obscure the special status of that root the work privileges by its self-constructed myth of origins. Racine's *Phèdre* may draw upon Augustine and Arnauld, Seneca and Garnier, Descartes and Corneille, but this polysemous intricacy does not decenter the *Hippolytus* as the acknowledged, pervasive subtext, whose presence as subtext an integral reading is compelled to acknowledge. We distinguish many presences with Racine, including the presence of Euripides; beyond all these, we recognize the explicit *adoption* of Euripides, and that adoption is itself a unique structural element that must be dealt with.

The text adopts its legitimate progenitor, of course, not without certain risks. As individuals, we have to recreate our origins in our memories and imaginations. If we are to stay sane, we have to pattern images of our origins that simplify and distort them. But certain kinds of distortion, or excesses of distortion, turn out to be destructive. There has to be a healthy circular interplay between our patterning of our beginnings and our free action as we try to move out from them. The interplay is never free from the risk of a pathological turn. Perhaps there is also an intertextual pathology. The past, as Augustine said, does not exist, but our editing of the past, our imaging, our violence upon it—these are the most powerful of our activities, and our destinies turn on the strength, the direction, the anguish, and the wisdom we draw from or against those versions of reality. This drama of each individual history attaches itself also to literary language. The poetic word achieves its brilliance against the background of a past which it needs in order to signify but which its own emergence is tendentiously and riskily shaping.[28]

5

Renaissance imitation at its richest became a technique for creating etiological constructs, unblocking—within the fiction of the work—the blockages in transmission which created humanist pathos. Imitation acts out a passage of history that is a retrospective version or construct, with all the vulnerability of a construct. It has no ground other than the "modern" universe of meanings it is helping to actualize and the past universe it points to allusively and simplifies. It seeks no suprahistorical order; it accepts the temporal, the contingent, and the specific as given. But it makes possible an emergent sense of identity, personal and cultural, by demonstrating the viability of diachronic itineraries. To analyze adequately the potentialities of the word to act out such itineraries, we would need a diachronic linguistics which at present we do not possess.

But what is meant by the phrase "universe of meanings"? The remainder of this chapter will be devoted to this question. I want to argue that the meaning of each verbal work of art has to be sought within its unique semiotic matrix, what might be called a *mundus significans*, a signifying universe, which is to say a rhetorical and symbolic vocabulary, a storehouse of signifying capacities potentially available to each member of a given culture. In an archaic society, what Lévi-Strauss calls a "cold" society, these capacities are few and more or less enduring;[29] in a complex, "hot" society, they are immensely numerous and constantly in flux. The *mundus significans* for most literate societies is a vast, untidy, changeful collection of techniques of meaning, expressive devices feasible for communication, a vocabulary grounded in the spoken and written language but deriving its special distinctness from the secondary codes and conventions foregrounded at its given moment. Only through them, and within the limits they allow, reflecting as they do the epistemological and other shared assumptions of their community, can a subject express himself into existence and individuate a moral style. The major author declares himself through his power in extending and violating the *mundus*, a power so dynamic and fruitful as to alter it irreversibly. Yet even his violations have to be understood in terms of the norms they challenge. The remote text of a major author remains remote to us partly because its affront to its *mundus* has lost, for us, its shock. The peculiar disadvantage of reading at our own particular historical moment is that we are losing our capacity for that kind of shock.

The resources of most literate societies (and doubtless of many illiterate) are so rich that its *mundus significans* at any given moment might well require a considerable literature to be *fully* described. But the beginnings of a catalogue can be sketched by way of rough example. The *mundus* of English culture in 1590 would include a polysemous allegorical tradition, dream vision, pastoral eclogue and elegy, emblems and emblem books, devices (*imprese*), "hieroglyphs," a vast and confusing body of mythographic materials, elements of liturgical and sacramental symbolism, interpretations of the "Book of Nature" including hermetic correspondences, astrological, mathematical, and scientific speculations, various typological and symbolic codes applied to holy scripture, beast fables, prose romance, native and Petrarchan conventions of love poetry, a number of Anglican and Puritan exegetical modes, Euphuistic examples from natural history, an amorphous and still unstable body of prosodic habits, a number of imitative conventions based on classical genres, a new, dense, exclamatory, metaphoric style and melodramatic theatrical technique developing in the nascent theater of Marlowe and Kyd while challenging older traditions of miracle, morality, and neoclassic comedy and tragedy—all of this set against the dominant intellectual disciplines embodied in the trivium. This list of what Daniel called "England's native ornaments" is far from complete, even after nonverbal signs are excluded, but it can serve to suggest how broad and disorderly a semiotic universe will necessarily appear. Yet each of the items in this list shares in varying degrees a common element: each requires of the reader or auditor a particular set of mental transactions that are understood to belong to the particular mode or convention or subgenre or intellectual sphere. To each *modus significandi* corresponds a *modus intelligendi*.

The acquisition of a set of responses is of course an important part of each individual's education, in the broadest sense, and since education and experience vary, it is understood that only a few if any will command all sets. They are not in any case *our* sets, and we can only approach them by the exercise of our historical imaginations. What is most remarkable about such a *mundus* is its way of combining immense conservatism and immense flexibility. Already in 1600, after ten years had passed, the later works of Sidney and Spenser, the works of Shakespeare, Nashe, Chapman, Marston, Drayton, the early Donne and Jonson and others would have transformed profoundly the *mundus* just described without however absolutely obliterating any single traditional element. Only from such a shifting and tangled matrix of semiotic reserves, it seems to me, can the *episteme* of a given culture be derived. And only from the tracing of microcosmic and macrocosmic shifts in the semiotic universe can a true literary history be written. "Literary evolution," remarks Jonathan Culler, "proceeds by displacement of old conventions of reading and the development of new."[30]

To read in terms of a *mundus* is not to close off the polyvalence of the text, but to seek its potency within the richness of the writer's play with his own codes. The codes themselves moreover cannot be isolated from the usages and structures of the language that supplies their counters. The *mundus* can be thought of as foregrounding certain semiotic potentialities against a background of neglected potentialities coextensive with the language. The *mundus* focuses that power in language to shape and respond to our mental activity. "What language expresses," wrote Durkheim, "is the manner in which society as a whole represents the facts of experience." One strong if controversial current of twentieth-century linguistics has enlarged his insight. Thus Whorf: "Every language is a vast pattern-system, different from others, in which are culturally ordained the forms and categories by which the personality not only communicates, but also analyzes nature, notices or neglects types of relationship and phenomena, channels his reasoning, and builds the house of his consciousness."[31] Doubtless the matter is not so simple. For Whorf, language tended to be primary and culture secondary. But in fact, language is enmeshed in a total cultural complex wherein its structures are "felt" or manipulated differently in different periods. The causal process works in two directions, or rather in a labyrinth of causalities. The extreme position toward which Whorf's unguarded thinking led him might be called "the fallacy of linguistic primacy." The conception of a *mundus significans* evades this fallacy because it supples a mediating space where the variable forces of history, culture, and language can interpenetrate.[32]

It is the transitory character of the literary code as it plays upon language that requires the exercise of the historical imagination. To read a text, we have to know not so much what as how the words mean, and this *how* depends on experience which is lost to us. Culture teaches us what to expect of a (contemporary) reader when we write, and how to translate into meaning the ambiguous contemporary constructions we read. At a deeper level it provides, or tries to provide, an explicit or intuitive *theory of relationships* to justify our translations. Thus it provides a certain vertical metaphysics to justify medieval allegory. A culture tells us how to understand the commerce between words and other words, things and other things, and between words and things. A reader's decoding of a message will necessarily be guided by his assumptions about this commerce, even (or especially) when they have never themselves been put into words. It is this shared but largely silent agreement about relationship and about signification that bedevils the estranged understanding. Clearly no modern reader will fully master the competence to read medieval allegory, a competence affective as well as conceptual, with the spontaneity of its early readers because we have not internalized those assumptions and intuitions in which the allegory is grounded.

Any theory of reading that ignores this historicity of the word and the code is incomplete.[33] Any theory is suspect which attributes to the text a Utopian simultaneity and a Platonic permanence. To deny the text its particularity and its solitude is to obscure those intuitions of relationship at work even in those works which want to challenge them. Each cultural moment, each writer, each poem asks us to learn its tropes all over again, and each learning is unique because each trope is unique. Each trope of a remote text violates our logic in its own peculiar way, and its violation must never defeat our patience even if ultimately we fail to defeat all of its resistance. In the very existence of that resistance lies a kind of security. For in this stubborn trope that will never yield entirely to our shaping minds we discover a radical entity that is nondeconstructible, a semiotic building block that is fiercely and distinctively whole. We cannot fathom its unreason; we cannot unravel its contingent being; it reaches us as a semiotic shard which is that it is. It will suffer our inquisitions but it will not allow us productively to unpiece its integrity. To take it at all, we have to take its irreducible and alien integrity.

The remoteness, the alterity of the remote trope is likely to be undervalued by the naive reader because the part of speech most subject to instability is the part that looks most continuous—namely, the copula. The copula looks continuous because the activities of predication and analogizing have remained durable mental and verbal habits, if not necessities. But in fact the force, the logic, the range, the *tyranny* of the copula vary with the society, the *mundus*, the creative mind, and the context it seems tamely to serve. Its essential variability is of particular hermeneutic significance because a copula is present explicitly or implicitly in most, though not all, metaphors.[34] The naive, unhistorical reading of remote texts attributes an identity of structure and force to the metaphors they contain which does not exist. The structure of the metaphor depends on the operation of the visible or invisible copula, and the copula in turn depends most directly of all parts of speech on the intuitions of relationship conceivable within its culture.

The variability of these intuitions is clearer when one considers a body of literature outside our own tradition. Here Phillip Damon's work on ancient modes of analogy provides valuable clarification.

> In the formulary utterances of *The Book of the Dead* there are many rudimentary epiphonemes which seem to be due less to stylistic artifice than to a special understanding of the category of relation. The logically inapposite details in such comparisons as:
>
>> Thy navel is the Tuat [the underworld] which is open, and which sends forth light into the darkness, and the offerings of which are *ankham* flowers,
>>
>> Thy two hands are like a pool of water in the season of abundant inundation, a pool fringed about with the divine offerings of the water gods,
>
> were probably conditioned to a large extent by practical, pre-poetic notions about the meaning of similarity. In funerary texts describing metempsychotic transformation, there is a strong and natural tendency to pile up random theriomorphic images after the copula *m* (the "as" of identification) in order to insist with maximum rhetorical force that the deceased has really become an animal. For instance:
>
>> I fly and I alight as a hawk which has a back four cubits wide, and whose wings are like mother of emerald of the south.
>
> . . . .
>
> This kind of elaboration, which had a proper function in assertions of identity, appears to have exerted a conceptual pressure on assertions of similarity, and to have encouraged an extralogical accumulation of sensuous detail even when, as after the copula "is," there was no question of consubstantiality. The motives behind this pressure are perhaps to be sought in . . . the primitive tendency to see qualities as external dimensions of essence and thus to feel that, in sufficiently formalized contexts, similarity implies identity.[35]

Damon's commentary is helpful and plausible, but of course it remains a hypothesis about something which we cannot know and which modern English might even be incapable of communicating. A mode of analogy is not finally reducible to cognitive apprehension or analysis because it is grounded in communal intuitions as well as doctrines of relationship. This imperfect expressibility of communal intuition is the root cause of the historicity of the signifier.

Our obvious removal from ancient Egypt should not blind us to the discontinuities within our own tradition, ruptures that are traceable in the various successive pressures placed on the copula. In a sense the copula is the most neutral, the most empty, most meaningless part of speech which nonetheless is necessary for meaning to exist. This emptiest of words has to be filled up by its context in the process of signifying, and in an extended context, the copula begins to acquire a character, a *habitus*, a signifying force of its own, which survives any single usage and begins to reflect meaning back on its context. As in Damon's examples, the copula may lead most directly to the intuitions of relationship, of knowing and being, which invisibly govern the discourse in which it participates. Vico thought the verb *sum* contains "all essences, which is to say all metaphysical entities" (*New Science*, #453).

We need a history of metaphor, which would involve at least tacitly a history of the copula, to teach us to wonder at the rhetorical shifts that punctuate our tradition. Horace opens his *Ars poetica* by granting some license to poets and painters but not, he says, too much: "not so far that savage should mate with tame, nor serpents couple with birds, lambs with tigers."

> sed non ut placidis coeant immitia, non ut
> serpentes avibus geminentur, tigribus agni.

Horace's strictures actually circumscribe the deeply conservative copula that he is willing to countenance, a copula dependent on congruence, convention, and decorum, resistant to paradox, oxymoron, and metaphoric daring. His conservatism and his intolerance contrast, perhaps are meant to contrast, with the rhetorical radicalism of another composer of odes, Pindar. But all of our literary history offers us nothing but constrasts. The structure of metaphors in a ceremonial society of medieval Europe must diverge from the structures of more modern metaphors.

> Done is a battell on the dragon blak!

The opening line of Dunbar's great resurrection hymn introduces a metaphorical equation (dragon blak—Satan) that has to be read as essentially unlike the equations of a modern poet, even a devotional poet like Hopkins.

> Not, I'll not, carrion comfort, Despair, not feast on thee:
> Not untwist—slack they may be—these last strands of man
> In me or, most weary, cry *I can no more.*

Modern metaphor presumes a strong tension of fragmentable terms which sacrifice their ontological wholeness, their "purity," their integrity to allow the formation of an unstable, unsituated, unbounded opening into temporary coherence, a sudden bolt of perception, transient, electric, and composite. The image of feasting on carrion is never allowed to reach a vividly visual level because it is too quickly fragmented, partially abstracted, to form a unit with fragments of the moral state of despair, just as in the following line the superb "slack . . . strands of man" forces the reader to choose only those elements of humanity relevant to "strands." The capitalized personification "Despair" is not permitted to assume the stability of an allegorical figure characteristic of an older rhetoric but is drawn into the dense labyrinth of imagistic transformations. The implicit copula linking Despair with carrion exists as a brief, fragile pulsation before an explosion.

Modern metaphor requires us to select elements from tenor and vehicle to create a *tertium quid* which is the product of their combination. When we encounter Hopkins's image "Natural heart's ivy, Patience," we have to conceive of an entity which is composed of both virtue and plant, an ad hoc creation which each reader reaches on his own. No two "modern" metaphors are identical because the given interplay between tenor and vehicle, the proportioning of their intermixture, depends on their unique particularity as well as on their unique context. But in a metaphor like Dunbar's, the product of a ceremonial society, things possess a wholeness which resists fragmentation and a location which resists displacement because determined by vertical references to a source of unity. Here the copula serves to bind likenesses which already have a rapport in the scheme of things, and the transaction to which it invites us is a ratification of evident concordance. Dunbar's line establishes an emblematic security which leaves both dragon and devil their cognitive stability. The presumed sensibility that produced the metaphor is transparent, impersonal; its meaning is firmly bounded; it produces no fresh perception but leaves rather an openness to participation. The signifier points to its signified with the repose of millennial repetition. The implicit copula carries no pulsation, fragments no unity, unveils no fragile epiphany; it carries with ceremonial solemnity and the weight of a hierarchy a scriptural correspondence that depends on each member's integrity. But the most intimate reverberations of this Paschal copula have to be listened for on the far side of a liturgical silence.

Part of the precious mystery of a remote text lies in its copulative insinuations.[36] This mystery is not simply the result of history; it is inherently poetic, and yet for the alerted reader, temporal distance deepens the promise as well as the obscurity, thickens an opacity which is at once dense and seductive. At the dawn of the medieval lyric, Guillaume d'Aquitaine writes abruptly and enigmatically, "Tot es niens" (All is nothing). One wants to sound the troubled undercurrents of that illogic, to gauge the tension that strains its little quiet-seeming bond. There is nothing ceremonial presumably about this copula, but it will not quite abide our inquisition; if it did, perhaps, we would understand better not only its context but some of the almost unimaginable nuances within its signifying universe. But how to approach those delicate flutterings of meaning without an instrument that *translates*, which is to say anachronizes? The mystery and the seduction are not limited to this most ancient poetry of the postclassical era. The mind must be very still to begin to register the force of the copula, expressed or unexpressed, that speaks from any *mundus significans* not our own. Here is Blake:

> The Human Dress is forged *Iron*,
> The Human Form is a fiery *Forge*,
> The Human Face, a Furnace seal'd,
> The Human Heart its hungry Gorge.

Donne:

> She'is all States, and all Princes, I,
> Nothing else is.

Mallarmé:

> Hilare or de cymbale . . . le soleil.

Chaucer:

> His herte, which that is his brestes eye.

Herbert:

> Prayer the Churches banquet, Angels age . . .
> The Christian plummet sounding heav'n and earth;
> Engine against th' Almightie, sinners towre,
> Reversed thunder, Christ-side-piercing spear . . .
> The milkie way, the bird of Paradise . . .

Scève:

> Tu es le Corps, Dame, et je suis ton umbre.

Pope:

> Round him much Embryo, much Abortion lay,
> Much future Ode, and abdicated Play;
> Nonsense precipitate, like running Lead,
> That slip'd thro' Cracks and Zig-zags of the Head.

Rilke:

> Gesang ist Dasein.

William of Shoreham:

> Marye, maide, milde and fre,
> Chambre of the Trinite . . .
> Thou art the boshe of Sinai . . .
> Thou art the slinge, thy sone the ston,
> That Davy slange Golye upon . . .
> Thou art the temple Salomon.

Nerval:

> Je suis . . .
> Le Prince d'Aquitaine à la Tour abolie.

Beneath its surface limpidity, each "is" conceals profundities of unreason. How does one fathom copulative depth? We have no gauge for that, or any system on which to base a taxonomy of the copula. Many pages would be required to circumscribe the implications of each unique act of predication. And the fuller the explication, the higher the risk of a modernizing falsification.

To recognize the variability of the copula is to call into question the stability of the term *metaphor*, a stability assumed by most rhetoricians across the centuries; since Jakobson it has been a cornerstone of modern linguistic thought.[37] This modern view may derive from Nietzsche, whose essay "On Truth and Falsity in their Ultramoral Sense" argues for a nominalism that oddly and inconsistently

excludes the metaphor. But the deepest wisdom may lie in a thoroughgoing
rhetorical nominalism. "The mind," wrote I. A. Richards, ". . . can connect any
two things in an indefinitely large number of different ways."[38] This variability
extended across history only increases the estrangement of the remote text. As
readers and interpreters we try to mitigate this estrangement by a faculty that
might be termed the "philological imagination." (Although some scholars today
believe that our hermeneutic instruments are more enlightened than in the past,
we should be wary of self-congratulation.)[39] The literary work, when its subtexts
are remote, contrives to deal with their estrangement through its chosen intertextual strategies. The remainder of this study is devoted to these strategies in the
poetry of the Renaissance.

Three • Imitation and Anachronism

It would be easy to oversimplify the emergence of new intertextual structures during the fourteenth and fifteenth centuries in Italy. Dante, like other medieval writers before him, counseled the practice of *imitatio* as an aid to literary art.[1] Some of his predecessors employed the very metaphors that have become familiar as Roman and Renaissance commonplaces. Yet the Renaissance repetitions and elaborations reach our ear with a changed accent. "In the history of culture," writes Charles Trinkaus, "nothing is truly original, but nothing is ever the same."[2] The description of the lack of sameness is likely to be a delicate, frustrating business, since it will never fully reflect the entanglements and irregularities of change. Cassirer suggested that the presence of a given idea at a given cultural moment counts less in itself than the degree of dynamic interplay it achieves with other ideas and forces.[3] This is a helpful guideline. Even if the fifteenth century could be shown to have produced no more explicit discussion of rhetorical imitation than the twelfth, the engagement of this element with the later cultural context would have to be seen as more active and more problematic.

The shift from one humanist Renaissance to another will be traced briefly in a later chapter (see chapter 5 below, pp. 84–88). Here the gap might best be epitomized if we return to the crucial gap between Dante and Petrarch. We have seen that Dante recognized changes in linguistic style corresponding to changes in cultural "style" ("mores et habitus") from the ancient world to his own. Yet these changes occurred within a continuum which for him was unbroken. Virgil may be hoarse from long silence, but he is greeted by Sordello as the glory of the Latin peoples in whom their language revealed its capacities (" 'O gloria de' Latin,' disse, 'per cui/mostrò ciò che potea la lingua nostra' "—*Purg.* 7.16–17). Sordello wrote only in Provençal and Italian, but he speaks to Virgil of "our language" (lingua nostra). As poets they belong to a single community. Dante had evoked another community, numerically smaller though linguistically broader, when he narrated his meeting in Limbo with Homer, Horace, Ovid, and Lucan in the company of Virgil. There the acceptance into a community is expressly formulated.

> . . . piú d'onore ancora assai mi fenno,
> ch'e' sí mi fecer della loro schiera,
> sí ch'io fui sesto tra cotanto senno.   [*Inf.* 4.100–02]
> [Then they showed me still greater honor, for they made me one of their number so that I was the sixth among those high intelligences.]

28

Dante walks with Virgil through the first two canticles as a disciple but also as a peer, until he passes beyond Virgil's purview and becomes the catechumen of Beatrice.

This experience of belonging to a community in spite of time became for Petrarch a fantasy which could be fulfilled only through some measure of self-deception. Although he writes of—and even to— the ancients with a new feeling of familiarity, he and his readers are aware of the pathos tingeing this intimacy. The long letter to Homer (*Familiares* 24. 12) ends with a self-subverting confession: "I realize how far from me you are" (Quam longe absis intelligo). The letter to Livy catalogues the Roman figures this historian permitted him to frequent in his mind, but its close projects them all into inaccessible remoteness.

> Written in the land of the living, in that part of Italy and in that city in which I am now living and where you were once born and buried, in the vestibule of the Temple of Justina Virgo, and in view of your very tombstone; on the twenty-second of February, in the thirteen hundred and fiftieth year from the birth of Him whom you would have seen, or of whose birth you could have heard, had you lived a little longer.[4]

The attempt to revive or fabricate a Roman community was itself open to the suspicion of profanation. Can one expose with impunity the Muses to the vulgarity of the modern world? A Latin verse epistle describing the poet's coronation at Rome raised the question with sleight of syntax.

>   . . . nec multa profatus;
> nam neque mos vatum patitur, nec iura sacrarum
> Pyeridum violasse leve est; de vertice Cirre
> avulsas paulum mediis habitare coegi
> urbibus ac populis.
> [I did not speak long; poetic custom forbids it, nor is it a little thing to violate the laws of the divine Muses; I led them, snatched from the summit of Cirrha, to dwell briefly amid the city crowd.][5]

One is allowed to understand the violation either as the long oration the poet chose not to make or as the act he did perform of leading the Muses through the urban rabble. Petrarch could not imagine without anxiety this guidance of the Muses into a new home, the guidance Virgil and Propertius boasted of. He could not imagine the companionable, progressively equalizing journey together of Dante and Virgil. The ending of the *Africa* reveals a different fantasized itinerary, wherein the future writer will walk backward against time, free and guiltless, into the luminous fields of antiquity.[6] But this image expresses little more than a desperate hope.

Petrarch precipitated his own personal creative crisis because he made a series of simultaneous discoveries that had been made only fragmentarily before him. It was he who first understood how radically classical antiquity differed from the Christian era; he also saw more clearly than his predecessors how the individual traits of a given society at a given moment form a distinctive constellation; he understood more clearly the philological meaning of anachronism. In view of his humanist piety and his literary ambition, these perceptions created a problem that he would bequeath to the generations that followed him: the problem how to write with integrity under the shadow of a prestigious cultural alternative. To be a humanist after Petrarch was not simply to be an archaeologist but to feel an imitative/emulative pressure from a lost source.

In Italy the word after Petrarch is cast out of the maternal circle of *Latinitas*; it begins to betray its exile, its finitude, its relativity. The sense of privation, which was certainly present in medieval culture, became better informed and less resigned, became an incitement. History betrayed a rupture, whereas medieval historiography tended to stress continuities—the five monarchies, the six ages, the nine worthies, the repetitions of the liturgical year, the millennial *autorità* evoked by Dante in reply to Saint John—even if it could not fail to take note of the disjuncture of Christian revelation. The Book containing that revelation existed in a continuous present. The *renovatio* to which medieval men repeatedly aspired was an actualization of values present in the Bible and the apostolic record. The apocalyptic forms that the dream of *renovatio* produced—as in a Joachim of Flora—involved the fulfillment of a pattern as eternal as the Trinity. Even if the passage to a "new" age were dramatic, an age that ideally would represent a return to enduring, predetermined values, medieval historiography knew no abysses. "Unlike the Humanists," wrote Franco Simone, "the men of the Middle Ages never lost the sense of continuity which they imagined passing from people to people, according to an idea of which the *translatio studii* is a mythical realization."[7] It is this sense of continuity that accounts for the appeal of medieval anachronism: Apollo as bishop, Mars as knight, "Queen" Belisea (Catiline's wife) attending mass on Easter morning in the church of Fiesole.[8] It is this which also accounts for the medieval attitude toward law as eternally given and untouchable, rather than the product of specific times, places, and men. Thus the sense of etiological itinerary was very weak. History before its ending knew no force of rupture, and this diachronic innocence explains in part the peculiar charm, security, and distinction of medieval literature.

In the literature of the Renaissance, intertextuality has to be analyzed as an interplay between stabilizing etiologies and a destabilizing perception of disjuncture. New etiological myths had to be produced which could contain the facts of loss and of anachronism, myths which could no longer assert the universal unity for which Dante fought and wrote. The Renaissance did produce such a myth or cluster of myths in its pervasive imagery of resurrection and rebirth, imagery still reflected in our period term. This was the etiological construct on the macrocosmic level of an entire civilization both in Italy and France, the means whereby the civilization incorporated the loss of antiquity into a myth that defined its own historical emergence. But this is a myth which can also be applied microcosmically at the level of the individual text, as a basis for interpretation and assessment. The characteristic risk of Renaissance imitation lay in the potential paralysis of its pieties, in a rhetoric so respectful of its subtexts that no vital emergence from the tradition could occur. The diachronic itinerary circles back to its starting point or peters out in a creative desert. But putting aside the reproductive hackwork, we see there is no question that imitative resurrection did act as a powerful creative principle in all realms of Renaissance civilization, so that the revivalist etiology can be invoked now as then without naiveté.

A passage in the prose of Lorenzo de' Medici provides a kind of metaphysics for this principle.

> It is the opinion of good philosophers that the corruption of one thing is the creation of another . . . and this comes about by necessity because, since form and species . . . are immortal, change must always take place in matter, and from this perpetual change there derives continuous generation of new things. . . . And according to Aristotle, privation is the beginning of all created things.[9]

Lorenzo's metaphysics can stand as a manifesto of a civilization and can explain incidentally how the civilization disposed of the anxiety of influence. In Harold Bloom's terms, the problem of the precursor is that he is not lost and not dead, thus not available for resurrection. His text has not suffered from any errancy, and thus no etiological itinerary away from it into the present is possible. The precursor constitutes the present; he determines the atmosphere the poet breathes. Between the precursor and follower, no discontinuity can intervene, since for Bloom discontinuity would be freedom.[10] This is doubtless why Petrarch could make more controlled use of Virgil than he could of Dante. The discovery of the ancient world imposed enormous anxiety upon the humanist Renaissance, but its living poetry represents a series of victories over anxiety, based upon a courage that confronts the model without neurotic paralysis and uses the anxiety to discover selfhood. The relationship to the subtext is deliberately and lucidly written into the poem as a visible and acknowledged construct.

It is no accident that the cultivation of memory received new and careful attention from Renaissance educators. In the educational treatises of Erasmus, the memory was understood as a crucial, creative faculty, already on its way toward becoming for Vico an instrument of the creative imagination.[11] In Rabelais's *Gargantua*, the tours de force of rote recall are the mark of a sterile, outdated pedagogical method wherein memory has no active, shaping force; it reproduces the identical.[12] For Erasmus the memory of the advanced pupil must produce a reactivation which is also a reformulation.[13] Verbatim repetition is rated less highly than paraphrase; still more desirable is a conversion or transposition whereby, for example, an ancient idea is reconceived and rephrased in Christian language.[14] Such a transposition already creates a small itinerary of the *sententia*. The creation of a passage mitigates the choice between the awareness of otherness and its refusal; it permits a fiction of historical flow that reconciles and bridges. This is the essence of Nancy Struever's valuable analysis: "Rhetorical *imitatio*, with its concept of virtuosity as both a command of past techniques which possess continuous sanctions and a sensitivity to the unique demands of the present situation, provides a model of continuity in change."[15] The paradox of this particular continuity is that it has to leap a thousand years. That is why even the act of memory always involves an implicit necromantic metaphor: a resuscitation. (The Christianity Erasmus's pupil learns is scriptural and patristic, itself resuscitated.) The very length of the itinerary from subtext to modern text permits more creative play, more of that distance which for Struever as for Bloom is liberating. "*Imitatio* is a source of freedom, the creation of a style is a prime expression of freedom of choice; and since the concept of freedom involves a sense of responsibility, the connection between the formal and the responsible is strict."[16] Thus out of that anteriority which humanist philology discovered within the word emerged a poetic, an ethic, and an altered attitude toward history.[17]

2

The sense of the loss of a precious past was a common element in the humanist enterprise not only in Italy but through Europe; outside of Italy however it tended to be less acute and more readily balanced by the hope of revival. What is unmistakable everywhere is an awareness of discontinuity coupled with the threat of inferiority. But in both France and England, the two northern countries to be dealt with in this study, there emerges within a few decades after the birth of a genuine humanism a resolution to right the scales of cultural history. Gargantua writing to his son confesses that in the new world of learning he would scarcely be admitted to the first grade, since his youth had been spent in an age of Gothic darkness. Yet this sense of disadvantage becomes the basis of hope, as he cheerfully instructs Pantagruel in a program of threefold restoration, overcoming at once original depravity, human mortality, and an age of ignorance by means of intellectual heroism. There is no doubt that hopeful calls for revival in authors other than Rabelais masked deep anxieties, fears of enduring feebleness, doubts of the given vernacular, worries over an irreversible decline in human capacities. Still these ambivalences of what Bloom calls belatedness did not cripple the renewal of a civilization.

In France and in England the resolution to revive is the more notable because in neither country did the elite perceive earlier models of accomplishment comparable to the "three crowns" of the Italian trecento—Dante, Petrarch, and Boccaccio. Writers in both countries were likely to feel that they had to begin the task of revival at the beginning, thus perceiving an independence both daunting and liberating. In France the rejection of the medieval heritage was by far the stronger (though not absolute), and perhaps not coincidentally the necromantic metaphors of disinterment, rebirth, and resuscitation were far more common. A characteristic example is the remark of Jacques Amyot in the dedication prefacing his translation of Plutarch's *Lives*: "Les nobles anciennes langues ... sont mortes et ... il les faut tirer hors des monuments des livres où elles sont ensepvelies."[18] Amyot goes on to evoke in lurid terms the "horreur de tenebres" and the "fondriere d'ignorance bestiale et pestilente" wherein men would be sunk without the knowledge of history. By 1559, when his translation was published, his imagery of burial and disinterment was already becoming obsessive in France as it had become in Italy. Ronsard's relatively brief preface to his *Quatre Premiers livres des Odes* (1550) uses verbs of resuscitation in three different passages.[19] Du Bellay organized his *Antiquitez de Rome* around the image, as we shall see, although there it would be caught in a texture of ironies. Later this metaphor would give way to images of progress or vicissitude. In England the image is a bit less common but instances can be found. Spenser uses it to pay tribute to Camden.

> Cambden, the nourice of antiquitie,
> And lanterne unto late succeeding age,
> To see the light of simple veritie,
> Buried in ruines . . .[20]

Bacon calls for a cultural history that would consult the principal works of each century "that so . . . by tasting them here and there, and observing their argument, style, and method, the Literary Spirit of each age may be charmed as it were from the dead." (Genius illius temporis Literarius veluti incantatione quadam a mortuis evocetur.)[21] Pallas, in Jonson's *Golden Age Restored*, invites the great dead English poets to

> Put on your better flames, and larger light,
> To waite upon the age that shall your names new nourish,
> Since vertue pressed shall grow, and buried arts shall flourish.[22]

In England the medieval past was not so consistently identified with night, burial, and death; perhaps also the act of disturbing the earth was attended with a more superstitious caution. The focus of England's sense of disjuncture lay most visibly in its embarrassment over its rude vernacular. Translators of the earlier Tudor period ritually deplored "our own corrupt and base, or as al men affyrme it: most barbarous Language,"[23] and comparable expressions are found in so many other contexts as well that the attitude has to be taken seriously.[24] The embarrassment of the English with their language should be read, I think, synecdochically, as an oblique lament over a broader cultural poverty. Not only the language was inadequate; the nation as a whole was seen as suffering from a kind of privation which translations from antiquity or even from the continental vernaculars could only underscore.

Thus in France and England as in Italy, the advent of humanism conferred a keener historical consciousness upon the literary mind and created an etiological problem: the task of constructing retrospectively a past from which a literary work could visibly emerge without damaging anachronism. For a humanist literature, this past was most commonly ancient and the etiological solution was embraced by the term *imitation*. Yet the remoteness of the ancient past grew increasingly evident in every country, and the resulting strain on the etiological construct was explicitly formulated at least as early as 1528, when Erasmus pitilessly insisted on the risk of anachronism in his *Ciceronianus*. "What effrontery . . . would he have who should insist that we speak, on all occasions, as Cicero did? . . . Since on every hand the entire scene of things is changed, who can today speak fittingly unless he is unlike Cicero?"[25] Much though not all of Erasmus's case against Ciceronianism would hold for the narrow imitation of more than one author. The problem of anachronism remained through the opening of the next century (1611), when Pierre de Larivey, adapting an Italian source, still found it a divisive issue.

> Je sçay bien que plusieurs ne prennent goust qu'à l'*antiquité*, dont ils font si grande estime qu'ils la logeroient volontiers au ciel, blasmant tous ceux qui ne les ressemblent et ne sont de leur opinion. Autres veullent que comme les aages sont variables et different l'un de l'autre, et d'autant qu'aujourd'huy l'on n'use des mesmes choses dont l'on usoit il y a vingt ans, qu'ainsi les modernes comedies ne doivent estre pareilles à celles qui estoient il y a mil six cens ans passez et plus, nostre vivre n'estant pareil au leur. Ceux-là disent qu'en Grece ou à Rome on usoit d'un sutre langage, d'autre façon de vivre, d'autres coustumes, d'autres loix, et—ce qui importe le plus—d'une religion toute contraire à la nostre Chrestienne et Catholique.[26]

In England, where the pressure to imitate was slacker and where the critical issues imitation provoked were less central, these alternatives posed by Larivey were felt as less problematic. Yet the striking ambivalence of those who did address them, including Donne, Jonson, and Carew, must give pause.[27] Humanist etiology in England was less urgent an issue only in degree.

Doubtless the humanist situation should be regarded as a local version of a situation universally human. The past always reaches us across a space which we want to deny. It reaches us incomplete, and in attempting to make it whole we merely create a new incompleteness. "Each new being," writes Erikson, "is received into a style of life prepared by tradition and held together by tradition, and at the same time disintegrating because of the very nature of tradition."[28] The imitative tensions of the Renaissance artist should not be cut off from this larger perspective on all human endeavor, a perspective that could be claimed to be theological. Thus Reinhold Niebuhr: "Men seek to complete history without regard to the contingent and finite character of the self, individual or collective, of the culture or civilization which they make the basis of their pretension."[29] Most of the present study will be concerned with a single chapter in the permanent drama of man's struggle with the mystery of time, but this enduring character of the drama should not be forgotten.

What was most dangerous in the humanist enterprise was the effort to exchange one recent past for another, distant one—a brave, perhaps absurd, and in any case profoundly unsettling design. One finds a warning against such a project even in the revolutionary thought of Nietzsche, who in his great essay on history alludes to such periods when the past is attacked at its roots and cut down.

The process is always dangerous, even for life; and the men or the times that serve life in this way, by judging and annihilating the past, are always dangerous to themselves and others. . . . Though we condemn the errors [of previous generations] and think we have escaped them, we cannot escape the fact that we spring from them.[30]

This dangerous element in the Renaissance resistance toward its medieval roots, this hazardous mythologization of an alternative, is also bound up in the tensions which the impulse to imitate produced and might ideally have been expected to resolve.

It is unclear how in fact the earliest authors began to write creative imitations that reflected a felt distance from the subtext. At the earliest stage, the task of writing was inseparable from the problem of reading. Valla's denial of the capacity to read during the preceding millennium (quoted above, p. 9) was not unique. Matteo Palmieri wrote in his *Vita civile*: "It would be better to say nothing than little of letters and liberal studies. These preeminent guides and true mistresses of every worthy discipline have been forgotten by the world for more than eight hundred years, so that no one has truly understood them."[31] A charge like this is unfair to medieval readers, but it begins to bear a kind of relevance if "truly" is taken to mean "with an informed historical imagination." Not the least problem facing the student of humanism is the question of how the assumptions of medieval readers were changed. The most important figure for the student of this problem is once again Petrarch.

It is by no means obvious how Petrarch made his Copernican leap. The effort he had to make can be gauged by means of the manuscript of Virgil that he kept with him through his life and annotated copiously. The manuscript itself contained the allegorizing commentary of Servius along with the text of the *Aeneid*, and its frontispiece illumination has been attributed to Simone Martini. In this miniature, Virgil appears crowned with ivy behind a thin curtain in a pose often assigned to biblical prophets or evangelists. The pointed finger of a grammarian, possibly Servius, directs the attention of a knight, Aeneas, to his creator. Below, a peasant with pruning hook and a shepherd with his flock also gaze upon the poet: they embody respectively the *Eclogues* and the *Georgics*. The miniature breathes the spirit of late medieval allegory, represented in a heavily stylized Gothic manner. Facing the manuscript and the civilization behind it, how could we expect Petrarch to erase the hermeneutic sedimentation of fourteen centuries? We know in fact that he did not. On the folios containing the first eclogue, he inserted an interlineated gloss based on a mechanical and reductive interpretation inspired by Donatus but spelled out now with a relentlessly heavy hand. If, as Donatus suggested, the figure of Tityrus represents Virgil enjoying the leisurely *otium* granted him by Augustus, Petrarch's gloss takes the rivers of Virgil's countryside to be students, the sacred springs to be their masters, the cool shade to be restful study, the hedges to be chronicles immortalizing the poet's name, and so on for the length of the poem.[32]

Now considering this kind of misreading, considering the massive hermeneutic unanimity of the Middle Ages, we may well ask how Petrarch could approach anything like a blending of horizons with those masters whom he perceived no longer as authorities, *auctoritates*, but as fathers, brothers, friends. How in fact could Petrarch, for all his nascent historical consciousness, begin to apprehend classical texts with an ear and a sensibility remotely akin to the ancients'? How could he pursue the rebirth of a culture that he could not even praise in a prose style it might have acknowledged? How could he compose poetry that neither ignored nor travestied the overwhelming power of an alien idiom? We approach here a deeply problematic area of speculation which far transcends Petrarch but which he can serve to illustrate as a nearly pure example. How in a society which is almost self-enclosed do we learn to decipher the signifiers of another dead society, another *episteme*? How do we begin to read truly and faithfully and profoundly the extant shards of a vanished civilization for which our own supplies only an incoherent and treacherous glossary?

It may be that no unequivocal reply to these questions is possible; it may be that we are left with a mystery. If so, it would have to contain the special mystery of genius, and in this case the peculiarly intricate, even antithetical gifts of Petrarch. Next to the anachronistic marginalia on the *Eclogues* could be placed the poet's heavy-handed *Bucolicum carmen*, whose laborious *églogues à clef* owe their artistic failure to the misguided hermeneutic set the marginalia reveal. Here is a pure example of the ways a wrong interpretive guess can produce stillborn imitation (though this result need not be inevitable). The poet's historical isolation prevented him from resurrecting Virgil, from handing down to posterity a poetic mode apprehended with even minimal understanding. A failure of transmission is due to a misreading of a remote style. Yet one could set against this double failure the late letter to the emperor Charles IV (*Seniles* 16.5) exposing the fraudulence of two epistles supposedly written by Julius Caesar and Nero. Petrarch's letter conducts a masterful analysis on historical and stylistic grounds of these documents' anachronistic self-betrayals. In its fierce indignation as in its method, it deserves comparison with Valla's *Declamatio* on the fake Donation of Constantine, which it anticipates by two generations.[33] The author of this letter possesses a sense of historical change which the reader of the *Eclogues* lacks. Doubtless a grasp of poetic codes is more difficult to achieve. But perhaps in any case a nascent historical sense is bound to appear in fits and patches. At this early stage, the humanist conflict between acceptance and denial of distance may simply have taken the form of intermittences between sensitivity and blindness.

Despite failures like the *Bucolicum carmen*, it is likely that the real school of sensitive reading lay in writing, that the mystery of acculturation is most accurately located in the mystery of creative imitation. But how precisely is the modern reader to understand what happens in an imitative literary work? How is he to regard the status of the model, or, to adopt a useful term from contemporary Slavic criticism, the subtext? What is one to do critically with poems that come to us displaying the constitutive presence of a subtext within the verbal structure, insisting on this presence as an essential component? I should like to suggest some solutions to these questions, but it seems to me of greater importance that they be posed in the first place. Some still think of the subtext as something external to the diachronic text, requiring no special attention or special theory. Even so fine a critic as Gérard Genette betrays this prejudice. "Des oeuvres littéraires considérées dans leur texte, et non dans leur genèse ou dans leur diffusion, on ne peut, diachroniquement, rien dire, si ce n'est qu'elles se succèdent. . . . Et la critique, fondamentalement . . . n'est pas, ne peut pas être historique, parce qu'elle consiste toujours en un rapport direct d'interprétation."[34] There is in fact everything to say diachronically about a large body of literature, even though as critics we are uncertain how to begin. The problem is how to embrace in Genette's direct interpretive relation a text that is ostentatiously diachronic.

3

Perhaps it should be stipulated first that each imitative literary work contains by definition what might be called a revivalist initiative, a gesture that signals the intent of reanimating an earlier text or texts situated on the far side of a rupture. For this purpose, maintaining a native contemporary convention does not truly count as imitation (although imitation itself could of course become conventional). The humanist text reaches across a cultural gap and takes the risk of anachronism. The reader then has the right to ask whether this initiative is completed and authenticated, whether the conflict of cultures and the potential conflict of attitude are put to use, whether something occurs within the imitation which truly renews. Here is Ronsard praising the Fontaine Bellerie:

> Tu seras faite sans cesse
> Des fontaines la princesse,
> Moi çelebrant le conduit
> Du rocher persé, qui darde
> Avec un enroué bruit,
> L'eau de ta source jazarde
> Qui trepillante se suit.

And here is this stanza's Horatian subtext:

> fies nobilium tu quoque fontium,
> me dicente cavis impositam ilicem
> saxis, unde loquaces
>   lymphae desiliunt tuae.[35]
> [You also will become one of the celebrated springs, as I sing of the oak planted over the hollow rocks from which your babbling waters leap down.]

Ronsard invites the reader of the complete ode to say whether the necromantic disinterment is brought off, whether the Latin text emerges still mummified from the tomb, or shrunken and thin, or merely ornamented, or whether rather an authentic resurrection has occurred. The reader can ask, *should* ask, not whether anachronism has been suppressed but whether it has been controlled and employed. If it has not and no true renewal is carried out, then the revivalist initiative has to be seen as abortive or failed or in bad faith. But if the revivalist initiative has been made good, if the necromantic metaphor has been validated, then how is this validating process to be described? At this point, it would seem useful to distinguish four types of strategies of humanist imitation, each of which involves a distinct response to anachronism and each an implicit perspective on history. For the sake of economy, I shall illustrate each of them here chiefly from Petrarch's immense canon, Latin and vernacular. Latter sections of this study will provide many more examples.

The simplest imitative strategy governs chiefly a few passages in the Latin poems that follow with religious fidelity their classical subtext. The longest of these is the dream of Scipio in books 1 and 2 of the *Africa*, an episode that visibly seeks to reproduce in epic verse a celebrated section of Cicero's *De re publica*. This reverent rewriting of a hallowed text bespeaks an almost ceremonial veneration for the "sacrosancta vetustas." Valla wrote of the Latin language as a "magnum sacramentum" or "magnum numen."[36] If some humanist writers of later generations betrayed that veneration with a facile and hollow fidelity, this fact does not affect the integrity of the original feeling. The version of history implied by this imitative strategy might be called *reproductive* or *sacramental*; it celebrates an enshrined primary text by rehearsing it liturgically, as though no other form of celebration could be worthy of its dignity. We recall Petrarch's exhortation to dig out old names and "hand them down to our grandchildren as objects of veneration." Poetic objects were still more venerable. The sacramental bonds that were loosening in the late medieval community are now restored as a product of the historical consciousness. Under this sacramental myth of history, writing becomes analogous to ritual as Eliade has described it; our conduct is referred to the archetypal beginning, *in illo tempore*, which in this case is the composition of the original poem. The model or subtext is perceived as a fixed object on the far side of an abyss, beyond alteration and beyond criticism, a sacred original whose greatness can never be adequately reproduced despite the number of respectful reproductions.

Although this sacramental type of imitation corresponded to a new and appealing impulse, it could not in itself produce a large body of successful poetry, nor could it effect a genuine solution to the intertextual dilemma. Clearly it could not function transitively; it could not open a window in the prison house of culture nor could it deal satisfactorily with the newly perceived problem of anachronism. Rather it condemned the reproductive poet to a very elementary form of anachronism, since any reproduction must be made in a vocabulary that is unbecoming the original and whose violations remain out of artistic control. Creative imitation in the Renaissance has to be seen as a challenge to the liturgical repetitions of an age lacking historical consciousness. The step from sacramental reproduction to

authentic imitation is the step Geoffrey Hartman invites us to take when he writes
that "as interpreters . . . we must set interpretation *against* hermeneutics."

> For the distinction between a primary source and secondary literature, or between a
> "great Original" and its imitations, is the space in which traditional hermeneutics
> works. It seeks to reconstruct, or get back to, an origin in the form of sacred text,
> archetypal unity or authentic story. To apply hermeneutics to fiction is to treat it as
> lapsed scripture; just as to apply interpretation to scripture is to consider it a mode,
> among others, of fiction. Both points of view, it can be argued, involve a category
> mistake.[37]

Sacramental imitation, we might say, involved a similar category mistake. It saw
an absolute beginning *in illo tempore* where it had no right to see one. Its pursuit
of a "great Original" led it paradoxically away from genuine contact with the
Original and also away from artistic discovery. Creative imitation enacts rather a
happy fall from the primary to the secondary, a civilized violence, a loving
sacrilege.

A second type of imitation appears in any number of Petrarch's Latin and
vernacular poems alike, where quite simply allusions, echoes, phrases, and images
from a large number of authors jostle each other indifferently. This eclectic
mingling of heterogeneous allusions recurs repeatedly in the Italian poems
throughout his entire career. The early sonnet that records the first vision of Laura
(sonnet 3) brings together elements from the Christian gospels, the *dolce stil
nuovo*, and Ovid's *Amores*. The "Triumph of Eternity," which he completed
during the last year of his life, brings together allusions or echoes of Cicero,
Horace, Saint Matthew, the *Apocalypse*, Saint Augustine, and Dante. Still other
elements were conventional topoi that might or might not have recalled a familiar
author but that had been reused over and over by many authors. This very simple
type of imitation was termed *contaminatio* by Renaissance rhetoricians and it is by
no means to be despised. Quite apart from Petrarch's sometimes brilliant manipu-
lations, it would become the compositional principle of such a masterpiece as
Poliziano's *Stanze per la Giostra*. We might call this type *eclectic* or *exploitative*,
since it essentially treats all traditions as stockpiles to be drawn upon ostensibly at
random. History becomes a vast container whose contents can be disarranged
endlessly without suffering damage. The art of poetry finds its materials everywhere, materials bearing with them the aura of their original contexts, charged
with an evocative power implanted by the poet or the convention from which they
are taken. At its slackest, eclectic imitation falls back into mere anachronism and
becomes indistinguishable from the ahistorical citations of the Middle Ages. But
when it is employed with artistic intelligence, the imitative poet commands a
vocabulary of a second and higher power, a second keyboard of richer harmonies,
which however are combined with rhetorical skill rather than esemplastic vision.
In sonnet 3 ("Era il giorno ch' al sol si scoloraro"), the most awesome event of
Christian story, the darkening of the sky at the crucifixion, loses most of its majesty
and serves chiefly to date the meeting with Laura as well as to explain the poet's

unsuspecting defenselessness against Love's arrows. No higher meaning emerges from the clash of this allusion with the Ovidian topos at the end (". . . non li fu onore / ferir me de saetta in quello stato") because both elements remain rhetorical counters, as does the commonplace of medieval physiology in line 10 (". . . aperta la via per gli occhi al core"). The sonnet as a whole reveals a kind of allusive sophistication but its dexterity remains a little cold.

Thus if the technique of eclectic imitation produced a number of engaging poems, it could not adequately fulfill the transitive responsibilities of poetry as Petrarch himself had formulated them. It could not mediate effectively between a past and a future if the past was fragmented, jumbled, in effect dehistoricized. It could not deal at any profound level with the problem of anachronism; it could simply play with anachronism within a hospitable texture. It could reconcile within its own frame momentary conflicts of heterogeneous motifs; it could tolerate the counterpoint of the voices it brought together; but it could not find out the drama of that counterpoint at a deeper pitch of conflict. When that conflict is sounded, we are already dealing with another type of imitation. To choose a hugely remote example, *Paradise Lost* looks at first glance also to depend on an eclectic strategy of *contaminatio*. But in fact it establishes firmly a strong if sometimes complex relationship with each work and each tradition that it draws upon, according to each its own cultural weight and situation. It underscores rather than obscures the historicity of its sources, and so it permits a flood of imaginative energy to flow through it unimpeded. Conversely Poliziano's *Stanze* achieves a kind of exquisite quintessence of European poetry, but its alchemy leaves no room for mediatory passage and reaches rather an elegant stasis.

Insofar as Petrarch's poetry behaves like Milton's rather than Poliziano's, it can be said to follow a third imitative strategy, which could be termed *heuristic*. Heuristic imitations come to us advertising their derivation from the subtexts they carry with them, but having done that, they proceed to *distance themselves* from the subtexts and force us to recognize the poetic distance traversed. To choose only the simplest and most familiar examples in the *Canzoniere*, one may cite sonnet 90:

> Erano i capei d'oro a l'aura sparsi . . .

which echoes repeatedly book 1 of the *Aeneid*; or sonnet 164:

> Or che 'l ciel e la terra e 'l vento tace . . .

which echoes a famous description in book 4 of the same poem; or sonnet 311:

> Quel rosignuol, che sí soave piagne . . .

which echoes a beautiful simile in the *Georgics*. Other examples could be cited which draw on other ancient poets. In all these cases, the informed reader notes the allusion but he notes simultaneously the gulf in the language, in sensibility, in cultural context, in world view, and in moral style. Each imitation embodies and dramatizes a passage of history, builds it into the poetic experience as a constitutive element. The imitation is able to act out this passage because the sensibility behind it is aware of itself as a cultural participant, aware of belonging to a cultural situation and helping to shape it. For Petrarch and for Renaissance humanism, a living culture is one which assumes historical responsibilities, one which remembers, preserves, resuscitates, and recreates; conversely a naive culture betrays its transitive responsibilities if it fails to remember and preserve. It is through a diachronic structure, an acting out of passage, that the humanist poem demonstrates its own conscientious and creative memory.

Out of the indefinite number of texts stretching behind it in endless regression, the humanist poem singles out one text as its putative genesis and it defines itself through its rewriting, its "modernizing," its *aggiornamento* of that text. It sketches an incipient myth of origins but refuses to posit a "great Original" which has to be remembered liturgically, and its refusal takes the form of a simultaneous myth of modernity. The poem becomes a kind of *rite de passage* between a specified past and an emergent present. Thus it contrives to deal with that dilemma which Paul de Man attributes to all literature. "The writer," de Man says, "cannot renounce the claim to being modern but also cannot resign himself to his dependence on predecessors." It is precisely this dilemma which heuristic imitation quite consciously confronts and builds deliberately into the literary work. It points to a dependence which it then overcomes by a declaration of conditional independence. "Modernity," de Man writes, "invests its trust in the power of the present moment as an origin, but discovers that, in severing itself from the past, it has at the same time severed itself from the present."[38] This discovery with its overtones of frustration and entrapment is skirted by the humanist ruse we have been studying, th⸱ double ruse of a myth of origin and a myth of modernist growth away from the origin. The term *myth* here does not of course mean necessarily deception, although it certainly means simplification. The passage of history will never be as simple as the *rite de passage* suggests. But by the reductive simplifications of its historical construct, the poem confronts the threat of history and asserts its own limited freedom from it. There is a term for the courage of the ancient of Renaissance artist who followed this strategy, who faced the threat of history and thereby found his artistic poise: the term is *classical*. The humanist poet is not a neurotic son crippled by a Freudian family romance, which is to say he is not in Harold Bloom's terms Romantic. He is rather like the son in a classical comedy who displaces his father at the moment of reconciliation.

Thus the imitative poem sketches, far more explicitly and plainly than most historically conscious texts, its own etiological derivation; it acts out its own coming into being. And since its subtext is by definition drawn from an alien culture, the imitative poem creates a bridge from one *mundus significans* to another. The passage of this rite moves not only from text to text but from an earlier semiotic matrix to a modern one. Thus the poem could be read as an attempt to heal that estrangement which humanism had constantly to face.[39]

Imitation of this type is heuristic because it can come about only through a double process of discovery: on the one hand through a tentative and experimental groping for the subtext in its specificity and otherness, and on the other hand through a groping for the modern poet's own appropriate voice and idiom. It is this quest, superbly achieved, that lies behind Ben Jonson's *Discoveries,* so that the full meaning of that title has to be located in this richly double sense. A discovery in Seneca's Latin only fulfills itself when it issues in Jonson's crisp and civilized English. The modern voice distinguishes itself from the older voice, finds its own public accent, but it does so, can only do so, after sensitively apprehending that other accent in something like its particular timbre and personal force. Finding its own idiom the modern voice discovers that new experience which is the modern poem and measures its modernity through the *ballet of latencies* that poem sets in motion.

In the successful humanist text, heuristic play will tend to render its codes and conventions more flexible. If the constructing of diachronic fictions is to escape the charge of bad faith, of mystification, of a destructive myth of presence, then it has to lead toward more open forms; it has to prove that its myths are liberating. The text calls given codes into question by means of anachronistic juxtaposition and goes on to produce a fresher, more polysemous code. Ben Jonson, inviting a friend to supper, Englishes Martial in order to work over English, to thicken its texture and complicate its resonance. The text cannot simply leave us with two dead dialects. It has to create a miniature anachronistic crisis and then find a creative issue from the crisis. Imitation has to become something more than a pseudoarchaeology contrived as an illegitimate solace. If Renaissance literature is troubled by an anxiety of validation, then it finds its true validation in the discovery of more hospitable codes.

The modern work that results will always lie open to the charge of what in the realm of the visual arts Panofsky called "pseudomorphosis."

> When a classical character had emerged from the Middle Ages in utterly non-classical disguise . . . and had been restored to its original appearance by the Renaissance, the final result often showed traces of this process. Some of the medieval garments or attributes would cling to the remodelled form, and thereby carry over a medieval element into the content of the new image.
>
> This resulted in what I would like to call a "pseudomorphosis": Renaissance figures became invested with a meaning which, for all their classicizing appearance, had not been present in their classical prototypes, though it had frequently been foreshadowed in classical literature.[40]

Most humanist poetry, by design or accident, deserves to be regarded in varying degrees as pseudomorphic; indeed, controlled pseudomorphosis tends to enrich a polyvocal *discordia concors.* What remains hard to know and discuss is the humanist poet's grasp of the classical text that initiated the creative process. We cannot expect that his reading approximate that of the text's original audience in order to produce a successful imitation. But we can expect that his response to his

subtext recognize an organic complexity. There is no lack of impoverished imitations that act out a historical passage only hazily defined, imitations whose subtext
is slackly and vaguely apprehended. One of Petrarch's most wooden sonnets—
"Ponmi ove 'l sol . . . " (145)—appears to fail because he mistook the tone of his
Horatian model. In this case, as in most of the *Bucolicum carmen*, misprision was
fatal. The heuristic circle tended to be productive so long as historical intuition
was assisted by an ear for moral style, even though at some point it involved a blind
leap.

This blindness has to be faced. Heuristic imitation fails to escape fully a certain
incompleteness of exchange. We meet it most visibly in the letters Petrarch
addressed to his favorite ancient authors, letters that transcend whatever element of
exhibitionism lay behind them and that are drenched in quixotic futility. The
deep yearning for a *transaction*, a yearning that was by definition unquenchable, is
best symbolized by the letter to Homer purporting to reply to a letter from that poet
actually composed by a friend whom Petrarch had put up to it. The ancients
whom he loved as friends maintained a marble or a bronze repose that could break
hearts. The humanist poet attempted to establish his artistic identity by a process
comparable to an infant's first grasp of self-consciousness as it sees itself the object
of its mother's gaze. But in this case the attempt fails; the perceived object cannot
recognize the subject. The subtext or its author cannot even appear to verify the
interpretation that the imitative text presumes. The filial gesture of critical affection never truly reaches its destination. The humanist wanted to endow the
ancient author with the "aura" evoked by Walter Benjamin: "The person we look
at, or who feels he is being looked at, looks at us in turn. To perceive the aura of an
object we look at means to invest it with the ability to look at us in return."[41] This
investment for the humanist could never definitively occur. Thus his dialogue
with the past always remained finally constructed. The intercourse with the
cultural other always came to a point where intuition had to replace historical
consciousness. The pathos of this incomplete embrace never altogether faded from
the humanist movement.

4

Heuristic imitation shades off into a fourth and last type, which is not altogether
distinct from it but which can be described separately for the purposes of exposition. This type could be said to grow out of heuristic imitation in such a way as to
respond to the radical incompleteness just analyzed. It also responds to that
resistance or ambivalence toward imitation that was a necessary and congenital
feature of humanism. Before any further consideration of imitative strategies, a
glance at this resistance is indicated.

It would be surprising if there had been no hostility toward the pressure to
imitate. Fortunately for the health of each national culture, there was a good deal.
A late, vibrant letter of Petrarch contains a stirring exhortation to literary inde-

pendence: "It is silly to trust only the ancients. The early discoverers were men too. If we should be discouraged by perceiving too many tracks of our predecessors, we should be ashamed. . . . And we should not be moved by that trite, vulgar saying that there is nothing new, and nothing new can be said."[42] This is not truly inconsistent, but it illustrates the complexities of a mind not easily circumscribed. We shall meet in a later chapter what looks out of context like an even stronger manifesto from Poliziano ("Someone says 'You do not express Cicero.' What then? I am not Cicero. I think I express myself."), a gesture toward independence which, like Petrarch's, has to be studied within the context of an entire career. The resistance of other minds is doubtless simpler. Leonardo's heresy was not limited to painting: "One must never imitate the manner of another, because as an artist he will be called the grandchild and not the son of Nature."[43] That irreverent wastrel Francesco Berni, a generation later, amused himself by arguing that all poets were essentially thieves.[44] Montaigne was more serious: "Qui suit un autre, il ne suit rien," he wrote; "il ne trouve rien, voire il ne cherche rien."[45] Shakespeare's Holofernes (an admittedly unreliable authority) would echo him: "Imitari is nothing. So doth the hound his master, the ape his keeper, the tired horse his rider."[46] "Never no Imitator, ever grew up to his Author," remarked Ben Jonson. And again: "I have considered, our whole life is like a Play: wherein every man, forgetfull of himselfe, is in travaile with expression of another. Nay wee so insist in imitating others, as wee cannot (when it is necessary) returne to our selves."[47] Donne (an iconoclast, it is true, whose jibes tend to betray respect) turned back the hoary Senecan image of digestion upon itself.

> But hee is worst, who (beggarly) doth chaw
> Others wits fruits, and in his ravenous maw
> Rankly digested, doth those things out-spue,
> As his owne things . . .[48]

This scattering of quotations is scarcely decisive, although it could be increased. But one is obliged to account for other kinds of evidence, such as the sharp increase in the millennial destruction and reappropriation of Roman ruins during the fifteenth and sixteenth centuries, when the cult of Rome appeared most devout. Was there a humanist will *not* to absorb, a sophisticated, refined fear or antagonism toward the buried, gigantic remains?[49]

Undoubtedly there was, and it is this fact which measures the positive force of the imitative impulse, an impulse which was able to come to terms with this resistance. One reads with astonishment a neoclassic expression of the same resistance, Doctor Johnson's observation: "No man ever yet became great by imitation."[50] How does one interpret that remark from the pen that produced "The Vanity of Human Wishes"? Doctor Johnson produced his own refutation, as did Ben Jonson, Donne, and Montaigne. Ben Jonson's uneasiness has to be weighed against his own imitative triumphs and against his positive advice to imitate. Even Donne invoked the archaeological metaphor without a trace of irony. "If I doe borrow any thing of Antiquitie, besides that I make account that I pay it to posterity, with as much and as good: You shall still finde mee to acnowledge it, and to thanke not him onely that hath digg'd out treasure for mee, but that hath lighted mee a candle to the place."[51] This paying of a debt to posterity is Donne's own homage to humanist transmission. Montaigne, speaking of Seneca and Plutarch, confesses that his book is "massonné purement de leurs despouilles."[52] The process called imitation was not only a technique or a habit; it was also a field of ambivalence, drawing together manifold, tangled, sometimes antithetical attitudes, hopes, pieties, and reluctances within a concrete locus. Margaret Ferguson wisely suggests that for Du Bellay the topic of imitation was "a kind of sacred space, a space in which all the poet's conflicting attitudes toward the ancient wage battle."[53] One might add "and not only for Du Bellay."

The humanism of the Renaissance as it evolved in Italy and spread through Europe assumed innumerable forms, produced manifold *mundi significantes*, gradually became estranged from its own origins. Yet it remains possible to speak of humanism as a coherent movement because it continued to circle around this space. The whole enterprise sustained conflicts between intuitions of intimacy and intuitions of separation, between the belief in transmission and a despair of transmission, between the denial of estrangement and the acceptance of estrangement, between reverence for the *maiores* and rebellion against them. Microcosmically the humanist text can be read as a reflection, an instance of these conflicts.

In order to contain them, and in order to protect itself against its failed quest for an exchange, the diachronic structure of the humanist text had to be carried farther in a fourth imitative strategy. It had to expose the vulnerability of the subtext while exposing itself to the subtext's potential aggression. It had to prove its historical courage and artistic good faith by leaving room for a two-way current of mutual criticism between authors and between eras. Thus we might say that Erasmus's *Praise of Folly* makes an imitative gesture when it twice sketches its own alleged literary genealogy, including the *Batrachomyomachia*, Apuleius, and above all Lucian. The text then goes on to authenticate that gesture by miming Lucian repeatedly while moving far away from him. Then, in its concluding hymn to Christian folly, Erasmus introduces values totally incompatible with Lucian and ancient comedy. The text makes a kind of implicit criticism of its subtexts, its authenticating models, but it also leaves itself open to criticism from the irreverent Lucianic spirit that it had begun by invoking. Thus *The Praise of Folly* creates a kind of struggle between texts and between eras which cannot easily be resolved. By exposing itself in this way to the destructive criticism of its acknowledged or alleged predecessors, by entering into a conflict whose solution is withheld, the humanist text assumes its full historicity and works to protect itself against its own pathos. In Heideggerian terms, the text can fulfill itself only as a projection into the future, an *Entwurf*, by acknowledging its *Geworfenheit*, its finite and contingent temporality, its existence in a specific cultural situation with its own particular and cultural vulnerabilities. This fourth type of imitation might be called *dialectical*.

Now there is a sense in which every imitative work that is not reproductive initiates this process of mutual criticism. Every creative imitation mingles filial rejection with respect, just as every parody pays its own oblique homage. The process is already anticipated in the *Commedia* of Dante, most notably in the thirteenth canto of the *Inferno*. Within Petrarch's canon, one clear example would be the *Secretum*, maintaining as it does its powerful and unresolved engagement with the *Confessions* of Saint Augustine. In this conflict of dialectical imitation, Oedipal aggression leads to self-perception and so finds its blessing. This process was clearly understood by the greatest practical critic of antiquity, Longinus, who described it in the thirteenth chapter of his treatise *On the Sublime*. Plato, he wrote, would have been less perfect a philosopher and less poetic a writer "unless he had with all his heart and mind struggled with Homer for the primacy, entering the lists like a young champion matched against the man whom all admire, and showing perhaps too much love of contention . . . but deriving some profit from the contest nonetheless. For, as Hesiod says, 'This strife is good for mortals.' "[54] This is not an insight that would have disturbed most humanists of the Renaissance. Something of Longinus's contention is present in the term *aemulatio*, which a number of humanist authors preferred to *imitatio*. Valla's veneration for the *Latina litteratura aeterna* did not prevent him from pointing out that one writes only to say something new and thus to take issue with earlier authorities.[55] It is in this dialectical imitative strategy that the tensions or conflicts inherent in humanism rise closest to the surface of the text and can be studied most usefully. And just as heuristic imitation involves a passage from one semiotic universe to another, so dialectical imitation, when it truly engages two eras or two civilizations at a profound level, involves a conflict between two *mundi significantes*. The text comes to terms most effectively with its own humanist problematics, its own incompleteness, by measuring its own signifying habits with those of the subtext. The text is the locus of a struggle between two rhetorical or semiotic systems that are vulnerable to one another and whose conflict cannot easily be resolved. In this dialectic, I think, one reaches the heart of the mystery of acculturation and perhaps its key. Anachronism becomes a dynamic source of artistic power.

One boundary of dialectical imitation is that complex form of assimilation we call parody. It is a moral style which Petrarch himself could not give us. His humanist piety was too devout and his makeup too humorless to permit any open gestures of ironic disrespect. But parody may well issue from creative imitation, and superior parody always engages its subtext in a dialectic of affectionate malice. Parody proper is intensely time-conscious and culture-conscious, and could be absorbed without strain by a poet with humanist training like Ariosto. The parodies of Dante in the *Orlando Furioso* are deliciously contrived without real damage to their subtexts, and the poem that contains them reveals a sensibility truly adult, skeptical, cosmopolitan, and disabused, but not incapable of respect for its predecessors. The same could be said of such different authors as Erasmus, Montaigne, Jonson, and Quevedo. In writers like these, the imitative modes nascent in Petrarch achieve their full development, and the literary text defines itself through its multiform, subtle range of sophisticated allusiveness.

The foregoing analysis of imitative strategies should not lead to the assumption that imitation cannot fail; it *can*, of course, and doubtless in more ways than it succeeds. It can fail if the original imitative gesture is made in bad faith, if the subtext is ornamental rather than constitutive, or if the subtext is misread so ineptly as to kill the possibility of a vital passage. It can fail if either subtext or surface text overwhelms the other by a disproportionate contrast of substance and value. The text can lapse into a misplaced scrupulosity of sacramental piety, or into a fruitless game of eclectic manipulation; or it can simply fail to produce an interesting model of history; it can fail to be heuristic. For each category of misfires examples could be found, but they do not in themselves invalidate their artistic genesis. The making of retrospective constructs represents an issue from the Hobson's choice of naive synchronism and lonely diachronism, the unwillingness and the willingness to recognize historical solitude. The third choice permits a kind of issue, but it imposes its own responsibilities and introduces its own risks.

The movement from ritualistic repetition to improvisational imitation always involves of course a heightened vulnerability. Indeed, this movement might be seen as an extension of that original hardy secularizing step that is the writing down of records and events. "Documents," writes J. G. A. Pocock, "tend to secularize traditions."

> They reduce them to a sequence of acts . . . taking place at distinguishable moments, in distinguishable circumstances, exercising and imposing distinguishable kinds and degrees of authority. They reduce time from a simple conceptualisation of social continuity to that of an indefinite multiplicity of continuities, which—since in the last analysis they represent different ideas of action, authority and transmission—cannot be altogether consistent with one another.

It was precisely this concrete specificity of history—"distinguishable moments" and "distinguishable circumstances"—that the new science of philology was designed to study, and it was disturbing to traditionalists like Frater Giovanni Dominici, as later to Savonarola, because it complicated the authority of the sacred text, shook its absolute status by calling attention to the specific circumstances of its production. "The traditionalist," writes Pocock, " . . . will always distrust the classicist, seeing in him the well-meaning author of a potentially radical doctrine."[56] This radicality is present a fortiori in that humanist imitation which asserts a limited but authentic shaping power of the imagination over the passage of history. Beneath the superficial flow of fashion and convention, artistic success and failure, one can make out a certain element of courage in this swing away from ceremonial pattern.[57] To imitate creatively is to assume the historicity of one's own particular place and moment and idiom, and thus to take on a kind of humility. The necromantic metaphor did not fully shield the men and women of the Renaissance against this swerve away from the security of ritual. Not only did the sacred text cease to be uniquely Judaeo-Christian, but the path of creative imitation led sooner or later to an implicit critique of the sacred.[58] Creative imitation, one might say, represents a kind of affirmation of the present, but an affirmation in jeopardy. The imitation approaches the status of the gentile, the ceremonial exile, because history in gaining specificity loses symmetry. Edward Saïd, paraphrasing Vico, writes: "To be a gentile [not a Hebrew or Christian] is to be denied access to the true God, to have recourse for thought to divination, to live permanently in history."[59] This history of the exile is secular and guilty. "The collective human fate. . . entails the historical creation . . . of an order of meaning different from . . . the order of God's sacred history. Man's beginning is a transgression, and so long as man exists, the fact of his existence asserts the beginning-as-transgression."[60] Myths of progress, of eternal return, and of apocalyptic endings or transitions, all protect the mind against the eccentricity of events. The retrospective etiological construct of the imitative art work also amounts to a protection because it does assign a kind of order: Petrarch's sonnet acts out a subjectification, a lyricization, of Virgil's quasi-epic simile. But this construct is not predictable; it collaborates with history but it is essentially the product of a free imaginative act. It bridges a rupture without any ceremonial sanction and so opens itself to a little more historical contingency than most literary texts conventionally accommodated.

In his admirable *Machiavellian Moment*, Pocock has stressed the element of courage in the shift from the Roman empire to the republic as a model within Florentine civic thought—a shift that occurs roughly during the century between Dante and Leonardo Bruni.[61] Pocock later points to the affinity between philological and political humanism: "Both isolated certain moments in the human past and endeavored to establish communication between these moments in the present."[62] This affinity in fact extended to literary humanism. The technique of imitation posed the problem of secularized repetition as it did the problem of discourse across time. Its profoundest, most characteristic solution required the writer both to assume the vulnerabilities of his own specific moment and to reach out for the specificity of his subtext. From this perspective the imaginative activity of imitation must be seen in its Italian origins as grounded in a far broader and deeper effort of an entire civilization. The experience of France and England would provide weaker analogies with the political sphere, and this comparatively shallower grounding would not lack consequences for the literature of each northern nation. But nowhere was the diachronic text a mere cultural accident; overriding caution and ambivalence, it responded to a vast cultural purpose.

5

This chapter might properly conclude with some remarks on the practical problems posed by the reading of imitations and especially imitative poems. The reader interested in thinking about Renaissance texts in this light has to make on his own a number of distinctions and decisions that in given cases can be slippery. He has to distinguish first of all *allusions,* usages of earlier texts that the reader must recognize in order to read competently, from *repetitions,* whose provenience may be obscure or irrelevant and matters little for the reading of the poem. When Du Bellay opens a sonnet

> Telle que dans son char la Berecynthienne
> Couronnée de tours, & joyeuse d'avoir
> Enfanté tant de Dieux . . .

the reader who misses the subtext from *Aeneid* 6 is in the position of one who reads

> The Chair she sat in, like a burnished throne . . .

and forgets *Antony and Cleopatra.* But other poems by Du Bellay make use of minor Italian poetasters now forgotten; certain sonnets of the *Olive,* for example, are based on sonnets appearing in contemporary fashionable Italian anthologies. Presumably the intentionality of the subtexts from Francesco Coccio or Bernardino Tomitano has a status different from that of Virgil's in the *Antiquitez.* The question has less to do with Du Bellay's private intention than with the claim an allusion could reasonably make upon a knowledgeable contemporary reader. It is arguable that the Giolito anthologies, where Du Bellay found Coccio and Tomitano among others, were sufficiently known in the elite circles for which he wrote to justify terming the use of them allusive. In this case, one could speak of imitations in the full meaning of that word used in this study. But in fact it is questionable whether allusions to the Italian poems would have been so immediately transparent to any reading public. In practice, this distinction can usually be made without difficulty, but borderline teasers arise. Petrarch enjoyed the status of a classic in sixteenth-century France, but what of Bembo? Probably he did also, though with less authority. Not infrequently external evidence is required to dispose of difficult cases.

Du Bellay's recourse to the Giolito volumes[63] can illustrate another necessary distinction. I have discussed *imitatio* in terms of otherness and discontinuity, keeping the relationship to antiquity preeminent and central. If one thinks of, say, Wyatt's relation to Petrarch, one has no trouble in making out an analogous cultural discontinuity. But cultural distance can be measured on a sliding scale; Wyatt's French contemporaries were not so far culturally from Petrarch as he was (one has only to think of Scève) nor were his English successors (for example, Sidney, Drayton, and Daniel). The English successors were less distant in part precisely because Wyatt had already written. How "other" must a subtext be if an imitation can justly be described as bridging a rupture rather than merely following a current convention? There is no perfectly reliable rule of thumb by which to answer this question. A decision must hinge essentially on one's judgment whether two *mundi significantes* are felt to clash at a sufficiently deep level of engagement. The semiotic worlds of Du Bellay and Petrarch do so clash, certainly, as they do not quite in the comparison of *Olive* with the Giolito volumes, despite its Petrarchizing ornaments.

Still another distinction has to be drawn between echoes so brief or peripheral as to be insignificant and a *determinate* subtext that plays a constitutive role in a poem's meaning. The imitative poem need not follow its "model" throughout, but the earlier poem must count as a major presence if one is to speak of imitation in a valid sense. The reader must also distinguish between the use of a single, specific subtext and a topos that conventional repetition has removed from the purview of any one author or work. Here the decision may in difficult instances require more learning than most twentieth-century readers command; it may also require knowledge of the imitative post's reading and taste. Petrarch's sonnet 164, "Or che 'l ciel . . ." (discussed below, pp. 115–19), draws upon an evocation of nightfall that by late antiquity had become conventional. One could argue that the majestic opening images of this sonnet simply represent a particularly rich example of the topos. However, Petrarch did not have access to all ancient Latin poetry, and he established a peculiarly close intimacy with Virgil, whose nightscape at *Aeneid* 4.522ff. had served as the principal fountainhead of the topos. I would argue that the allusion made in 164 is essentially to Virgil, but evidence could be marshaled to support the opposite conclusion. Where one is indubitably dealing with a topos, the etiological itinerary is far more jagged and less than fully knowable. It is also to some degree dehistoricized: if the topos has been everywhere, then it derives specifically from nowhere. The reader is not expected to know its history but to recognize its conventionality, to know it as a product of history. Reading an eclectic texture of topoi is a sharply different activity from reading heuristic or dialectical imitations.

Yet it is possible to speak of dialectical imitation in the case of some poems belonging to conventional subgenres (eclogue, pastoral elegy, epithalamion), which commonly consist of such an eclectic texture. Spenser's "Epithalamion" is saturated in a patrician Catullan and Renaissance tradition, but is a poem nonetheless that insists repeatedly on its own provinciality, its own quaint parochialism, pointing to the rustic manners of its little community, worrying about the disheveled coiffure of the local nymphs, apologizing for its own hastiness, and reversing convention by leaving bride, groom, and reader as wretched earthly clods plunged in dreadful darkness. There is a willful, sometimes humorous, but highly significant choice to underscore its own isolation, its bourgeois modesty as well as its depth of feeling, and in this very emphasis there lies a silent critique of a tradition that comes to look in retrospect a little showy and external. By affirming its lack of pretension, the "Epithalamion" quietly establishes an alternating current of contention with its past.

The long poem of the Renaissance constitutes a special problem for the student of *imitatio*. Superficially all long poems are eclectic imitations, pulling in innumerable subtexts and clusters of topoi, alluding sometimes to conventions and modes by means of a kind of synecdochic shorthand analyzed by Rosalie Colie.[64]

Yet most long poems also tend to reach out to a single privileged predecessor and bind themselves to that authenticating model with particularly intricate knots. Poliziano, despite his heavy reliance on *contaminatio*, binds his *Stanze* to Claudian in this way; Ariosto privileges Boiardo, Tasso privileges Virgil, d'Aubigné the Old Testament, Spenser Ariosto, and Milton the Book of Genesis. The reader must stay alert to the local play of allusion and convention, the interplay for example between Ovid and Virgil within Ariosto's Boiardesque framework, or in *The Faerie Queene* the several matrices admirably sorted out by Angus Fletcher. In a poem of middle length like "Lycidas," the reader needs to note the subtle and gradual shift from the Theocritean and Virgilian subtexts at the opening to the Spenserian at the close, culminating with the unmistakable resonance in the final line of the elegy proper:

To all that wander in that perilous flood.

One has to remain alive to all the local texture of allusion in the longer Renaissance poem while keeping an eye on the poem's ongoing interplay with the major subtext and its massive subterranean outlines. In the big poems this interplay is virtually always dialectical.

A series of distinctions made by humanist schoolmasters and scholars is of lesser interest to the modern reader: this is the series *translatio, paraphrasis, imitatio, allusio*, which tries to draw boundary lines as the version of the original becomes increasingly free. In addition to these four exercises, Renaissance pupils were also introduced to multiple translations of a single original (*variae interpretationes*) and, what must have called for more imagination, replies to it (*responsa*).[65] Once removed from the classroom, divisions between the four principal categories are likely to seem arbitrary; parts of many imitations might well be regarded as translations, while most Renaissance "translations" are already interpretations. The wider the cultural gulf, the more inevitable this interpretive element. A comparison of sixteenth- and seventeenth-century adaptations of, say, Anacreon shows how various even faithful versions could be and how blurred the lines between translation, paraphrase, and imitation. Perhaps these divisions will recommend themselves more to the writer than the reader, serving as general guidelines to govern his individual judgments. Dryden distinguished three degrees of translation: *metaphrase* (following an author "word by word, and line by line"), *paraphrase* (which strives to render the sense rather than every word), and *imitation* ("where the translator [if now he has not lost that name] assumes the liberty, not only to vary from the words and sense, but to forsake them both as he sees occasion; and taking only some general hints from the original, to run division on the groundwork, as he pleases").[66] Since he is here intent on rendering a foreign text into English most effectively, Dryden quite sensibly chooses the second option. Yet he concedes that he might lean toward imitation were his business not with translation: "By this way, 'tis true, somewhat that is excellent may be invented, perhaps more excellent than the first design. . . . To state it fairly;

imitation of an author is the most advantageous way for a translator to show himself, but the greatest wrong which can be done to the memory and reputation of the dead." After several pages in defense of paraphrase as a mean between extremes, Dryden confesses in his last paragraph that he himself, in the version of Ovid to follow, has taken "more liberty than a just translation will allow." Which may in fact be a confession that his original distinctions were too rigid to be of value.[67]

The present study will not concern itself greatly with such categories. But there remains one more distinction which the attentive reader of imitations will find himself obliged to deal with, one which mercifully is easier in drawing than the others even if problematic in its consequences. It concerns the line between what might be called simple imitation, where history, time, and intertextuality are not thematized, and complex imitation, where they are. In most diachronic poems, the interplay does not interfere with the explicit themes, does not overlap or qualify them in ways available to analysis. Ben Jonson writes:

> Kisse me, sweet. . . .
>   First give a hundred,
> Then a thousand, then another
> Hundred, then unto the tother
> Adde a thousand, and so more:
> Till you equall with the store,
> All the grasse that Rumney yeelds,
> Or the sands in Chelsey fields,
> Or the drops in silver Thames . . .

The sprightly rewriting of Catullus 5 and 7 leaves the diachronic interplay altogether distinct from the synchronic meaning. The interplay supplies a kind of frame within which the synchronic poem is experienced. Or perhaps better than *frame* is the Renaissance term *surround,* a design with a life of its own that presses in upon the picture it contains without destroying the picture's integrity. That is simple imitation, which sets as it were quotation marks around the poem proper but refrains from interrupting it. For complex imitation, one has only to look at the companion piece to Jonson's little lyric.

> Come my *Celia*, let us prove,
> While we may, the sports of love;
> Time will not be ours, for ever:
> He, at length, our good will sever.
> Spend not then his guifts in vaine.
> Sunnes, that set, may rise againe:
> But if once we loose this light,
> 'Tis, with us, perpetuall night.

Yes and no. Catullus's "*perpetua . . . dormienda*" has not been absolute; his good has not altogether been severed, since in fact an English Jacobean has grown very He or attempted to, has in any case perpetuated Catullus's light as well as his darkness. Whatever reading one finally reaches of this second lyric, one has to account for the *impingement* of the diachronic on the synchronic and the counter reflection in the other direction. The octave of Du Bellay's "Berecynthienne" sonnet, which rewrites amply and nobly the simile of Virgile's Anchises. is answered ominously. by the clanging first line of the sestet in a kind of iron dismissal:

> Rome seule pouvoit à Rome ressembler.

The interaction between statement and imagistic itinerary is inextricable, and nowhere more than in *Les Antiquitez de Rome*, perhaps the most densely ironic instance of all complex imitations. When the imitative interference approaches this degree of complexity, no taxonomy of types is possible; each text is unique and the reader has to work out his own hermeneutic calculus.

Reading imitations makes even larger claims on the historical imagination than most reading, and underscores even more cruelly our cultural solitude. It asks us not only to intuit an alien sensibility from a remote *mundus significans*, but also that sensibility's intuitions of a third. Nothing perhaps is more calculated to impress on us our temporal estrangement. Yet nothing perhaps immerses us so forcibly in the flow of literary history; no exercise plunges us so deeply into the currents and eddies of this continuous flow of energy. "All poetry actually deals in anachronism," Goethe wrote, astonishingly;[68] we are scarcely beginning to learn how to reckon the accounts of this commerce.

Four • Themes of Ancient Theory

To study the imitation of models (*mimesis* in Greek, *imitatio* in Latin) in ancient theory is to confront immediately a problem that will recur throughout the history of this subject.[1] Some of those who wrote about it were concerned with the education of boys, often at a fairly elementary stage; others were concerned primarily with adolescents or young men already beginning a serious professional career; others were writing mainly for adults. Some were concerned with a broad liberal education, others specifically with the training of orators, others with poets or what we would call creative writers. Although any given discussion of imitation generally indicates with sufficient clarity its field of application, it is impossible to trace doctrines exclusively within each field. Educational precepts blended too gradually into literary counsel to permit a firm line between them. Rules for orators and advice to poets were contained within perspectives embracing an entire society. Thus the study of ancient imitative theory possesses a real unity, but its history is obliged to zigzag through a series of heterogeneous contexts.

This history can properly begin with brief remarks by two major Greek authors of the fourth century B.C. Aristotle writes in the *Poetics* that "Imitation is natural to man from childhood, one of his advantages over the lower animals being this, that he is the most imitative creature in the world, and learns at first by imitation."[2] Since Aristotle goes on to speak of the pleasure derived from pictorial representations, it might appear that the term *mimesis* used here means what it generally means throughout the *Poetics*, the imitation of "nature." But the statement that man learns first by imitation would on the other hand be more easily applicable to children copying or repeating the observed actions of adult "models." Aristotle apparently subsumes both meanings of *mimesis* under a single, more general concept. Later writers would separate out these meanings, though not without occasional contaminations and overlappings. The universalization of the imitative impulse provided in any case an authoritative basis for its literary justification. This universalization would recur in Quintilian's *Institutio oratoria*.

> Omnis vitae ratio sic constat, ut quae probamus in aliis facere ipsi velimus. Sic litterarum ductus, ut scribendi fiat usus, pueri sequuntur, sic musici vocem docentium, pictores opera priorum, rustici probatam experimento culturam in exemplum intuentur; omnis denique disciplinae initia ad propositum sibi praescriptum formari videmus. [10.2.2]
> [It is a universal rule of life that we should wish to copy what we approve in others. It is for this reason that boys copy the shapes of letters that they may learn to write, and that musicians take the voices of their teachers, painters the works of their predecessors, and

peasants the principles of agriculture which have been proved in practice, as models for their imitation. In fact, we may note that the elementary study of every branch of learning is directed by reference to some definite standard that is placed before the learner.][3]

Both Aristotle and Quintilian assimilate the learning process in children to adult activities presumed to be inherent in human existence. This assumption is one reason why no sharp distinction can be drawn between pedagogic and artistic imitative doctrine throughout most of antiquity.

One natural conclusion to be drawn from this Aristotelian conception is that imitation characteristically proceeds from the observation of models immediately present. Young children can only try to reproduce the acts they see performed around them, and this immediacy becomes by implication a feature of adult reproductions. This immediacy is also presumed by Aristotle's older contemporary Isocrates, writing specifically about education. For him the teacher is ideally not only a source of information and explanation, but a dominant, formative single model whose example shapes permanently the thought and praxis of his pupils. This ideal appears twice in Isocrates' works, once in *Against the Sophists:*

> The teacher . . . must in himself set such an example of oratory that the students who have taken form under his instruction and are able to pattern after him will, from the outset, show in their speaking a degree of grace and charm which is not found in others.

and again in the *Antidosis.*

> This . . . will be agreed to by all men, namely, that in all the arts and crafts we regard those as the most skilled who turn out pupils who all work as far as possible in the same manner. Now it will be seen that this is the case with philosophy. For all who have been under a true and intelligent guide will be found to have a power of speech so similar that it is evident to everyone that they have shared the same training. And yet, had not a common habit and a common technique of training been instilled into them, it is inconceivable that they should have taken on this likeness.[4]

Cicero would later praise Isocrates himself precisely for this capacity of exemplary influence reflected in the resemblance of his students among themselves. Cicero in fact would carry the idea much further. It would appear that for this great Greek teacher the "common habit and technique of training" are inseparable from the common model, the teacher, just as training in speech is inseparable (the context of the quotation from *Against the Sophists* also makes this clear) from instruction in philosophy. Isocrates like Aristotle is concerned with the unmediated impact of human beings on younger human beings closely exposed to the force of their example.

There is some evidence that the imitation of models was discussed in the lost works of Theophrastus, Aristotle's follower and nephew. Quintilian at any rate writes that according to Theophrastus the reading of poets is very useful to the orator (10.1.27).[5] No one can say how much Theophrastus made of this, but if the relationship advocated between reading and speaking contained an implication that poets among others might be useful as models, then this relation would clearly be one without precedent in extant texts. Those who enjoy further reaches of speculation might conjecture that, given Theophrastus's known dependence on his uncle's work, it is likely that rhetorical imitation was mentioned in Aristotle's lost dialogue on poets. What *can* be said with assurance is that the usefulness of poets to orators, however formulated, obviously depended on an experience of reading rather than direct learning from a teacher. It would appear also that Theophrastus was sensitive to the historicity of style, since Cicero refers to his remarks on the stylistic developments introduced by Herodotus and Thucydides (*Orator* 12.39). We have no reason to believe that this was a subject of great interest to Theophrastus's predecessors.

It was on the other hand of considerable interest to the scholars of Hellenistic Alexandria, and especially to the greatest of them, Aristarchus (second century B.C.). For Horace, this scholar's name had virtually become shorthand for the ideal practical critic (*Ars poetica* 450). For our purposes he is important, together with his Alexandrian forerunners, because he contributed that historical sophistication to the reading of texts which permits the growth of philology. Aristarchus silenced critics who objected to alleged Homeric breaches of decorum (Nausicaa doing the laundry, insults exchanged by gods, kings carving the meat) by pointing to changes in social customs. His replies to these criticisms thus established the fallacy of anachronism (anticipated to be sure by Aristotle, *Poetics* 1461a). As an editor and commentator on Homer, he insisted on establishing the meaning of a word by reference to all its Homeric contexts, in preference to its usage in later centuries. He refused to alter certain grammatical constructions merely because they were no longer current. In effect, Aristarchus defended Homer as the representative of his own *mundus significans*. The result was to open a space between model and imitator. This Alexandrian consciousness of the historicity and consequently the remoteness of older texts can be regarded as a permanent acquisition of Graeco-Roman culture.

This consciousness is probably operative in the thought of the remarkable poet-philosopher-critic Philodemus (born 110 B.C. in Greece and educated there, later established in Rome). The remarks on imitation in the fragmentary remains of his *Poetics* attack those unsympathetic to older poetry simply because it is old, but attack equally those respectful of imitative poetry simply because its models are good.[6] No poet excels consistently in all genres; even in his own, writes Philodemus, his consistency may be open to question.[7] Justice cannot be described as the imitation of Aristides, or politics as the imitation of Pericles. Whom was Homer himself imitating? The upshot of these reflections for Philodemus was advice to pursue literary imitation cautiously. From our own vantage point, limited to be sure by enormous gaps in the available literature, we can take note of a broad swing across the centuries separating Isocrates and Philodemus. The decline of Greek civilization has produced a gap between imitator and model. No longer the result of an unmediated human impact, imitation is now a relationship between reader and book, the book from a lost era of distinction whose virtues, because lost, lend themselves to oversimplification. Philodemus is the first Greek author known to have denounced the idolatry of misplaced imitation, what I have called sacramental imitation, which reifies the energy of a venerated classic and thus loses touch with it. Philodemus recognizes the problematic character of imitation across a historical expanse, although his response to this problem as recorded in the extant texts, namely caution, is not in itself suggestive.

Most of the major ancient critics writing after Aristarchus reveal in one fashion or another their sensitivity to this problematic character, even if the sensitivity is unavowed. Greek critics had to deal with the decay of their tradition. Roman critics had to deal with a sense of inferiority to Greece. Both had to deal with linguistic, literary, and social change. The classic looms inimitable and unavoidable, nourishing and threatening. The tradition commands allegiance and must be maintained, but its maintenance requires innovation, which is to say some degree of rejection. As the cultural center of gravity shifts to Rome, the crucial problems surround the *translation* of a tradition. Is it possible? demeaning? appropriate? anachronistic? Are etiologies extensible across a sea and a linguistic frontier? And can one, in an era of decline, hope to reactivate momentum lost? The continuing dialogue over imitation is conducted against the background of these uncertainties.

Among those who faced most directly the decay of Hellenic civilization was a Greek who settled in Augustan Rome a generation after Philodemus, the antiquarian and critic Dionysius of Halicarnassus. Dionysius wrote a treatise in three books on the subject of the imitation of models; this has been lost, but a passage from it is quoted in an extant compostion and there are also scattered remarks in other works that survive. Since Dionysius knew Latin well, it is possible though not certain that his thinking shows some Roman influence. He is the first Greek author of whom it can be said with assurance that imitation of the classics formed the basis of his literary program. He felt an acute sense of loss, not only of the classics themselves but of the classical (that is, fifth and fourth century) temper. The expression of this loss in the introduction to his *On the Ancient Orators* approaches more closely the humanist pathos of the Renaissance than any other single ancient text. Dionysius, who has nothing kind to say of any Greek writer of the first three centuries B.C., placed what hope he could muster in classical imitation as a technique of recovery. His polemics against the debased rhetoric of the Hellenistic era ("Thus was wisdom driven out by ignorance, and sanity by madness")[8] recall the humanists' polemics against the medieval darkness separating them from all that was noble.

The technique for recovering excellence devised by Dionysius begins with precise analysis of the best Attic orators and historians in order to isolate the specific virtues (*aretai*) of each. This technique, "of great potential benefit to mankind," can be approached by asking three questions: "Who are the most important of the ancient orators and historians? What manner of life and style of writing did they adopt? Which characteristics of each of them should we imitate, and which should we avoid?"[9] To answer these questions it is helpful to compare two writers one of whom imitated or emulated the other. Dionysius provides such comparisons, conducted somewhat mechanically; the longest one rates Herodotus against Thucydides.[10] Armed with this precise array of comparative virtues, the aspirant writer is then in a stronger position to form his own classicizing style. Thus we are really dealing with a double set of imitative resemblances, the first between those not separated by a wide temporal gap and the second between those who are so separated. One corollary of Dionysius's method is the assumption that the postclassical imitator should choose many models rather than one in forming his own style. No single author was perceived as embodying all the virtues. This advocacy of multiple models would be echoed by some later ancient writers but opposed by others. During the Renaissance the debate over this question would provoke an enormous literature.

It is unclear to what degree Dionysius saw his method to be attended with inherent difficulties. The restoration of sound rhetoric which he believed (or professed to believe) to be occurring in the Roman Augustan Age he prudently explained either by "the instance of some god, or by the return of the old order of things in accordance with a natural cycle, or through the human urge that draws many towards the same activities."[11] This seems to leave open the question whether classical imitation can achieve anything of itself without supernatural aid. In one fragment imitation is defined as "an activity receiving the impression of a model by inspection of it."[12] The metaphorical reception of an impression suggests a passivity and facility which however are qualified by the activity of inspection, requiring energy and subtlety. In this same fragment the term "imitation" (*mimesis*) is coupled with a second term that would frequently accompany or replace it throughout its history, namely "emulation," *zelos*, defined felicitously as "an activity of the soul impelled toward admiration of what seems to be fine." In his actual comparisons of the Greek historians and orators, Dionysius employs *zelos* or its cognates at least as often as *mimesis*. He does not use it however in speaking of the postclassical imitator in the introduction to *On the Ancient Orators*. He may not have considered it possible for a postclassical writer to emulate, which is to say seriously rival, a true classic.

The concept of emulation found in Dionysius's letter to Pompeius, containing a long quotation from the lost treatise on imitation, assumes not only the element of challenge but also a specific precursor one wants to rival or surpass. One can emulate either subject matter or language or both. Although the fragmentary quotations and epitomes are too brief to allow for certainty, it would seem that for Dionysius imitation within a single era *is* emulation, always contains this element of rivalry. But none of his examples are Latin, and the separation in time between precursor and emulator is not very great. Dionysius's method, basically comparative, justifies itself in part by this assumption of rivalry. We have already met this

Greek respect for emulation in a passage from Longinus (see above, page 46) with its allusion to Hesiod. Longinus's comments leave no doubt concerning his own favorable attitude, nor does Dionysius's definition as an admiration of the soul for the fine. *Zelos* in these Greek presentations is unambiguously, courageously positive and seems to permit no suspicion of Bloomian evasion.

Two serious questions however are posed by the manifold usages of this term and its counterparts during antiquity and the Renaissance. First, one may ask whether the term has any value for textual analysis as distinguished from pedagogic or genetic precept. I have attempted in the previous chapter to sketch a theory of dialectical imitation, a theory intended as an analytic instrument. The terms *zelos* and *aemulatio* as alternatives possess millennial authority, but they suffer from the disadvantage of a psychologistic tincture calculated to blur formal analysis. To advise emulation rather than close imitation in a pedagogical situation may conceivably free an apprentice writer to follow his models less mechanically. But for the reader-critic to seek to distinguish, ex post facto, emulative texts from imitative may lead to a wasteful multiplication of categories. To the degree that a text by an emulator bears a resemblance to a subtext, it can be analyzed in imitative terms. The spirit or intention of its author must remain subject to guesswork. If an attitude of rivalry toward a given subtext or toward the tradition is explicitly thematized, then its expression needs to be noticed, but it does not constitute in itself a structural relationship. If there are formal resemblances as well, the expression of rivalry creates an interaction between theme and structure that results in complex rather than simple imitation.

The second question posed by this term stems from the conflict one can discern in imitative theory between a will to recognize the problematic character of imitation and a will not to recognize it. As the models recede, as the Aristotelian analogy of the child watching its parent grows less and less apt, as (for example, in the case of Dionysius) the experience of discontinuity grows more acute, then the conflict between these two wills is exacerbated. The precise proportion of resemblance and difference becomes harder to control, and the prestige of the classic becomes more intimidating. Thus one may ask whether the concept of emulation may not become a means of sidestepping that prickly nexus which is imitation, whether it may not displace attention away from the troubling issue of structural similarity to a psychologistic category easier to deal with. However rooted in Greek tradition, a theory of emulation held by a historically sophisticated thinker is open to the charge of fudging the problem of resemblance.[13]

If in fact theories of emulation are symptoms of felt conflict, so in a more open and creative way are metaphorizations of imitative relationships. If abstract, discursive language is insufficient to register imitative complexity, then it may possibly be captured at a secondary, figurative level. Unmediated relationships in Aristotle and Isocrates need no governing metaphors. In Dionysius's definition of *mimesis* there is a tacit reflection of difficulty in the faintly suggested conflict between the active inspection of something external and the passive reception of an impression from it. Another incipient metaphor lurks in a distinction between two kinds of *mimesis*.

> An imitation is related to the ancient models in two different ways: the first relationship is the natural result of being for a long time in close contact with the model and living with it; the second resembles it but results from the application of rhetorical rules. About the first kind there is little one can say; about the second one can say only that all the models have a natural grace and charm of their own, while their contrived imitations, even if they are as perfect as imitations can be, always have something labored and unnatural about them.[14]

It is easy enough to write about "unnatural" and contrived imitation. Nothing can be predicated about the organic kind except a metaphorical intimacy, a "living together." This reversion to a secondary discourse, this recourse to figuration, is the best evidence that Dionysius intuited a resistance in his chosen subject.

2

In Roman discussions of *imitatio* during the first century B.C., metaphorization is a good deal denser in poetry than in the prose rhetorical treatises where the subject most commonly arises. This contrast may simply reflect the different norms of decorum supposed to govern two unlike bodies of writing. There is abundant evidence in both bodies of tension surrounding the literary dependence of Rome on Greece. It is true that most major writers tended to share a remarkably similar hope for the development of their own culture through imitation of the Greek classics. G. M. A. Grube describes their program in these terms:

> Latin literature was . . . the self-conscious creation of men who were thoroughly familiar with a kindred literature which they knew to be far more developed than their own. The educated Romans of the late Republic and the early Empire were bilingual. They deliberately set out to forge their own language into an instrument by means of which they could hope to rival the Greeks with masterpieces of their own which, imitative in all external matters of form, would yet breathe the Roman spirit and celebrate Rome's achievement.[15]

Grube's unfortunate separation of form and spirit is faithful to comparable separations made by the Romans themselves. The actual ineffable entanglement of Greek elements in Roman civilization, the intricate processes of assimilation and resistance which occurred, did of course produce the masterpieces envisioned by this program, but not without conflicts of admiration and envy, classicism and chauvinist pride. These conflicts are writ large in the discussions of *imitatio*. Neither Cicero nor Horace nor Quintilian produced a formulation of the imitative classicist program that was stable, coherent, enduring, and self-sufficient. None of them found a final equilibrium for his classicism just as none found language that could capture the delicate interplay of cultures at work, say, in a Horatian ode.

Seneca came closer in his highly metaphoric sketch of an imitative syncretism. The restlessness behind the failures need not of course be regarded as impoverishing; without it doubtless the masterpieces would not have emerged. In them one finds the stability missing in the discursive accounts. The *Aeneid* makes its peace with Homer and the Greeks by engaging them everywhere but thematizing them almost nowhere. However even if the discursive accounts never attain this peace, they do not lack interest; part of the interest lies precisely in their shifts and self-subversions.

The breadth of the gap between imitator and model, the degree of mediation between them which increases so sharply in Greek theory, becomes an issue even more highly charged by Roman ambivalence toward that conquered civilization which, in Horace's phrase, made her savage victor captive (*Epistulae*, 2.1.156). Education of well-born Roman boys was already considerably Hellenized at the opening of the first century A.D.; this was a situation in itself likely to irritate Roman pride. The *Rhetorica ad Herennium*, written by an unknown author during the eighties, strains to be self-sufficiently Roman, but it could not conceivably have received the form it took without the example of Greek forerunners like Demetrius and Hermagoras. Imitation is mentioned at the outset as a means of acquiring the faculties needed for speaking well. It is that which "stimulates us to attain, in accordance with a studied method, the effectiveness of certain models in speaking" (1.2.3). (Imitatio est qua impellimur, cum diligenti ratione, ut aliquorum similes in dicendo valeamus esse.)[16] The method (*ratio*) is not further defined, nor are the models (in the Latin vaguely designated as "aliquorum") here specified. But a curious ramification does appear in the preface to the fourth and last book. There the author defends at length his decision to supply his own *exempla* (examples, models) rather than use quotations from earlier writers as, he says, Greek writers generally do.[17] The author first argues (4.5) that it would be better to draw on one author for "examples" than many. But in 4.6 he argues that it would be still better to draw on no other author. One needs to demonstrate one's own competence by supplying one's own passages for imitation. "Not thus did Chares learn from Lysippus how to make statues. Lysippus did not show him a head by Myron, arms by Praxiteles, a chest by Polycleitus. Rather with his own eyes would Chares see the master fashioning all the parts; the works of the other sculptors he could if he wished study on his own initiative" (4.6.9). Thus this apparently unimportant issue really concerns the distance from the student of his models (as well as the apparent superiority of a single model). The author wants to reduce this distance. Some gap however is inevitable in dealing with rhetoric, since the technical terms are Greek. All the more reason not to use borrowed examples.

> Haec quoque res nos duxit ad hanc rationem, quod nomina rerum Graeca quae convertimus, ea remota sunt a consuetudine. Quae enim res apud nostros non erant, earum rerum nomina non poterant esse usitata. [4.7.10][18]
> [I have been led to this method by another consideration also—the remoteness from our own usage of the technical terms I have translated from the Greek. For concepts non-existent among us must seem rather harsh at first.]

As the following discussion makes still clearer, the fact that Greek terms are inescapable but remote constitutes a source of potential embarrassment and defensive justification.

Cicero's first, youthful rhetorical treatise, *De inventione*, probably a little earlier than the *ad Herennium*, shows somewhat less embarrassment toward its Greek sources. For the history of imitative theory it is most notable as the locus classicus of a topos that Renaissance authors would repeat tirelessly: the story of the painter Zeuxis who, commissioned by the citizens of Crotona to decorate their temple of Juno, chose five maidens of the town as models for his painting of Helen, since none alone was perfectly beautiful without defect. Thus has Cicero done in this work.

> Quod quoniam nobis quoque voluntatis accidit ut artem dicendi perscriberemus, non unum aliquod proposuimus exemplum cuius omnes partes, quocumque essent in genere, exprimendae nobis necessarie viderentur; sed, omnibus unum in locum coactis scriptoribus, quod quisque commodissime praecipere videbatur excerpsimus et ex variis ingeniis excellentissima quaeque libavimus. Ex eis enim qui nomine et memoria digni sunt nec nihil optime nec omnia praeclarissime quisquam dicere nobis videbatur. [2.2.4][19]
>
> [In a similar fashion when the inclination arose in my mind to write a text-book of rhetoric, I did not set before myself some one model which I thought necessary to reproduce in all details, of whatever sort they might be, but after collecting all the works on the subject I excerpted what seemed the most suitable precepts from each, and so culled the flower of many minds. For each of the writers who are worthy of fame and reputation seemed to say something better than anyone else, but not to attain pre-eminence in all points.]

The Latin verb "libavimus" (extracted) has weaker metaphoric force than the Loeb translator's "culled the flower," but it does carry the suggestion of a culinary analogy. The writers drawn upon by Cicero are clearly Greek, but in this work the faint metaphor is the only sign that he feels their remoteness to be problematic, as the *auctor ad Herennium* would. The divergence of these two early treatises on the desirable number and distance of *exempla* is significant of an enduring division in the Roman mind.

Cicero's attitude has changed in the mature rhetorical work written over thirty years later, the *De oratore*. There the gap between model and imitator collapses into the direct contact of Isocratean pedagogy, although this Roman process whereby a student forms himself upon a distinguished native orator is understood to follow a pattern that is originally Greek. Skill in oratory is transmitted through careful observation from generation to generation—by proximity, metonymically or syntagmatically. But this entire activity of generational transmission parallels Greek transmission—by transference, metaphorically or paradigmatically. The fullest and most interesting account of these relationships appears in book 2, where the supposed speaker, Antonius, advances opinions that are transparently the author's (2.88–98). He begins by citing the example of a younger speaker present at the fictive conversation, a certain Sulpicius, who had succeeded in moderating and polishing his innate exuberance by studying the style of the distinguished orator Crassus (who is also supposed to be present). The choice of the model was crucial, precisely appropriate for the development of Sulpicius's style. The young man's temperament would have led him naturally to Crassus

> sed ea non satis proficere potuisset, nisi eodem studio atque imitatione intendisset, atque ita dicere consuesset, ut tota mente Crassum atque omni animo intuere-
> tur.   [2.21.89][20]
> [. . . but could never have made him proficient enough, had he not pressed forward on that same way by careful imitation, and formed the habit of speaking with every thought and all his soul fixed in contemplation of Crassus.]

Antonius's stress thus falls on *selecting* that model most appropriate for the student's combination of gifts and on *observing*, "looking" with the mind. There then follows a negative example, one Fufius, who copies only the external manner-isms and even the imperfections of his chosen model. The looking expressed by the verb "intueretur" clearly implies a piercing to the core of the chosen model's skill and manner, and then in a second choice, isolating those excellences that deserve close reproduction.

Antonius then abruptly turns to a historical survey that contains several original ideas and introduces new dimensions to Cicero's reflection.

> Quid enim causae censetis esse, cur aetates extulerint singulae singula prope genera dicendi? Quod non tam facile in nostris oratoribus possumus iudicare, quia scripta, ex quibus iudicium fieri posset, non multa sane reliquerunt, quam in Graecis; ex quorum scriptis, cuiusque aetatis quae dicendi ratio voluntasque fuerit, intellegi potest. Antiquissimi fere sunt, quorum quidem scripta constent, Pericles atque Alcibi-ades, et eadem aetate Thucydides, subtiles, acuti, breves, sententiis magis quam verbis abundantes. Consecuti sunt hos Critias, Theramenes, Lysias. . . . Non potuisset accidere ut unum esset omnium genus, nisi aliquem sibi proponerent ad imitandum: omnes etiam tum retinebant illum Periclis sucum; sed erant paulo uberiore filo. Ecce tibi exortus est Isocrates, magister rhetorum omnium, cuius e ludo, tanquam ex equo Troiano, meri principes exierunt; sed eorum partim in pompa, partim in acie illustres esse voluerunt.
>
> Atque et illi, Theopompi, Ephori, . . . multique alii naturis differunt, voluntate autem similes sunt et inter sese et magistri, et ei, qui se ad causas contulerunt, ut Demosthenes, Hyperides, . . . aliique complures, etsi inter se pares non fuerunt, tamen omnes sunt in eodem veritatis imitandae genere versati, quorum quamdiu mansit imitatio, tamdiu genus illud dicendi studiumque vixit. Posteaquam, exstinctis his, omnis eorum memoria sensim obscurata est et evanuit, alia quaedam dicendi molliora ac remissiora genera viguerunt.   [2.22.92–23.95][21]
> ["Why now is it, do you suppose, that nearly every age has produced its own distinctive style of oratory? Of this truth we can judge less easily in the case of our own orators, since they have left but very few writings on which a judgement could be based, than as regards the Greeks, from whose works the method and tendency of the oratory of every generation may be understood. Quite the earliest of whom we have any authentic

remains are Pericles and Alcibiades, with Thucydides of the same generation, all of them accurate, pointed, terse and wealthier in ideas than diction. These were followed by Critias, Theramenes and Lysias. . . . Their uniformity of style could never have come about, had they not kept before them some single model for imitation: they all still retained the peculiar vigor of Pericles, but their texture was a little more luxuriant. Then behold! there arose Isocrates, the Master of all rhetoricians, from whose school, as from the Horse of Troy, none but leaders emerged, but some of them sought glory in ceremonial, others in actions.

And indeed the former sort, men like Theopompus, Ephorus, . . . and many more, while differing in natural gifts, yet in spirit resemble one another and their master too; and those who betook themselves to lawsuits, as did Demosthenes, Hyperides, . . . and several others, although of varying degrees of ability, were none the less all busy with the same type of imitation of real life, and as long as the imitation of these persisted, so long did their kind of oratory and course of training endure. Afterwards, when these men were dead and all remembrance of them gradually grew dim and then vanished away, certain other less spirited and lazier styles of speaking flourished."]

Whether or not the individual names strewn through this passage all have meaning for us, it can teach us a good deal about Cicero's conception of the history of oratory, which was of course for him the supreme discipline bridging letters and public life.[22] Antonius sketches at once a retrospect of Attic oratory and a potential prospect for Rome. The original points can be more or less matched to specific terms. The *aetas*, or generation, of orators is distinguished as the fundamental historical unit, each dominated by a single exemplary figure who at once imposes himself and is freely chosen by a school of gifted followers. The family resemblance of each generation of orators is perceived by Cicero as positive; it produces what he calls the *genus dicendi* of the age, its particular oratorical character. A few lines below, this term is replaced by the phrase *dicendi ratio voluntasque*, which implies an orderly method, a willed, self-conscious attempt by the speakers of each era to achieve a common temper, a cultural style of their own. There is an implication that the elite of each generation can develop deliberately this common moral style through the intelligent, creative, mutual exercise of imitation, which thus becomes, in Elaine Fantham's expression, "the prime cause of stylistic growth."[23] It also serves to organize and rationalize the age's *mundus significans*. This shared will does not erase the variety of individual oratorical temperaments (*naturae*), but it establishes a community where each temperament finds its place. The system is patriarchal but not despotic. It depends upon a loyalty to a master and a tradition, a loyalty here called *memoria*. When Antonius remarks that remembrance of the Isocratean school grew dim and disappeared, he is not of course saying that the members of the school were literally forgotten but that the will to maintain the tradition, to sustain growth through imitation, slackened and died. Remembrance here is an active, communal faculty that serves to keep history open.

The passage is informed by mature and original reflection. But it must be admitted that as a Roman prospect, rather than an Attic retrospect, its bases are shaky. Antonius's alleged reason for citing the Greek oratorical tradition rather than the Roman (fewer Roman speeches were written down) is more than a little disingenuous. Roman oratory before the date of this fictive conversation could not begin to rival Greek. Crassus, the dominant figure in the conversation, the model imitated by Sulpicius and perhaps the most distinguished orator of his age, was himself trained by Greeks and had studied in Greece. The Roman orators of the generation following Crassus, as they are later characterized in *De oratore* 3.26–37, are less notable for a common *genus dicendi* than for their wide range of individual talents ("specie dispares, genere laudibiles"). The citation in book 3 of Isocrates, who had imposed a common style on comparable variety, using the spur with Ephorus and the bridle with Theopompus, cannot conceal the absence of a Roman figure of Isocratean stature. Cicero doubtless hoped himself to play such a role, but he had not at this writing yet succeeded. Thus unmediated, Isocratean imitation within a Roman context remains an ideal still unrealized in the *De oratore* and perhaps unrealizable.

This latent instability may account for Cicero's shift nine years later in the dialogue entitled *Brutus*, written during the Atticist controversy. Here it is accepted by all speakers that the *genus Atticum* is the most worthy of imitation, and for Cicero himself the supreme model is clearly Demosthenes (see especially *Brutus* 285–91). This assumption recurs in a much slighter contemporaneous work, *De optimo genere oratorum*, an introduction to unwritten translations of Aeschines and Demosthenes, where references to the effort of translation (14, 23) are doubled by an apparent doubt concerning the feasibility of any translation commensurate with the originals.[24] The program of *De oratore* must have seemed attractive because it avoided imitation across a gap, mediated imitation of the supremely great. The *Brutus* reopens this gap, but the solution of that work in turn proved far more short-lived. In the *Orator*, composed later the same year (46 B.C.), all imitation of historical models gives way to the imitation of a perfect ideal present only to the mind.

> Ut ... in formis et figuris est aliquid perfectum et excellens, cuius ad cogitatam speciem imitando referuntur ea quae sub oculos ipsa non cadunt, sic perfectae eloquentiae speciem animo videmus, effigiem auribus quaerimus.   [9][25]
> [As there is something perfect and surpassing in the case of sculpture and painting—an intellectual ideal by reference to which the artist represents those objects which do not themselves appear to the eye, so with our minds we conceive the ideal of perfect eloquence, but with our ears we catch only the copy.]

Now one copies a supreme idea of eloquence. Can one regard this ultimate recourse to Plato, whom Cicero cites (10), as an implicit admission that the comparisons and disjunctures of human history are finally too threatening for this great Roman classicist? Cicero significantly never produced a governing metaphor to clarify his successive conceptions of imitation. He never produced a theory of transformation. His strongest theory depended on an enduring, continuous civic vitality which at the end he was clear-sighted enough to perceive as moribund. The Platonism of the *Orator* can be read as a gesture of despair over what mattered most to Cicero; it can also be read as another tacit acknowledgment of the imitative problematic.

3

The Augustan Age in Rome produced some of the greatest imitative poetry ever written. It demonstrated for future eras, including the Renaissance and including our own, the potential power of a poetic based on the bridging of discontinuities. In this respect the Romans differed from their Greek masters. Nietzsche praised Greece as "a true unhistorical culture—and in spite of that, or perhaps because of it, an unspeakably rich and vital culture." The Greeks, he wrote, were unhistorical because after falling under the influence of several Eastern civilizations "they again came into possession of themselves, and did not long remain the epigoni of the whole East, burdened with their inheritance. . . . After that hard fight, they increased and enriched the treasure they had inherited by their obedience to the oracle ['Know thyself'], and they became the ancestors and models for all the cultured nations of the future."[26] Nietzsche praised Greece in these terms near the beginning of his career, but near its close, he wrote, "The Greeks . . . *cannot* be to us what the Romans are. One does not *learn* from the Greeks—their manner is too strange. . . . Who would ever have learned to write from a Greek! Who would ever have learned it *without* the Romans!"[27] This shift from Greece to Rome as cultural model does not mean that the late Nietzsche came to undervalue Greece but that he came to measure at its true worth a "historical" civilization, whose gifts lay in its collaboration with historical process.

The *Aeneid* is the classic statement of the Roman task because Virgil made it an epic of what I should like to call *transitivity*, that is to say of historical mediation, of threatened but preserved continuities. For it was Rome's function, as we see it now in hindsight, to transmit the traditions of Greek culture still living to the European west. What is extraordinary is the recognition by the greatest Roman authors that this was in fact to be their role in what Auerbach called the drama of western literature. They understood, that is—Virgil, Horace, and Cicero among others—not only the value and dignity of transmission but also the necessity of living transmission, of cultural re-creation. The *Aeneid* is the classic statement of this high role because it gives substance to the role in two distinct ways. First, it narrates and valorizes a myth of precarious continuity; and second, its minor forms (episodes, descriptions, speeches, similes, characters) call attention to their Greek provenience and specifically to their Homeric provenience. Virgil deals with the Homeric shadow, his own anxiety of influence, by putting it into his poem, by facing it literally on every page and by transmuting each minor form through context into something new and Roman. Thus his fable of transitivity was orchestrated everywhere by a transitive technique that demonstrated the fact of preservation but also the fact of transmutation. This special historical character of Virgil's poem makes it the central and supreme expression of Roman civilization.

It is clear that Horace's poetry also was deeply transitive, although in this case we lack almost all of the Greek subtexts that would permit us to study the precise workings of his art. On the other hand Horace's poetry abounds in allusions to and discussions of this art. Here the metaphorization of *imitatio* is as copious as it is thin in Cicero. For the modern student the difficulty lies in reconciling the conflicting implications of successive metaphors or the conflicting implications of the same metaphor repeated in shifting contexts. Alternatively the difficulty lies in understanding the significance of their near-irreconcilability. Taken together, these discussions stretched out over a career of writing demonstrate the arduous and intricate task of a transitive culture.

One common metaphor appears in the epistle to Julius Florus (1.3), where the speaker, inquiring about an acquaintance with poetic aspirations, asks,

> Quid Titius, Romana brevi venturus in ora?
> Pindarici fontis qui non expalluit haustus,
> fastidire lacus et rivos ausus apertos?   [9–11][28]
> [What of Titius, soon to be on the lips of Romans, who quailed not at draughts of the
> Pindaric spring, but dared to scorn the open pools and streams?]

Fairclough, the Loeb editor and translator, interprets the contrast between "fontis" and "lacus et rivos" as "the contrast between those Greek writers who could easily be reproduced, and the inimitable Pindar." Anybody apparently could draw water from artificial pools and tanks, but few from natural springs in distant hills requiring a long itinerary. There is implicit scorn for those who draw their water from the easily accessible ("apertos") sources, as well possibly as a touch of urbane irony toward the ambitious young man with sublime intentions.[29] Here already appears a gambit we shall meet more than once in Horace, a pairing of opposed negative directions leaving a very narrow space between them. Where *should* one look for water? The question is not made easier by the subsequent allusion to a certain Celsus, who must be warned against touching (for the purpose of imitation) the books in the Palatine library but must rather seek his own private wealth ("privatas ut quaeret opes") lest he be stripped of his borrowed plumage like a crow. The poem is indirectly telling us how difficult apt imitation is. But if Fairclough is right, there is also an ambivalent reflection of the theme of transitivity. The Pindaric spring *flows*, as lesser standing pools do not. The imitation Titius dreams of would be a remarkable achievement if it were brought off, because the stream would actually be directed through time in an act of transitive creativity. The vital power inherent in Pindar's poetry seems to be conflated with the vital flow of history, sweeping from that distant, almost unattainable source. Pindaric odes move with a fearful energy lacking in lesser versifiers and requiring special courage from that follower who has not paled ("non expalluit") at the prospect of drinking from their stream. However urbane the irony, the respect for this awful force is genuine.[30]

This respect is confirmed in a late ode, *Carmina* 4.2, where the Pindaric spring has become an irresistible swollen torrent.

> Pindarum quisquis studet aemulari,
> Iule, ceratis ope Daedalea
> nititur pinnis vitreo daturus
>   nomina ponto.
>
> Monte decurrens velut amnis, imbres
> quem super notas aluere ripas,
> fervet immensusque ruit profundo
>   Pindarus ore.   [1–8]

[Whoever strives, Iulus, to rival Pindar, relies on wings fastened with wax by Daedalean craft, and is doomed to give his name to some crystal sea. Like a river from the mountain rushing down, which the rains have swollen above its wonted banks, so does Pindar seethe and, brooking no restraint, rush on with deep-toned voice.]

The destructiveness implicit in the verbs "ruit" and "fervet" rolls down over whom? Perhaps over the emulator evoked in the preceding stanza, whose itinerary would resemble Icarus's. Rather than the flight of the tempest-breasting Pindaric swan, Horace himself will choose, with overstated modesty, the itinerary out and back of the bee gathering its thyme from many plants, artfully but without power.

> Ego apis Matinae
> more modoque
>
> grata carpentis thyma per laborem
> plurimum circa nemus uvidique
> Tiburis ripas operosa parvus
>   carmina fingo.   [27–32][31]

[I, after the way and manner of the Matinian bee, that gathers the pleasant thyme with repeated labor around groves and the banks of well-watered Tibur, I, a humble bard, fashion my verses with incessant toil.]

A significant word here is "plurimum" (modifying "laborem" and not "nemus"). Horatian imitation is said to draw on many models, syncretically, because it is allegedly incapable of the grand Pindaric note. Yet here in the ode as a whole something like the force of Pindar is genuinely conveyed, and there is no Icarian catastrophe. The ode does mediate Pindar, does achieve a degree of transitivity in the face of its imagery. The poet, his reader, and his poetic apprentice, Jullus Antonius, are obliged to have it both ways.

Alternative itineraries are proposed in the epistle to Maecenas (1.19). There the poet is complaining that the mob of poetasters ape the morals and manners of their betters; then he turns upon them witheringly.

> O imitatores, servum pecus, ut mihi saepe
> bilem, saepe iocum vestri movere tumultus!   [19–20]

[O you mimics, you slavish herd! How often your pother has stirred my spleen, how often my mirth!]

These lines, often quoted sixteen centuries later, are ostensibly directed at those who ape a true poet's life rather than his work, but by a kind of deft swerve characteristic of Horace, they serve to introduce a serious discussion of this poet's authentic textual imitation.

Libera per vacuum posui vestigia princeps,
non aliena meo pressi pede. Qui sibi fidet,
dux reget examen. Parios ego primus iambos
ostendi Latio, numeros animosque secutus
Archilochi, non res et agentia verba Lycamben.   25
Ac ne me foliis ideo brevioribus ornes,
quod timui mutare modos et carminis artem,
temperat Archilochi Musam pede mascula Sappho,
temperat Alcaeus, sed rebus et ordine dispar. . . .
Hunc ego, non alio dictum prius ore, Latinus   32
volgavi fidicen. Iuvat immemorata ferentem
ingenuis oculisque legi manibusque teneri.   [21–29, 32–34]

[I was the first to plant free footsteps on a virgin soil; I walked not where others trod. Who trusts himself will lead and rule the swarm. I was the first to show to Latium the iambics of Paros, following the rhythms and spirit of Archilochus, not the themes or the words that hounded Lycambes. And lest you should crown me with a scantier wreath because I feared to change the measures and form of verse, see how manlike Sappho tempers the muse of Archilochus with her rhythm; how Alcaeus also tempers that Muse, differing in his themes and arrangements. . . . Him, never before sung by other lips, I, the lyrist of Latium, have made known. It is my joy that I bring things untold before, and am read by the eyes and held in the hands of the civilized.][32]

The imitative process is subjected to a swirl of metaphorization that blurs the focus and weakens the force of any single figure. The succession of metaphors can be traced in the verbal expressions: "set foot" (posui, pressi), "will rule" (reget), "showed" (ostendi), "following" (secutus), "tempers" (temperat), "made accessible" (volgavi), "bearing" (ferentem). The boldest, most dramatic assertion is the first, which presents the poet as an undaunted, self-reliant pioneer, penetrating a trackless wilderness. Here Horace's ironic urbanity deserts him, so that the following series of weaker, heavily qualifying formulations constitutes an awkward withdrawal from the original self-puffery. The boast of the explorer traversing virgin country must be immediately qualified for the reader in two respects. First, it is not itself original, but derives from Lucretius and Propertius.[33] Second, the expression "per vacuum" has to be reconciled with "Parios . . . iambos" and all that follows. The allegedly virgin soil first entered by this solitary scout has in fact already been crossed by Archilochus and Alcaeus; the primacy asserted extends only to Roman travelers. The original heroic itinerary gives way to more precise tracings: Horace has followed the Greek satirist Archilochus in his meters and in his poetic manner or moral style ("animos"), not in subject matter. The thrust of the argument seems to minimize the importance of "animos," which is central to Horace's art. By line 26 the boastful tone has turned defensive, and the fearless explorer appears open to the charge of timidity ("quod timui mutare..."). There is again an underlying paradox in 32–34, where the Latin lyrist makes Alcaeus known to a Roman public unfamiliar with him by bringing back from his explorations the hitherto unspoken ("immemorata"). The status of that which is brought back is unclear; the act of divulgation obviously needs an object existing prior to itself, just as the act of transport needs an object found and placed in the saddle bags. In some sense the unspoken *has* been spoken, just as the "vacuum" (21) is not truly a desert. The verb "temperat" (moderates, tones down), which dominates the central lines of the paragraph and which receives emphasis by placement and repetition, implies unambiguously a previous entity, what is called the muse of Archilochus, to be moderated. "Temperat" suggests a polyvocality in the imitations of Sappho and Alcaeus which Horace, in the more uncompromising images that frame his paragraph chiastically, denies his own work. To make sense of the assertion of originality, one has to privilege subject matter ("res") at the expense of meter ("numeros, modos"), spirit and manner ("animos"), even, more broadly and vaguely, artistic form or skill ("carminis artem"), since Horace admits to retaining these from his forerunners. If a coherent imitative program can actually be derived from this paragraph, it would have to be extracted tortuously, by playing off the images against each other and defining a complex activity no single formulation in the Latin captures.

The remarks scattered throughout the *Ars poetica* touching on the imitation of models must also be read as a series of checks and balances. The apprentice poet is told to handle Greek models night and day (268–69), since the Roman tradition retains so much crudity (258–74), yet there is praise for those Romans who have dared ("ausi") to abandon Greek paths (285–88). Letters would match arms in Roman glory if writers knew better how to use a file. The imitator must shun the vulgar open road of trite conventionality, must refuse to translate word for word, and must refrain from too timid a respect for rules.

> publica materies privati iuris erit, si
> non circa vilem patulumque moraberis orbem,
> nec verbo verbum curabis reddere fidus
> interpres, nec desilies imitator in artum,
> unde pedem proferre pudor vetet aut operis lex.   [131–35][34]
> [In ground open to all you will win private rights, if you do not linger along the easy and open pathway, if you do not seek to render word for word as a slavish translator, and if in your copying you do not leap into a narrow place, out of which either shame or the laws of your task will keep you from stirring a step.]

This new version of the imitative itinerary leads from an overworn road to a nightmare of fatal constriction ("artum"). The servile reproducer leaps self-destructively into the confinement of shame (for too much originality?) and of decorum ("operis lex").[35] This last expression leads to the heart of Horace's poetic and must give us pause. Decorum, here the constricting principle, is that rule of genre which mattered supremely to Horace.[36] Its importance is affirmed in a passage beginning at line 86 and assumed everywhere. Yet to crawl out of his claustration, the classicist poet must violate, to some degree, this rule. He must find a resolution to this conflict which Horace fails to supply. Elsewhere, in a passage we have already met, Horace erects further obstacles to his own classicism by lamenting the mutability of language and all things human: "We are doomed to death—we and all things ours" (Debemur morti nos nostraque—63). The tragedy of the leaf on the tree remembered by Dante, the tyranny of relentlessly shifting usage, complicates further the profit from handling Greek models night and day. Decorum, imitation, tragic change meet in the text of this charmingly, frivolously volatile poem and are left in a conflict that is barely taken notice of. Perhaps a kind of notice can be read into the bizarre, final paragraph where the manic poet goes wild, and the tight spot into which the reproductive imitator leapt now becomes the Aetna of Empedocles. What has made this madman a poet in the first place? Perhaps, Horace suggests, he "has defiled [by urinating on] ancestral ashes or in sacrilege disturbed a hallowed plot."

> nec satis apparet, cur versus factitet, utrum
> minxerit in patrios cineres, an triste bidental
> moverit incestus. [470–72]

We are left at the very end with the whimsical guilt of this "incestus," sacrilegious defiler of paternal ashes. Is this another subversion of those who worship Greek gods? If there is any meaning at all under the black whimsy, it could only be an implication that poets are destined by the nature of their craft to insult their fathers, to pursue cultural alternatives that violate native pieties. Briefly, through the mock-horror of the concluding hilarity, a darker vision of imitative continuities flashes and disappears.

In the late "Epistle to Augustus" (*Ep.* 2.1), there are no signs that Horace's ambivalences have been moderated. This not wholly attractive essay mingles native pride, envy of Greece, admiration for its greatness, and condescension toward its perceived decadence. The primitive Romans, sturdy, thrifty, content with little, have left a tradition that needs to be purged. Greece, a capricious little girl, left models that need to be followed. The Saturnian poison has not yet been eradicated.

> . . . sed in longum tamen aevum
> manserunt hodieque manent vestigia ruris.
> serus enim Graecis admovit acumina chartis
> et post Punica bella quietus quaerere coepit,
> quid Sophocles et Thespis et Aeschylus utile ferrent.
> temptavit quoque rem, si digne vertere posset,
> et placuit sibi, natura sublimis et acer:

nam spirat tragicum satis et feliciter audet,
sed turpem putat inscite metuitque lituram.   [159–67]
[. . . yet for many a year lived on, and still live on, traces of our rustic past. For not till
late did the Roman turn his wit to Greek writings, and in the peaceful days after the
Punic wars he began to ask what service Sophocles could render, and Thespis and
Aeschylus. He also made essay, whether he could reproduce in worthy style, and took
pride in his success, being gifted with spirit and vigor; for he has some tragic
inspiration, and is happy in his ventures, but in ignorance, deeming it disgraceful,
hesitates to blot.]

Horace will countenance no fructifying "pseudomorphosis" in the enduring
traces of old Roman crudity. In this passage as elsewhere he seems to disapprove of
that mixed idiom, that mixing of Chian and Falernian wines (*Sat.* 1.10.20ff.),
which his own polyvocal art vindicates superbly. The crucial term above, "vertere"
(transfer), leaves a question open which only his work, not his theory, can answer.
The last line quoted seems to define *imitatio* as a local and soluble problem for
contemporary Roman playwrights. With a little less carelessness, ignorance,
laziness, the transfer apparently could be made. This is the implication drawn in
many of his texts, but in the confusing interplay of competing itineraries, of
precept and counterprecept, of metaphors cutting athwart metaphors, there is
rather evidence of a continuing, irreducible mystery. The relation of the Roman
challenge to the perennial, universal challenge has the form of a synecdoche which
Horace appears never to have recognized.

4

The treatment of *imitatio* during the first century A.D. is colored progressively by
the sense of decline that seems to have been virtually universal during that era.
Thus imitation, when it is perceived as desirable, tends to emerge as a technique
for mitigating the general lowering of standards. A canon of Roman classics joins
the older Greek canon; perhaps part of the status of a classic lies precisely in its
pastness, its *lost* excellence. The role which the finest Greek authors of the fifth and
fourth centuries played for Dionysius, Cicero, and Horace could now be played as
well by the Latin masters of the golden age.
     The feeling of decline and the new status of the Roman classics are both evident
in the following passage by Seneca the elder, writing a preface to his collection of
the scholastic exercises called *Controversiae.*

My boys, you are doing something necessary and useful in not being satisfied with the
models provided by your own day and wanting to get to know those of the last
generation. For one thing, the more patterns you examine, the greater advantage to
your eloquence. You should not imitate one man, however distinguished, for an
imitator never comes up to the level of his model. This is the way things are; the copy
always falls short of the original. Moreover, you can by these means judge how sharply
standards are falling every day, how far some grudge on nature's part has sent

eloquence downhill. Everything that Roman oratory has to match the arrogant Greeks (or even prefer to them) reached its peak in Cicero's day: all the geniuses who have brought brilliance to our subject were born then. Since then things have got worse daily.[37]

For this old man, writing in his nineties, imitation both arrests the gradual decline and also underscores it. Imitation will teach the pupil, if only by his own mediocrity, how great men once were. The choice of many models is justified by the inevitable failure of the copy to equal any single original; multiple imitation, if it does not repair, diffuses the humiliation. No real transitivity seems possible. The tone is tart rather than pathetic, but the assumption of a fall is absolute.

The son of this old man produced one of the most interesting discussions of imitation ever written, although arguably it consists of a theory of reading as much as of writing. It remains the most coherent and self-sufficient discussion by any Roman, perhaps because it sticks constantly to a figurative level of argument. The remarkable 84th moral epistle by Seneca the younger makes no direct allusion to a decline, although other epistles (for example, 114) do so. Still, one can discern in Seneca a slackening of belief in the transitive vocation of Rome. The metaphors of itineraries found in Lucretius, Propertius, and Horace tend to be negative in Seneca if they appear at all: "A man who follows another not only finds nothing; he is not even looking" (Qui alium sequitur, nihil invenit, immo nec quaerit.— *Ep. Mor.* 33). Instead, Seneca's dominant analogies, mellification and digestion, stress a process of transformation. There is a shift from the penetration of a containing outer world to the absorption of the outer world within the self. In a subtle way the emphasis on the breakdown of the elements absorbed checks the passing on of a tradition. "No past life has been lived to lend us glory, and that which has existed before us is not ours" (Nemo in nostram gloriam vixit neq quod ante nos fuit, nostrum est.—*Ep. Mor.* 44).[38] Seneca is not concerned with the flow or passage onward of a heritage; he is concerned with what a single individual can do with it. This shift may reflect indirectly his own pessimism over the literary standards of his time.

Epistle 84 begins with brief comments on travel, then veers off to praise the mutual benefits of reading and writing for each other. This leads in turn to a reprise of the Lucretian–Horatian apian simile.

Apes, ut aiunt, debemus imitari, quae vagantur et flores ad mel faciendum idoneos carpunt, deinde quicquid attulere, disponunt ac per favos digerunt.   [3]
[We should follow, men say, the example of the bees, who flit about and cull the flowers that are suitable for producing honey, and then arrange and assort in their cells all that they have brought in.]

After a quasi-scientific review of theories concerning the chemistry of mellification (does it happen automatically? does the bee add something? is fermentation the key factor?), Seneca returns from this "digression" to conclude the simile, or rather to interpret it by means of a second.

Nos quoque has apes debemus imitari et quaecumque ex diversa lectione congessi-
mus, separare, melius enim distincta servantur, deinde adhibita ingenii nostri cura et
facultate in unum saporem varia illa libamenta confundere, ut etiam si apparuerit,
unde sumptum sit, aliud tamen esse quam unde sumptum est, appareat. Quod in
corpore nostro videmus sine ulla opera nostra facere naturam: alimenta, quae accepi-
mus, quamdiu in sua qualitate perdurant et solida innatant stomacho, onera sunt; at
cum ex eo, quod erant, mutata sunt, tum demum in vires et in sanguinem transeunt.
Idem in his, quibus aluntur ingenia, praestemus, ut quaecumque hausimus, non
patiamur integra esse, ne aliena sint. Concoquamus illa; alioqui in memorian ibunt,
non in ingenium.   [5–7]
[We also, I say, ought to copy these bees, and sift whatever we have gathered from a
varied course of reading, for such things are better preserved if they are kept separate;
then, by applying the supervising care with which our nature has endowed us,—in
other words, our natural gifts,—we should so blend those several flavors into one
delicious compound that, even though it betrays its origin, yet it nevertheless is clearly
a different thing from that whence it came. This is what we see nature doing in our
own bodies without any labor on our part; the food we have eaten, as long as it retains
its original quality and floats in our stomachs as an undiluted mass, is a burden; but it
passes into tissue and blood only when it has been changed from its original form. So it
is with the food which nourishes our higher nature,—we should see to it that whatever
we have absorbed should not be allowed to remain unchanged, or it will be no part of
us. We must digest it; otherwise it will merely enter the memory and not the reasoning
power.]

Whereas Lucretius and Horace had stressed the activity of gathering, Seneca
stresses metamorphosis; movement through metaphorical space gives way to the
body's invisible concoction of unlike elements into one. By reviewing theories of
mellification without selecting any one, Seneca essentially allows the process of
assimilation to remain mysterious. We do not, perhaps cannot, know exactly how
nectar becomes honey, how food becomes tissue and blood; analogously the
assimilation of our reading is a process not to be codified, although the will is
called upon to ensure the thoroughness of absorption. Seneca's analogies—for he
does make them his own, following his own precept—may have had such an
extraordinarily long life because he is tactful enough to leave a space for an
invisible event.

Seneca differs from his classicist forerunners and even from his father by
presenting the element of difference not as an inexorable, historical given but as a
chosen, calculated effect. "Let it appear other than that from which it was taken."
This otherness is the token of completed, willed transformation. Thus the emphasis on the unrecognizability of the final product is not, what it would become for
some Renaissance theorists like Vida, a counsel of dissimulation to hide one's
thefts, but rather the simple evidence of mature individuality.

Hoc faciat animus noster: omnia, quibus est adiutus, abscondat, ipsum tantum
ostendat, quod effecit. Etiam si cuius in te comparebit similitudo, quem admiratio tibi
altius fixerit, similem esse te volo quomodo filium, non quomodo imaginem; imago
res mortua est.   [7–8]

[This is what our mind should do: it should hide away all the materials by which it has been aided, and bring to light only what it has made of them. Even if there shall appear in you a likeness to him who, by reason of your admiration, has left a deep impress upon you, I would have you resemble him as a child resembles his father, and not as a picture resembles its original; for a picture is a lifeless thing.]

The preference for the filial over the painterly relationship seems to rest on the former's organicity; the organic can be controlled but not programmed. There is also in this filial analogy, as the context makes clear, an understood element of *un*likeness. The painting is contrived to reproduce its subject as faithfully as possible, but the son is allowed to recall his father's features with only a vague "family resemblance." The phrasing places the stress on this saving degree of noncorrespondence while assuming an underlying continuity. Not much is made of this little simile, and it would be inappropriate for the glossator to wrench his author's emphases, but one does need to notice how the image saves Seneca's imitator from the unfilial sacrilege of Horace's berserk versemonger. Seneca's son grows away from his father without ceasing to reveal his parentage, the impress of his precursor. The filial status allows for independence by the same natural law that allows sons to acquire their own faces. Seneca the younger like Seneca the elder advises recourse to many models, but after his own fashion and without any Oedipal crisis.

Seneca goes on to produce a brilliant paradox that, almost alone in this little essay, would *fail* to become a topos, perhaps because it resists easy resolution. "Won't your model be obvious?" he asks rhetorically.

Puto aliquando ne intellegi quidem posse, si imago vera sit; haec enim omnibus, quae ex quo velut exemplari traxit, formam suam impressit, ut in unitatem illa conpetant. Non vides, quam multorum vocibus chorus constet? Unus tamen ex omnibus redditur.   [8–9]
[I think that sometimes it is impossible for it to be seen who is being imitated, if the copy is a true one; for a true copy stamps its own form upon all the features which it has drawn from what we may call the original, in such a way that they are combined into a unity. Do you not see how many voices there are in a chorus? Yet out of the many only one voice results.]

A true copy makes recognition impossible. The paradox, like the analogies, creates an area of uncertainty for speculation to play with. It suggests that purely discursive description is inappropriate. The word "imago," which has just been dismissed as dead, is then reanimated by the metaphor of the chorus, which will be developed at some length. It is with this analogy that the discussion of imitation proper ends. It deserves to be climactic because it offers, as no other ancient text explicitly does, support for what modern criticism calls polyvocality. For Seneca the mind and the text must blend many arts, many precepts, many models chosen from many periods of history: "multae . . . artes, multa praecepta . . . , multarum aetatum exempla" (10). The epistle then closes with an apparent swerve away to familiar Stoic morality. One may of course legitimately read injunctions to avoid greed and pleasure as irrelevant to what has preceded. But one is also free, and perhaps wiser, to understand retrospectively the polyvocality stemming from imitative assimilation as a moral achievement. From no ancient writer did the humanism of the Renaissance derive its faith in the morality of style more directly than from Seneca.

Seneca's exposition by analogy, and the particular analogies he chose, dehistoricize imitation. The blending into one substance of subtexts from many eras produces syncretic imitation that frees the writer from the kind of responsibility toward one's present and future culture felt by Cicero and Horace. There is no communal *voluntas* of the kind evoked by the *De oratore*. In an age of perceived decay, history may be felt to be intractable. Metaphorization and syncretism allow one to avoid historical specificity; they correspond to the Platonizing turn by Cicero at the end of his career. In the treatment of imitation by Quintilian, the last important Roman of the pre-Christian age to discuss it, an attempt is made to reintroduce historical specificity. Metaphorization is less common (although the digestive analogy makes a perfunctory appearance at 10.1.19) and the writer's transitive vocation is reasserted: "This glory . . . shall be theirs, that men shall say of them that while they surpassed their predecessors, they also taught those who came after."[39] Yet the treatment of imitation is curiously divided agianst itself. Although the *Institutio oratoria* is known as a work of rational method, on this subject it becomes curiously contradictory. Quintilian, the author of a lost treastise on the decline of eloquence, betrays his own discomfort with history.

Quintilian's formal treatment of *imitatio* occupies the second chapter of his tenth book. This chapter opens with the statement that a large part of the art of oratory lies in imitation ("Neque enim dubitari potest, quin artis pars magna contineatur imitatione"). This affirmation of its essential role has already appeared at the opening of the first chapter, where imitation is partially assimilated to the activity of reading, and the purpose of reading seems to be the study of potential models. "Practice [in writing] without the models supplied by reading will be like a ship drifting aimlessly without a steersman" (Citra lectionis exemplum labor ille carens rectore fluitabit—10.1.2). Thus the long review of the principal authors that follows in this first chapter can properly be seen as a prolegomenon to the discussion of imitation proper in the second. After affirming the universality of imitation in a passage already quoted (p. 54), Quintilian's argument then makes a curious turn.

> Sed hoc ipsum, quod tanto faciliorem nobis rationem rerum omnium facit quam fuit iis, qui nihil quod sequerentur habuerunt, nisi caute et cum iudicio apprehenditur, nocet.   [10.2.3]
> [But the very fact that in every subject the procedure to be followed is so much more easy for us than it was for those who had no model to guide them, is a positive drawback, unless we use this dubious advantage with caution and judgment.]

This sentence acts as a hinge leading to a demonstration of the hazards of imitation. The activity that has just been asserted to be universal is now contrasted unfavorably with the creativity of those primal discoverers who had no one to lead them. The "iis" of this hinge sentence are never named; they are mythified heroes of Edenic genius next to whom the imitator's effort will always pale, after whom the follower must necessarily follow. The only hope would be to outdo them, by shunning the paths they have marked out. Quintilian's reasonable and orderly mind reveals here an irrational nostalgia for Origination. The real distinction for the modern would be to resemble the originators in their creation *ab nihilo*.

> Quid enim futurum erat temporibus illis, quae sine exemplo fuerunt, si homines nihil, nisi quod iam cognovissent, faciendum sibi aut cogitandum putassent? Nempe nihil fuisset inventum. Cur igitur nefas est reperiri aliquid a nobis, quod ante non fuerit? [4–5]
> [For what would have happend in the days when models were not, if men had decided to do and think of nothing that they did not know already? The answer is obvious: nothing would ever have been discovered. Why, then, is it a crime for us to discover something new?]

The discussion that ensues postulates two antithetical poles—origination and duplication; any middle ground is excluded. One pole is heroic, the other shameful. "It is a positive disgrace to be content to owe all our achievement to imitation" (Turpe . . . illud est, contentum esse id consequi quod imiteris—7). The only progress history can show was made by those who refused to follow. It is also easier to push on for oneself than to try to repeat another's achievement.

This question of relative difficulty recurs more than once. In what I have called the hinge sentence, the belated creator's task is awarded a relative if qualified facility. But in the critique of imitation, the task of the follower is progressively represented as hard, futile, near-impossible.

> Adde quod plerumque facilius est plus facere quam idem. Tantam enim difficultatem habet similitudo, ut ne ipsa quidem natura in hoc ita evaluerit, ut non res quae simillimae, quaeque pares maxime videantur, utique discrimine aliquo discernantur. Adde quod, quidquid alteri simile est, necesse est minus sit eo, quod imitatur. [10–11]
> [Further, it is generally easier to make some advance than to repeat what has been done by others, since there is nothing harder than to produce an exact likeness, and nature herself has so far failed in this endeavor that there is always some difference which enables us to distinguish even the things which seem most like and most equal to one another. Again whatever is like another object, must necessarily be inferior to the object of its imitation.]

There is a touch of sophistry in Quintilian's pointing to the difficulty of a perfectly faithful copy, since few imitators make this their goal. But this stress on the easier role of the originator may help to explain the remark in the preceding chapter that however superhuman the genius of Homer, "there is greater diligence and exactness in Virgil, just because his task was harder."[40] There would seem to be a fear, which this chapter wants to exorcise, that diligence is all that is left to the belated man, who must lack natural energy.

Namque eis, quae in exemplum adsumimus, subest natura et vera vis; contra omnis imitatio ficta est et ad alienum propositum accomodatur.   [11]
[For the models which we select for imitation have a genuine and natural force, whereas all imitation is artificial and moulded to a purpose which was not that of the original orator.]

The distance between the original and the copier threatens to become absolute, uncrossable, mythic. In the middle, excluded by these either/or formulations, lies among many the figure of Cicero, since in other passages he is said to have been a tireless imitator of the Greeks as well as the supreme model for Romans (10.1.108, 112).

   This extended antitransitive critique of the imitative process, the product of an age haunted by the fear of sterility ("hiuius infelicatis, ut nunc demum nihil crescat"—8), yields to a series of blander and more derivative precepts that would nevertheless have a long and powerful influence. Now the distance from the model shrinks again to manageable length. One must consider whom to imitate, and which qualities in him; one must also estimate one's own powers; one should not violate the rules of each genre or species of writing; one should avoid choosing a single guide for all situations; one's study of an author should include decorum and disposition as well as language. Only at the close of this chapter riven by ambivalence does a potential reconciliation emerge.

Haec si perviderimus, tum vere imitabimur. Qui vero etiam propria his bona adiecerit, ut suppleat quae deerant, circumcidat, si quid redundabit, is erit, quem quaerimus, perfectus orator.   [28]
[If we have thoroughly appreciated all these points, we shall be able to imitate our models with accuracy. But the man who to these good qualities adds his own, that is to say, who makes good deficiencies and cuts down whatever is redundant, will be the perfect orator of our search.]

This compromise then makes possible the transitive glory of those who surpass their predecessors and teach their posterity. But that *laus* lies in the shadow of the blurred argument it concludes. The reader may extrapolate from this chapter an attitude of emulative rivalry toward the great models which is also nourished by them, but no single passage conveys this attitude. The nautical image we began with permits no compromise: we accept the steersman, who ensures our dependence, or we throw him overboard and accept our drift through time.

   The tensions in Roman reflection upon tradition and the individual talent are subsumed and elevated in the historic vision of Quintilian's probable contemporary, Longinus. The author of *On the Sublime* betrays no crippling sensitivity to the Roman ascendancy over his own Hellenic tradition, nor any sentimental grief over that tradition's virtual demise. He is not concerned with instruction, as had been in various ways Seneca, Quintilian, the Cicero of the *De oratore*, and the Horace of the *Ars poetica*; he is concerned with understanding the force of certain exemplary texts as they strike the reader with unique impact. He returns to the theme of Dionysius, *zelos*.[41] For Longinus, the ambivalence toward the master is recognized, "sublimated," freed to enter into those mysterious currents of imaginative energy which fecundate the serial masterworks of a civilization and which in their mysterious fructifying power attain a kind of religious majesty. "The imitation and emulation of previous great poets and writers" lead to the sublime because the currents of energy flowing from them possess a holy aura, an aura conjured by a simile of extraordinary grandeur.

> For many men are carried away by the spirit of others as if inspired, just as it is related of the Pythian priestess when she approaches the tripod, where there is a rift in the ground which (they say) exhales divine vapor. By heavenly power thus communicated she is impregnated and straightway delivers oracles in virtue of the afflatus. Similarly from the great natures of the men of old there are borne in upon the souls of those who emulate them (as from sacred caves) what we may describe as *effluences*, so that even those who seem little likely to be possessed are thereby inspired and succumb to the spell of the others' greatness.[42]

In these overpowering wafts of divinity the initiate breathes in a numinous strangeness that impregnates him like a woman. The strangeness does not inhere in the temporal removal of the source but in its faculty for supernatural possession. The effluence reaches the initiate through a rift which is not a division but a channel. The source-text takes its authority from its capacity to affect. It is uncannily awesome as it issues from a sacred darkness, but it is also perpetually available and thus perpetually present. On the far side of a tradition's decline, history ceases to be a factor. The writer's itinerary is not backward through time but upward toward greatness. There is to be sure an image of historic flow which succeeds in intimating the polyvocality, the number of voices of the contributory rivers: "Plato . . . from the great Homeric source drew to himself innumerable tributary streams."[43] But another image, which we have met before (chapter 3, p. 46), brings Plato and Homer together to wrestle with each other. In this Olympian perspective from above the flow, the later figure grapples with the older as a kind of Jacob struggling with that divine forerunner whom he cannot best but whose formidable antagonism constitutes a kind of blessing. This compelling vision of dialectical imitation is in itself a creation of immense imaginative force.

The term *zelos* in this thirteenth chapter is clearly not psychologistic but descriptive; it corresponds to a pressure which the author finds in the *texts* of Plato. The reader is left to reconcile the male experience of wrestling with the female experience of possession by a divine effluence. Not only the images but the conceptual space between images leave room for a mystery which the text hieratically refuses to dispel. Still another space opens as the image of bodily struggle is succeeded by an image whereby the masters light the modern writer, still contending with them, up to the ideal that *he* has created for himself. Now we must reconcile the master as antagonist with the master as guide along an itinerary upward he allows the modern to choose. The past may reach us according to one figure as an insubstantial effluvium, according to another as a solid body we wrestle with, and according to a third as a light cast ahead to illuminate the dark path to the self. These figures will not really abide the logic of our reasonable reconciliations; they maintain their paradoxical density and invite meditation at their own rare level of discourse, *peri hupsous.*

Longinus would not be a major influence on Renaissance criticism, but all of the major Roman critics who wrote about imitation would be. There are few themes of Renaissance imitative theory not present in these Roman authors— some themes perhaps only in nucleus, but most of them already well developed. In this respect Renaissance theory can be called imitative in its own right, and would be a proper object of imitative analysis. Such an analysis would of course have to take acccount of the obvious differentiating factors. Among these: the wider rupture between antiquity and the Renaissance, the medieval scapegoat-epoch on which to blame the rupture, the more radical challenge to the writer's native tongue, the literal loss of texts, the change in religious faith, and—during the earlier stages—a stronger sense of cultural inferiority. These factors help to explain the darker tinges of Renaissance humanist pathos. Ancient criticism seldom allowed itseld broad pathetic gestures; perhaps this is the reason why its insecurities emerge on the whole indirectly and symptomatically. But it did struggle nonetheless for insight into the enigmatic interaction between a tradition's liberating constraints and constraining freedoms. Ancient pedagogy is open to the charge that it codified this interplay artificially and mechanically. But to study the major critics who pondered it is to find it not only analyzed but exemplified. The ancients rightly saw the imitative impulse as a constant of our condition. Their civilization did not produce a single, coherent, communal description of this impulse's proper role in a creative society. Antiquity never reached a shared estimate of its removal from its classics. It produced rather terms and themes about which reflection circled, repeatedly and restlessly, variously and stubbornly, in a prolonged conversation bearing on the grounds of its prolongation.

Five • Petrarch and the Humanist Hermeneutic

The belief in the value, for students as for mature writers, of fashioning their compositions on models of excellence was perpetuated by the teaching and practice of many medieval men. During the revival of classical letters beginning in the twelfth century, this belief crystallized into an important pedagogical-literary doctrine. Earlier the loose, informal consensus of the ancients concerning the major authors had been codified into a stricter canon of *auctores*, authorized classics suitable for imitation. The prestige of medieval *imitatio* was heightened by the support of two writers from late antiquity: Saint Augustine, who recommends it briefly as a useful means of acquiring rhetorical skill, and Macrobius, who discusses Virgil's rewriting of his forebears at length in the *Saturnalia*. During the so-called Carolingian Renaissance, imitation was approved by Alcuin, the most influential scholar of the era, although he warned against its abuse. The twelfth century produced discussions by John of Salisbury and Pierre de Blois among others, discussions that occasionally anticipate in specific ideas and images those of Petrarch and later Renaissance theorists. A tradition of classical imitation in Latin verse, begun as early as the ninth century, was maintained virtually unbroken throughout the entire medieval period. Thus some version of imitative doctrine or composition was almost always present in medieval civilization whenever it reached a certain stage of development. Yet despite the superficial resemblances with earlier and later periods, these versions retained a recognizably medieval character that to be studied seriously would require a distinctive methodology. Large areas of vernacular literature moreover were left relatively untouched by pressure to imitate the ancients, in Italy until the fourteenth century at the earliest and still later in the north. For these reasons, medieval *imitatio* will concern this study only as a background against which its Renaissance counterpart defined itself. I trust that my descriptive distinctions will not be misinterpreted as normative.

Augustine's approving reference to imitation occurs in a passage of the *De doctrina christiana* unlikely to have given comfort to many of those later preceptors who would otherwise have valued his authorization. The saint is arguing that rhetoric is a subject to be learned quickly by boys or not at all, a subject unworthy to occupy the time of grown men. For those who lack this training, he writes, imitation is an easy way of dispensing with the rules.

> Quapropter, cum ex infantibus loquentes non fiant nisi locutiones discendo loquentium, cur eloquentes fieri non possunt nulla eloquendi arte tradita, sed elocutiones eloquentium legendo et audiendo et, quantum assequi conceditur, imitando?[1]

[Therefore, as infants cannot learn to speak except by learning words and phrases from those who do speak, why should not men become eloquent without being taught any act of speech, simply by reading and learning the speeches of eloquent men, and by imitating them as far as they can?]

Imitation for Augustine would seem to be the recourse of the autodidact in a hurry to make up for educational lacunae. In Macrobius, it is treated not as a pedagogical tool but as poetic praxis, an object of literary criticism calling for a nice exercise of judgment and taste. Augustine and Macrobius thus illustrate between them the breadth of the spectrum along which any given discussion of imitation in any era situates itself. Despite this breadth, it is important, I think, to see the spectrum as a single continuous extension, not a set of mutually exclusive alternatives. It is a whole because learning to write well is not a distinct activity from writing well; the work of the child's classroom cannot be segregated from the work of the adult's desk.

In his preface to the *Saturnalia*, Macrobius virtually quotes Seneca's 84th epistle to justify his composition of a florilegium. Here he is not really concerned with imitation but with the kind of direct appropriation of various texts which produced this book. Later his convivial group of friends will talk about the use Virgil makes of his poetic forerunners, notably Homer. Although some criticism of his very heavy use is heard, the authorized voices praise the intertextual density of his art and the judgment that went into its weaving.

> Eustathius deinde:—Maxime, inquit, praedicarem quanta de Graecis cautus et tamquam aliud agens, modo artifici dissimulatione, modo professa imitatione transtulerit, ni me major admiratio de astrologia totaque philosophia teneret.
> [I, added Eustathius, should give the highest praise to [Virgil's] use of Greek models—a cautious use and one which may even have the appearance of being accidental, since he sometimes skillfully conceals the debt, although at other times he imitates openly—did I not admire even more his knowledge of astronomy and the whole field of philosophy.]

> Denique et judicio transferendi et modo imitandi consecutus est ut quod apud illum legerimus alienum, aut illius esse malimus, aut melius hic quam ubi natum est sonare miremur.[2]
> [Virgil showed such judgment too in his borrowings, and such was the manner of his imitation, that when, in our reading of him, we come across another's words, we either choose to regard them as Virgil's own or else realize with surprise that they sound better now than they did in their original context.]

At one point Macrobius seems to assign the imitative faculty a central function in the composition of literature.

> ... hunc esse fructum legendi aemulari ea quae in aliis probes et quae maxime inter aliorum dicta mireris in aliquem usum tuum opportuna derivatione convertere, quod et nostri, tam inter se quam a Graecis, et Graecorum excellentes inter se saepe fecerunt.[3]
> [The reward of one's reading is to seek to rival what meets with one's approval in the work of others and by a happy turn to convert to some use of one's own the expressions

one especially admires there. For this is what our writers have often done, borrowing both from one another and from the Greeks; and this is what the greatest of the Greeks often did among themselves.]

Macrobius may himself be converting Quintilian here (*Inst. Orat.* 2.8); Ben Jonson would write, "Sometimes it is the reward of a mans study, the praise of quoting an other man fitly."[4] But the greater part of the talk in Macrobius turns not on general precepts but on specific "debts" Virgil allegedly incurred. Many chapters consist of nothing but bare catalogues of parallel passages, but some of these do receive critical comments ranging from the external and trivial to the sensitive. Among the latter might be cited the remarks on the similes in Homer and Virgil describing a horse race (5.11.21–22) and on those describing a boiling cauldron (5.11.24–25). In discussing the two poet's epic catalogues, Macrobius contrasts Homer's use of formulaic repetition as he introduces each new contingent with Virgil's care in varying his introductions. Credit is given to Virgil's "wealth of phrases" (has copias) but there is also appreciation of Homer's repetitive simplicity.

> Stat in consuetudine percensentium, tamquam per aciem dispositos enumerant, quod non aliis quam numerorum fit vocabulis.[5]
> [He has, as a rule, taken up the usual attitude of one holding a review and given us, as it were, the "parade state" of the troops deployed, the substance of which is, simply, a statement of the numbers present.]

Macrobius at his liveliest impresses the reader as an interesting practical critic, deserving some portion of his prestige as a medieval *auctoritas*. But there is evidence that both his insights and his catalogues are secondhand. Although he undoubtedly read Greek, it would appear that he knew Homer only through snippets in the manuals and compilations that were his primary sources.[6] If he knew Aulus Cellius, Quintilian, and Plutarch, he did not know directly Plato or the Greek tragedians. By the close of the fourth century it was not easy for an educated Roman to procure the classic Greek texts. Thus the *Saturnalia* is useful as an index to the knowledge of the classical rear guard before its defeat, as it shored its fragments against a new faith and a new barbarism. If there are no itineraries or transformations in his imagery, if there is no sense of rupture, these absences are due not to possession but to lack, the beginning of that millennial lack which the humanists would represent as an interment. But before this millennium had run its course, the syncretism of Macrobius's compilations would render him more accessible, would facilitate his assimilation by the humanism of the Middle Ages.

The medieval system based on a classical canon can be seen developing in Alcuin's *Rhetoric*, which takes the form of a dialogue between the author and Charlemagne. Toward the close Charlemagne asks, "How can our speech attain the authority which that of the ancients had?" (Qualiter ad auctoritatem priscorum potest oratio nostra pervenire?). This might be rephrased: "How can a man of our age achieve the status of an *auctor*?" Alcuin replies:

Legendi sunt auctorum libri eorumque bene dicta memoriae mandanda: quorum sermone adsueti facti qui erunt, ne cupientes quidem poterunt loqui nisi ornate. Neque tamen utendum erit verbis priscis, quibus iam consuetudo nostra non utitur.[7] [Their books ought to be read, and their words well impressed upon our memory. Whoever has fashioned his style upon theirs cannot consciously express himself in a manner devoid of refinement. Nevertheless, we should not employ antique words that our present usage does not recognize.]

Alcuin gives no further details concerning the modalities of imitative fashioning, apparently assuming that acquaintance and memory suffice. That in fact skillful imitation of the classics was possible even during the most somber periods of the Dark Ages is proven by such a poem as the tenth-century Virgilian epic *Waltharius*, which retells a Germanic legend with some power in accomplished hexameters. A twelfth-century text by Bernard of Utrecht reflects familiarity with the fact that ancient authors imitated their predecessors.[8] The proto-Renaissance of the twelfth century produced a fresh spurt of Latin verse imitation, including an impressive epic poem, the *Alexandreis* by Walter of Chatillon. The most notable theoretical comments of the century on imitation appear in a letter by Pierre de Blois (died ca. 1200) written to justify his own debts to classical texts against the attacks of an unnamed critic. The sections of Pierre's letter that concern us constitute almost an anthology of conventional images destined to characterize *imitatio* for centuries to come.

Et quae invidia est, si, quod ex multiplici librorum lectione decerpsi, ferventiore studio digerente, in materiam virtutis et exercitium prudentiae coalescit? Nam, sicut in libro Saturnalium, et in libris Senecae ad Lucilium legimus, apes imitari debemus, quae colligunt flores, quibus divisis, et in favum dispositis, varios succos in unum saporem artifici mistura. . . . Quidquid canes oblatrent, quidquid grunniant sues, ego semper aemulabor scripta veterum: in his erit occupatio mea; nec me, si potero, sol unquam inveniet otiosum. Nos, quasi nani super gigantum humeros sumus, quorum beneficio longius, quam ipsi, speculamur, dum antiquorum tractatibus inhaerentes elegantiores eorum sententias, quas vetustas aboleverat, hominumve neglectus, quasi iam mortuas in quandam novitatem essentiae suscitamus.[9]
[Why should that be accounted envy which fuses into a single study of virtue and exercise of prudence all that I have taken from my wide reading and digested with keen ardor? For as we read in the *Saturnalia* and in Seneca's epistles to Lucilius, we must imitate those bees gathering flowers whose various nectars are turned to honey and are mingled to create a single savor. . . . However the dogs bark and the swine grunt, I shall always continue to imitate the writings of the ancients: to them shall I devote my labor, nor will the sun ever find me unoccupied, if my strength remains. We are like dwarfs mounted on the shoulders of giants; with their assistance we can see further than they can; clinging to their works, we restore a new life to their more elegant thoughts, which time or the neglect of men had already left as dead.]

The simile of dwarfs on the shoulders of giants bespeaks both a humility and a pride, since it is the dwarfs who see further.[10] But of these serial images, the most significant is doubtless the last evoking a resurrection. It may owe something to an elegy by Hildebert de Lavardin, but whether or not totally original it expresses a consciousness of cultural privation, along with a hope of overcoming it, more common in the fifteenth century than in the twelfth. This important text by Pierre is evidence that humanist pathos and humanist anger at neglect ("hominum . . . neglectus") can be found during the High Middle Ages. But in gauging the significance of this text for the century as a whole, one has to recall Cassirer's warning that what matters for a given era is not so much the presence of a given idea as its dynamic force. Literate men of the twelfth century knew and loved the classics available to them, but the idea of a renascence into a living present of a thing immeasurably removed did not acquire the dynamic power to move their civilization. It could not aquire this power because the precise understanding of their removal was inaccessible.[11] Even in Pierre the sense of difference tends to be quantitative, comparable to the difference in size between a dwarf and a giant, rather than the qualitative separation of two historical moments and two patterns of culture.

Pierre may have found his simile of giants and dwarfs in the *Metalogicon* (1159) of his slightly older contemporary John of Salisbury. John's account in that work of the teaching methods adopted by his master, Bernard of Chartres, constitutes the fullest description we possess of medieval imitative pedagogy. It is also a more representative reflection of its century's view of imitation.

Quibus autem indicebantur praeexercitamina puerorum, in prosis aut poematibus imitandis, poetas aut oratores proponebat, et eorum jubebat vestigia imitari, ostendens juncturas dictionum et elegantes sermonum clausulas. Si quis autem ad splendorem sui operis, alienum pannum assuerat, deprehensum redarguebat furtum; sed poenam saepissime non infligebat. Sic vero redargutum, si hoc tamen meruerat inepta positio, ad exprimendam auctorum imaginem, modesta indulgentia conscendere jubebat faciebatque, ut qui majores imitabatur, fieret posteris imitandus.[12]
[[Bernard] would also explain the poets and orators who were to serve as models for the boys in their introductory exercises in imitating prose and poetry. Pointing out how the diction of the authors was so skillfully connected, and what they had to say was so elegantly concluded, he would admonish his students to follow their example. And if, to embellish his work, someone had sewed a patch of cloth filched from an external source, Bernard, on discovering this, would rebuke him for his plagiary, but would generally refrain from punishing him. After he had reproved the student, if an unsuitable theme had invited this, he would with modest indulgence bid the boy to rise to real imitation of the classical authors, and would bring about that he who had imitated his predecessors would come to be deserving of imitation by his successors.]

Several elements in this passage deserve attention. The vestigial evocation of transitivity at the close shows that this aspiration of Roman civilization was preserved to some degree by the Latin Middle Ages. The close connection maintained between the appreciation of stylistic elegance and the skills required for composition show an alertness to the interplay between reading and writing. There is also a certain sensitivity to degrees of imitative mastery. Plagiarism is rebuked; a kind of crude imitation is introduced into the elementary exercises; mature imitation is anticipated as a potential goal, at which point the imitator would become a model himself. What is missing from this passage as from Pierre's is the requirement of self-knowledge, the consideration of the *suitability* for a unique individual of a given *auctor*.

We do not find in John the sense of loss present in Pierre de Blois. But it certainly exists in other medieval writers. Chrétien de Troyes, at the opening of *Cligès*, writes that "pre-eminence in chivalry and learning once belonged to Greece. Then chivalry passed to Rome, together with that highest learning which has now come to France." But "of Greeks and Romans no more is heard, their fame is passed, and their glowing ash is dead."

> . . . des Grezois ne des Romains
> Ne dit an mes ne plus ne mains,
> D'ax est la parole remese
> Et estainte la vive brese.[13]

These lines are affecting, but it is important not to misinterpret their poignance. If the glory of the ancients is gone, those books of theirs which have survived are there to be copied and rewritten. The poetic Aeneas is guided by no fading light, no glowing ashes, from over his shoulder, but he is not lost. The medieval writer works within a system of texts that are all equally available for extension, completion, higher realization. Although this writer may know that some of his texts were produced by a society now disappeared, he has no way of measuring its difference, as Chrétien's reference to Greek and Roman chivalry makes clear. Thus medieval intertextuality can properly be thought of as metonymic, Renaissance intertextuality as metaphoric. Gerald L. Bruns remarks that for the medieval writer, the inherited text is tacitly unfinished; "it is never fully present but is always available for a later hand to bring it more completely into the open."[14] What the later hand writes fills in, lengthens, deepens, clarifies, without any strain of disjuncture. "A text always contains more than what it says, or what its letters contain, which is why we are privileged to read between the lines, and not to read between them only but to write between them as well, because the text is simply not complete—not fully what it could be."[15] Intertextuality is metonymic because the later text touches, connects with, grows out of, the earlier one. All writing enjoys a neighborly community. Thus there is no perceived threat of anachronism, no clash of *mundi significantes*, no itinerary from one concrete historical moment to another.[16]

The earliest direct forebears of Renaissance humanism begin to appear in northern Italy toward the close of the thirteenth century. They combine philological curiosity with the production of more philologically informed imitative poetry. Padua was the most important center, though not the only one.[17] A Paduan jurist, Lovato dei Lovati (died 1309), found access to Latin authors virtually lost (Catullus, Lucretius, parts of Livy and Cicero) at the library of the abbey of Pomposa, wrote a treatise on the versification of Seneca's tragedies, an epic poem (not extant), and verse epistles that reveal a new intuition of the spirit of his ancient models. A more considerable figure, Albertino Mussato (died 1329), also studied Seneca's prosody, wrote a history in the manner of Livy and Sallust, and most significantly composed a Senecan verse tragedy, the *Ecerinis*, based on the career of the Paduan tyrant Ezzelino da Romano. Mussato's drama is less dependent on individual fragments, images, and motifs of ancient literature than with the structure, tone, dignity, and manner of his Roman model apprehended as a whole. This apprehension is balanced by the decision to dramatize the life of a modern man, a life of burning relevance to the Paduan community. Given this holistic understanding and this choice of a modern subject, given also Mussato's relative skill in matching the rhythms and intensity of his Senecan subtexts, the *Ecerinis* must be regarded as a protohumanist document. It begins to sketch an itinerary into the present from a past whose specific foreignness is at least dimly grasped. Thus Mussato's intertextuality is no longer metonymic. His drama signals the loss of the medieval community of texts and the lengthening of a relationship in time calling for a different *translatio*, the span of a metaphoric bridge from one unlike realm to another. The *Ecerinis* asserts its own historical specificity, its separateness, by its contemporary political reference, while embodying a formal continuity which the separation reveals to be precarious.

The remarks on *imitatio* in Dante's *De vulgari eloquentia* (2.4.2; quoted in chapter 3, note 1 above) stress the correctness of composition to be learned by naive (vernacular) poets from the study of Roman works written according to rules. One imitates, according to this passage, to learn a professional, technical discipline (*ars regularis*) in place of caprice and intuition. This advice coexists, as we have seen, with the recognition of profound linguistic and cultural change both in this treatise and in *Paradiso* 26. The lingering sense of community expressed in Sordello's phrase addressed to Virgil—"la lingua nostra"—coexists with the universal human transience affirmed by Adam. The actual imitative passages in the *Commedia*, such as the Pier delle Vigne episode in *Inferno* 13 or the simile at *Inferno* 3.112ff. or Adam's speech itself, are superb adaptations which demonstrate both estrangement and filiation. Isolated passages like these disclose Dante's mastery in controlling and manipulating potential anachronism. The assurance of the modern imitator seems to be reinforced by the perception of historical specificity, even if specificity becomes estrangement in the pathos of Virgil's progressively anachronistic role throughout the *Purgatorio*.

Thus the opening of the trecento witnesses an incipient withdrawal of the *auctores* from their perennial presence, a ripping of the medieval network, an emergent linearity in history that is neither necessarily tragic nor necessarily redemptive.[18] It is never easy to say why things happen in literary history. In the case of Lovato and Mussato, one can point to the greater availability of ancient texts and to the classicizing coteries that grew up in Padua and in other north Italian cities. One can point to the study of law pursued by both men as favoring a recognition of the ties connecting language to a concrete social context. One can point also to the civic cult of antiquity that led to the laureation of Mussato by his fellow citizens, a ceremony whose repetition in his own career Petrarch would contrive and mythify. Before the genius of a Dante, explanation must abdicate. Whatever the "causes" of the prehumanistic shift, the early years of Petrarch's life saw an incipient change in the uses to which men might put the past, a change pregnant with opportunity and pain, which would make possible the pivotal role of his talent in the drama of European letters. The growth of historicism called for a new poetic, for Petrarch a daunting itinerary lit by the dim brilliance of a vanishing city.

2

A well-known letter from Petrarch to Giovanni Colonna di San Vito evokes a promenade the two men had made together through the wilderness of ruins then covering most of Rome. As he recalls to his friend the sites they had visited, the poet identifies them not as they appeared to the naked eye but as they prompted his historical imagination: "Each step," he writes, "stirred our tongue and mind" (Aderat . . . per singulos passus quod linguam et animum excitaret). The organization of the long touristic catalogue that ensues bears no relation to the disposition of historic sites in Rome—most of which were lost or so overgrown as to be unrecognizable—but follows rather the course of ancient Roman history: "Hic Evandri regia . . . hic Caci spelunca; hic lupa nutrix" (Here was the dwelling of Evander . . . here the cave of Cacus, here the nourishing she-wolf),[19] and so on through the early kings, the republic, the empire, and the Christian martyrs. Since neither Petrarch nor his friend could identify more than a fraction of the actual scenes where the historical or legendary events were supposed to have been enacted, the letter exhibits the imaginative projection onto a landscape of a historical coherence which that landscape could only begin to suggest. Petrarch essentially *read* an order into the Roman wilderness, intuited a plan beneath the shattered temples and grazing sheep whose overwhelming human drama rendered the surface accidents of the city merely evocative pretexts. Oblivious like all his contemporaries to the atmospheric appeal of ruins in themselves, Petrarch might be said to have divined the subterranean plan of a living city in the way a scholar might puzzle out conjecturally the precious and nearly obliterated text of a palimpsest whereon a debased modern text had been superimposed.

The pursuit of a deeper historical reality beneath unpromising modern appearances leaves its mark on many of Petrarch's works, and especially on those letters that reflect his touristic curiosity. Thus the young Petrarch describes his pleasure in the city now called Cologne as having stemmed from the fanciful reconstructions it provoked:

Proximis aliquot diebus a mane ad vesperam civitatem iisdem ducibus circumivi, haud iniucundum exercitium, non tam ob id quod ante oculos erat, quam recordati-

one nostrorum maiorum, qui tam procul a patria monumenta Romanae virtutis tam
illustria reliquissent.   [*Fam.* 1.5]
[During the next few days I wandered about the city from morning to night under the
guidance of my friends. It was a very pleasant occupation, not so much because of what
I actually saw, as from the recollection of our ancestors, who left such illustrious
memorials of Roman virtue so far from the fatherland.]

A few years later, during his first visit to Rome, he wrote that he had been actually
hesitant to arrive, "metuens ne quod ipse michi animo finxeram, extenuarent
oculi et magnis semper nominibus inimica presentia" (fearing that the sight of
actuality would bring low my high imaginations. Present reality is always hostile
to greatness.—*Fam.* 2.14). But in this case, he added, the present was greater than
he expected. It was greater, of course, precisely because it offered sufficient stimulus
for the imagination to win its contest with the diminished present.

A long letter to Philippe de Vitry about the itinerary of Cardinal Gui de
Boulogne through Italy evokes this prelate's future visit to Rome in terms of the
Christian relics he will find there, each of which preserves intact the memory of a
past event. The letter then turns to the pagan past of Rome, which also awaits the
traveler, and here Petrarch's prose blends almost inextricably the objects of
common sight with the objects of the mind's eye:

Mirabitur septem colles unius muri ambitu circumclusos, cuntis olim terris ac
montibus et pelagis imperantes, et latas vias captivorum agminibus tunc angustas;
arcus suspiciet triumphales subactorum quondam regum ac populorum spoliis
honustos; Capitolium ascendet omnium caput arcemque terrarum, ubi olim cella
Iovis fuerat, nunc est Ara Coeli, unde, ut memorant, Augusto Cesari puer Cristus
ostensus est.   [*Fam.* 9.13]
[He will gaze in wonder at the seven hills enclosed within a single wall, once supreme
over all lands, seas, and mountains; and the broad streets, all too narrow for the hordes
of captives. He will look up at the triumphal arches, once loaded with the spoils of
subjugated kings and peoples. He will ascend the Capitoline hill, the world's head, the
citadel of all the lands, where aforetime was Jove's seat, where now stands the *Ara
Coeli*. There, they say, the infant Christ was displayed to Caesar Augustus.]

In each instance the eye rushes past the contemporary appearance into the
imaginative image of history or legend, situated by the adverbs "tunc,"
"quondam," "olim." The present condition of the arches seems almost irrelevant
to the contemplation of their once magnificent function. In still other texts,
Petrarch's historical vision strives unsuccessfully to discern the tokens of a
prestigious past now concealed too effectively by the modern landscape. This at
any rate seems to be the case when, as the verse letter to Virgil describes it, Petrarch
visited supposedly Virgilian haunts near Mantua:

Hinc tibi composui quae perlegio, otia nactus
Ruris amica tui; quonam vagus avia calle
Fusca sequi, quibus in pratis errare soleres
Assidue mecum volvens, quam fluminis oram

Quae curvi secreta lacus, quas arboribus umbras,
Quas nemorum latebras collisque sedilia parvi
Ambieris, cuius fessus seu cespitis herbam
Presseris accubitu, seu ripam fontis amoeni;
Atque ea praesentem mihi te spectacula reddunt.   [*Fam.* 24.11]
[It is in this city [Mantua] that I have composed what you now are reading. It is here
that I have found the friendly repose of thy rural fields. I constantly wonder by what
path you were wont to seek the unfrequented glades in thy strolls, in what fields were
wont to roam, what streams to visit, or what recess in the curving shores of the lake,
what shady groves and forest fastnesses. Constantly I wonder where it was that you
rested upon the sloping sward, or that, reclining in moments of fatigue, you pressed
with your elbow the grassy turf or upon the marge of a charming spring. Such
thoughts as these bring you back before my eyes.][20]

At first the questing imagination seems to wander unappeased; and yet the
ultimate goal is attained, since Virgil's human presence emerges as a reality—
"praesentem"—even from the random questioning of stream and wood.

This habit of seeking out everywhere the latent vestiges of history is shared today
by every tourist, but in Petrarch's century it was a momentous acquisition. His
inquisitions of landscape reveal him in the act of discovering history, and they
reveal how creative, how inventive was this act for which he is properly famous.[21]
The letters and poems that reflect the exercise of his historical imagination exhibit
him in the process of living through this discovery, not only in his study but also in
the daily experiences of his peripatetic life. To say that Petrarch "discovered"
history means, in effect, that he was the first to notice that classical antiquity was
very different from his own medieval world, and the first to consider antiquity
more admirable. Even if anticipations of these attitudes may be found, he was the
first to publicize them so effectively as to influence profoundly his immediate
posterity.

Thus Petrarch took more or less alone the step an archaic society must take to
reach maturity: he recognized *the possibility of a cultural alternative*. With that
step he established the basis of a radical critique of his culture: not the critique that
points to a subversion of declared ideals, but rather the kind that calls ideals
themselves into question. It is this immense shift of perspective that is signaled by
Petrarch's original way of looking at places, and especially his view of Rome.
Before him, writes Peter Burke, the Roman ruins were noticed, but their historical
significance was scarcely perceived. "They were thought of as 'marvels,' *mirabilia*.
But they were taken as given. People seem not to have wondered how they got
there, when they were built, or why the style of architecture was different from their
own. The most they will do is to tell 'just so stories' or explanatory myths about the
names of places."[22] With the rare exception of such a protohumanist as Hildebert
de Lavardin, this statement is true; its accuracy can be measured by the continuing
use, well after the age of Petrarch, of the twelfth-century "guidebook" *Mirabilia
urbis Romae*, whose mingling of Christian miracle and topographic error beto-

kens an incapacity or unwillingness to peceive the passage of history. To gauge the originality of Petrarch, one can set against the *Mirabilia* the extended passage in book 8 of the *Africa* that evokes the edifices of republican Rome with loving detail and reverent prolixity, even if not with archaeological precision. It was this Rome that Petrarch had gone to see and did see, despite the hostility of "present reality."

The effort of the imagination that produced these pages of the *Africa* reversed, in a sense, the imaginative effort behind the eighth book of the *Aeneid*—and to a lesser extent the treatment of place throughout that poem. For the *Aeneid* systematically introduces places as yet unfamiliar to its heroes but deeply charged for the Roman reader: Actium and Carthage, Cumae and Avernus, the Forum and the Janiculum. The *Aeneid* requires of its reader a simultaneous double vision that superimposes the past landscape on the present, thus providing a peculiar pleasure compacted of recognition and nostalgia. This process is sustained most continuously in lines 337–61 of book 8, lines that follow Evander and Aeneas as they walk from the Carmental shrine to what was to become the Forum, and that stress repeatedly the modest pastoral simplicity of each hallowed site:

Hinc ad Tarpeiam sedem et Capitolia ducit
aurem nunc, olim silvestribus horrida dumis.   [*Aeneid* 8.237–48]
[From there he conducted them to Tarpeia's Place and the Capitol, which is now all gold, but was once wild and ragged, covered with woodland undergrowth.][23]

The reader is required to hold before his eyes two plans, two historical incarnations at once, and to shift his focus so quickly from the upper to the lower and back again that he grasps with a thrill the staggering impetus of time. Petrarch's eighth book makes no explicit reference to the city of his own age, to the Capitol once again "silvestribus horrida dumis," but the late medieval reader could not fail to perceive the Rome of the *Africa* as an archaeological construct. He would retrace in his mind the same promenade taken by the poet and Giovanni Colonna: he would superimpose present decay upon past glory and measure now the ironies of history. More painfully, he would confront a cultural alternative that appeared to dwarf his own crude and divided Christendom. For Petrarch, refusing Hildebert's conception of a fortunate Roman fall—"Maior sum pauper divite, stante iacens" (I am greater in poverty than in wealth, prostrate than erect)—saw the vestigial text of the Roman palimpsest as still more precious than its rude overlay.

Similar uses of landscape appear elsewhere in Petrarch's work where history is not at issue. The beautiful canzone that begins "Chiare fresche e dolci acque" (*Canzoniere* 126) situates the speaker in a landscape by a stream where once he had seen Laura bathing and where he repeatedly returns to recapture this privileged moment. He even pictures her, in his fantasy, returning some day to seek *him*, only to find his grave. The poem thus depends on two distinct superpositions of presence upon absence, past upon present. Several of the poems *in morte* will also represent the poet seeking and finding Laura present in the places she once frequented:

Cosí comíncio a ritrovar presenti
le tue bellezze a' suoi usati soggiorni.   [282]
[Thus I begin to discover again the presence of your beauty in its accustomed haunts.]

Fantasies like these constitute a kind of erotic, or perhaps narcissistic, complement
to the fanciful re-creation of a historical site.

To move from these uses of the actual landscape to less literal interests and
unearthings was only a small step for Petrarch, as it would be for the humanist
movement he unknowingly fathered. The image that propelled the humanist
Renaissance and that still determines our perception of it, was the archaeological,
necromantic metaphor of *disinterment*, a digging up that was also a resuscitation
or a reincarnation or a rebirth. (See above, chapter 3, pp. 30–33.) The discovery of
the past led men literally to dig in the ground, and the recovery from it of a
precious object needed only a touch of fancy to be regarded as a resurrection. But
the resurrection of buried objects and buildings could not be sharply distinguished
from the resurrection of literary texts as they were discovered, copied, edited,
disseminated, translated, and imitated by the humanist necromancer-scholar.
Petrarch found it natural to use the term *ruinae* for the lost or fragmentary literary
remains of antiquity,[24] and he himself would be praised by later humanists for
having brought the Latin language back to the light of day from among the ruins
with which it had been entombed.[25]

This commonplace Renaissance equation between the literal unearthing of
antiquities and the unearthing or resurrection of ancient culture was already
current during Petrarch's lifetime. Benvenuto of Vicenza (died 1323) celebrated the
discovery of a manuscript of Catullus by composing a poem "de resurectione
Catulli poete Veronensis."[26] Boccaccio employed the same metaphor in at least
three separate contexts in order to praise three great trecento artists: Dante, Giotto,
and Petrarch himself.[27] Filippo Villani, writing a short time after Petrarch's death,
praised Giotto for having "revived the bloodless and almost extinct art of painting."[28] Several passages in Petrarch's work can be associated with the same
image.[29] Thus the effort to decipher and recreate the buried reality of a place can be
assimilated to the re-creation of a culture that was buried in various literal and
progressively figurative ways. The title of a work by Valla—"Repastinatio," a
digging up again—might have been used appropriately for any number of humanist writings.[30]

Vestigial traces of necromantic superstition are by no means absent from the
awe that produced this imagery. We catch an echo of it in the canzone "Spirto
gentil" (*Canzoniere* 53), which evokes a senile Rome overcome by sleep, to be
awakened perhaps by the unnamed hero who is being addressed. The call for
Rome's reawakening is followed immediately by a vision of the ancient walls, the
tombs of Roman heroes, the entire ruined city, and the souls beneath the earth of
the Scipios, Brutus, and Fabricius, hoping and rejoicing at the prospect of an
imminent *renovatio*: "tutto quel ch'una ruina involve, / per te spera saldar ogni
suo vizio" (All that a ruin envelops, hopes through you to remedy every loss). The

allusions to an underworld of heroes and the metaphoric portraits of a stupefied or widowed Rome waiting to be revived, contain in germ the full-blown necromantic imagery of the later Renaissance. Petrarch, like Boccaccio, situated the otherness of the past beneath his feet and formulated his hopes of renewal in terms of a return to life.

3

The force of the necromantic superstition at the heart of the humanist enlightenment gave rise to a curious artistic phenomenon. It produced buildings and statues and poems that have to be scrutinized for subterranean outlines or emergent presences or ghostly reverberations. Renaissance art requires us to penetrate its visual or verbal surface to make out the vestigial form below, a revived classical form or a medieval form transmuted by a classicizing taste. Sir Kenneth Clark remarks that the Venus of Boticelli's *Primavera* "raises her hand with a gesture of a Virgin Annunciate; and the figure of Spring, fleeing from the icy embraces of the East Wind, is a Gothic nude."[31] Anthony Blunt, discussing Lescot's design for the facade of the Cour Carrée of the Louvre, points out that the "triple repetition of the pavilion seems to be an echo, probably unconscious, of the late medieval chateau facade divided by three round towers, to be seen for instance at Josselin or Martainville."[32]

Other examples from the visual arts would be easy to find. But it is above all the humanist literature of the Renaissance that requires an "archaeological" scrutiny, a decipherment of the latent or hidden or indecipherable object of historical knowledge beneath the surface. I propose to call this activity *subreading*. In the case of Petrarch, we can follow the ways in which subreading the landscape came to resemble subreading a culture. The crucial moment occurs when the poet turns from landscape to the literary remains of antiquity and struggles to pierce their verbal surfaces to reach the living particularity of the past they bear within them. This subreading seems to me to be a central activity of Petrarch's mind, an activity that can be distinguished from medieval hermeneutics and that he bequeathed to his humanist heirs.

Subreading an ancient text involved first of all an intuition of its otherness, an intuition that neither filial reverence nor fraternal affection could altogether dim. It also involved a dynamic and continuous interplay between the reader and the distant voice whose very accent and idiom he sought to catch. The first and essential discipline created by the humanist movement was the science of philology, which was designed to deal systematically with the otherness and distinctiveness of ancient literature. Philology, queen of the *studia humanitatis*, testified to the humanist discovery that cultural styles and verbal styles alter with time, like languages. Thus the first problem for the humanist was to deal with the temporal, cultural, and stylistic gap between the text and himself. Fully to bridge that gap required an effort of subreading that would unearth the alien presence carried by a text in all its subtle integrity. More arduous even than the reading of ruins is the intimate, delicate, and subtle conversation with a voice of the ancient past. The subreader tries to catch the inflections of a remote idiom, the cultural and personal quiddities obscured by millennial history. Petrarch's own capacity to subread is proven by his distinction as a gifted textual scholar. Writing to Boccaccio about the cult of Virgil on the part of Giovanni Malpaghini, his copyist and an aspiring poet, he remarks that he understands the seduction that the young man feels, rapt with the sweetness of another's wit—"alieni dulcedine raptus ingenii." We will not greatly distort the meaning of this phrase if we link the sweetness with the *alien* character of Virgil's genius. Petrarch himself was perhaps the first modern man to be intoxicated by this sweetness.

The reading of poetry before Petrarch had been described in terms of a different activity: not the bridging of time but the piercing of a veil. The activity of subreading needs to be distinguished from the conventional medieval hermeneutic methods with which it would at first coexist and which it would later progressively replace. It resembles neither the fourfold method of scriptural exegesis adapted by Dante and described in his letter to Can Grande, nor the Alexandrian method that presumed a poetic truth concealed by an allegorical veil. Petrarch himself echoes this latter presumption in several works, including his coronation address and the ninth book of the *Africa*: "sub ignoto tamen ut celentur amictu, / nuda alibi, et tenui frustrentur lumina velo" ([Poets may] conceal in an unfamiliar garment things which otherwise are bare, and may baffle our vision with a fine veil, 9.100–01). But he also expressed doubts about the propriety of this presumption in the interpretation of Virgil: once through the mouth of Augustinus in the *Secretum*, and again at greater length in the late letter to Federico Aretino containing an allegorical interpretation of the *Aeneid*, which he there assigns to his youth and which he is no longer prepared to support.[33] Petrarch never explicitly recognized the disparity between the traditional hermeneutic presumptions and the presumptions that emerge in other works of his, most notably in the three letters on imitation (*Fam.* 1.8, 22.2, 23.19). But we can perceive these rhetorical and philological presumptions silently challenging the allegorical in his own mind, as we can follow this challenge or tension or split dividing humanist theory of the next two centuries.

The two hermeneutics are by no means mutually exclusive, but they do bring sharply dissimilar expectations to the literary text. The older method presupposed a fullness of knowledge awaiting the successful interpreter—knowledge that is whole and entire because it can be unlocked by a single operation of the appropriate intellectual key. This method aligned author and reader in a single universe of discourse wherein no cultural distance could exist because, with the sole exception of the Christian revelation, historical change was virtually unknown. The new "archaeological" hermeneutic, on the other hand, presupposed a considerable distance and withheld a single all-divulging key. Instead of a relation between "veil" and "truth" that, once discovered, is easily grasped and formulated, there emerges an interplay of entities that resists total description because it operates in the elusive domain of style. Style by definition cannot be described perfectly even if it can be categorized. And the poetic substance enmeshed in, or half-buried beneath, the verbal surface is now perceived as reaching the reader from far off, from a remote and prestigious world radically unlike his own.

Examples of the older method are not difficult to find in the corpus of Petrarch's work. One of the least convincing is the allegoristic wrenching of Virgil's first eclogue (see above, p. 35). In this particular instance, the effort of subreading failed; misled by a risky hermeneutic convention, Petrarch's literary intelligence could not locate the alien poetic substance latent in the words on his codex. The reductive hermeneutic presuppositions that underlay his gloss were supported by reverend authority and would continue to exercise an influence on literary theory as late as the seventeenth century. But their influence on the actual composition of poetry would decline sharply after the trecento, and Petrarch himself followed them systematically only in his *Bucolicum carmen.*

What in fact Petrarch did choose repeatedly to do as poet was to write verse that could itself be subread and demanded to be subread, verse bearing within it the latent presence of an ancient author. In so doing, of course, he again anticipated the course of the humanist imagination. We move here from the humanist subreading of an ancient text to the subreading required by a modern humanist text. Each activity, though distinct, can illuminate the other. The composition of humanist poetry can best be approached through the theory of imitation.[34] Petrarch's fullest and most interesting discussion of it occurs in the letter to Boccaccio already cited (*Fam.* 23.19), which begins by portraying Giovanni Malpaghini. Petrarch goes on to describe himself as pleased with Giovanni's poetic progress but fearful that too crude a fidelity to their common master Virgil might vitiate his verse:

Curandum imitatori, ut quod scribit simile non idem sit, eamque similitudinem talem esse oportere, non qualis est imaginis ad eum cuius imago est, quae quo similior eo maior laus artificis; sed qualis filii ad patrem, in quibus cum magna saepe diversitas sit membrorum, umbra quaedam et quem pictores nostri aerem vocant, qui in vultu inque oculis maxime cernitur, similitudinem illam facit, quae statim viso filio patris in memoriam nos reducat, cum tamen si res ad mensuram redeat, omnia sint diversa; sed est ibi nescio quid occultum quod hanc habeat vim. Sic et nobis providendum, ut cum simile aliquid sit, multa sint dissimilia, et idipsum simile lateat, nec deprehendi possit, nisi tacita mentis indagine, ut intelligi simile queat potius quam dici. Utendum igitur ingenio alieno, utendumque coloribus, abstinendum verbis. Illa enim similitudo latet, haec eminet. Illa poetas facit, haec simias. [*Fam.* 23.19]
[A proper imitator should take care that what he writes resemble the original without reproducing it. The resemblance should not be that of a portrait to the sitter—in that case the closer the likeness is the better—but it should be the resemblance of a son to his father. Therein is often a great divergence in particular features, but there is a certain suggestion, what our painters call an "air," most noticeable in the face and eyes, which makes the resemblance. As soon as we see the son, he recalls the father to us, although if

we should measure every feature we should find them all different. But there is a
mysterious something there that has this power. Thus we writers must look to it that
with a basis of similarity there should be many dissimilarities. And the similarity
should be planted so deep that it can only be extricated by quiet meditation. The
quality is to be felt rather than defined. Thus we may use another man's conceptions
and the color of his style, but not his words. In the first case the resemblance is hidden
deep; in the second it is glaring. The first procedure makes poets, the second makes
apes.]

In this admirable passage, more enlightened than most discussions of the
subject by later theorists, Petrarch is describing an object of knowledge that, unlike
the "truth" represented by medieval allegory, cannot by definition be fully and
succinctly delimited. The resemblance of a poem to its model or series of models
will never be fully articulated, even supposing that it will be fully grasped. Rather,
one subreads, patiently and intuitively, the dim, elusive presence of the model in
the modern composition. This presence can no more be circumscribed than can
the mysterious resemblance of a son to a father, or the confused relations between
the levels of a buried city. Petrarch himself says this in one crucial sentence of the
passage just quoted: "Sic et nobis providendum, ut cum simile aliquid sit, multa
sint dissimilia, et idipsum simile lateat, nec deprehendi possit, nisi tacita mentis
indagine, ut intelligi simile queat potius quam dici." This silent searching of the
mind, "tacita mentis indagine," is considered never to complete its meditative
investigation. That is because the object of knowledge is perceived to be composed
not by a kernel of moral, religious, or philosophic wisdom, but by what might be
called a *moral style*—a texture of feeling, thought, rhetoric, and tone defining itself
allusively against a ground of literary tradition.

Petrarch's letter itself needs to be subread since its central comparison—likening
the goal of proper literary imitation to the resemblance of a son to his father—bears
just this resemblance to a much briefer simile in Seneca we have already met (pp.
74–75). As we subread the father's features, indistinctly but unmistakably, in his
son's, so we subread Seneca in this letter, and so we subread Virgil in the *Africa* and
other poems. We pursue the diffused, the incomplete, the latent, even as we
recognize that their presence cannot fully be violated by verbal definition. Petrarch
points to this fleeting latency when he uses the word's etymological ancestor: "ut . . .
idipsum simile lateat." The interplay between the surface text and the antecedent
or subtext involves subtle interpenetrations, an interflowing and tingeing, an
exchange of minute gradations, that cannot be measured wholly or formulated. If
the allegorical meaning participated in being, this humanist interplay is forever
becoming. Reading and subreading it means dealing with the implicit, the
incipient, the virtual, and the inexpressible—"ut intelligi simile queat potius
quam dici."

The humanist poet's interplay with antiquity also involves what might be
called a subreading of the self. As Petrarch warned Malpaghini, the very sweetness
of otherness constitutes a risk, since it may change the poet into an ape; it may so

fill the spirit with another's presence that one's own selfhood will be dimmed. Here he seems to adumbrate the idea that true respect for another's wit requires a certain reciprocity. As the ultimate symbols of this reciprocity, we might take his epistles in prose and verse to the ancient authors who mattered most to him, epistles that characteristically reflect a certain humility but do not lack traces of their author's pride and, in the case of Cicero, his disapproval. Petrarch read (and subread) the ancients with less risk, with fuller appreciation, and with sharper philological acuity than Malpaghini not only because he was a great poet but also because he was a great egoist. This means that he brought to his reading a mind blessed with or condemned to compulsive self-questioning, a mind greedy of experience and quick to change its tenor, a mind forever in the process of becoming, obsessed with its own movements and turnings but intermittently open nonetheless to other minds and worlds.

If Petrarch was the first great humanist, his primacy can teach us that the fullest apprehension of otherness requires a continuous circle of adjustments. The subject who attempts to subread must be ready to play with subjective styles of perception, must question and test himself as he sharpens his intuitions, must finally subread his own consciousness to discern that inner likeness, that virtual disposition capable of conversing with a voice from the depths of time. Only thus can he taste without risk that sweetness of the alien that will wither the unguarded and the pallid self. Renaissance anthologies are full of poems by the Malpaghinis, who never mastered this humanist circle of continuing adjustments. In the poetry of mature humanism, subreading the alien text required subreading the range of potential styles of response in one's innermost being, imitation with the inner ear and then imitation with the pen. Imitation at its most powerful pitch required a profound act of self-knowledge and then a creative act of self-definition.[35] Of course the reverse requirement is equally stringent: the definition or creation of literary voices, literary styles, required the progressive apprehension of voices and styles from outside the self.

This process of dynamic self-discovery is adumbrated in another, somewhat earlier letter to Boccaccio that also deals with imitation. Here the analogy is sartorial:

Alioquin multo malim meus michi stilus sit, incultus licet atque horridus, sed in morem toge habilis, ad mensuram ingenii mei factus, quam alienus, cultior ambitioso ornatu sed a maiore ingenio profectus. . . . Omnis vestis histrionem decet, sed non omnis scribentem stilus; suus cuique formandus servandusque est, ne . . . rideamur. Et est sane cuique naturaliter, ut in vultu et gestu, sic in voce et sermone quiddam suum ac proprium, quod colere et castigare quam mutare cum facilius tum melius atque felicius sit.   [*Fam.* 22.2]

[I much prefer that my style be my own, rude and undefined, perhaps, but made to the measure of my mind, like a well-cut gown, rather than to use someone else's style, more elegant, ambitious, and ornamented, but suited to a greater genius than mine. . . . An actor can wear any kind of garment; but a writer cannot adopt any kind of style. He should form his own and keep it, for fear . . . we should laugh at him. Certainly each of us has naturally something individual and his own in his utterance and language as in his face and gesture, It is better and more rewarding for us to develop and train this quality than to change it.]

The perfunctory and quite insincere formulas of modesty need not detain us, but the perception that literary composition requires a lucid estimate of the self is important and valuable, and cuts deeper than the corresponding passage in Quintilian. Petrarch sees that a man's style is as personal as his face, and that both reflect the essential core of selfhood—"quiddam suum ac proprium"—that makes him unique. Only after grasping his own selfhood can the artist create ("formare") and preserve his literary style. Actually, the conception of selfhood shifts slightly but significantly in the course of this passage. The sartorial analogy implies a conception that is basically static. The gown I wear either fits or fails to fit; I may choose between gowns but I cannot alter the fit once I put one on. But the argument that follows this analogy allows us to glimpse a more dynamic self-cultivation. By recognizing our capacity to develop and train ("colere er castigare") not only our style but also our essential individuality, Petrarch recognizes the potentially creative interplay between the alien and the self. Thus, for the humanist poet the beginning of creativity does not lie in a *cogito*, a *prise de conscience*, as it must, according to Georges Poulet, for the modern poet; it lies, rather, in a double groping—toward the otherness of the ancient text and toward a modern sensibility, a modern voice, that can mediate the ancient. And we as readers of humanist poems have to follow the interplay of that mediation, shifting our focus back and forth from the surface text to the fragments buried below it.[36]

Thus these two letters on imitation can be made to yield a kind of embryonic theory of humanist composition, a theory that is clarified by other passages and other images in these same texts. Both letters make use of an apian analogy which was to become a humanist cliché but which in these Petrarchan contexts retains a fresh power of suggestion.

> Standum denique Senecae consilio, quod ante Senecam Flacci erat, ut scribamus scilicet sicut apes mellificant, non servatis floribus, sed in favos versis, ut ex multis et variis unum fiat, idque aliud et melius.   [*Fam.* 23.19]
> [This is the substance of Seneca's counsel, and Horace's before him, that we should write as the bees make sweetness, not storing up the flowers but turning them into honey, thus making one thing of many various ones, but different and better.]

The familiar apian analogy implies a capacity for absorption and assimilation on the part of the poet, a capacity for making one's own the external text in all its otherness. That Petrarch did in fact perceive this process to be crucial in his own creative experience is clear:

> Legi apud Virgilium apud Flaccum apud Severinum apud Tullium; nec semel legi sed milies, nec cucurri sed incubui, et totis ingenii nisibus immoratus sum; mane comedi quod sero digererem, hausi puer quod senior ruminarem. Hec se michi tam familiariter ingessere et non modo memorie sed medullis affixa sunt unumque cum

ingenio facta sunt meo, ut etsi per omnem vitam amplius non legantur, ipsa quidem
hereant, actis in intima animi parte radicibus.   [*Fam.* 22.2]
[I have read Virgil, Horace, Livy, Cicero, not once but a thousand times, not hastily but
in repose, and I have pondered them with all the powers of my mind. I ate in the
morning what I would digest in the evening; I swallowed as a boy what I would
ruminate upon as a man. These writings I have so thoroughly absorbed and fixed, not
only in my memory but in my very marrow, these have become so much a part of
myself, that even though I should never read them again they would cling in my spirit,
deep-rooted in its inmost recesses.]

Here the analogy is digestive, and it too can be traced back to Seneca as well as
forward at least to Francis Bacon, but the formulation here corresponds to something of moment in the poet's own artistic formation. It betokens an intimacy of
conversation with the ancient text, a habitual interiorization of its letter and
essence, and a freedom to transform, to recreate this sweetness of an alien wit into
the honey of one's own personal creation.

One might argue that already in these digestive and apian analogies there lies in
germ the obsessive analogy of a rebirth. The metamorphosis of the ancient into
renewed modern life within the poet's consciousness constitutes a kind of
renascence. This metamorphic implication is more visible in a much earlier usage
of the bee simile:

Neve diutius apud te qualia decerpseris maneant, cave: nulla quidem esset apibus
gloria, nisi in aliud et in melius inventa converterent. Tibi quoque, siqua legendi
meditandique studio repperis, in favum stilo redigenda suadeo.   [*Fam.* 1.8]
[Take care that the nectar does not remain in you in the same state as when you
gathered it; bees would have no credit unless they transformed it into something
different and better. Thus if you come upon something worthy while reading or
reflecting, change it into honey by means of your style.]

Petrarch seems already to see that this kind of assimilation must occur if the
modern text is truly to recall its paternal model imprecisely but unmistakably.
Only this profounder and more secret act of "imitation" permits the authentic
subreading of a latent otherness in the modern work and invests it with its unique
historical depth. The alien text has been absorbed so thoroughly that its presence
haunts the polyvocal modern text, slowly reveals itself to the silent searching of the
mind, resonates faintly in the third ear. In that resonance lies its renascence. The
reader divines a buried stratum, as a visitor to Rome divines the subterranean
foundations of a temple.

In Petrarch's own poetry, this latent stratum can be felt only intermittently, and
more commonly in the Latin works than in the vernacular. Neither body is
lacking in pseudoimitation, in perfunctory assimilation and distorted self-
definition. Most noticeably, the *Africa* is marred by failings that from our
perspective can be attributed to a double incapacity: first, to grasp the alien
substance of ancient epic in its artistic fullness; and second, to gauge lucidly the
character of the writer's own poetic vocation. In fact, Petrarch's most successful

and influential poetry needs to be subread less consistently than does the poetry of his great humanist successors—Poliziano and Tasso, Ronsard and Du Bellay, Jonson and Milton, among them. Yet there are instances of "imitation" in something like the creative sense we have been considering, and these instances, however scattered and brief, are full of interest; in terms of the history of European poetry, they are highly significant.

The poetry initiated by Petrarch in these scattered instances was to become a major current of Renaissance literature, a current whose signal successes amid the perennial mediocrity proved that the double quest of the humanist artist could fecundate the imagination. Before the current spent itself, Petrarch's poetry was itself to achieve the status of a classic; after the dead poetic interval of the earlier quattrocento, and after the genuine poetic renewal of the full European Renaissance, his work joined the ancients' as the object of innumerable attempted resuscitations, some of them splendidly successful. The poems of this current, enriched by a new and subtle polyvocality, might be described as *chronomachias,* battlegrounds for a conflict of eras, a struggle of period styles. In an authentic struggle, the contemporary always wins—which is to say that the poetic voice learns from the baptism of otherness to find its own unique salvation. Merleau-Ponty has written:

> L'histoire vraie vit . . . tout entière de nous. C'est dans notre présent qu'elle prend la force de remettre au présent tout le reste. L'autre que je respecte vit de moi comme moi de lui. Une philosophie de l'histoire ne m'ôte aucun de mes droits, aucune de mes initiatives. Il est vrai seulement qu'elle ajoute à mes obligations de solitaire celle de comprendre d'autres situations que la mienne, de créer un chemin entre ma vie et celle des autres, c'est-à-dire de m'exprimer.[37]

It was this arduous route that the great humanists of the Renaissance chose—and Petrarch first of all—in their momentous search for a self-expression that was, then as always, self-discovery.

4

Petrarch's *search* for self-discovery was complicated by the division, narcissism, and volatility of that self. As one moves from his conceptions of imitation to his poetic practice, these particularities of his personality intrude themselves as constituent elements of his writing. Quite possibly the discovery of history came the more readily to him because he was by birth a dislocated individual. His parents were already in exile in Florence when he was born in Arezzo; much of his youth and maturity were spent in and around Avignon, site of the "exiled" holy See. Thus Petrarch was born deracinated, and while young was marked by that "avara Babilonia" which mingled and corrupted indifferently men of various estates and tongues. Petrarch did not frequently refer to this uprooting, but we can judge its importance to him from the tears shed by Franciscus when the subject arises in the *Secretum.* "Are you unaware," he asks Augustinus, "of this stepmother Fortune's cruelty, which in a single day destroyed with one brutal stroke all my hopes and wealth, my family and home?" (Illa ne tibi inaudita est Fortune novercantis immanitas, cum uno die me spesque et opes meas omnes et genus et domum impulsu stravit impio?)[38] Avignon anticipated the modern city in its power to cut men off from their *attachments* to a class, a place, and a community. Petrarch grew up without strong attachments of this sort, without a ceremonial identity, and his bookish genius transformed a dislocation in space into a dislocation in time, into a nostalgia for a City that was not Florence but rather the Rome of the republic.

This dislocation appears to have been one of the factors that heightened his self-perception. On the opening page of *De remediis utriusque fortune* appears a quotation from Saint Miniato that treats the problem of self-consciousness in a peculiarly modern spirit.

> I see that nature has provided all irrational animals with a remarkable protection, namely a lack of knowledge of themselves; only to us who are human do I see memory, intelligence, and foresight turned into torment and weariness.[39]

The sense of time, the possession of three faculties corresponding to the three realms of earthly temporality, permits that reflexive capacity to examine our selves and our conduct which makes us responsible and problematic animals. The exacerbated self-consciousness is of a piece with the intensified historical consciousness—the two sources of that originality which, quite apart from his poetic gifts, constitute Petrarch's signal importance in the history of the European mind. As the quest for a community was displaced from the geographical frame to the historical, ceremonial absolutes were undermined by the recognition of alternatives, and through the dawning perception of cultural otherness there emerged new criteria for judgment, including self-judgment. The opacity of the other, the distinct particularity of the other, led to a recognition of the uniqueness of the self which ceremonial symbolism could not represent. The rootless, self-questioning personality, half in love with and half perplexed by its reflexive inquisitions, was haunted by Fortune as Chronos, by the privations of mutability and the enormous holocaust of history. There may have been a fatality in the fact that the earliest diachronic poetry of the modern era, the first poetry deliberately to dramatize the passage of history, would dramatize a descent into a selfhood unsure of its status.

In the writing of Petrarch this lack of assurance affected that vocation for historical mediation, for what I have called transitivity, which he felt quite as strongly as had his Roman masters. Petrarch refers in several contexts to his felt responsibility as interpreter of the classical heritage not so much or not only for his contemporaries as for posterity. In an early letter (*Fam.* 1.9) he calls this task a form of charity (*charitas*).[40] Later passages return to the theme with varying degrees of hopefulness.[41] There were indeed grounds for qualifying the hope. The effort of mediation, which Petrarch correctly understood to be creative, would require a complex set of gifts involving a patient and subtle discipline. It would require what Nietzsche called the plastic power (*plastische Kraft*) enabling a man to assimilate and make healthy use of history. The ideal of mediation lacks in itself any hint of the means whereby a passive inheritance is rendered transitive; it lacks the magic formula by which humanist turns necromancer. The whole enterprise, the whole drama of Petrarch's humanism centers on the effort to win through to hermeneutic and creative responses that could deal productively with ancient literature in something vaguely resembling its own terms. His effort was inhibited by his intrusive egoism and deracinated loyalties, which, if they led him to momentous new experiences, troubled his capacity to control them.

One may set against the relatively confident passages of the letters on imitation the following sonnet (*Canzoniere* 40) alluding to a specific but unnamed imitative work (the *Africa?* the *De viris illustribus?*) for which the writer needs a certain manuscript in the possession of the sonnet's Roman addressee.

> S'amore o morte non dà qualche stroppio
> a la tela novella ch' ora ordisco,
> e s' io mi svolvo dal tenace visco,
> mentre che l'un coll'altro vero accoppio,   4
>   i' farò forse un mio lavor sí doppio
> tra lo stil de' moderni e 'l sermon prisco
> che, paventosamente a dirlo ardisco,
> infin a Roma n'udirai lo scoppio.   8
>   Ma però che mi manca a fornir l'opra
> alquanto de le fila benedette
> ch' avanzaro a quel mio diletto padre,
>   perché tien' verso me le man sí strette   12
> contra tua usanza? I' prego che tu l'opra,
> e vedrai riuscir cose leggiadre.[42]

[If Love or Death does not cut short the new cloth that now I prepare to weave, and if I loose myself from the tenacious birdlime while I join one truth with the other,
I shall perhaps make a work so double between the style of the moderns and ancient speech that (fearfully I dare to say it) you will hear the noise of it even as far as Rome.
But, since I lack, to complete the work, some of the blessed threads that were so plenteous for that beloved father of mine,
why do you keep your hands so closed toward me, contrary to your custom? I beg you to open, and you will see delightful things result.]

The declaration of a humanist poetic intent is qualified by the conditional phrases of the first quatrain and the "forse" (perhaps) of line 5. If it survives the threats of love and death, the work to come will consist of a fabric ("tela") made from two interwoven styles historically dissimilar (Christian modern and ancient classical) which correspond to two structures of truth. To finish, the writer requires a text by a beloved father (Livy? Augustine?) that he now lacks. The fabric of the father's work is to be undone, ravelled out, so that only its blessed threads remain to be rewoven in a new design and then to be subread later within a tissue altogether new. If it suffers no rip ("stroppio"), the result of this interweaving will be so original as to cause a splash, an explosion ("scoppio") (8) that, the writer adds with express timidity, may be audible even in Rome. Whereas the metaphorical shifts of the letters on imitation seem to succeed each other more or less harmoniously, this sonnet offers a series of metaphors not easily accommodated. The single verb *accoppiare* (4) means "to couple, to marry, to pair, to yoke." Which emphasis should the reader choose? Is the act of imitative acculturation a serene marriage, a sexual union, a forcible yoking of animals or their violent breeding? How smoothly are the two truths wedded in this double labor? The primary meaning of the metaphoric "visco" (3)—birdlime, snare—is apparently the passion for Laura to which "l'amore" (1) also refers, but the presentation of the "visco" as something distinct from "amore" suggested by the conjunction "e" (3) and the proximity of this sticky trap to the act of coupling in line 4 suggest a more generalized snare inherent in this act. The concluding word, "leggiadre"—"graceful, delightful"— has to be reconciled with the force of "scoppio" (8). The filial metaphor evoking the spiritual father appears in a context locating the father as absent in that mythical, unattainable city where perhaps only explosions can reach him. Simultaneous filiation and lack, confidence and apprehension, freedom and claustration, harmony and violence, suggest that the actual imitative texts Petrarch produced would disclose his own ambivalences. The texts do indeed reveal various antithetical pulls; but they are not necessarily crippled works of art for thus exposing their tensions. *Virescit vulnere virtus.* At their strongest, Petrarch's humanist poems fulfill their imitative impluse, authenticate their transitive function, while reflecting the private and historical vulnerability of their tormented author.

Six • Petrarch: The Ontology of the Self

Before we consider Petrarch's creative use of *imitatio* proper in his poetry, it might be instructive to look at a failed imitation which is not altogether literary but which will illustrate the hazards of his poetic enterprise and indeed of the humanist enterprise. The experience is recounted in one of his best-known prose texts, the letter to Dionigi da Borgo San Sepolcro (*Fam.* 4.1), purporting to describe his ascent, in the company of his brother Gherardo, of Mont Ventoux in Provence. This text deserves its fame: it is rich in both biographical and literary interest, and it is the work of a great writer who was also a great actor upon the stage of his century. But from our own special perspective, it will have to stand as a negative object lesson. It is true that certain basic questions surrounding this letter have not been fully resolved. It is not certain whether Petrarch did climb Mont Ventoux, nor, if he did, whether he composed the letter immediately after his descent (as he says he did), nor even, if he did write it then, whether he lengthened it with interpolated passages written many years later. Scholars are divided on these questions,[1] but their controversy is not paramount for our purposes. If Petrarch never made the climb, his volition to make it is clear; if he did make it, what he left us, whenever written, is a highly stylized version of his experience. In either case, what we have is literature growing out of an existential impulse. In my discussion, I shall speak for simplicity's sake as though Petrarch did literally climb the mountain, without further inquiry as to whether this "Petrarch" is to some degree a fictional character.

The most extraordinary thing about the adventure is the initial fact that Petrarch wanted to embark upon it. It is by no means clear that he himself understood his own impulse. He accounted for his decision by referring to an incident in Livy (40.21.2–22.7). This is the way he explains it in the opening of his letter.

Altissimum regionis huius montem, quem non immerito Ventosum vocant, hodierno die, sola videndi insignem loci altitudinem cupiditate ductus, ascendi. Multis iter hoc annis in animo fuerat; ab infantia enim his in locis, ut nosti, fato res hominum versante, versatus sum; mons autem hic late undique conspectus, fere semper in oculis est. Cepit impetus tandem aliquando facere quod quotidie faciebam, precipue postquam relegenti pridie res romanas apud Livium forte ille michi locus occurrerat, ubi Philippus Macedonum rex . . . Hemum montem thesalicum conscendit, e cuius vertice duo maria videri, Adriaticum et Euxinum, fame crediderat, vere ne an falso satis comperti nichil habeo, quod et mons a nostro orbe semotus et scriptorum dissensio

dubiam rem facit. . . . Titus Livius falsam famam opinatur; michi si tam prompta montis illius experientia esset quam huius fuit, diu dubium esse non sinerem.[2]
[Today I ascended the highest mountain in this region, which, not without cause, they call the Windy Peak. Nothing but the desire to see its conspicuous height was the reason for this undertaking. For many years I have been intending to make this expedition. You know that since my early childhood, as fate tossed around human affairs, I have been tossed around in these parts, and this mountain, visible far and wide from everywhere, is always in your view. So I was at last seized by the impulse to accomplish what I had always wanted to do. It happened while I was reading Roman history again in Livy that I hit upon the passage where Philip, the King of Macedon . . . ascends Mount Haemus in Thessaly, since he believed the rumor that you can see two seas from its top: the Adriatic and the Black Sea. Whether he was right or wrong I cannot make out because the mountain is far from our region, and the disagreement among authors renders the matter uncertain. . . . Livy supposes the rumor to be false. I would not leave it long in doubt if that mountain were as easy to explore as the one here.]

Petrarch's report that the reading of Livy crystallized a hankering which he had long entertained is curious in view of Livy's own attitude toward the incident in question. Philip, who chooses to make the ascent, is anything but an appealing figure; the ascent itself is arduous and fruitless; visibility at the summit is impeded by fog; and the legend that both seas could be sighted from it is treated as a joke. After returning, those who had reached the summit concealed the truth lest, Livy writes, the futility of the journey should expose them to riducule—"ne vanitas itineris ludibrio esset." Petrarch's impulse to imitate Philip would be hard to explain if we lacked evidence that Petrarch the man tried repeatedly to imitate the conduct as well as the style of the ancients, in large things as in small. It has been argued that Petrarch rejected his apparently inoffensive illegitimate son by way of imitating Cicero's paternal troubles.[3] Thus he seems to have seized upon a brief and unlikely incident in Livy as an authenticating pretext for his own admirable and spontaneous impulse.

During the account that follows, however, Petrarch leaves Livy far behind. After explaining his choice of his brother Gherardo as his companion and sketching briefly the circumstances of their setting forth, he dwells at some length on his temporary separation from Gherardo, a future Carthusian monk, who chooses to follow the hard and steep path to the summit while Francesco, the writer, wanders vainly below in search of an easy path. Here the factual account of a literal outing seems to modulate into Christian allegoresis, and lest there remain any doubt, Petrarch the correspondent quotes Petrarch the Christian alpinist drawing the equation himself.

"Quod totiens hodie in ascensu montis huius expertus es, id scito et tibi accidere et multis, accedentibus ad beatam vitam. . . . Equidem vita, quam beatam dicimus, celso loco sita est. . . . Eo pervenire volunt omnes, sed, ut ait Naso, 'Velle parum est; cupias, ut re potiaris, oportet.' . . . Veruntamen, ubi multum erraveris, aut sub pondere male dilati laboris ad ipsius te beate vite culmen oportet ascendere aut in convallibus peccatorum tuorum segnem procumbere; et si . . . ibi te 'tenebre et umbra mortis' invenerint, eternam noctem in perpetuis cruciatibus agere."

["What you have so often experienced today while climbing this mountain happens to you, you must know, and to many others who are making their way toward the blessed life. . . . The life we call blessed is located on a high peak. . . . Every man wants to arrive there. However, as Naso says: 'Wanting is not enough; long and you attain it.' . . . Having strayed far in error, you must either ascend to the summit of the blessed life under the heavy burden of hard striving, ill deferred, or lie prostrate in your slothfulness in the valleys of your sins. If 'darkness and the shadow of death' find you there . . . you must pass the eternal night in torments."]   [39–40; 734]

The "darkness and the shadow of death" (tenebre et umbra mortis), quoted from Psalm 107, are to be taken most immediately for the darkness of hell, but in the larger context of the entire letter, with its dramatic geographical and moral panoramas, these shadows have to be linked with the spiritual ambiguities and intermittences that will emerge as the author's particular torment. In terms of the local narrative, the wayfarer's little autoexhortation succeeds promptly in putting an end to his self-indulgence and brings him quickly to the mountain peak, almost as though the moral character of his errancy had to be articulated in order to be dealt with.

Thus we encounter here during the ascent what we shall encounter again at the summit: a will to purify the mountain of its physical substance, to sublimate it into the *summus* which is the end of life, just as the existential actuality of the climb is purified to make room for a Christian *peregrinatio*. A consecrated literary mode, allegoresis, authorized by the Christian tradition, threatens the timid, provisional, exploratory mode of secular autobiography, weakly validated by a text from Livy and resting on a hazy humanist etiology (I climb because Philip climbed). On the one hand a mode whose force in Petrarch's own creative imagination will fade or is fading; on the other hand, a nascent humanist mode, *imitatio*, which is still insecure and perhaps displaced from the written page to a physical effort in an objective landscape. If allegoresis is still alive in a text like this one, we may ask whether its true function is not to colonize the external world less as a servant of Christian morals than as an instrument of an ego's jealousy toward any distractions from its own absorbing drama.

The objective field of reference seems to gain a momentary victory when, his dilatory weakness behind him, the writer stands upon the actual summit and triumphantly looks about him: "Respicio." The narrative opens out into authentic externality: there is a little flat ground commanding an immensity of space, and below the weary climber's feet are gathering actual clouds, no longer the shadows of death. The wind is blowing hard, with force enough, it appears, to compel the enchanted poet to mingle sensory impressions with his sentimental and bookish train of thought.

Respicio: nubes erant sub pedibus; iamque michi minus incredibiles facti sunt Athos et Olimpus, dum quod de illis audieram et legeram, in minoris fame monte conspicio.

Dirigo dehinc oculorum radios ad partes italicas, quo magis inclinat animus; Alpes ipse rigentes ac nivose per quas ferus ille quondam hostis romani nominis transivit. [I looked around me: clouds were gathering below my feet, and Athos and Olympus grew less incredible, since I saw on a mountain of lesser fame what I had heard and read about them. From there I turned my eyes in the direction of Italy, for which my mind is so fervently yearning. The Alps were frozen stiff and covered with snow—those mountains through which that ferocious enemy of the Roman name [Hannibal] once passed.] [41; 736]

Later, as he gazes into the distance at the Lyonnais, the Mediterranean, Aigues Mortes, and below him at the Rhone, he stands for these moments upon a peak that is truly solid and elevated, so that the nostalgia for Italy, the story of Hannibal's crossing of the Alps, the desire to see his friend Giacomo Colonna, the examination of his past life, and the other characteristic meditations of his learned, centripetal mind, are provided with a substantial and dramatic setting. Here is a place where, as an arresting line from a great canzone has it, no shadow of another mountain reaches—"ove d'altra montagna ombra non tocchi"; here Petrarch might have won through to a steadiness of vision and a fruitful interchange between his mind and the solid externality of the majestic site. He seems on the brink of such an interchange after surveying the panorama below:

> Que dum mirarer singula et nunc terrenum aliquid saperem, nunc exemplo corporis animum ad altiora subveherem. . . .
> [I admired every detail, now relishing earthly enjoyment, now lifting up my mind to higher spheres after the example of my body. . . .] [44; 738]

The moment might even have prompted him to assess the motives that prompted his ascent: the will to experiment with his sensibility; the will to dramatize his restless mobility; the will to pose against the expanse of history; the will to dominate with his romantic imperial egoism the widest extension of space.

But the centripetal reflection falls short of that lucidity; and in fact the burden of this reflection lies precisely in the mind's forever falling short or digressing or fading away before reaching a true conclusion; it lies in the hectic impermanence of all motions of the soul, all meanings of the voice, and in the bitter poignancy of this self-reproach, qualified with measured hope of progress, the place and the occasion are forgotten until the mind deliberately throws off its burden to return to them.

> De provectu meo gaudebam, imperfectum meum flebam et mutabilitatem comunem humanorum actuum miserabar; et quem in locum, quam ob causam venissem, quodammodo videbar oblitus, donec, ut omissis curis, quibus alter locus esset oportunior, respicerem et viderem que visurus adveneram—instare enim tempus abeundi, quod inclinaret iam sol et umbra montis excresceret, admonitus et velut expergefactus—, verto me in tergum, ad occidentem respiciens.
> [I was glad of the progress I had made, but I wept over my imperfection and was grieved by the fickleness of all that men do. In this manner I seemed to have somehow forgotten the place I had come to and why, until I was warned to throw off such

sorrows, for which another place would be more appropriate. I had better look around and see what I had intended to see in coming here. The time to leave was approaching, they said. The sun was already setting, and the shadow of the mountain was growing longer and longer. Like a man aroused from sleep, I turned back and looked toward the west.]   [43; 738]

The various flights of the conflicted, volatile, self-scrutinizing mind are recorded in detail, and they culminate in the impulse to open a copy of Saint Augustine's *Confessions*. Petrarch opens and reads.

> "Et eunt homines admirari alta montium et ingentes fluctus maris et latissimos lapsus fluminum et oceani ambitum et giros siderum, et relinquunt se ipsos."
> ["And men go to admire the high mountains, the vast floods of the sea, the huge streams of the rivers, the circumference of the ocean, and the revolutions of the stars—and desert themselves."]   [44; 740]

Stunned by this new rebuke and certain that the words had been written for him, Petrarch descends with contrition and writes out this letter immediately, he says, because "I was afraid the intention to write might evaporate, since the rapid change of scene was likely to cause a change of mood if I deferred it." Then he concludes by asking Dionigi to pray for him.

> Pro quibus ora, queso, ut tandiu vagi et instabiles aliquando subsistant, et inutiliter per multa iactati, ad unum, bonum, verum, certum, stabile se convertat.
> [Pray for these thoughts, I beseech you, that they may at last find stability. So long have they been idling about and, finding no firm stand, been uselessly driven through so many matters. May they now turn at last to the One, the Good, the True, the stably Abiding.]   [46; 742]

In view of this conclusion, the intellectual curiosity of the opening appears all the more puzzling, not to say paradoxical ("I would not leave it long in doubt . . . whether Philip was right or wrong"). There is no contrition in these opening pages. The text as a whole betrays an authorial consciousness so deeply divided that its integrity begins to blur. The text in fact becomes a locus for struggles between antagonistic voices or forces within the writer, struggles to which he himself refers,[4] which dramatize that *mutabilitatem* we have seen him deploring, and which issue in stalemates or Pyrrhic victories. Most patently there is a conflict between Livy and Augustine. For the conversion, if that is what it is, produced by the passage from the *Confessions* is itself an imitation of Augustine, and Petrarch in fact points out the imitation. Having read the passage, he is persuaded that it was written for himself and himself alone, just as once, he recalls, Augustine was likewise persuaded after opening to a passage from Paul's epistle to the Romans. Petrarch's experience imitates Augustine's, just as Augustine's, by his own admission in the *Confessions*, imitated an experience attributed to Saint Anthony Abbot by his biographer Athanasius. Petrarch contrives an imitation of Augustine as an interruption of his imitation of Livy's Philip, an interruption which is also a judgment but which falls short, again, of conclusive permanence.

Thus there is a conflict between Livy and Augustine that is by no means resolved in the letter, and there is a more generalized conflict between humanist and Christian, curiosity and compunction, between echoes of Ovid, Seneca, Virgil, and echoes of the Psalms, the Gospels, and Saint Paul. There is a conflict between Petrarch's self-image as a persistent striver asserting his personal coherence and mastery ("Tireless labor overcomes everything," he quotes from the *Georgics*—38; 732), and as a helpless pawn of Fortune whirled about by ceaseless flux ("as fate tossed around human affairs, I have been tossed around in these parts"—36; 730). There is a conflict between a self-conscious, self-observing actor and a self-blinded, naive agent who invites our irony. And there is the conflict between the ascent conceived as a literal occurrence and the ascent as mythic literature. All of these conflicts fall short of resolution in the letter as they do repeatedly in Petrarch's work and in his life. They contribute to that impression of *oxymoronic* irresolution that seems to govern so much of his work, a coexistence of opposites that seldom find an equilibrium, giving way one to the other in a fatal succession which Petrarch's art can render brilliantly but not bring to rest.

The struggle however which counts most for our purposes is rather that one we have already discerned between the effort of the material mountain to achieve objectivity against the drift toward allegoresis in the writer's sensibility. There is a struggle pursued even more deeply in the very language of Petrarch toward a capacity for reference beyond the consciousness which gives it being, a struggle repeatedly frustrated by the poet's imperial ego. The last of the oddly assorted quotations that adorn this text is the opening of a famous passage in the *Georgics* (2.490ff.) that has been commonly referred to Lucretius.

> Felix qui potuit rerum cognoscere causas
> atque metus omnes et inexorabile fatum
> subiecit pedibus strepitumque Acherontis avari!
> [Happy the man who succeeded in baring the causes of things
> And who trod underfoot all fear, inexorable Fate, and
> Greedy Acheron's uproar.]   [46; 742][5]

Petrarch cites these lines, anachronistically, to illustrate his Augustinian medita-tion on the obligation to overcome one's worldy appetites, but the citation is doubly anachronistic because the profound knowledge of material things in themselves, experimental knowledge in the Lucretian sense, is precisely what Petrarch has shown himself incapable of attaining. The language of Lucretius, like the language of the *Georgics*, brings feeling to bear on a universe of externals; it attaches to things names which adhere and which designate. To take cognizance—"cognoscere"—in this full sense is to subdue the fear of eternal night (Virgil's "Acherontis avari"; the Psalmist's "tenebre et umbra mortis") by a means which Petrarch's imagination seems doomed to forego, because those of its words—here as in the *Canzoniere*—that appear to refer beyond their creating consciousness are subject to a collapse of reference, an implosion into subjective allegory. Petrarch's words are truly shadowed by a failure of denotative firmness, a failure of lucid and humble contemplation that accepts a realm of experience beyond the reach of the voracious ego, beyond allegoresis.[6]

The interior experience that is plotted by allegory remains, curiously, at once restless and stationary, "immobile," as Bosco remarked, "in its perplexity."[7] That sentence (quoted above) which opens most promisingly a possibility of interchange between self and nature ("I admired every detail . . .") concludes with the turn to Saint Augustine, and this turn then leads to a moral judgment upon the ascent that will bring the traveler down the mountain sorrowful and repentant. The mountain, as we last see it, is blurred by Christian symbolism.

> Quotiens, putas, illo die, rediens et in tergum versus, cacumen montis aspexi! et vix unius cubiti altitudo visa est pre altitudine contemplationis humane, siquis eam non in lutum/terrene feditatis immergeret.
> [How often, do you think, did I turn back and look up to the summit of the mountain today while I was walking down? It seemed to be hardly contemplation, were the latter not plunged into the filth of earthly sordidness.]   [45; 740–42]

The judgment upon the ascent is recorded as though it issued from the voice of the saint speaking to the narrator from without and striking him with the impact of a conversion. But the lines from Augustine which meet his eyes correspond to an internalized voice speaking as a Christian conscience, just as the admonitions of Augustinus in the *Secretum* will correspond to the same voice. The conversion is a pseudoconversion because there is no true gain in self-knowledge. The impact of the peripety at the summit does not protect the writer on his return from concern that his mood will change if he delays to write. The apparent singularity and unique significance of the peripety, registered by the perfect and historical present indicative tenses, are smothered by the valedictory appeal in the subjunctive for constancy and stability, an appeal that evokes only the speaker's continuous, ongoing need. The whole experience comes to be *one more example* in an indefinite series.

It fails of uniqueness, we might say, because of a failed assimilation. There might have been—and the text briefly allows us to hope for it—an original, secular experience in which Petrarch would have perceived something external decisively, in which the admirable impulse to commit this heady, experimental act would have flowered in authentic contact with the nonself. That contact would then inevitably have led, since we are dealing with Petrarch, to a new situating of the self, and this consequence in turn might have perpetuated the interplay between inner and outer realms. But the letter threatens rather to fall into the opposite cycle, also approached in the *Canzoniere*, a sterile, narcissistic sequence wherein the external, if it is apprehended at all, triggers a purely internal series of delusions and disillusions. Thus the letter could be described as the locus of still another conflict pitting an alert and creative consciousness against an imprisoning narcissistic consciousness.

The whole letter can be read as leading up to the concluding prayer for rest—"ut tandiu vagi et instabiles aliquando subsistant"—a prayer for an existential repose that is also a semiotic repose, an end to that unstable ambiguity of signification we shall meet again in Petrarch's poetry. It is striking that within the plot of this anecdote it is the "imitation" of Livy's king that provokes an outward orientation, a disposition toward firm reference, and it is the imitation as well as the reproof of Augustine that pull away from secure reference. As the story of a single or a double imitation, the letter is of interest because it demonstrates the difficulty of dominating and *using* anachronistic conflict.

The depth of this conflict is clear enough. Livy's book stages its mythologized history against a geographical setting that is firmly respected and precisely rendered. It also assumes that the patterning of events it narrates is discernible only through sequences that are irreversible and that influence future events. But the Augustianian vision of history dissolves geography as a major constituent factor and presumes a repetitive monotony in all events falling short of that decisive experience which transforms man and history.[8] It is at this level that the crucial anachronism exists and that the failure to bridge it becomes critical. The text quickly exchanges the slender recollection of the king of Macedonia for the intense and profound but inconclusive response to Augustine; in doing so, it can stand as a model of the weakness of the historical imagination in the years just after its rebirth. The text wants at the end to be an imitation of Augustine—an easier imitation in one sense since the crucial experience is suprahistorical—but in this case it fails out of spiritual instability. Augustine remains anyway as a remote ideal, but Livy falls away, falls out of the letter and history with him. The historical imagination did not in this instance provide Petrarch with an instrument sufficiently powerful to deal with the antihistorical inertia of his culture and the ahistorical elements of his own personality which acted to reinforce that inertia. The imitative impulse proves to have been sentimental precisely in the Meredithian sense, and the transitive potentialities of the experience are closed off along with the heuristic. There is no clear passage opened up between Livy's text and Petrarch's, except for an ambivalent repudiation; the passage from Augustine's text can only serve to underscore the pathos of the repetition's inadequacy. A crisis of retrospection emerges because the retrospective fiction represents historical passage too simplistically as a fall into shadow, a moral fall that conceals a semiotic fall, and out of this simplicity no enrichment of the moral style can derive. To dwell on this failure is not peevishly to derogate a very great man, but to describe the drama of his life-effort and to measure the dimension of his true achievement. It is also to circumscribe the crisis that Renaissance humanism had to face to come into being while it was scarcely more than nascent in one man's mind.

2

The study of imitation in Petrarch's vernacular poetry might well begin with *Canzoniere* 90.

Erano i capei d'oro a l'aura sparsi
che 'n mille dolci nodi gli avolgea,
e 'l vago lume oltra misura ardea
de quei begli occhi ch 'or ne son sí scarsi;   4
    e 'l viso di pietosi color farsi,
non so se vero o falso, mi parea:
i' che l 'esca amorosa al petto avea,
qual meraviglia se di súbito arsi?   8
    Non era l 'andar suo cosa mortale
ma d 'angelica forma, e le parole
sonavan altro che pur voce umana;
    uno spirto celeste, un vivo sole   12
fu quel ch ' i' vidi; e se non fosse or tale,
piaga per allentar d 'arco non sana.

[Her golden hair was loosed to the breeze, which turned it in a thousand sweet knots,
and the lovely light burned without measure in her eyes, which are now so stingy of it;
and it seemed to me (I know not whether truly or falsely) her face took on the color of
pity: I, who had the tinder of love in my breast, what wonder is it if I suddenly caught
fire?

Her walk was not that of a mortal thing but of some angelic form, and her words
sounded different from a merely human voice: a celestial spirit, a living sun was what I
saw, and if she were not such now, a wound is not healed by the loosening of the bow.]

This sonnet is haunted by the passage from the first book of the *Aeneid* in which
Aeneas encounters Venus disguised as a huntress near Carthage and recognizes her
as his mother only as she leaves him. Petrarch's opening line is a variation on
Virgil's "dederatque comam diffundere ventis" (she had let her hair stream in the
wind). Ovid's description of the fleeing Daphne's hair may also serve as a subtext.[9]
Lines 9–10 makes reference to Virgil's "vera incessu patuit dea" (her gait proved
her a goddess), as what follows in the Italian makes reference to

> . . . namque haud tibi vultus
> mortalis, nec vox hominem sonat.   [*Aeneid* 1.319, 405, 327–28]
> [You have not the countenance of human kind and your voice has no tones of
> mortality.]

Petrarch plays with the ambiguity of the woman's creaturely status which
underlies the dramatic interplay in the *Aeneid*, but he reverses of course the
direction taken by appearances: Venus is a goddess who looks like a woman, but
Laura is a woman who looks like a goddess. If there were any doubt about Laura's
status or the poet's perception of it, the parenthetical concession in line 4 would
dispel it: "ch'or ne son sí scarsi." Remembering his first encounter with her as
epiphanic, the poet writes from a perspective of years which call her divinity into
question by dimming her beauty but affect not at all the intensity of his original
wonderment. Thus the epiphanic revelation to Aeneas is reversed to permit a
delicate admixture of nostalgia, a hovering regret at Laura's bodily decline. This

regret sounded in line 4 receives the faintest possible echo in the conditional of line 13: "se non fosse or tale."

But the crucial distancing of surface text from subtext lies in the dramatic presentation of their respective epiphanies. The *Aeneid* stages a progressive *recognition* of divine radiance; the sonnet exposes a *perception* of divinity to the doubts, qualifications, and insecurities of a sensibility struggling to validate its own vision. The graceful and seductive opening lines appear to be introducing a portrait composed of vivid details, but this portrait fails of completion because the poem embeds it in psychologistic process: in the shift from a verb of more or less pure description ("avolgea") to a second somewhat more impressionistic verb ("ardea"), and then to a third which admits the speaker's bias ("parea"); in the confession of phenomenological uncertainty ("non so se vero o falso"); in the stock pun ("l'aura"), which subverts the claim of the opening lines to pure representation and confuses slightly the image (is there really a breeze?); in the confession of a predisposition to enchantment: "i' che l'esca amorosa al petto avea"; in the contradictions between Laura's asserted superhumanity (lines 9–12) and her vulnerability to time; in the semiretraction of line 13; in the fragmentation of the woman, so characteristic of the *Canzoniere*, into detached features and attributes— hair, eyes, face, voice, bearing; and in the implicit restoration of truth by line 14 to the frankly subjective realm (whatever the truth of her beauty now, my suffering is no more reduced thereby than a wound is healed when the archer's bow is unstrung.) The ostensibly descriptive strokes with their apparent basis in epic impersonality prove to be counters in a purely internal flux that reaches not even a local stay in this sonnet any more than a permanent stay in the macrocosmic volume. This repeated betrayal of representational denotation involves a kind of *fall* inherent in Petrarchan imitation, since the classical subtext always appears to be proof against such betrayals.

The problem of objectivity is posed most repeatedly and crucially of course in the representation of "Laura." Aside from the self whose voice we hear, we are made aware always of this second presence whose fictive autonomy, on the far side of the poet's mediating sensibility, seems to fade as soon as it emerges. This presence is designated by a series of periphrases or metaphors or pronouns, none of them constant and none of them allowing us to form a clear visual image. At the most we are given parts of the body with indeterminate modifiers—"belle membra," "bel fianco," "angelico seno," "trecce bionde"—or some other feature or faculty or organ—eyes, smile, hands, face, heart. The most common image for this presence is the *lauro* (laurel tree) and *l'aura* (the breeze—by extension, the relief or the refreshment). In a very few cases, the proper name *Laura* appears. But it is not clear that the name *Laura* is everywhere commensurate with the laurel, since Petrarch repeatedly uses this image to allude to his own coronation and to the fame which this ceremony recognized and enhanced. Thus at the conclusion of canzone 119 ("Una donna piu bella assai che 'l sole . . ."), a poem dedicated to poetic Glory, personified as a beautiful woman, the poet is crowned with a garland of laurel.

. . . di verde lauro una ghirlanda colse,
la qual co le sue mani
intorno intorno a le mie tempie avolse.   [ll. 103–05]
[She gathered a garland of green laurel, which with her own hands she wound round
my temples.]

The univocality of this text is unusual; in most cases it is difficult to know to what
extent the laurel corresponds to fame or the desire for fame as against a woman
who is almost never named and who appears in part as an instrument by which
fame is acquired. Thus in symmetry with a divided authorial voice there corresponds a divided, almost unnamable, and hazy presence that eludes precise definition and description, eludes even descriptive focus. This presence, which in one
poem bears primarily the attributes of a woman, in another of a tree or of a breeze,
in another of a passion for fame or mercy, for acceptance, for *recognition*—this
presence may most helpfully be regarded as that externality which the speaker of
the *Canzoniere* desires but fails to possess, that fluid and intangible entity which
would bring relief by responding to a stable, knowable, recognizable self. One
word for this relief, one frequent word, is *pace* (peace). The state of *pace* or *riposo*
or *salute* would presumably be attained when the blurred external phenomenon
fell into focus, could be described without periphrase or fragmentation, and when
it could respond to a speaking self capable of whole emotions and unriven
language.

   Thus in a sense Petrarch's poetry is always in search of a recognition from an
external agency that the poetry cannot succeed in circumscribing. It is true that a
certain haziness consistently surrounded the figure of the beloved in the medieval
love lyric, and not least in the work of the *stilnovisti*, who refer not infrequently to
her necessary subjectivization in the lover's imagination.[10] Petrarch widens the
gap between the beloved's "reality" and her image within the lover's mind, and he
calls into question the possibility of their correspondence. By shifting the dramatic
center of gravity conclusively away from the woman, away even from any relationship, to the poet's own imprisoning consciousness, he renders her still dimmer,
more remote, more invisible and unknowable than she had been before.

   Robert M. Durling and John Freccero have severally discussed in two seminal
essays the attitude toward "Laura" as idolatry in the precise meaning attached to
this word in the Old Testament.[11] This collocation, which Freccero extends to
include the thought of Saint Augustine, is supported by a reference in sestina 30
("Giovene donna sotto un verde lauro"), quoted by both critics, to "l'idolo mio
scolpito in vivo lauro" (my idol sculpted in a living laurel). Freccero's brilliant
analysis of this relationship opposes Petrarch's laurel to Augustine's fig tree, this
latter being a true allegorical sign which "stands for a referential series of anterior
texts grounded in the Logos." Petrarch on the other hand makes of the laurel "the
emblem of the mirror relationship *Laura-Lauro*, which is to say, the poetic lady
created by the poet, who in turn creates him as poet laureate."[12] This relationship
leads, according to Freccero, to a new problematic poetics: "In order to create an

autonomous universe of autoreflexive signs without reference to an anterior Logos—the dream of almost every poet since Petrarch—it is necessary that the thematic of such poetry be equally autoreflexive and self-contained, which is to say, that it be idolatrous in the Augustinian sense."[13] The only objection to this reading, in my view, concerns the status of the created "lady." Within the limits of this book she never is created, and so is unable to create her supposed lover as laureate; the poetry seems to strive toward this mutual creation without success, so that the closed system of an autonomous universe remains permanently out of reach. *Idol* is a useful term in this connection only if one stays alert to the repeated collapse of its Hebrew meaning (a graven image) into the psychologistic meaning both critics recognize as secondary (*eidolon*, phantasm). This collapse can be translated into the hermeneutic difficulty of picturing and understanding, in sestina 30, how a lady can be seated under a laurel that in part symbolizes her and into which she will later be metamorphosed in the form of a carved image. Freccero writes again: "The lady celebrated by Petrarch is a brilliant surface, a pure signifier whose momentary exteriority to the poet serves as an Archimedean point from which he can create himself."[14] The question is whether this service ever really works. One might argue rather that he creates himself out of failed signifiers. Visual and semiotic imprecision come and go together in the *Canzoniere*, and both bear witness to an incorrigible fugacity of verbal plenitude.

Thus the imitation of Virgil in poem 90 acts out an etiology, a historical passage, that could be described as a fall into constricting subjectivity and blurred verbal reference. To describe this passage as a fall is not to pronounce an evaluative judgment on the poem or on the other imitative poems which present the same etiology. It is simply to give a name to the version of history, the construct or fiction of cultural process, extending from subtext to modern text. If this itinerary needs to be read as a fall, one can appropriately look to Petrarch's sense of cultural inferiority as one determining cause. But the sense of inferiority has not, in most of his vernacular imitations, crippled his creative talent. By inviting the reader to subread an ancient text whose presentational modes are visibly at odds with its own, the modern text underscores its own particularities and avoids the trap of anachronism. It dramatizes a *lyricization* of epic materials. It is this peculiarly Petrarchan lyricization that the heuristic imitation discovers and permits us to discover in the long line it stretches across the discontinuities of time.

3

Petrarch's imitative poems reveal other types of lapsarian insecurity (which as one reads and subreads are not, of course, experienced apart from each other). Poem 164 can serve as an example of a second type.

Or che 'l ciel e la terra e 'l vento tace,
e le fere e gli augelli il sonno affrena,
notte il carro stellato in giro mena

e nel suo letto il mar senz' onda giace,   4
   vegghio, penso, ardo, piango, e chi mi sface
sempre m' è inanzi per mia dolce pena:
guerra è 'l mio stato, d' ira e di duol piena,
e sol di lei pensando ò qualche pace.   8
   Così sol d'una chiara fonte viva
move 'l dolce e l'amaro ond' io mi pasco;
una man sola mi risana e punge;
   e perché 'l mio martir non giunga a riva,   12
mille volte il dí moro e mille nasco:
tanto da la salute mia son lunge.
[Now that the heavens and the earth and the wind are silent, and sleep reins in the
beasts and the birds, Night drives her starry car about, and in its bed the sea lies without
a wave,
I am awake, I think, I burn, I weep; and she who destroys me is always before me, to my
sweet pain: war is my state, full of sorrow and suffering, and only thinking of her do I
have any peace.
Thus from one clear living fountain alone spring the sweet and the bitter on which I
feed; one hand alone heals me and pierces me.
And that my suffering may not reach an end, a thousand times a day I die and a
thousand am born, so distant am I from health.]

The eleventh line of this sonnet echoes the *Remedia amoris* of Ovid, and the
thirteenth echoes Bernart de Ventadorn.[15] But neither subtext is of major heuristic
significance. The important one is again Virgilian. Of the several nightscapes in
the *Aeneid* that bear some resemblance to Petrarch's opening quatrain, the closest
in imagery and dramatic force is the passage in book 4 that portrays the nocturnal
anxiety of Dido.

Nox erat, et placidum carpebant fessa soporem
corpora per terras, silvaeque et saeva quierant
aequora: cum medio volvuntur sidera lapsu,   524
cum tacet omnis ager, pecudes pictaeque volucres,
quaeque lacus late liquidos, quaeque aspera dumis
rura tenent, somno positae sub nocte silenti
lenibant curas, et corda oblita laborum.   528
At non infelix animi Phoenissa, nec umquam
solvitur in somnos . . .   [4.522–30]
[It was night, and tired creatures all over the world were enjoying kindly sleep. Forests
and fierce seas were at rest, as the circling constellations glided in their midnight
course. Every field, all the farm-animals, and the colorful birds were silent, all that lived
across miles of glassy mere and in the wild country's ragged brakes, lying still under the
quiet night in a sleep which smoothed each care away from hearts which had forgotten
life's toil. But not so the Phoenician queen. Her accursed spirit could not relax into
sleeping.]

The Virgilian passage is easily made out below the Italian, but it has nonetheless
been greatly altered—of necessity. Nothing in the culture of the trecento resembled

the august sorrow and spacious majesty of Virgil's mature manner; nothing resembled the balance of a moral vision that registered at once the beauty and grandeur of the world, the pain visited randomly on noble and ignoble alike, the ineluctable course of a history that is both cruel and redemptive. Petrarch's lyricism had no business with that epic balance and the potential anachronism he courted shows in the distance between their respective nightscapes. Virgil's night is primarily a repose of living things, of birds and beasts (line 525), of the "corpora" (523) with its richly suggestive vagueness, and the even vaguer "quaeque . . . quaeque" (526). This impression of a densely inhabited quietude gives way in Petrarch to an *elemental* stillness, wherein living creatures are noticed a little neutrally in only a single line, but where the cosmic presence of heaven, earth, and wind are at rest, where the starry carriage of a personified Night follows its orderly circuit, and where a universal quiescence culminates in the arresting fourth line with the immense peace of the sea. The imperial imagination of Roman epic, whose vocation was the ordering of history and space, yields to a private intuition of natural forces, an intuition entertained no longer by a transparent narrator but by a speaker who is chief actor and sufferer and mythic center.

The presence of the subtext in the first quatrain, however transformed, serves to sustain an apparent firmness of objective reference through four marvelously evocative lines, and then with the turn in line five, the four explosive verbs in the first person crash upon the nocturnal stillness, almost as though bursting from the deferral of subjective feeling. They bring in their aftermath a series of oppositions and paradoxes that are peculiarly obtrusive because they so patently have no place in the silent cosmos: "dolce" and "pena," "guerra" and "pace," "dolce" and "amaro," "risana" and "punge," "martir" and "salute," "moro" and "nasco." These paradoxes leave no single affirmation unqualified after the four serial verbs have asserted their own opposition to the outer stillness, and the rhetoric that governs these ten lines of subjective expression positively seems calculated to permit no statement free of contradiction. In a broad sense, everything in these lines is engaged oxymoronically with its contrary. Thus the noun "martir" in line 12, although it happens not to be qualified oxymoronically by an adjective, nevertheless *is* qualified in the larger context of the sonnet by the presence of the repeated adjective "dolce" (ll. 6 and 10) and by the verbs "risana" (11) and "nasco" (13). Analogously the copula in the closing line is not free of the pressure generated by the preceding paradoxes of feeling: the speaker is at once far from his salvation and near it, since the lady's face is always before him (5–6) and he finds some peace in the thought of her (8). We can read the last line without qualification only if we take "salute" (14) to refer to that psychological and ontological integrity that would also be semiotic repose, that ultimate peace he seems to glimpse fragmentarily ("qualche pace") in the dim presence of "her." *This* "salute," a fulfillment of yearning and simultaneously a fullness of language, is truly, unambiguously distant, and its distance is reflected in the oxymoronic verbal texture. We have the right then to speak of a fall into oxymoron, understood both as a rhetorical instrument and a norm of personal emotion.[16]

The Virgilian subtext functions as a kind of surrogate for the sentimental and semiotic integrity the remainder of the sonnet is pursuing. For the verbs there are untouched by oxymoronic subversion: they call into being, with grand simplicity, a universe of elemental force subdued in stillness, and they seem to promise a poetic idiom capable of rendering this cosmic quietude without apparent semiotic instability. Although in fact the *Aeneid* is shot through with internal dissidence, and nowhere more visibly than in that fourth book Petrarch is drawing on, this sonnet leads us to perceive the Virgilian idiom as secure, entire, and generously sweeping, impervious to the erosions of context. Thus the sonnet dramatizes a kind of fall out of a fiction of absolute verbal incarnation into a discourse divided against itself, threatened at every syllable with the disintegration of statement, but capable through this very risk of rendering a more intimate, insidious, and labyrinthine consciousness. The echo of Bernart de Ventadorn confirms the "modernity" of this discourse, which absorbs and renews the paradoxical impertinence of Ovid in its own profounder idiom.

The oxymorons of sonnet 164 are not incidental ornaments; they reflect the contradictory character of private experience throughout the *Canzoniere*. "Amor ... vol," wrote Petrarch, "che tra duo contrari mi distempre" (55). (Love ... wishes me to be untuned between two contraries.) Oxymorons are paradoxes which refuse resolution and which refuse separation into distinct opposed entities. The oxymoron is so loaded a figure in this poetry because it is its tendency to allow no single word fullness of denotation. The "fall" into an oxymoronic style follows closely from the other "falls" already analyzed. We encounter a collapse of reference that is also a collapse of unalloyed meaning, a collapse into divided, flawed, internecine meaning. This collapse and this division of meaning in the oxymoron constitute a powerful *modus significandi*, a brilliant expressive device which, in the radicality of its use by Petrarch, ceases to be a cliché of the rhetoric of love and becomes an original, disturbing vehicle for statement. The language is forever falling back into a consciousness so mercurial as to seem ineffable. The succession of each mood, feeling, image, analysis seems to contaminate its predecessor, to pile up into paradoxical simultaneities; the language seems always to be straining to represent an inner state more mobile, more divided and elusive, than itself so that even its reflexive reference to the consciousness that grounds it is finally frustrated. The division of meaning is meaningful; it corresponds to the shifts, velleities, reflexivities, antagonisms, and ruptures of a psyche torn by moral conflict, ill at ease within a body, and suspicious of its own good faith. In this very division of meaning lies the root of a new moral style. Thus a conventional figure that had threatened to degenerate in earlier poetry into a somewhat obvious, precious, even tiresome rhetorical tic, can be viewed in Petrarch as the most visible verbal equivalent of the speaker's flawed capacity for expression.[17]

In sonnet 164, the four verbs of line 5 constitute the first announcement of this "fall," an exchange of epic breadth for lyrical immediacy but also an exchange of a unique moment for indefinite continuity. The single present moment—"*Or* che 'l ciel . . . tace"—is assimilated into repetition, signaled by the adverb "sempre" (6) and the noun "stato" (7), so that already the concluding verb of line 5—"sface"—has to be understood retrospectively to signify a serial, endless undoing. This shift from a narrative past or present to an iterative present tense is extremely common throughout the *Canzoniere*. It is not too much to say that the iterative present is the dominant verb tense of the entire work, recording the fluctuations of the speaker's feeling so as to extend it indefinitely into a vague past and future.

> Pace non trovo e non ò da far guerra,
> e temo e spero; ed ardo e son un ghiaccio. [134]
> [Peace I do not find, and I have no wish to make war; and I fear and hope, and burn, and am of ice.]

> Nuoto per mar che non à fondo o riva;
> solco onde, e 'n rena-fondo, e scrivo in vento. [212]
> [I swim through a sea that has no floor or shore, I plow the waves and found my house on sand and write on the wind.]

It is the verb form most characteristically Petrarchan and historically the most influential. It carries the weariness, the monotony, and the hopelessness of the speaker's suffering, so that every specific incident that interrupts or detaches itself from the indefinite repetition is finally embedded in it, even the concluding prayer to the Virgin calling for a repose, a definitive interruption that is still denied. This iterative present tense acquires a meaning in Petrarch's poetry it had scarcely ever found in his predecessors; by underscoring the endlessness of his experience, the poet thematizes the force of his syntactic norm. The nightscape in the sonnet that concerns us is conspicuously free from this force, since its singularity is established at the outset. It is free from repetition just as it is free from oxymoron; here as elsewhere in the work, the movement from subtext to surface text involves a descent into oxymoronic iteration.

The definition of a more intense and imprisoning form of repetition might be said to constitute the plot of canzone 50, "Ne la stagion che 'l ciel rapido inchina." Each of the first four stanzas evokes the turning of a representative figure—pilgrim, peasant, shepherd, seaman—from labor to rest at nightfall; each stanza then goes on to contrast this nightly ritual, with its associations of rhythmic, hard-won, and simple rest, to the unnatural and tormented wakefulness of the restless speaker. The contrast of sonnet 164 is made more homely, but the evocations of universal repose do not lack grandeur and they tend to cluster again about a Virgilian (and in this case Dantesque) nucleus.

> E i naviganti in qualche chiusa valle
> gettan le membra, poi che 'l sol s'asconde,
> sul duro legno e sotto a l'aspre gonne.
> Ma io, perché s'attuffi in mezzo l'onde,
> e lasci Ispagna dietro a le sue spalle
> e Granata e Marrocco e le Colonne,

e gli uomini e le donne
e 'l mondo e gli animali
aquetino i lor mali,
fine non pongo al mio ostinato affano
e duolmi ch'ogni giorno arroge al danno.   [ll. 43–53][18]

[And mariners in some closed valley throw down their limbs, when the sun hides himself, on the hard wood and under the coarse canvas. But I, though he dive into the midst of the wave and leave Spain behind his back and Granada and Morocco and the columns, and men and women and the world and animals calm their ills, I put no end to my obstinate trouble: and I grieve that each day adds to my losses.]

The *long* delay between pronoun and verb ("io . . . fine non pongo") through all that polysyndeton acts out marvelously the frustrated wait for rest. But the principal burden of this stanza, like that of the others, is the distinction between two versions of the iterative present tense: the universal and appropriate iteration of the opening and its subtext ("gettan" above), and the pathetic, incessant, nonrhythmic iteration ("pongo," "duolmi," "arroge") of the speaker's travail.[19]

Oxymoronic iteration was of course deeply rooted in the tradition of the Provençal and Italian love lyric. The iteration in an early sonnet by Giacomo da Lentini is already on the verge of oxymoron:

Lo visso me conforta ispesamente,
l'adorno viso che mi fa penare.
[The face gives me solace many times, the gracioius face through which I feel pain.]

Guinizelli was alluding to a familiar convention when he wrote

Così 'n le nostre voglie
contrar aire s'accoglie.
[Thus contrary emotions are brought together in our wills.]

The conventional content of the lover's iterative experience tended to be the ceaseless alternation between polarities of hope and fear, warm and cold, joy and sorrow, an alteration already familiar to the trecento physician Dino del Garbo, whose hermeneutic/physiological commentary on Cavalcanti's "Donna me prega" stresses what he calls the *alterationes* of erotic psychology. Glossing Cavalcanti's phrase "Move cangiando colore," Dino attributes the physiological effects of love—laughter and tears, blushing and pallor—to a duality inherent in all experience of love and especially in the lover's imagination.[20] It is these *alterationes* which are commonly preserved in the iterative present tense of Petrarchan poetry and it is they which establish the oxymoron as the dominant Petrarchan trope. For Petrarch accelerated the *alterationes* of the *stilnovisti* to the point of a perpetual overlapping; not only do I hope and fear, but I suffer from a ceaseless fearful hope, in a cycle that turns each pole into its antithesis as soon as its name has been uttered. Thus any given word denoting feeling in Petrarch is threatened by its antithesis, which in turn will be threatened. It was this repetitious oxymoronic structure of erotic experience that led one of the speakers in Bembo's *Asolani* to conjecture that each man must possess two souls leading him in opposite directions, since no one with a single soul could desire antithetical goals and feel antithetical emotions.[21] Examples of Dino's stereotyped alternations are by no means lacking in Petrarch's work; one finds an accumulation in the *Trionfi*, for example, that almost descends to parody.

> . . . stanco riposo e riposato affanno,
> chiaro disnore e gloria oscura e nigra,
> perfida lealtate e fido inganno . . .   [*Trionfo d'Amore*, 4.145–47]
> [. . . weary rest and restful travail, illustrious shame and black, dim glory, perfidious loyalty and faithful deception . . .]

But the *Canzoniere* as a whole brings a fresh energy to the oxymoron and rediscovers its range of meanings. No Italian poet before Petrarch, to my knowledge, made so creative use of these literary/physiological/psychological commonplaces. The result is a more radical and pitiless rhetoric of self-negating action, pushing the iterative process into finer and more intimate paradoxes.

> Ardomi e struggo ancor com' io solia,
> l'aura mi volve, e son pur quel ch' i' m' era.   [112]
> [I am burning up and suffering still just as I used to, the breeze turns me about, and I am still just what I was.]

> Io son pur quel ch' i' mi soglio,
> né per mille rivolte ancor son mosso.   [118]
> [I am still what I used to be, nor for a thousand turnings about have I yet moved.]

> Né pur il mio secreto e 'l mio riposo
> fuggo ma più me stesso e 'l mio pensero.   [234]
> [Nor do I flee only my hiding place and my rest, but even more myself and my thoughts.]

The autoanalysis produces insights which are not precisely oxymoronic but which presuppose the trope as a norm, bearing witness not merely and tritely to Dino's *alterationes* but rather to the fatal paradoxes of human identity. Petrarch recuperated the topoi of a worn-out rhetorical vocabulary, renewing and deepening them by finding out their hidden existential logic.

One can study this recuperation further in one of Petrarch's most affecting imitations, the sonnet *in morte* 311, where one can observe in particular how the fall into oxymoron, as I have called it, is intricately involved with the fall into subjectivity. The sonnet reaches back across the Provençal lyric[22] to a simile in the *Georgics* comparing the lament of Orpheus for Eurydice to the complaint of a nightingale for her lost young.

> Quel rosignuol, che sí soave piagne
> forse suoi figli o sua cara consorte,
> di dolcezza empie il cielo e le campagne
> con tante note sí pietose e scorte,   4
>   e tutta notte par che m' accompagne,

e mi rammente la mia dura sorte:
ch' altri che me non ò di chi mi lagne
ché 'n dee non credev' io regnasse Morte.   8
     O che lieve è ingannar chi s' assecura!
Que' duo bei lumi assai piú che 'l sol chiari
chi pensò mai veder far terra oscura?
     Or cognosco io che mia fera ventura   12
vuol che vivendo e lagrimando impari
come nulla qua giú diletta e dura.
[That nightingale that so sweetly weeps, perhaps for his children or for his dear
consort, fills the sky and the fields with sweetness in so many grieving, skillful notes,
and all night he seems to accompany me and remind me of my harsh fate; for I have no
one to complain of save myself, who did not believe that Death reigns over goddesses.
Oh how easy it is to deceive one who is confident! Those two lights much brighter than
the sun, who ever thought to see them become dark clay?
Now I know that my fierce destiny wishes me to learn, living and weeping, how
nothing here both pleases and endures!]

The Virgilian subtext of the first six lines reads as follows:

Qualis populea maerens philomela sub umbra
amissos queritur fetus, quos durus arator
observans nido implumis detraxit; at illa
flet noctem, ramoque sedens miserabile carmen
integrat, et maestis late loca questibus implet.
Nulla Venus, non ulli animum flexere hymenaei:
solus Hyperboreas glacies Tanaimque nivalem
arvaque Riphaeis numquam viduata pruinis
lustrabat. . . .   [Georgics 4.511–19]
[As the nightingale, mourning beneath the poplar's shade, bewails the loss of her
brood, that a cruel ploughman spied and plucked unfledged from the nest; she weeps all
night and, perched on a bough, renews her pitiful song, filling the region round with
sad lament. No love, no wedding song could bend his soul; alone he would roam the
northern ice, the snowy Tanais, and the fields ever wedded to Rhipaean frosts.][23]

Although the Virgilian allusion is clear, Petrarch's alterations are revealing. The
specificity of the occasion (*this* nightingale singing *now*) is imbedded in the
iteration carried most clearly by the participles "vivendo" and "lagrimando" in
line 13. The iteration in this case is supplemented by generalizations of an
aphoristic character in lines 9 and 14 that move still further away from the specific.
This movement leads again into a series of implicit oxymorons: painful sweetness,
mortal goddesses, precarious security, dark brightness, tropes which would be
altogether out of place in Virgil's epyllion. Virgil's characteristic trope, the simile,
in its turn finds no place in the Italian, in fact ceases to be a simile, and this change
of status underlies many other changes. Whereas in the sonnet the speaker *hears*
the nightingale, shares a common location with it, Virgil's simile is based on a

series of distinctions, including a distinction of place, which are as necessary to the simile as the likeness of grief. The nightingale singing from within the nocturnal darkness of a poplar is a southern image, familiar to a Roman audience, whose softer intimacy and Mediterranean grace set off the bleak Hyperborean icescape where Orpheus stonily mourns. The simile mirrors the narrative tenor but also pulls away from it, widening the paradigmatic distance between the elements it opposes—singer and bird, Eurydice and the bird's young, Aristaeus and plough-man, snow and poplar. Virgil's rhetoric reflects the Ciceronian ideal of congruity, to be reformulated later as a poetic principle by Horace in his Epistle to the Piso, an ideal of harmonious decorum that clearly presupposes points of congruence between complexes that are essentially separate. The same presupposition under-lies Aristotle's remark that the ability to use metaphor (and by extension simile) well implies a perception of resemblances (*Poetics*, chap. 22). Virgil's firm control of likeness within unlikeness is complemented by his firm control of spatial relations (the solitary bird in the poplar's shade fills centrifugally the wide fields with its song) and of causal relations (the ploughman sees the young in the nest, then plucks them from it, causing the parent bird to grieve and thus to sing). This tiny anecdote is represented as capable of recurrence, but each single instance is clearly distinct and enclosed, objective and autonomous.

The relationships in Petrarch are altogether different. We do not know in fact whether the nightingale has lost its young or—a significant addition—its "cara consorte"; the only given fact is the song itself in its beauty. The "forse" (perhaps) of the second line indicates that the loss and ensuing grief form part of a fantasy of the poet's hypothetical imagining, which tells us more, is intended to tell us more, about him than about the bird. Petrarch fails to supply an agent such as the "durus arator" for this hypothetical bereavement; what matters is not the incident but the bittersweet affectivity of the song: the sweetness ("dolcezza") which is exquisite ("soave") and artfully modulated (Sapegno's gloss for "scorte"), and in this very sweetness, absent in Virgil, more painful, more cruelly wounding in their own right, since the speaker has also been denied these vulnerable attachments which his fantasy, in its perverse reflexive cruelty, has attributed to the nightingale in order to dramatize his own solitude. The nightingale's song indeed is scarcely distinguished from the appearance it creates of accompanying the speaker's own lament, and this *appearance*, expressed by the verb "par" in line 5, reveals explicitly how dependent the song's reality is upon the speaker's consciousness. The verb "par" is the means whereby the bird is drawn into the speaker's sensibil-ity, annexed, interiorized, transformed into a function of his own psyche, an emblem of his suffering. The closing line will deny that any earthly thing pleases, thus refusing retrospectively even that sweetness which had been the poem's starting point. The objective externality affirmed at the opening has been effec-tively denied, has collapsed into a privacy on the verge of solipsism.

This privacy, which appears to open outward only to reassert its hegemony, which takes notice of the moment only to absorb it, is thus constrained to remain ill at ease with the filtered sensations that reach it. With this observation, we reach a point where both modes of "falling" reveal their unity. The absorption of sweetness by pain, sensation by feeling, world by consciousness, is an absorption of event by repetition and description by oxymoron. In the cruel and exquisite art of the nightingale's song, sensation and feeling are intermingled but at odds, with an insidious involvement rare in antiquity but familiar to the Christian, that sentient oxymoron. The result of this disequilibrium is to cast doubt on the nature and stability of the self.

One could argue that the fundamental subject of the *Canzoniere* is not so much or not only the psychology of the speaker as the *ontology* of his selfhood, the struggle to discern a self or compose a self which could stand as a fixed and knowable substance. This struggle, with its intermittences and truces, its partial victories, its circularities, its temptations by despair, its numbing rehearsals and reenactments, is finally a failure, since the closing poems envision the redemptive composition of a self at peace only in the form of a prayer for that which is not yet given. This ontological theme is introduced by the opening sonnet, in the line "quand'era in part altr'uom da quel ch'i' sono," as it is introduced again and again through a long sequence of moving restatements. The struggle to compose a self is in fact said to be visible in the successive emotions betrayed by the speaker's face, quick to reflect the turbulence of his mind.

> e 'l volto che lei segue ov' ella il mena
> si turba e rasserena,
> ed in un esser picciol tempo dura;
> onde a la vista uom di tal vita esperto
> diria: "Questo arde, e di suo stato è incerto."   [129.9–13]
> [. . . and my face, which follows wherever my soul leads, is clouded and made clear again, and remains but a short time in any one state; and at the sight anyone who had experienced such a life would say: "This man is burning with love and his state is uncertain."]

It is the "stato," the "essere," of the speaker which emerge as the work's dominant concern and which remain to the end "incerto." The feelings of guilt, fear, debasement, and weariness belong to a Christian sensibility but lack the reassurance of the Christian sacraments, so that even the concluding prayer to the Virgin is a private and lonely act, even, despite its destination, proto-Reformist.

Traces of the ontological problem are visible in sonnet 311, in the shifts of the speaker's role from listener to sentimentalist as objective reference fades, and then again from sentimentalist to moralist and metaphysician. The sonnet fails to follow the classical process whereby a speaker defines himself against an external context dependent in turn upon his own emergent consciousness. As the external context in the *Canzoniere* tends to lose actuality and the object fades into adumbration, the self emergent from the descriptive act has to modify its outline or produce another makeshift that is equally vulnerable. One obvious instance in 311 is the speaker's repudiation of his former credulity for his present posture of wan enlightenment. The rhetorical reflection of this pattern here as elsewhere lies in the serial repudiations of the oxymoronic language. One syntactic form of modification appears in the Chinese box sentence that encloses clause within clause as though reaching for an infinitely regressive self-consciousness. Thus the sentence composing the second tercet places an aphorism ("nulla qua giú diletta e dura") within a clause presenting this as a lesson the speaker has learned (*"impari come ..."*), this in turn placed within a clause presenting this learning as the desire of the poet's savage destiny ("mia fera ventura vuol che ..."), and this clause finally within the main clause indicating the poet's recent recognition of his destiny's will. An analogous structure governs lines 6–8, where the poet's ignorance that (seeming) goddesses are subject to death is presented as the content of his self-reproach, whose iteration constitutes the basis of that harsh lot which the nightingale's song brings back to him. Each statement seems contained in a parenthesis in order to be dealt with by an encompassing mental transaction which then proves itself to be so contained, as though no absolute encompassment were possible. *Nulla qua giú dura*: nothing here below endures, least of all verbal affirmation and the self it seems to imply.

Virgil's poetry in this regard is not altogether here below. From the perspective of Petrarchan imitation, Virgil's signifiers, however subtle and complex, possess a stability of definition and reference that becomes in this new context their outstanding attribute. They compose a style that is inhospitable to oxymoron as to metaphor, since both of these tropes assert, not the enduring resemblance of discrete entities (as in the simile), but a precarious and provisional unity that flares and disappears. This counterlogical force, depending as it does on a temporary offense to reason, is calculated to disturb the orderly arrangement of distinctions underlying Roman rhetoric. These distinctions' stability in turn depends on fictions of *continuity* that not only support his rhetoric but are thematized variously throughout Virgil's work. Just as the action of the *Aeneid* hinges on the preservation of communal continuity, the long rumination on life and death that comprises the *Georgics* culminates positively in the *begonia*, the technique of engendering bees from the carcass of a bull. The exemplary death of Eurydice finds exemplary compensations in this technique, in the doctrine of metempsychosis (4.219–27), in the immense effort of the poem to superintend hazardous growth into life, and in the limited but nevertheless restorative power of song. The verb *integrare* employed in the nightingale simile meant not only "to renew" but also "to refresh" and even "to heal." This poetry of hard continuities and circular restorations could be regarded as thematizing *semiotic* continuity, a firm capacity for steady reference whose expressive modalities remain serenely under public control. Virgil's poetry uses legend to create, in addition to fictions of etiological mythography, fictions of semiotic incarnation, fictions of verbal plenitude and permanence unshadowed by Christian dualism.

The erosion of this plentitude in Petrarch's art is related, I believe, to his lifelong anxiety of temporality. The obsessive fear of time and mutability, which is one of his commonest themes and which was also a true sickness of his soul, has to be understood in its relation to the mutability of signification. The endless revision of his poetry testifies to a deep-rooted sense of its incompleteness, a falling short of total statement which was also a symptom of the man's private self-perception. The confession in the *Secretum* of this existential falling short, "Sentio inexpletum quoddam in precordiis meis semper" (I always feel something unfilled in my heart),[24] would be repeated in the concern of the aged poet for his eternally imperfect work: "Sentio . . . quia si centum adhuc annos viverem semper aliquid nescio quid deesset" (I feel that even if I were to live to be a hundred something mysterious would still be missing) (*Seniles* 12.1). The production of spoken or written words is an act irremediably trapped in temporality, contaminated with the mutable, incapable of that simultaneity which is denied all mortal discourse: ". . . ex quo loqui cepimus, mutatio aliqualis incessit, et modo per singulos sillabarum tractus vite aliquid excidit." (From the moment we decide to speak, some alternation intervenes and as we pronounce each single syllable, some part of our life slips away.)[25] The act of speech betrays its contingency and its incompleteness in its inescapable subservience to succession; poetry remains a time art. The debates that comprise the *Secretum* are represented to be proof against the contamination of the mutable because they take place beneath the gaze of Veritas. Without her privileging presence, says Franciscus at the close, the discussion would have wandered in darkness ("tenebris"). In this it would have resembled all other speech. It is against the portentous and demeaning fact of temporality that the symbol of the evergreen laurel is fabricated; the laurel is an emblem of precisely that eternality to which poetry and the poet aspire. But the laurel itself is a divided and unreliable emblem. Were the laurel to become a pure symbol, perfectly expressive and perfectly grounded, the demon of temporality would be exorcised.

The fall into iteration, like the fall into oxymoron, dramatized by Petrarch's imitative poems involves more than a syntactic or rhetorical category; both involve a mode of being in the world. Arnaud Tripet has written sensitively about Petrarch's resistance to an *alterité* of the external universe.[26] But it must be added that this resistance, this instinct of withdrawal, coexists with that passion for a reception, a recognition by an ineffable otherness, also present in his language. It is present in the very restlessness which seeks a name or a formulation which will do this otherness justice. That otherness which the historical Petrarch did reach in the form of friends and correspondents and which, in the form of classical culture, he did begin to apprehend and to introduce into his poetry, this otherness in its more intimate and simultaneously more exalted aspect he fled while pursuing, courted without hope, with the oxymoronic emotion which this very thing, if it were ever obtained, would resolve. "Nebbia o polvere al vento," he wrote with profound insight, "fuggo per più non esser pellegrino" (331.22–23) (A cloud or dust in the wind, I flee in order to be no longer a traveler). The ancient texts, for him, were exempt from this unstable play of displacements, and in his poetic use of them he reveals how deeply interiorized was his respect for their privilege.

Seven • Petrarch: Falling into Shadow

In *Canzoniere* 23, "Nel dolce tempo de la prima etade," the so-called "canzone delle metamorfosi," other characteristic itineraries of Petrarchan imitation can be traced. In this early poem substantially revised in middle age, the metamorphoses are all Ovidian and all visited upon the speaker, who is transformed successively into a laurel tree (like Daphne), a swan (like Cycnus), a rock (like Battus), a spring (like Byblis), a voice imprisoned in stone (like Echo), and a stag pursued by hounds (like Actaeon). There is also a briefer allusion to the fate of Phaeton. The *commiato* invokes the myths of Aegina and Ganymede; the myth of Danae is recalled but rejected. Ovidian myth saturates the poem, although no mythical personage is named with the exception of Jove. Each metamorphosis is represented as a new and prodigious form of cruelty imposed by the lady upon the wretchedly Protean lover.[1]

The first and most important of these imitative passages follows its subtext most closely.

> Qual mi fec'io, quando primer m'accorsi
> de la trasfigurata mia persona,
> e i capei vidi far di quella fronde
> di che sperato avea già lor corona,
> e i piedi in ch'io mi stetti e mossi e corsi,
> com'ogni membro a l'anima risponde,
> diventar due radici sovra l'onde
> non di Peneo, ma d'un piú altero fiume,
> e 'n duo rami mutarsi ambe le braccia!   [ll. 41–49]
> [What I became, when I first grew aware of my person being transformed and saw my
> hairs turning into those leaves which I had formerly hoped would be my crown, and
> my feet, on which I stood and moved and ran, as every member answers to the soul,
> becoming two roots beside the waves not of Peneus but of a prouder river, and my arms
> changing into two branches!]

Most of these details derive directly from the *Metamorphoses* (1.550–51):

> in frontem crines, in ramos bracchia crescunt;
> pes modo tam velox pigris radicibus haeret.
>   [Her hair was leaves,
> Her arms were branches, and her speedy feet
> Rooted and held.]

If the allusion is clear, however, the precise status of Petrarch's imagery is not. Clearly we have here neither simple mythography nor simple allegory, but

127

something like metaphor which draws a little on both. We are not, that is, to suppose that the speaker literally passed through this and the other metamorphoses; if we did suppose this, we should be hard put to explain his concluding statement that despite the number of his metamorphoses he has never abandoned the laurel ("né per nova figura il primo alloro / seppi lassar"—nor for any shape could I leave the first laurel—ll. 167-68). Some of the Ovidian details permit a metaphoric decipherment: for example, in the passage quoted the feet which normally move in obedience to the soul could be said to be rooted because the speaker is immobilized by awe at the sight of the beloved. But the transformations of hair and arms resist any such facile decipherment, particularly in view of lines 43-44, which exclude an interpretation based on the pursuit of fame. In fact to reduce any of the metamorphoses to this kind of interpretation would be to impoverish them. They need to live in their own slightly mysterious rhetorical region. When the poet is transformed into a stag like Actaeon after glimpsing the lady nude, the hounds that pursue him might conceivably be allegorized as feelings of guilt or shame. But this detail merely concludes a little scene that no allegorical or metaphorical key altogether fits: the fount where she bathes, the sun shining its strongest, the water she splashes on the speaker's face—these are elements in an anecdote that must somehow be accepted without forcing too far the hermeneutic questions we bring to it. The poetry locates itself near the misty borders of three modes or figures—metaphor, allegory, mythography—and so creates an original *modus significandi* whose workings are disturbingly elusive. They are also clearly and deliberately at odds with Ovid. The visual precision by which Ovid transforms the human or immortal body into some other living thing accounts for part of his charm, but Petrarch in fact blurs visualization; we are not led, nor even allowed, to picture his metamorphoses because they remain to some uncertain degree emotive and internal. We can picture them no more than when he writes in another Daphne poem, with haunting imprecision, that the lady seats herself upon grass and makes a shade for herself with her arms (". . . far de le sua braccia a se stessa ombra"—*Canzoniere* 34). The imagery of the canzone of metamorphoses seems to designate psychic events that refuse to reveal themselves, remain in an opacity casting a semiotic shadow like that darkening the speaker, "lunga stagion di tenebre vestito"—long dressed in darkness (l. 106). The metaphoric shadows of the speaker's suffering seem to find a counterpart in his rhetorical expression.

Other metamorphoses of the *Metamorphoses* crowd themselves upon the subreader's attention. The consciousness chronicling its own history is one which attributes all the multiform experience of classical fable to itself and only itself, drawing into its single orbit, with characteristic self-regarding imperialism, the various destinies of nine figures, divine and human, male and female, active and passive, aggressors and victims. "The lover . . . becomes, in a sense, the object of meditation, the incarnation of his own obsession," writes Terence Cave of this poem.[2] This multiple absorption is itself a challenge to its subtext. But the absorption also has a tendency to equalize if it does not flatten this multiform experience. The metamorphic change is presented in each case as pathetic; it dramatizes afresh the speaker's suffering without that element of compensation which in varying degrees allows Ovid to close so many of his myths on a note of healing. Petrarch, that is to say, does not greatly distinguish the degree of pathos governing, say, the transformations into the laurel, the spring, and the stag, and in this failure to distinguish departs from his subtexts. In Ovid, the fate of Actaeon is quite unambiguously disagreeable, whereas the fate of Byblis is just as clearly redemptive: "what better thing could be done for her?" asks the narrator (9.658). Ovid's myth of Daphne (*Met.* 1.452ff.) lies between these extremes and tempers its pathos skillfully and typically with an understated sense of fitness. The nymph's stubborn virginity is presented as a little deviant, but her plea for transformation is granted by the Peneus and Apollo accepts it, according her a kind of affectionate apotheosis as his adopted emblem to which the laurel in its turn assents with a formal inclination of its leafy top. The stress at the end is on accommodation, and the continued life of the natural growth provides an acceptable finality which, as so often in Ovid's poem, atones in part for the loss of bodily freedom.

Petrarch suppresses this sense of accommodation and repose. It is absent from the imitation of the Daphne story as it is absent from the Byblis imitation later.

> . . . gittaimi stanco sovra l'erbo un giorno.
> Ivi, accusando il fugitivo raggio,
> a le lagrime triste allargai 'l freno,
> e lasciaile cader come a lor parve;
> né già mai neve sotto al sol disparve,
> com'io senti' me tutto venir meno,
> e farmi una fontana a pie' d'un faggio.   [ll. 111–17]
> [I threw myself tired onto the grass one day. There, blaming the fleeing ray, I loosed the rein to sad tears and let them fall as they willed; nor did ever snow under the sun disappear, as I felt myself entirely melt and become a fountain at the foot of a beech.]

The curious presence of an Augustinian subtext in this Ovidian imitation needs to be noticed. It is drawn from the climactic episode of the *Confessions*, the conversion of the saint as he is seated beneath a fig tree: "I flung myself down . . . under a certain fig tree, and gave free rein to my tears. The floods burst from my eyes."[3] This anachronistic Augustinian intrusion matters because the alteration of ancient myth in this canzone depends largely on Augustinian anthropology. The shadows that clothe the speaker, "lunga stagion di tenebre vestito," are Christian shadows because they call into question the status and worth of matter. "The dualism 'soul against body,'" wrote Leo Spitzer, "so dear to Christian poetry, is not associable with classical Latin words which are lacking in any suggestion of the psycho-physical perplexities of the Christian mind, of that *suture* between body and soul which Montaigne recognized in Christianity."[4] The absence in Petrarch of qualifications to pathos, the absence from his "metamorphoses" of any restorative repose, derive in part from the assumption that any descent deeper into brute matter can only degrade. The poetic equivalent of this repose would be an imagistic incarnation, a fullness and freedom of objective representation which the poetry withholds. The poetic interest indeed seems to lie in the capricious withdrawal from representation, the fading away of reference. Physical details are not allowed to assume that full *enargeia* granted them by the *Metamorphoses*, but coexist darkly with a psyche that is neither in harmony with the body nor clearly distinct from it. The descent deeper into matter was degrading for Petrarch despite (or because of?) the fact that matter itself lacked solidity, within the poem as without. External matter is known only through images which, when received, distract the soul with their bewildering clutter, and the body, through the agency of its physical senses, abets this process. Augustinus speaks of it in the *Secretum*.

Conglobantur siquidem species innumere et imagines rerum visibilium, que corporeis introgresse sensibus, postquam singulariter admisse sunt, catervatim in anime penetralibus densantur; eamque, nec ad id genitam nec tam multorum difformiumque capacem, pregravant atque confundunt.[5]
[The countless forms and images of things visible, that one by one are brought into the soul by the senses of the body, gather there in the inner centre in a mass, and the soul, not being akin to these or capable of learning them, they weigh down and overwhelm with their contrariety.]

Franciscus replies by citing correctly the source of this doctrine in his interlocutor's *De vera religione*.[6] "Blind we are led by the blind," wrote Petrarch to Giovanni Colonna, "nor do we know what is to be wished or feared by us, perceiving only through the shadow of the flesh" (Ceci cecis ducibus innitimur, nec quid optandum metuendum ve nobis sit, per umbram carnis agnoscimus).[7] It is this "shadow of the flesh" that informs the canzone of the metamorphoses (and not only this canzone) with its mazy visual and rhetorical ambiguities, instabilities of image and meaning that are poetically disturbing because they ultimately reflect the unstable ontology of the speaking self.

The poem itself speaks of a "malign fall" in a passage that bridges a metaphoric plunge from heaven like Phaeton's and the transformation into a swan like Cycnus's.

... già mai poi la mia lingua non tacque
mentre poteo, del suo cader maligno ...   [ll. 58–59]
[From then on my tongue was never silent about its evil fall, as long as it had power.]

The "cader maligno" is tactically placed to refer to either mythographic episode, and doubtless we would not much wrench the phrase if we applied it to all of the speaker's metamorphic disguises. Each transformation does truly represent a fall that is moral as well as sentimental and even finally ontological or theological, because the fall widens the division between soul and body, humiliates the soul by the descent into a prodigious brutishness that yet paradoxically seems impalpable. It is tempting to conclude that the success of the poet's or the swan's quest for its lost hope:

> ... solo, lagrimando,
> là 've tolto mi fu, dí e notte andava
> ricercando ...   [ll. 55–57]
> [Alone and weeping I went night and day where it had been taken from me.]

would be signaled rhetorically by an end to the figurative ambiguity and
ontologically by a harmonious integration of body and soul. But this success is
never achieved.

The result of this disequilibrium is, for the subreader, the impression of an
immense distancing of the Ovidian texts in a direction which can be grasped and
by means of processes which, however elusive, can be described. The poem
provides a direction and a version of poetic history that we can intuitively
apprehend, "tacita mentis indagine." We are led from the relative wholeness of
Roman mythography, with its visual and rhetorical clarity, its calm
impersonality, its security within nature, its accommodations with suffering, its
refusal of psychologistic paradox, and its capacity for repose—we are led from all
this to the turbulent egoism, the problematic divisions and restless intensities of a
voice pathetically in quest of its own integrity. The direction then of the
constructed historical movement is downward, just as on the crest of Mont
Ventoux, the Augustinian example is introduced only as an unavailable
alternative. Heuristic imitation has indeed produced a discovery which proves on
examination to be itself a fall. The poem presents entanglements, or in Spitzer's
term "perplexities," of spirit and matter, vehicle and tenor, metaphor and myth,
which are vulnerable to the comparisons they invite. We are led in other words to
subread a text that is more secure, semiotically and metaphysically, than the
surface text that evokes it. The surface text seems almost to suffer from a kind of
poetic gnosticism, a rhetorical bad conscience which distrusts imagistic
incarnation and admits it only obliquely through the chiaroscuro of imitation. As
a diachronic composition, it has created its own "cader maligno," a fall into
division. The sense of privation where the nascent humanist impulse found its
origin has now been displaced but is still acted out in the poem's troubled
retrospection.

2

The closing lines of canzone 23 celebrate the pleasure of the laurel's shade.

> ... né per nova figura il primo alloro
> seppi lassar, ché pur la sua dolce ombra
> ogni men bel piacer del cor mi sgombra.   [ll. 167–69]
> [... nor for any new shape could I leave the first laurel, for still its sweet shade turns
> away from my heart any less beautiful pleasure.]

How rich and how ironic is this particular image of pleasant shade—"dolce
ombra"—are questions that doubtless remain open to debate. What lies beyond

debate is the complex resonance of the word *ombra* and the imagery of shade and shadows within the macrocosm of the *Canzoniere* and throughout Petrarch's writing.[8] We have already met many instances of this imagery. Within the *Canzoniere* alone it receives many richly variegated tints, although this may be scarcely surprising in poetry whose organizing symbol is a laurel tree. Many usages follow 23 in associating the laurel shade with Laura's effect or influence upon the speaker; this is commonly represented as restorative, but not always.

> . . . l' arbor sempre verde ch' i' tant' amo
> benché n' abbia ombre piú triste che liete.   [181]
> [. . . the evergreen tree that I so love, although it has more sad than happy shadows.]

> l'ombra sua sola fa 'l mio cor un ghiaccio.   [197]
> [Her very shadow turns my heart to ice.]

Elsewhere it suggests the mortal body of Laura:

> . . . quel velo
> che qui fece ombra al fior degli anni suoi.   [268.38–39]
> [. . . the veil that here shadowed the flower of her years.]

or more generally ephemeral beauty:

> Questo nostro caduco e fragil bene
> ch' è vento ed ombra ed à nome beltate . . .   [350]
> [This brittle, frail good of ours, which is wind and shadow and is called beauty . . .]

or the fraility and mortality of all earthly things:

> . . . quant' io miro par sogni, ombre e fumi.   [156]
> [Whatever I look on seems dreams, shadows, and smoke.]

> Veramente siam noi polvere ed ombra.   [294]
> [Truly we are dust and shadow.]

(this last usage echoing a celebrated Horatian line);[9] or else, with a more clearly Christian coloring, those vain appearances that seduce the poet from the truth:

> vorre' 'l ver abbracciar, lassando l' ombre.   [264.72]
> [I wish to embrace the truth, to abandon shadows.]

and in at least one passage, a prayer to God for deliverance from earthly love, the epithet "ombroso" directly links the shadows of Christian darkness with the charms of Laura:

> Guarda 'l mio stato, a le vaghezze nove,
> che 'nterrompendo di mia vita il corso
> m' àn fatto abitador d' ombroso bosco.   [214.31–33]
> [Guard my state from those new beauties which, breaking off my life's course, have made me a dweller in the shady wood.]

In several significant passages, the word *ombra* or its cognates is associated with the composition of poetry. For example, the laurel is said to have permitted the poet's slender gift to flower in its shade:

> . . . fiorir faceva il mio debile ingegno
> a la sua ombra, e crescer negli affanni.   [60]
> [. . . made my weak wit flower in its shade and grow in my troubles.]

or the activity of poetic creation is described as the depiction of an enveloping shadow:

> . . . i' depinsi poi per mille valli
> l' ombra ov'io fui.   [66.34–35]
> [I depicted then through a thousand valleys the shade where I had been.]

The wealth of meaning accreted around the image enriches those contexts where Petrarch employs an Italian verb analogous to the English verb *adumbrate*, as in the sonnet which asserts its author's aspirations weakly to shadow forth one or two of Laura's physical attributes, though not the higher attributes of her soul:

> Le lode, mai non d' altra et proprie sue, . . .
> pur ardisco ombreggiare, or una or due.   [308]
> [Still now and again, I dare to adumbrate one or two of the praises that were always hers, never any other's.]

Again in the great canzone 129, "Di pensier in pensier . . . ," that poem which lays bare most pitilessly the erotic pathology of the speaker's fantasy-ridden obsessions, the act of consciously creating the fantasized woman according to the spirit's own desperate needs and specifications is carried, brilliantly and profoundly, by another cognate of the same noun.

> I' l' ò piú volte (or chi fia che m' il creda?)
> ne l' acqua chiara e sopra l'erba verde
> veduta viva, e nel troncon d' un faggio,
> e 'n bianca nube . . .
> e quanto in piú selvaggio
> loco mi trovo e 'n piú deserto lido,
> tanto piú bella il mio pensier l' adombra.   [ll. 40–43, 46–48]
> [I have many times (now who will believe me?) seen her alive in the clear water and on the green grass and in the trunk of a beech tree and in a white cloud . . . and in whatever wildest place and most deserted shore I find myself, so much the more beautiful does my thought shadow her forth.]

The verb derives from the Latin *adumbrare*—to shade in, to sketch (whence *adumbratus*—sketched, hence imperfect, shadowy, unreal). In this canzone, the phantasm of the beloved, which is said to outshine all stars, is only adumbrated, shadowed forth; it belongs to that shadow world of definition which is here all the speaker's being, and when it fades, the result is a kind of death.

Poi quando il vero *sgombra*
quel dolce error, pur lí medesmo assido
me freddo, pietra morta in pietra viva.   [ll. 49–51]
[Then, when the truth dispels that sweet deception, right there in the same place I sit
down, cold, a dead stone on the living rock.]

Sgombra means conventionally "clears out" or "removes"; here the context and
the rhyme oblige one to make out a meaning something like "dis-shadows." It is
precisely this act of dis-shadowing, of correcting his hallucinated vision, that
empties the speaker of his being, and with it his creative gift.[10]

All of these various uses of a single imagistic nucleus seem to circle around all
that is problematic in the poet's experience and in his art. Even when the shadow is
hospitable and nourishing, we are aware of its dangerous duplicities, if only
because the tree that casts the shadow is a locus of tenebrous power and ontological
insecurity. The shadow is already present in that moral and ontological dimness
beclouding the central self at the opening of canzone 129.

    . . . a la vista uom di tal vita esperto
diria: "Questo arde, e di suo stato è incerto."   [ll. 12–13]
[. . . at the sight anyone who had experienced such a life would say: "This man is
burning with love and his state is uncertain."]

It is the virtue of the *Canzoniere* to locate itself at the center of this uncertainty and
to acknowledge the shadowiness of the art that has to realize it. It is hard not to
glimpse in this recognized adumbration a new implication half emergent from the
traditional imagery employed in the coronation oration, where Petrarch asserts
the relation between the work of the poet and that of the historian or philosopher
to resemble the relation between a cloudy sky and a clear one, "since in each case
the same light exists in the object of vision, but is perceived in different degrees
according to the capacity of the observers."[11] The imagery we have been examining, if pushed to dogmatic limits, would seem to suggest that this capacity will
never, in the case of poetry, attain perfect knowledge. Poetry itself, according to the
opening sonnet, is reducible like all wordly things to a dream. It is admittedly
dangerous to juxtapose discursive and poetic statements without regard for specific
contexts and purposes. But we ought to notice nonetheless a passage from a letter
that seems to describe poets as naturally shadow-loving animals.

    Sunt qui clam pergant et velut aperta evitantes, *umbris gaudeant*, neque se profanari et
    nimia familiaritate contemni . . . velint. Hi sunt poete.   [*Fam.* 10.5]
    [Some you see journeying furtively, avoiding open ground and taking pleasure in
    shadows; they wish not to be sullied by contact nor to attract scorn by too much
    familiarity. . . . These are poets.]

This rejoicing in shadows and shunning of open places cannot be restricted
exclusively either to the poet's social or professional conduct; it cannot really be
excluded from that commerce with *ombre* to which the *Canzoniere* returns so

often. It seems to want repeatedly to expose an ambiguous delight in shadow and a shadow upon delight—an existential condition which is also an artistic condition, whether the play of context valorizes or deprecates it. In a writer where so much is Augustinian, nothing of course is more so than this darkening intuition. "Avertere ab umbra tua," wrote the saint, "revertere in te."[12] (Turn away from your shadow, turn back to yourself.) But the poet could never revert.

3

The presence of this umbrageous consciousness in Petrarch has significance for his poetic imitations because the classical subtexts he employs tend to emerge as though they were somehow almost shadow-free, more or less clear and whole on pinnacles of light "ove d' altra montagna ombra non tocchi" (129.53). This is true even when the subtexts themselves refer to shadows, as several do in sonnet 188, where a fall into "the shadow of the flesh" is thematized less obliquely than in the canzone of metamorphoses.

> Almo sol, quella fronde ch' io sola amo,
> tu prima amasti: or sola al bel soggiorno
> verdeggia e senza par, poi che l' addorno
> suo male e nostro vide in prima Adamo.   4
>   Stiamo a mirarla: i' ti pur prego e chiamo,
> o sole, e tu pur fuggi, e fai dintorno
> ombrare i poggi e te ne porti il giorno,
> e fuggendo mi toi quel ch' i' più bramo.   8
>   L'ombra che cade da quel' umil colle
> ove favilla il mio soave foco,
> ove 'l gran lauro fu picciola verga,
>   crescendo mentr' io parlo, agli occhi tolle
> la dolce vista del beato loco
> ove 'l mio cor co la sua Donna alberga.
> [Life-giving sun, you first loved that branch which is all I love; now, unique in her sweet dwelling, she flourishes, without an equal since Adam first saw his and our lovely bane.
> Let us stay to gaze at her, I beg and call on you, O sun, and you still run away and shadow the hillsides all around and carry off the day, and fleeing you take from me what I most desire.
> The shadow that falls from that low hill where my gentle fire is sparkling, where the great laurel was a little sapling, growing as I speak, takes from my eyes the sweet sight of the blessed place where my heart dwells with his lady.]

The speaker is standing at the site where Laura was born and passed her childhood ("ove 'l gran lauro fu picciola verga"); the season is winter, since now only the evergreen laurel retains its leaves; the hour is dusk ("te ne porti il giorno"). The speaker addresses the sun as Apollo, the first lover of Daphne/laurel/Laura, calling upon him to halt his flight which deepens the shadows over his beloved's natal hillside and will soon conceal it from sight. On first acquaintance the sonnet seems a little slight, possibly a little more straightforward than most of its companions, muted certainly, and even perhaps lacking in point. Does it matter greatly if the growing darkness obscures for a few hours the poet's view of Laura's natal home?

The phonic structure of the sonnet at any rate is exceptionally dense, weaving as it does an elaborate network of anagrams, paronomasias, internal rhymes, repetitions, assonances, consonances, and echoes:[13] "Almo sol"/"sola amo"/"sola al"/ "suo male"; "Stiamo"/"chiamo"; "fuggi"/"poggi"/"fuggendo"; "toi"/"tolle"; "ombrare"/"ombra"; "soave loco"/"beato loco"; the assonance in lines 5–6 ("dintorno . . . giorno"); the parallel enjambments in lines 2–3 and 6–7; the anagram "bramo"/"ombra" connecting the second quatrain with the first tercet. The effect of this phonic density is an impression of a text under peculiarly firm control, packed with structural reflectors, organized by deceptive cadences, approximated parallels, virtual chiming, evanescent recalls that fade and then, almost, return. This density caught by the outer ear is in fact matched by an analogous intertextual system whose allusive network impresses the literary ear with its own matted texture of allusions.

There are allusions first of all to other texts within the *Canzoniere*. Two consecutive sonnets *in morte* (320 and 321) again use Laura's birthplace as their fictive setting, and the second evokes again an image of darkness falling over hills:

> . . . veggendo a' colli oscura notte intorno.
> [. . . seeing dark night around the hills.]

But the darkness in this case is produced by the lady's disappearance.

> O del dolce mio mal prima radice
> ov' è il bel viso onde quel lume venne
> che vivo e lieto ardendo mi mantenne?
> [O first root of my sweet harms, where is the lovely face whence came the light that kept me alive and glad though burning?]

The site is the root of the poet's evil, his oxymoronic "dolce . . . mal." The line seems to conflate two expressions in 188—the allusion to Eve ("l' addorno suo male e nostro") and to Laura's infancy, when the great laurel was but a twig ("picciola verga"). The link is strengthened when one examines a prose text contemporaneous with sonnets 320 and 321, the brief life of Adam from the *De viris illustribus*. It concludes with a kind of apology for its presence within the volume.

> Ex omnibus seculis floridiora carpenti preterire non libuit radicem ipsam, amaram quamvis et asperam, unde tamen frondosi omnes virentesque prodeunt rami, de quibus interlegere aliquid institui.[14]
> [As one plucking the most thriving examples from all the centuries, I could not neglect

their root itself, however bitter and harsh, whence nevertheless issued all the green and leafy boughs from which I have decided to make my selection.]

There seems to be an association between the image of a root and a source of suffering, an oxymoronic association that centers on the drama of progressive growth into inevitable but flowering pain. A variant of the same image appears in the "Trionfo d'Amore":

Ma pur di lei che 'l cor di pensier' m' empie
non potei coglier mai ramo né foglia,
sí fur le sue radici acerbe ed empie.   [4.82–84]
[But yet I could never pluck branch or leaf from her who fills my heart with thoughts,
so bitter and evil were her roots.]

If the roots are harsh and bitter here, the evil stemming from the root is sweet ("dolce") in 321 and embellished ("addorno") in 188, as in the little biography the root of original depravity produces green and flourishing branches. The common motif in these three last-mentioned texts leads to the question whether our original sonnet, 188, was not also written when the others were, about 1351, three years after Laura's death. (The *Trionfi*, more difficult to date precisely, were composed during the period 1352–74.) There is no evidence of the composition of 188 before this date, nor would this be the only instance of a poem written later but inserted into the group *in vita*. I believe that it postdates her loss. But whatever its date, it gains immensely in meaning and force if it is understood to express forebodings of a looming tragedy.[15]

Sonnet 319, which directly precedes the pair just mentioned, strengthens this inference by associating the *ombroso* imagery directly with death in its opening words.

I dí miei piu leggier' che nesun cervo
fuggir come ombra.
[My days, swifter than any deer, have fled like a shadow.]

echoing a biblical subtext which may be present in 188 as well: "Dies mei sicut umbra declinaverunt" (Psalm 102—Vulgate 101), where the context makes it clear that the implied image is again organic. The King James Version reads: "My days are like a shadow that declineth, and I am withered like grass." Organic imagery is applied specifically to Laura's life cycle in still another Petrarchan text, canzone 127, "In quella parte dove Amor mi sprona." The poet there describes his habit of perceiving spring as a symbol for his beloved's early youth, and the summer sun, warming all things, as a flame of love mastering his heart. Then summer comes to an end.

. . . quando il dí si dole
di lui che passo passo a dietro torni,
veggio lei giunta a' suoi perfetti giorni.   [ll. 26–28]
[When the shorter day laments that the sun turns back step by step, I see her arrived at her fullest days.]

"Perfetti" can mean "perfected" or "fulfilled," but it can also mean "completed" and thus "ended." It is this completion that deepens the winter shadows in 188.[16] The anxiety of mortality in Petrarch penetrates his perennial obsession with temporality, carried in the sonnet most powerfully by the parenthetical phrase "crescendo mentr' io parlo" (l. 12). "Ora, mentre ch'io parlo, il tempo fugge" (Now, as I speak, the time is passing) he had written in an early sonnet (56), echoing Ovid ("Dum loquor, hora fugit") and Horace ("Dum loquimur fugerit invida Aetas"),[17] and went on to ask (in reference to a slight from Laura) what shadow was so cruel to blight the seed of the fruit so close to its ripening.

> Qual ombra è sí crudel che 'l seme adugge
> ch' al disiato frutto era sí presso?

Here the evil is not itself rooted, but fruition and blight are linked again, and the laurel shade is seen as unambiguously withering.

The extraordinarily thick texture within sonnet 188 of echoes of other Petrarchan texts (many quite possibly unconscious, but nonetheless expressive and meaningful) is scarcely more dense than the texture of imitative allusions to texts by other authors, most of these necessary and funtional. In addition to the echoes of Horace and Ovid in line 12 and the fainter hovering echo of Psalm 102, one may perhaps catch a note of Dante's *petrosa* sestina, another poem of winter and twilight set among hills.

> Al poco giorno e al gran cerchio d'ombra
> son giunto, lasso!, ed al bianchir de' colli,
> quando si perde lo color ne l'erba . . .
> [To the shortened day and to the great circle of shade I have come, alas! and to the whitening of the hills, when the color is lost from the grass. (Durling trans.)]

Dante's shadow is antiorganic, bleak and motionless, a finality at the end of a wan pilgrimage. It records the chilling conclusion of a decline. But the dominant subtexts in sonnet 188, those which are structurally determinate, are, as so often, Roman and reflect less desolate organic cycles. The opening apostrophe clearly imitates the opening of Horace's "Carmen saeculare."

> Alme Sol, curru nitido diem qui
> promis et celas aliusque et idem
> nasceris . . .
> [Nourishing Sun, who with your gleaming chariot bring and conceal the day and are reborn different yet the same . . .]

Some editors hear in line 11 of the sonnet a subtext from a bantering passage in Ovid's *Remedia amoris*. The frivolous speaker of that poem is urging the hopeful lover to choke his passion promptly before it grows to be uncontrollable. Delay only gives passion strength: *mora dat vires,* and turns grass into lusty crops.

> Quae praebet latas arbor spatiantibus umbras,
>   Quo posita est primum tempore virga fuit;

Tum poterat manibus summa tellure revelli:
  Nunc stat in inmensum viribus aucta suis.[18]
[What was it once, that tree with its great shade over the strollers?
  Sapling, or less, which one might have pulled out of the ground.
Now it is grown to full height, and arches over with shadow,
  Firm in its root, immense, come to the full of its bloom.]

If this image underlies the eleventh line of Petrarch's sonnet, it has altered its tone with its context; what is most odd, and what curiously argues for its presence as a subtext, is the recurrence here again of a shadow, the hospitable "umbras" of the mature tree.

I am inclined to believe, though I cannot prove, that Ovid's banter was conflated in Petrarch's mind with a more sober line from the *Georgics* expressing a related thought: "tarda venit seris factura nepotibus umbram" (2.58) (The slowly maturing tree will provide shade for remote descendants). What is undeniable is that this latter line is quoted toward the end of the *Secretum*, following closely upon a passage of great significance for the sonnet that concerns us. Augustinus is there admonishing Franciscus to use the passing of days and seasons as spurs to moral reflection, and one such moment he singles out is familiar.

Quotiens vergente ad occasum sole umbras montium crescere conspicis, dic: "Nunc vita fugiente umbra mortis extenditur; iste tamen sol cras idem aderit; hec autem michi dies irreparabiliter effluxit."[19]
[As often as you behold at sunset the shadows of the mountains lengthening on the plain, say to yourself: "Now life is sinking fast; the shadow of death begins to overspread the scene; yonder sun to-morrow will again be rising the same, but this day of mine will never come back."]

Again the twin anxieties of temporality and mortality are interfused, and they are focused by an image of shadows whose lengthening is expressed by the verb "crescere," Latin cognate of the analogous verb in the sonnet ("crescendo mentr' io parlo"). The Augustinus of the *Secretum* does not identify the source of his image, but no literate reader would forget the beautiful line which closes the first of Virgil's eclogues. There the exiled Meliboeus is invited by Tityrus to delay his departure from Arcadia and to linger another night as Tityrus's guest. Smoke has begun to rise from the shepherds' roofs, he says, and shadows from the high mountains are growing longer: "maioresque cadunt altis de montibus umbrae." It is an image of repose within a majestic setting which is at one with the pastoral rhythms it encloses, even if this harmony is qualified in its context by the imminence of exclusion and loss.[20] The line had already figured as a subtext in Petrarch's early canzone 50, where it signals to the peasant the welcome end of a weary day's labor, forming a part there also of a vignette informed with simple and rhythmic tranquility.[21]

In the *Secretum*, however, as in sonnet 188, this shadow ceases to be rhythmic; it encroaches irreversibly; it renders ominous the linearity of Christian time. It is particularly associated with the act of speech in that little phrase "crescendo mentr' io parlo:" The temporality of speech is more oppressive in Petrarch than in Ovid or Horace because extension in time invokes the threat of deviation or digression. For Augustine, life in time is a *distentio*, a word meaning both "duration" and "distraction" (*Confessions* 9.29). Language itself, for both Augustine and Petrarch, does not escape this distraction or error leading the soul away from salvation. That sorrowful remark in the *De remediis* on the fugacity of speech ("as we pronounce each single syllable, some part of our life slips away"—see above, p. 126) discloses its fallen character. Despair over the irredeemable *distentio* of language darkens the sonnet that concerns us. One definition of the *ombra* in that poem would be the original infection of words.

At the opening of the sonnet, however, there is no shadow; there is a fraternity between the speaker and the sun god, who first loved the laurel as Daphne; there is the animating, nourishing beneficence of the sun as source of warmth and light; there is the beauty of the place ("il bel soggiorno"); there is above all the enduring, peerless beauty of the evergreen beloved. All of these affirmations are crowded into the opening two and a half lines of the sonnet and reinforced by the allusion to the "Carmen saeculare," where the periodic absence of light is not presented negatively as a threatening shadow but reverently as a recurrent phase of a divine and appropriate repetition ("curru nitido diem qui promis et celas"). The periodic concealment of the day does not seem to darken for Horace the splendor of Apollo's chariot; it remains, apparently, always brilliant, "nitido," whatever the hour, just as the religious mystery of the sun's daily birth ("aliusque et idem nasceris") into a paradoxically changeful identity suggests a perennial organic cycle, unclouded by anxieties of loss. The allusion to the *Remedia amoris*, once its teasing context is set aside, also rests on an assumption of a nonproblematic cycle, in this case a gradual growth into a fullness whose shadows are purely hospitable. This fulfillment is only underscored if one hears in this image an echo of its counterpart in the *Georgics*.

But the Ovidian subtext can be heard in any case only after Petrarch's sonnet has turned away from the nourishing fraternity and constancy of its opening two and a half lines. These initial affirmations abruptly disappear from the poem, and what follows will transform the life-warming Apollo into a force of change and mutability, a source of that shadow which will deepen through the remainder of the poem as the poet speaks. Against this gathering obscurity, the lady's oxymoronic gentle fire ("soave foco") glints to small avail, just as the natural growth of the laurel from its first shoot seems also threatened by the deepening darkness. The parallelism in lines 10–11 of the two periphrastic metaphors for Laura—"soave foco" and "gran lauro"—tends to involve the organic cycle in oxymoron. The fire—not in this case the lover's ardor but its cause, the lady herself—despite its sweetness becomes an object of concern, indeed is the object of that mounting anxiety which emerges as the poem's main burden. The poem stages once again a fall, now a degeneration from a purely fostering cycle into a threatened or tainted or ambivalent cycle that will destroy Laura and that divides the poet as well as his poetry from vital process. In lines 1–2, the speaker and the sun are united; after Adam's fall is invoked in line 4, they are opposed and the poet's appeal for constant fraternity goes unheard. The poem stages this fall *sequentially*, in the abrupt surrender of its initial reverences and affirmations, but also *iconically*, by subjecting its classical subtexts to transformations that subvert them. This is true of the little Ovidian image; it is also true of the classical laments for the ebbing of time ("Dum loquimur fugerit invida Aetas"), because when classical time leads to loss and death it offers a solace in the simultaneous renewal it also brings and in the pure simplicity it attributes to natural cycles. The body that suffers death need not thereby, for Horace, be called into question. He could not have written, as Petrarch did:

> Hec michi nascenti lex cum corpore data est, ut ex eius consortio multa patiar, aliter non passurus.[22]
>
> [A law was imposed on me together with my body when I was born, that from its association with me I must suffer many things which I would not suffer otherwise.]

or again:

> Ex contagio corporis huius, ubi circumsepta est, multum a primeva nobiltate sua degenerasse ne dubites.[23]
>
> [In [the soul's] contact with the flesh, wherein it is imprisoned, it has lost much of its first splendor.]

This law is present in sonnet 188 and it governs along with the other elements the subtext from Virgil. The shadow that lengthens about Tityrus and Meliboeus gathers them into a unity with the Arcadian landscape about them, and if Meliboeus will be required to leave it, his exile will only heighten our perception of its beautiful integrity. His darkening shadow is as yet unfallen; it is innocent of psychologistic or theological or rhetorical perplexities. It lies on the far side of a gulf whose near side is marked by the Psalmist's withered grass and declining days, Dante's stony chill, Augustine's repudiation of the pure phenomenon, the sunset-in-itself, and by the bitter Edenic root whose branches are blighted but flourishing. Petrarch's intertextual proliferation avoids anachronistic chaos by organizing its subtexts on either side of this gulf, and by dramatizing the slide across it as an entry into division and into anxieties of adumbration. The only repose left in the sonnet lies in the last word—"alberga," in the heart's lodging with its lady at her birthplace, but the place and the lady are menaced and the stability is provisional. Virgil's anecdote of hospitality has deteriorated into a premonition of ravishment.

The adumbration in the sonnet as in the canzone of metamorphoses is theological. Between Apollo as animating lover and as fugitive-thief, between the laurel as evergreen and as deciduous, falls the embellished evil of Eve—that first Laura, and like her oxymoronic. The shadow extending from the one woman to the other is postlapsarian; it stands for a fall into tragic linearity, into an estrangement of mind from body, into an oxymoronic Christian frailty which however lacks the option of redemption. The text performs a disruption of classical equilibriums by a modern metaphysical fissure, a darkening of history that turns the animating world into a thieving, fleeting principle of privation. Less problematic rhetorically than the canzone of metamorphoses, the sonnet keeps its reserve as Petrarch's vernacular poems seldom do. But few of the poems for Laura approach so closely the thematizing of what he perceived as the loss of ancient plenitude.

Precisely because the sonnet does thematize this fall in lines 3–4 (and thus becomes an example of "complex imitation"), it must be distinguished from the other imitative poems (23, 50, 90, 164, 311) that tacitly dramatize the same movement. By presenting the fall as explicit, the sonnet tends more closely toward something like tragic confrontation. There is also a hinted anticipation of an end to the iterative action expressed in the verb "bramo" (line 8). When the sun concludes its action of taking away the beloved, extinguishing her fire, that conclusion can be envisaged as a potential punctuation mark, breaking off permanently the present iteration. There may be a fainter allusion to the speaker's eventual death as well as Laura's. At any rate it is possible to await a silence, an interruption of desire and speech. For this sonnet, it does not matter that in fact Laura's death would not impose silence upon the poet. The conceivable interruption leaves room for an attitude responsive to tragedy, an attitude that would transcend the essentially antitragic repetitive frustrations still dominant at the present moment of speech. There is equally a tendency in the poem to allow a degree of objective solidity to the hill, even a dimension of externality to the darkness, however richly and ominously symbolic. Thus the sonnet leaves open an issue away from the phantasmic into tragic resignation, a genuine interplay between sensibility and world which would permit an ultimate repose. The sonnet is pervaded by fear but it seems to anticipate a resolution when both fear and desire would be out of place. In this respect it is a very rare instance within the context of the whole collection.

Insofar as one discerns a veering in this poem toward tragic resignation, one can begin to speak of dialectical imitation. That is to say, its shadowed sorrow may adumbrate a response to loss as humane, as morally satisfying, as that of the "Carmen saeculare" or the first eclogue. The poem does stage a fall, from the life-giving cycles of pagan faith to a harsher Christian linearity, but it is possible to read in this harsher pattern a finer, more appropriate attitude toward pain and death. The poem would constitute an oblique criticism of the ancient texts and values it invites us to subread, while simultaneously exposing its own Christian, postlapsarian vulnerabilities: the starkness of its spiritual loneliness, its exclusion from Roman solaces. The Christian element is all the starker because for Petrarch divine mercy and grace generally appear so inaccessible. The poem presents a densely impacted chronomachia that pits Apollonian against Adamic myth, Horace, Ovid, and Virgil against a bleak concordance of Christian voices—Dante, Augustine, the Psalmist, the manifold echoes of Petrarch's own canon. The struggle thus presented does not end by canceling out all parties nor by sinking into an aporetic vortex. It remains, in a fugal, unresolved resonance, to transform anachronism into the polyvocal agon of an emergent, self-discovering culture.

4

In the foregoing discussion of Petrarch, I have tried to argue that his poems were among the first written after antiquity to spring from an acute sense of cultural removal, that the poems deal with this removal by constructing "itineraries," etiological versions of historical passage bridging the perceived gap, and finally that in each instance the itinerary defines itself in one sense or another as a "fall," locates itself on a descending gradient corresponding to the poet's feelings of inferiority (although in the last poem analyzed a countercriticism appeared to emerge). The fall dramatized in each of these remarkable texts shows how their author made sense of history as a poet.

Imitative poems including Petrarch's can profitably be studied in the terms of what the Soviet critic Mikhail Bakhtin called "meta-linguistics," a term he coined in his critique of conventional stylistic studies for their attention to the merely superficial and univocal externals of linguistic activity. *Metalinguistics*, as defined in Bakhtin's study of Dostoevsky, refuses to consider the word (*slovo* in Russian: "word" or, less often, "discourse") in isolation from the life of exchange and dialogue which he sees as inherent in it.

> The word is not a thing, but rather the eternally mobile, eternally changing medium of dialogical intercourse. It never coincides with a single consciousness or a single voice. The life of the word is in its transferral from one mouth to another, one context to another, one social collective to another, and one generation to another. In the process the word does not forget where it has been and can never wholly free itself from the dominion of the contexts of which it has been a part.[24]

The literature of the humanist Renaissance intensified this awareness of the word's passage; it is already intensified in Petrarch. Humanist literature at its richest would find its profit in the circumstance, underscored by Bakhtin, that the words we receive from our linguistic community are "filled" or "inhabited" by the voices of others.

> When each member of a collective of speakers takes possession of a word, it is not a neutral word of language, free from the aspirations and valuations of others, uninhabited by foreign voices. No, he receives the word from the voice of another, and the word is filled with that voice. The word arrives in his context from another context which is saturated with other people's interpretations. . . . Every trend in every epoch has its own characteristic perception of the word and its own range of verbal possibilities. The ultimate semantic authority of a creative writer is by no means capable in every historical situation of being expressed in the direct, unrefracted, unconditional author-

ial word. When one's own personal "final" word does not exist, then every creative plan, every thought, feeling and experience must be refracted through the medium of another person's word, style and manner, with which it is impossible to directly merge without reservation, distance and refraction.[25]

This intertextual capacity—or necessity—of the word, which Bakhtin analyzes suggestively in the novels of Dostoevsky, thickens the translinguistic orchestration of all the central masterpieces of the high Middle Ages in each major European language: those by Guillaume de Lorris and Jean de Meun, Gottfried of Strasbourg, Dante, Chaucer, the Archpriest of Hita, and Villon. The works of all these writers mingle a number of vividly differentiated voices assigned to fictive characters. Where the tradition of these densely polyvocal works (Bakhtin's term, anticipating Frye's, is "Menippean satire") was not prolonged by Renaissance authors, the new literature is likely to sound purer but thinner, as Marot and Ronsard sound after Villon, Wyatt after Chaucer, and Petrarch after Dante. The presence within the text of controlled diachronic relationships can be viewed as compensating for a loss of polyvocal density and reintroducing a creative calculation of refractions. Or, more precisely, the poet of the later generation chooses to work with a double system of refractions, a *lavor doppio* opposing and accommodating two alien conventions, one remote and buried, one at hand and in danger of shrinkage. The special character of the intertextual refractions in postmedieval poetry lies in the distinct proveniences of the voices within the word.

Thus in the most Augustinian of all his poems, the canzone "I' vo pensando" (264), which invokes divine grace as well as Christ crucified in its opening stanza—in this long debate of compunction, ambition, and passion, with its anguished confession of a shadowed will ("vorre 'l ver abbraciar, lassando l' ombre"—see above, p. 132), the voice heard most powerfully in the counterpoint of subtexts is Ovid's, and it is from Ovid that the Christian anxiety of the close takes its rhetoric.

ché co la morte a lato
cerco del viver mio novo consiglio;
e veggio ' l meglio, ed al peggior m' appriglio.   [ll. 134–36]
[. . . for with Death at my side I seek new counsel for my life, and I see the better but I lay hold on the worse.]

video meliora proboque, deteriora sequor.   [*Metamorphoses* 7.20–21]
[I see and approve the better, follow the worse.]

Conversely, sonnet 292 *in morte* (Gli occhi di ch' io parlai . . .), one of the starkest laments for the lost body of the profane love, finds its closing rhetoric in the Vulgate version of Job.

secca è la vena de l' usato ingegno
e la cetera mia rivolta in pianto.
[Dry is the vein of my accustomed wit, and my lyre is turned to weeping.]

Versa est in luctum cithara mea. [Job 30:31]
[My harp is turned to mourning.]

In the single words "meglio" and "peggior" of the canzone, the devotional, confessional accent with its terrible sense of unworthiness and its formal debate structure enters into a dialogue or a struggle with the Ovidian story of Medea. More than in Dostoevsky or most writers of the last two centuries, the provenience of the voices in dialogue forces itself into the reader's mind; each side is *ticketed*. The opposition takes place along a passageway through time.

One way to study the metalinguistic activity of a humanist text is to isolate what might be called the mistranslation, the word or image or motif that seems at first glance to follow the meaning of its counterpart in the subtext but in fact is shifting away from it under the pressure of context. Sometimes the entire clash engendered by an imitative work will be epitomized within a single word; sometimes the historical passage from past to present can be located in this one mistranslation. The word "ombra" in sonnet 188, corresponding to the "umbrae" of Virgil's first eclogue, is clearly a very rich example. In the nightingale sonnet (311), the adjective "pietose" (roughly "pathetic" or "affecting") can be taken as the equivalent of Virgil's "miserabile" or "maestis": yet in fact "pietose" is paired with the adjective "scorte" (artfully modulated), and it cannot be separated from the "dolcezza" of the preceding line. The "pietose" notes in Petrarch's usage are more lyrical, more skillful, more caressing to the ear, more *human*, and yet because of these very qualities more piercing and more subtly painful. This is another way of saying that the pathos is internalized, ceases to be a predication of the song and becomes a projection of the auditor. The almost ineffable but nonetheless real distance between the two images is focused in this one word, which emerges as a node of diachronic interaction, centering the play of cultures and of moral styles. We shall need to consider other mistranslations in analyzing the works of later Renaissance poets.

It will not, I think, distort our perspective on later poets to have lingered so long over Petrarch. Because he was a figure of immense significance, both as poet and as reader of history, for the civilization of the following centuries, the particular behavior of his poems as diachronic constructs is of greater moment than their number or even their undisputed intrinsic value would warrant. For Petrarch left as a legacy to the European Renaissance not only his books but the vision of history for which each imitative poem served as *speculum*. He left a legacy that was double-edged generally for a culture and privately for each humanist poet. The remainder of this study will be devoted primarily to individual poetic responses to Petrarch's difficult legacy, which of course ceased to be purely Petrarchan once the humanist movement proper gathered headway. His special privilege lies in that transitive role for which he deliberately cast himself and which he accepted responsibly, assuming in good faith the burden one carries to cross a threshold.

Eight • Poliziano: The Past Dismembered

The death of Petrarch in 1374 was followed by a period of poetic aridity in Italy that lasted over three quarters of a century. The new wave of humanist energy that began to gather strength early in the quattrocento did not immediately produce an important body of poetry either in Latin or the vernacular. Somewhat more surprisingly, it also failed to produce interesting discussions of imitation. This failure may be due in part to the pedagogic method of the commonplace book, which tended to foster syncretic textures of fragmentary allusions or topoi and left little room for extended reflection.[1] The educational treatises of the quattrocento have curiously little to say about *imitatio*; this may be due to their emphasis on *curriculum*—the resquisite range of subjects and canon of authors—rather than *method*. At the opening of the last decade of the century, the *De poetice* of Bartolommeo della Fonte contains a few derivative remarks on the need for judgment both of the writer's self and his model before he sets out to emulate it.[2] But the vogue of imitation as a theoretical issue seems to have been triggered by della Fonte's more gifted colleague at the Studio of Florence, Angelo Poliziano, who exchanged polemics at about the same time with a young humanist, Paolo Cortesi, on the propriety of following a single model, Cicero. This exchange was followed by a flood of theoretical debate throughout western Europe that subsided only in the latter sixteenth century.

The one treatise on imitation we possess between Petrarch and Poliziano in no way ranks with their briefer but incisive discussions. This is the heretofore unpublished *De imitatione* by Gasparino Barzizza (died 1431).[3] As its editor George Pigman suggests, Barzizza's little essay may not have been intended for publication but for the private use of his students; it remains at any rate at a very elementary and even mechanical level. Imitation is discussed almost entirely in terms of diction, although invention and disposition are said to require parallel procedures. Verbal imitation is effected in four ways: addition, subtraction, transposition, and alteration.[4] Each is explained in language so simple as to be childlike. An example of addition: if one's model is Cicero and he writes "Scite hoc inquit Brutus" (Brutus says this deftly), one can expand this to read "Scite enim ac eleganter hoc inquit ille vir noster Brutus." Barzizza also lists the five standard metaphors for imitation: apian, digestive, filial, echoic, choral. He could have found all but the fourth in Seneca. What is striking is their status as routine topoi so early in the humanist Renaissance. The longevity of the first two in particular after this demonstration of their familiarity, and what is more, their reascent to something like eloquence at the hands of an Erasmus, a Du Bellay, a Montaigne, a Jonson,[5] reinforce a lesson no twentieth-century reader will ever fully absorb. For the evidence that these metaphors were already felt as commonplaces, and the evidence that boys of that era learned imitation at a primary stage in their studies, this plodding schoolbook is chiefly valuable.

Its limitations should not in any case be allowed to obscure the vaster intellectual adventure in which it played a humble part. During the era stretching from Petrarch to Poliziano, the humanist movement established itself in Italy as a dominant intellectual force. Major texts of antiquity were rediscovered; the composition of Latin prose and poetry came to approximate ancient Roman style; education in the best schools came to be based chiefly on classic Roman authors and also included some Greek. A far sharper perception of the alien specificity of ancient civilization was achieved, and along with this a perception of period styles during the course of that civilization. In his inaugural lecture delivered at the Florentine Studio, Poliziano reveals his own sensitivity to the shift of *mundi significantes* as the universally admired Augustan age of letters was succeeded by the silver age, which many humanists regarded as decadent.

> Neque statim deterius dixerimus quod diversum sit. Maior certe cultus in secundis est, crebrior voluptas, multae sententiae, multi flores, nulli sensus tardi, nulla iners structura, omninoque non tantum sani et fortes sunt omnes et laeti et alacres et pleni sanguinis atque coloris. Quapropter ut plurima summis illis sine ulla controversia tribuerimus, ita priora in his aliqua multoque potiora existere iure contenderimus. [We should not automatically call worse what is different. In the later authors there is assuredly more elaboration, more frequent pleasure, many *sententiae*, many flowers, and there is nothing sluggish; no structure is inert; not only is everything healthy but it is strong, joyous, animated, full of blood and color. Thus while we recognize without debate the great merits of those [earlier] supreme masters, we must rightly affirm that in these [later authors], certain new qualities appear with more distinction.][6]

All these ages, Poliziano argues, provide matter for imitation and nourishment, as Lucretius's bees find nectar in all meadows. This new alertness to period style is visible not only in the growth of connoisseurship through all the arts, but in the facility that produced fakes: Alberti's Latin comedy corresponds to the youthful statue by Michelangelo successfully passed off as antique. Poliziano composed Greek poetry that could *pass* as Greek among native speakers, although he personally never left the shores of Italy. This kind of distinction is the most persuasive token of the enormous gain in quattrocento historical and linguistic sensitivity.

Yet the spectacular gains were irregular, insecure, and overshadowed by a persisting sense of estrangement. Many ancient texts were available in manuscripts incomplete or faulty—and *divergently* faulty—to the point of heartbreak. No usable dictionaries existed for either ancient language; Greek was generally learned by the arduous comparison of facing Latin translations, usually those done by Theodore of Gaza. Confronting a mutilated or nonsensical manuscript, the scholar had no recourse but to consult another manuscript that might be less reliable. The relatively systematic organization of philologic research in universities, as against the more brilliant but erratic research of humanists employed in courts and chancelleries, assumed major importance only at the end of the quattrocento. I have already quoted that remarkable confession of Poliziano which must have cost him no little pain: "There is no single book of Roman antiquity, I believe, which we professors fully understand" (nullus apud Latinos . . liber [ut arbitror] quem professores ad liquidum intellegamus).[7] And I have quoted also (see above, p. 9) his tribute to those intrepid adventurers who seek out the obscure and forgotten mysteries ("tam remota tamque oblivia") of the distant past. The increase of humanist knowledge heightened ironically the sense of the unknown; the wider the diameter of light, the greater the circumference of darkness—and the keener the awareness of potential estrangement. Poliziano's own alertness to the risk of anachronism is revealed in such an insignificant phrase as his boast of having translated a certain ancient text *coloribus servatis*, with its particular cast, its moral style, intact.[8] It is true that the dedicatory epistle to the *Raccolta Aragonese* stresses the continuity of ancient Latin and vernacular Italian poetry. But this passage from an official document may have less to teach us than a private jotting in the poet's journal: "Nuovi ragionamenti fanno nuovi casi: e nuovi casi vogliono nuovi modi." (New reasoning produces new examples, and new examples require new modes of thought.)[9] The Christian sense of universal fragility we find in Poliziano's sermons ("nulla in fra gli uomini è stabile"— nothing human is stable)[10] is not fully distinguishable from a secular anxiety of millenary loss. Instances of the necromantic metaphor can be found throughout his work, from the early praise of the book dealer and copier Vespasiano da Bisticci:

Felix, cui liceat revocare in lumina vitae
  Mortua priscorum tot monumenta virum.[11]

to the late praise of Ficino for having brought back Platonic philosophy from the underworld as Orpheus wanted to bring back Eurydice. Yet as we shall see, the imagery of neither compliment escapes the problematic. Moreover in a city that had lost the civic spirit and communal liberty of the Salutati-Bruni era, the necromantic metaphor began to be co-opted for the propaganda of Poliziano's patrons. The Virgilian slogan "Le tems revient" appeared on a banner carried by Lorenzo during a Florentine tournament.

It is against this checkered background of ignorance and knowledge, against the perpetual Renaissance conflict of perceived continuity and rupture, that one must read the well-known letter of Poliziano on the subject of imitation. It is not his only pronouncement on the subject, but it is rightly regarded as the richest and the most representative. It was composed toward the close of the author's relatively short career, at a time when he saw himself primarily as teacher and scholar, only secondarily as a poet, writing almost exclusively now in Latin. The recipient of the letter was a young man, Paolo Cortesi, who had made the mistake of sending the master a sheaf of letters composed by various hands in strict imitation of Cicero.

Poliziano's brief, withering polemic would receive a somewhat longer reply from Cortesi. During the sixteenth century the same scenario would be played out by Giovanfrancesco Pico della Mirandola (nephew of the philosopher) and Pietro Bembo, and then again by Erasmus and Scaliger among others.[12] Of all the contributions to this sizable literature, Poliziano's has the merit of concision. I quote it in full.[13]

> I return to you the letters which you have gatherd so diligently, in the reading of which, speaking frankly, I am ashamed to have wasted my time. Except for a very few, they do not deserve to be read by a cultivated person or to have been collected by you. I shall not indicate which I approve or disapprove. I prefer that no one's pleasure or displeasure in them be swayed by my judgment. However there is one question of style on which I take issue with you. If I understand you, you approve only those who copy the features of Cicero. To me the form of a bull or a lion seems more respectable than that of an ape, even if an ape looks more like a man. Nor, as Seneca remarked, do those most highly reputed for eloquence resemble each other. Quintilian ridicules those who think themselves Cicero's brothers because they end their sentences *esse videatur*. Horace scolds those who are imitators and nothing else. Those who compose only on the basis of imitation strike me as parrots or magpies bringing out things they don't understand. Such writers lack strength and life; they lack energy, feeling, character; they stretch out, go to sleep, and snore. There is nothing true in them, nothing solid, nothing efficacious. Someone says: "You don't represent Cicero." What of it? I am not Cicero; I think I represent myself.
>
> Then there are some, dear Paolo, who beg for their style like bread, bit by bit, and live by the day. Unless the book is at hand to draw from, they can't string three words together, and even these they muddle with awkward transitions and disgraceful barbarisms. Thus their style is always tremulous, wobbly, weak—unkempt and ill-fed, so to speak; these I can't tolerate. And they have the temerity to pass judgment on the learned, whose style has been enriched by abstruse erudition, broad reading, and prolonged practice.
>
> But to return to you, Paolo, whom I love deeply, to whom I owe much, whose mind I greatly respect, I hope that you will detach yourself from that superstition whereby what is entirely yours cannot please you and you never take your eyes off Cicero. When you have read Cicero and other good authors widely and at length, when you have pondered, learned, digested them, filled your breast with the knowledge of many things and propose to compose something yourself, then I hope that you will swim as they say without cork and take counsel with yourself, putting aside that fretful and demoralizing concern with reproducing Cicero alone and finally venturing all your own powers in the effort. For whoever contemplates with awe those ridiculous features of your models cannot adequately represent them, believe me, but only hamstring the velocity of his mind, block the road, as it were, of a true runner, and to use the Plautine expression, act as a remora. One who takes care to place his foot in another's tracks cannot run well, nor can one write well if he lacks the courage to leave the beaten path. Bear in mind finally that to draw nothing from the self and to imitate always is the mark of an unhappy mind. Farewell.

It would be well to exclude at the outset an anachronistic reading of this document that would see in it a manifesto of a modern expressionism. The last sentences of the first paragraph, if taken out of context, might lend themselves to a view of their author as an unfettered individualist fighting free of the constraints of tradition. But this of course is precisely what Poliziano was not, in or outside of this letter. The self which he wants to express is that self nourished and matured by the digestive absorption of others that is described in the third paragraph. Only the man whose heart and stomach are filled with the substance of others is able thus to portray himself. The Ciceronian is not overstuffed by a hypertrophy of learning, as the post-Romantic observer might consider him to be; without his model he is rather undernourished, unkempt, and ill-fed, betraying that scarcity of *recondita eruditio* which leaves his beggarly prose so trembling and unsteady.

It is true that for Poliziano the digestive phase is understood to be preceded by a phase of analytical withdrawal, the philological act of *placing* the word and the text in their own era, at their own distance, in order to experience their peculiar savor, their uniqueness as historical artifacts. There is a rigor, an impersonality, in this moment of lucid apprehension that is absent from the Petrarchan metaphor of innutrition. And this is a moment that does not fade even after the assimilative act occurs. The capacity to savor implies a necessary, preliminary stage in the innutritive process. As these metaphors suggest, a *wissenschaftlich* detachment was not altogether distinct from an Epicurean detachment, the refined composure of an erudite connoisseur. Yet it is a mistake to be deluded by this composure into denying the assimilative act that follows and fulfills the preliminary distancing.[14] The poetry of Poliziano is there to guarantee the validity of that profound absorption which the letter defines and celebrates.

What is really at issue between Poliziano and Cortesi is the human capacity for achieving an *integration* of the self, which then becomes an integration of style, out of the contamination of multiple models. The young Cortesi, speaking in this dispute for the generation to follow, denies the possibility of forming a stylistic unity out of the flotsam of literary history. In the battle of metaphors that focuses this polemic, he opposes to the fullness of Poliziano's well-fed eclectic avoiding the footprints of a single forerunner the dissonant clashing of stones in a landslide, the chaos of a pawnbroker's shop, cluttered with the bric-a-brac of its motley customers, or the confusion of the traveler who strays from the highway and wanders among the thorns. The ill-assorted meats on the plate of the eclectic for Cortesi can only produce indigestion. In these images of satiety, confusion, and disorder, given the cult they introduce, it is perhaps not too much to discern a humanist *crisis of receptivity*. One way, that is, to interpret the Ciceronianism of the high Renaissance is in terms of a glut, if not of knowledge, then of the will to knowledge, the end of a long chapter of omnivorous passion. Is it paradoxical that the supremely civilized man of Poliziano's letter takes the form of a bull or a lion, preserving a wildness of predatory appetite? To surrender this appetite is to act the remora, *facere remoram*, to cancel the dynamism of civilization.

Thus the decision whether to draw upon a single master (Cicero) or the entire breadth of the canon translates a choice between rival conceptions of assimilation and rival possibilities of humanist wholeness. These were in fact issues around which Poliziano's entire career had turned. And assimilation is a crucial motif running through the thought of the fifteenth century. It is already significant in the profound and original thought of Nicholas of Cusa.

> Si hanc divinam simplicitatem infinitam mentem vocitaveris, erit ipsa nostrae mentis exemplar. Si mentem divinam universitatem veritatis rerum dixeris, nostram dices universitatem assimilationis rerum, ut sit notionum universitas. Conceptio divinae mentis est rerum productio; conceptio nostrae mentis est rerum notio. Si mens divina est absoluta entitas, tunc eius conceptio est entium creatio; et nostrae mentis conceptio est entium assimilatio. . . . Si omnia sunt in mente divina ut in sua praecisa et propria veritate, omnia sunt in mente nostra ut in imagine seu similitudine propriae veritatis, hoc est notionaliter: similitudine enim fit cognitio.
> [If you affirm the divine mind to be the entire truth of things, you affirm our mind to be the entire assimilation of things, since it contains the totality of impressions. For the divine mind to conceive of things is thereby to produce them; for ours, to conceive of them is to form an impression. If the divine mind is absolute being, it need only conceive beings to create them; the conception of our mind is the assimilation of entities. . . . If all things are contained in the divine mind as in their proper and precise truth, all things are in our mind as in an image or resemblance of their proper truth, which is to say as impressions; all knowledge is achieved by means of resemblance.][15]

There is much in this passage of the *Idiota* that speaks to us today, not least the argument that human knowledge is by necessity figural or metaphoric. What for our purposes is seminal is this proud affirmation of the mind's vocation as container and assimilator, second only to the divine function of creation. The older meaning of *assimilatio* (comparison) is associated with the process of mental reception, the modern English meaning. In fact, Nicholas was still closer to the vision of late Italian Neoplatonism because he saw in this human capacity for reception a complementary capacity for assimilating itself to the multiplicity outside itself. The act of drawing this multiplicity into the self is somehow akin to giving one's self to the movement, diversity, disjunction outside it. Paradoxically the mind absorbs the otherness of the external creation by yielding itself up. This double movement of absorption and surrender reappears in the thought of Ficino, where the metaphoric activity of the assimilative mind disappears and the distinction between divine and human creativity is further blurred.

> Neque credendum est animum sibi minus unire quae capit quam corpus. Corpus enim cibos vel diversissimos in suam vertit substantiam anima concoquente. Ita et animus quae accipit, immo concipit, in se vertit, et multo magis, siquidem dimensiones corporum mutuam in corporibus impediunt unionem; spiritalia vero sunt unioni admodum aptiora. Itaque rationes rerum intellectarum magis in substantiam transeunt intellectus, ut vult Plotinus, quam in substantiam corporis alimenta.
> [One must not believe that the soul unites what it receives less with itself than does the body. The body transforms the most varied nourishment into its own substance, through the digestive process of the vital principle. Similarly the soul transforms what it receives and even what it conceives into itself still more thoroughly, for the physical dimensions of bodies are an obstacle to their union, whereas spiritual entities are better

adapted to union. Thus the principles of things understood penetrate more deeply the substance of the intellect, according to Plotinus, than does nourishment the substance of the body.][16]

Elsewhere Ficino writes: "Our soul tends to become all things, as God is all things."[17] This giving up of the self to the nonself no more constitutes an annihilation of the subject than does the diffusion of the One in the many; it is simply one more of man's divine prerogatives, and perhaps the central prerogative. It is once again a phase of an activity that remains circular and assimilative.[18] It is only in this larger conception of dynamic interchange that one grasps the deepest interpretation accorded the familiar formula attributed to Cosimo de' Medici: "Every painter paints himself" (Ogni pintore dipinge se.) Later formulations can be found in Pico and in Patrizzi; perhaps one hears an echo of the idea in Leonardo's remark: "Whoever paints a figure and cannot be that figure, cannot reproduce it." (Chi pinge figura, se se non po' esser lei, non la po' porre.) The assimilationist impulse, cut off in this case from the impulse to self-surrender, reaches its culmination in the thought of Charles de Bouelles, who designated self-knowledge as the goal of all human endeavor and made assimilation of the outer world the single means to this goal. This conception doubtless carried the Renaissance trend as far as it could go. The mind of the sage swells to contain the universe itself, and this ingestion becomes his life.

It would be a serious error to place in the center of this metaphysical current the reflection of Poliziano, whose reservations concerning Neoplatonic speculation are well known. But it would be equally wrong to segregate him from the milieu in which he moved and breathed. The assimilationist images of the letter to Cortesi and the Studio lecture cannot be read as mere transcriptions of the corresponding images in Petrarch. There is, that is to say, a seriousness in the concept of self-creation by mellification or innutrition which the egoism of Petrarch would ultimately have repudiated. Yet Poliziano also distinguishes himself from the metaphysical thought of his century by substituting for the act of self-surrender the act of philologic apprehension. Cortesi's response goes so far as to question the very possibility of a richly assimilated selfhood. Who wants the clutter of a pawnshop? Isn't there a limit to each man's capacity for absorption? Nietzsche for one thought there was.

There is a degree of sleeplessness, of rumination, of "historical sense," that injures and finally destroys the living thing, be it a man or a people or a system of culture. To fix this degree and the limits to the memory of the past, if it is not to become the gravedigger of the present, we must see clearly how great is the "plastic power" of a man or a community or a culture; I mean the power of specifically growing out of one's self, of making the past and the strange one body with the near and the present.[19]

Nietzsche deals here in his own idiom with that question of the wholeness of the assimilative individual which brought the long affirmative stage of humanism to the point of crisis. The dispute between the two humanists at the close of the quattrocento turns precisely upon what Nietzsche calls *plastische Kraft*. The Ciceronian cult can be regarded as a misguided or pathological response to an authentic issue, a response that is a superstition rather than a liberation. What in Poliziano looks to the naive eye like an individualism repudiating tradition is more properly understood as a defense of every man's unlimited "plastic power," the strength to absorb and remain free. Underlying the exchange of letters is this deeper problem of receptivity whose solution in any given case is by no means obvious.

Along with this crisis of assimilation in the Ciceronian dispute one can make out a crisis of historicism. As the quarrel was fought and refought repeatedly, one can discern a conflict between heuristic and reproductive imitation, between history as freedom and history as ceremonial repetition. The Ciceronian (Cortesi, Bembo, Longueil, Erasmus's Nosoponus) is inclined to believe in pure repeatability, in imitation as secular ritual, and to reduce by implication anachronistic distance. The anti-Ciceronian (Poliziano, Giovanfrancesco Pico, Erasmus) is inclined to deny the sacred status of the original text and to stress the creative freedom of the imitator, a freedom which is inescapable given the fact of cultural change. This dimension is present in the exchange that concerns us, but in the letter of Cortesi there are hints of a movement away from any concern with history, however understood. There is in fact already here in germ that massive shift of emphasis from imitation of texts to imitation of "nature" which would gradually take place over the course of the cinquecento. We can watch this shift acted out in two successive sentences. Cortesi has just stated that he prefers to be an ape of Cicero than a student of anybody else. But there is a great difference between wishing to imitate someone and no one.

> Ego autem statuo non modo in eloquentia, sed in aliis etiam artibus necessariam esse imitationem. Nam et omnis doctrina ex antecedenti cognitione paratur, et nihil est in mente quin fuerit prius in sensibus perceptum.
> [I hold imitation to be necessary not only in eloquence but also in the other arts. All knowledge is based on an antecedent cognition; there is nothing in the mind which has not first been perceived by the senses.][20]

The pivotal word is "antecedent" (antecedenti). Is this the antecedence of a model anterior in time or the antecedence of sensory to mental apprehension? Cortesi has it a little both ways. Cicero in any case deserves to be the unique model of all writers because his preeminence attains the flawless wealth of nature itself, a higher, perfected, ideal nature. To take this direction is to dehistoricize Cicero and suppress the etiological passage from his particular moment to the present. It is to bypass that moment of philological savoring which places the text at its unique and proper distance. It is also implicitly to redefine the risk of anachronism—not as a failure of the historical imagination but as a failure of skill to reach an enduring standard. In this incipient reinterpretation of imitation a certain diachronic sensibility stands threatened and another crisis begins to gather.

Thus along with the familiar anxiety of estrangement, so acute in Poliziano, the quarrel over imitation at the close of his life signals a potential crisis of assimilation and another of historicism itself. In his letter, all three seem to be mastered with an imperturbable and arrogant assurance that in his own image might be called leonine. This is curious, almost ironic, since the same issues join to create the troubled fascination of his poetry.

2

Poliziano's richest and most important poem, the *Stanze cominciate per la giostra di Giuliano de' Medici*, seems to have been intended originally as a celebration of the victory in a civic tournament by Lorenzo's younger brother. It would also have dramatized Giuliano's interest in a young woman then living in Florence, Simonetta Vespucci. But the ill-starred poem had to change its notes to tragic or apocalyptic when Simonetta died in 1476, a year after the tournament; and when Giuliano himself was murdered during the Pazzi conspiracy of 1478, the poet must have abandoned any thought of completing it. The *Stanze* remain a marvelous fragment of less than two books, but even as a fragment arguably the poetic summit of the quattrocento. Before its composition, earlier poems about civic tournaments had begun to constitute a kind of emergent subgenre, but the *Stanze*, far more ambitious in every sense, bear little resemblance to them. I give here the summary of the poem contained in the admirable introduction by David Quint to his translation of the poem.

> After invocations to Love, and to Lorenzo the Laurel (Book I, stanzas 1–7), the action of the poem opens in a pseudo-classical landscape around Florence. Here Giuliano, his name Latinized to Julio (Julius), lives as a hunter, close to nature. An adolescent, he is ignorant of love, and an angry Cupid decides to punish him for his mockery of lovers (8–24). As Julio enters a forest to hunt, the god places a white doe in his path (25–32). Giving chase to the animal, Julio comes to a clearing where the deer vanishes and a beautiful "nymph" appears in its place (33–37). She reveals her name, Simonetta; she is married and lives in Florence (38–54). She leaves and Julio returns home a changed man, desperately in love (55–57). The rest of Book I is taken up with a description of the garden and palace of Venus on Cyprus; its primary literary source is Claudian's *Epithalamium*. Poliziano has added the description of the doors sculpted by Vulcan with their mythological scenes of love (97–119). Cupid, meantime, flies back to the garden where he finds his mother on her couch with Mars (120–25).
> In Book II, Cupid discusses with Venus the amorous fate of Laurel and Julio. He will take pity on Laurel, who has been faithful to the rule of love. But Julio will have to prove himself in battle in order to gain the hand of Simonetta (II, 1–15). Venus sends out the little cupids to wound all the noble young men of Florence and make them eager to bear arms for love (16–21). Meanwhile she dispatches Pasithea to obtain a dream from the god of sleep (22–26). The dream is intended for Julio: in a vision that owes much to Petrarch's "Triumph of Chastity," he sees Simonetta overpower Cupid and tie him to Minerva's olive tree, apparently symbolizing a victory of chastity and

reason over love. The goddess Glory then descends and disarms Simonetta. Glory and Julio fly off to the field of battle, where Julio carries the day. But on his return he finds Simonetta enveloped in a dark cloud. She emerges as Fortune and as his personal Genius to govern his life and eternalize them both (27–37). On awakening, Julio prays to Minerva, Glory, and Cupid for victory, both in battle and in love (38–46). Here the poem abruptly stops, never reaching the action of the tournament itself.[21]

Before we consider the language in which this abortive story is told, something needs to be said about the *mundus significans* Italian poetry could draw upon in 1475. Precisely a century had passed since the deaths of Petrarch (1374) and Boccaccio (1375), a century dominated by the medium of prose and the prestige of Latin. Vernacular poetry had been largely limited to popular modes, to carnival songs, *ballate, rispetti, canzoni a ballo*, in drama the *sacre rappresentazioni*, or else the raucous proletarian compositions of a Domenico Burchiello. The energies of the classicizing humanist Latin culture were out of touch with the popular vernacular energy. And when in 1441 a kind of contest was organized in Florence (the *certame coronaria*) for vernacular poems in a formal style on a set subject (true friendship), the results in their stiffness and frigidity betrayed this segregation of energy. A serious vernacular idiom had to be reinvented, beginning with what was available: ancient Latin and Neo-Latin texts, medieval Provençal and Italian, Dante, Petrarch, Boccaccio, and the popular modes. For Poliziano as for few others one may add to this short list the corpus of extant Greek poetry. No single body of texts in this list constituted a living vernacular canon on which a humanistically trained poet could build. In the absence of a wholly original genius, some form of syncretic verbal imagination was needed to establish a viable Italian voice. In the work of that gifted dilettante, Lorenzo de' Medici, one can trace a process of restless experimentation drawing in turn on each available tradition but failing to produce any single work of indisputable authority. The very prestige of Latin poetry, together with the prestige of the *tre corone* of the trecento, did not simplify the task of reinvention. It was a task at the broad generic level but also at the local verbal and rhetorical level. The *Stanze* are the first poem of the century that might truly be said to have solved the problem.

The *Stanze* are in fact profoundly eclectic. The language owes most doubtless to Petrarch, but to the poet of the *Trionfi* rather than the *Canzoniere*, which means that the oxymoron is no longer the radical trope. There *is* no such trope, or rather this trope is simply conflation—*contaminatio*. In a certain sense, the *Stanze* represent the perfect example of that magisterial assimilation to be celebrated much later in the letter to Cortesi. We can take as an example the opening of a stanza describing nightfall after Giuliano's meeting with Simonetta, a stanza whose imagery will be in part familiar.

La notte che le cose ci nasconde
tornava ombrata di stellato ammanto,
e l'usignuol sotto l'amate fronde
cantando ripetea l'antico pianto;

ma sola a' sua lamenti Ecco risponde,
ch'ogni altro augel quetato avea già 'l canto;
dalla chimmeria valle uscian le torme
de' Sogni negri con diverse forme. [1.60]
[Night that hides the world from us was returning, covered by a starry mantle, and the nightingale, singing under her beloved branches, repeated her old lament; but only Echo answered her weeping, for by now every other bird had stilled its song: the swarms of black Dreams came out of the Cimmerian valley in their different forms.][22]

Poliziano's readers were not expected to miss the faint presence of Petrarch's sonnet 311 ("Quel rosignuol . . .") in lines 3–4, and even that sonnet's subtext from the *Georgics*. But the opening line is taken verbatim from Dante's *Paradiso*. Is it an accident that in that context also one finds an image of a mother bird and her young? Poliziano's commentators appear not to have noticed that his phrase "amate fronde" in line 3 is drawn as well from the same passage, a long simile that warms the young birds with a maternal presence Petrarch and Virgil deny them.

Come l'augello, intro l'amate fronde,
  posato al nido de' suoi dolci nati
  la notte che le cose ci nasconde,
che, per veder li aspetti disiati
  e per trovar lo cibo onde li pasca,
  in che gravi labor li sono aggrati,
previene il tempo in su aperta frasca,
  e con ardente affetto il sole aspetta . . . [*Par.* 23. 1–8]
[As the bird among the loved branches, having sat on the nest of her sweet brood through the night that hides things from us, anticipates the time on the open spray that she may see their longed-for looks and find the food to nourish them for which her heavy toils are welcome to her, and with ardent longing awaits the sun. . .]

As this bird awaits the sun, so Beatrice awaits the vision of the eighth sphere. It is an image of solicitous love, of hospitable retreat, of joyful suspense and nascent radiance, but Poliziano has chosen that single line which in isolation might be read negatively as an image of absence. The Dantesque passage is contaminated in line 2 with a phrase from Claudian's *De raptu Proserpinae*.

stat pronuba iuxta
stellantes Nox picta sinus tangensque cubile
omina perpetuo genitalia foedere sancit. [2.362–64]
[Night clad in starry raiment, stands by her as her brideswoman; she touches the couch and blesses the union of marriage with a bond that cannot be broken.][23]

This is the culminating moment, terrible and majestic, of that dark epic, also unfinished, which completes the rape of the girl and consummates her wedding in the bed of the chthonic god. Poliziano substitutes for the ornamental Latin "picta" (dressed in embroidery) the somewhat unexpected "ombrata"—covered or shadowed (can night be shadowed by stars?), which weakens faintly the stellar brilliance. The Dantesque image of serene repose is not altogether violated by the recall of Claudian, since the wedding in his poem suspends death on earth and torture in the underworld, bringing a simulacrum of epithalamic reassurance to the frightened bride. But the element of rape is nonetheless sustained by Poliziano's allusion to the Philomela story in line 4. All of these subtexts hover on the border of consciousness as the humanist reader takes in this evocation of a solemn, tranquil, and restful twilight haunted by ghosts of violence and loss. The subtexts are like those echoes of the nightingale heard in line 5, which also introduces the Ovidian story of Echo and Narcissus (already present earlier in the antierotic taunts of the virginal Giuliano, which draw on the *Metamorphoses*). Or else the subtexts glimmer dimly like the diverse, confusing shapes in lines 7–8 issuing from the Homeric Cimmerian vales, darkening with illusions and half-shades the linear purity of the description. This flood of black dreams at the close of the stanza works to reinterpret retrospectively the first line, suggesting a more sinister concealment of things, a redefinition of a Dantesque paradisiac composure by a pagan Erebean insubstantiality. The muted play of subtexts partakes of this Erebean vagueness, but it is nonetheless essential to the magisterial subtlety of the poet's art. If the intertextual play were suppressed, little would be left.

In this conflative alchemy lie at once the brilliance and the limits of the poet's creative achievement. It rests on an art of eclectic assimilation that can only yield itself to and only absorb other texts. The historical pretext of the poem, the tournament, is delayed; the historical figure Giuliano de' Medici is scarcely recognizable in the character Julio. The real substance of the poem is a tissue of subtexts.[24] The *Stanze* compose a mosaic, each of whose stones is likely to prove a tiny composite of still smaller elements. The effect of this subtle and haunting intercontamination of a hundred subtexts is a kind of alchemical quintessence of the European poetic tradition. What the *Stanze* do not give us is a sense of transformation; there is no sense of a modern sensibility or moral style into which the past is reborn. The rhetoric is purely conflational and thus purely synchronic; historical process is excluded because there is no visible *terminus ad quem*. The historicity of the word is exorcised by a kind of miracle of simultaneity that abolishes anachronism and seems to deny all loss. The ideal would appear to be a kind of Utopian plenum of the past, an ideal that leads in practice to a vacuum of the modern. There is no continuous itinerary because a modern *modus significandi* is not established; what might be a modern idiom only allows itself to be glimpsed or triangulated intermittently. Anachronism is controlled, not by a denial of distance, which would be neomedieval, but by a homogenization of specific alterities.

In the presence of certain Ovidian subtexts there emerges a kind of irony that may have escaped the poet's control. The young Julio, in his disdain for love and his pleasure in the hunt, recalls Euripides' Hippolytus, but in his proud and self-sufficient rejection of erotic advances, he recalls two figures in the *Metamorphoses*. The stanza that presents this rejection:

Ah quante ninfe per lui sospirorno!
Ma fu sí altero semple il giovinetto,
che mai le ninfe amanti nol piegorno,
mai poté riscaldarsi il freddo petto.
Facea sovente pe' boschi soggiorno,
inculto semple e rigido in aspetto. . . .   [1.10]
[How many nymphs signed for him! But the amorous nymphs could never make the
arrogant boy yield, nor could his cold breast be warmed. He often made his home in the
forest, always unkempt and hardened in aspect.]

is indebted both to Ovid's story of Narcissus:

Multi illum iuvenes, multae cupiere puellae;
sed (fuit in tenera tam dura superbia forma)
nulli illum iuvenes, nullae tetigere puellae.   [3.353–55][25]
[Many youths and many maidens sought his love; but in that slender form was pride so
cold that no youth, no maiden touched his heart.]

and his story of Daphne:

Protinus alter amat; fugit altera nomen amantis;
silvarum latebris captivarumque ferarum
exuviis gaudens innuptaeque aemula Phoebes;
vitta coercebat positos sine lege capillos.
Multi illam petiere; illa, aversata petentes,
impatiens expersque viri nemora avia lustrat
nec quid Hymen, quid Amor, quid sint conubia, curat.   [1.474–80]
[Straightway he burned with love; but she fled the very name of love, rejoicing in the
deep fastnesses of the woods, and in the spoils of beasts which she had snared, vying
with the virgin Phoebe. A single fillet bound her locks all unarranged. Many sought
her; but she, averse to all suitors, impatient of control and without thought for man,
roamed the pathless woods, nor cared at all what Hymen, love, or wedlock might be.]

But these Ovidian antecedents can only underscore the absence of a resolution in
the *Stanze* comparable to those of the *Metamorphoses*. In the fates of Narcissus and
Daphne, as in those of so many other Ovidian figures, the metamorphosis out of
the human represents doubtless a loss but nonetheless a solution that integrates the
creature into a dynamic, living cosmos. But in the *Stanze* this integration is
lacking. Julio is not convincingly metamorphosed after his meeting with Simonetta within the abortive narrative as we have it. In book 1 we scarcely see him after
this meeting, and in book 2 he is fragmented emblematically between Cupid,
Pallas, Gloria, Fortuna, and Simonetta herself. Time and Death, which enter the
poem in its opening stanza, are felt to be present and to share in this decomposition. He is presented in an original state followed by a passage that is then aborted
by a dispersal. This is analogous to the destiny of the word in the poem's verbal
texture. There is an origin, say in Ovid, which is left behind by the word's passage
into the surface text, but the end of the passage is a contamination with Euripides
or Petrarch or Claudian.

If the *Stanze* have in fact any single major subtext, it is the epithalamion by Claudian entitled "De nuptiis Honorii Augustii," composed for the marriage of the emperor Honorius. The flight of Cupid to his mother's palace, followed by a description of her palace and garden, was a central element of the later Roman epithalamion, beginning with Statius; Poliziano's version is especially close to Claudian's and in some stanzas imitates it closely. (He shared a taste for the poetry of the later empire with Huysmans' Des Esseintes.) Poliziano's descriptive prolixity, like Claudian's, tends to clog the narrative, and his mythographic vision, like Claudian's, tends to dwarf the historical pretext. But Poliziano's sensibility is the subtler, his control of detail more discriminating; insofar as his poem succeeds in distancing itself at all from this major subtext, the passage traversed is felt as a movement toward a more fastidious refinement.

Both poems take their occasion from a public event that has been to some degree degraded. Honorius's marriage, at a late stage of imperial decadence, brought him as bride Maria, daughter of the Vandal general Stilicho, whom he would later have murdered. The civic tournament at Florence was won in 1469 by Lorenzo and in 1475 by Giuliano; emptied of its chivalric function and of genuine competition, the *giostra* had become a frivolous entertainment designed to enhance Medici prestige. It diverted energies harmlessly away from the kind of civic contention that during the commune had had tangible political results. Poliziano's intended mythicization of the *giostra*, like Claudian's apotheosis of the emperor's wedding, served clear political ends. This fact does not in itself discredit either poem as an art work—it is equally true of the *Aeneid*—but it means that the relation of myth to history would pose an artistic problem requiring a solution. In the fragmentary work as we have it, the problem remains unresolved, the *giostra* remains unwritten, and history makes itself felt precisely as that force which in actuality cut short the poem.

The opposition between creativity and violence remained the organizing theme throughout Poliziano's career. His philological labor counted as a contribution to culture in its perennial struggle against time the destroyer. In his long verse celebration of poetry, *Nutricia*, that art is given to men to redeem them from bestial savagery and lead them to civilized concord. But in the drama *Orfeo*, the poet is hideously dismembered by the wild fury of the Bacchantes. In the *Stanze*, the civilizing power of creative language is displaced onto the power of creative love: the antisocial, narcissistic Julio, whose predatory wildness betrays itself during the hunt, is meant to be tamed and civilized by his encounter with Simonetta. The mythographic emblem of this process will appear when Amore finds the head of a tamed Mars in the lap of Venus.[26] The creative principle seems victorious in this first book, but in the apocalyptic presentiments of violence in book 2, this victory is menaced with a reversal. The struggle of government, love, and letters, arranged paratactically, against fortune, death, and time, is actually introduced in the poem's opening stanza.

Le gloriose pompe e' fieri ludi
della città che 'l freno allenta e stringe
a' magnanimi Toschi, e i regni crudi
di quella dea che 'l terzo ciel dipinge,
e i premi degni alli onorati studi,
la mente audace a celebrar mi spinge,
sí che i gran nomi e i fatti egregi e soli
fortuna o morte or tempo non involi. [1.1]

[My daring mind urges me to celebrate the glorious pageants and the proud games of the city that bridles and gives rein to the magnanimous Tuscans, the cruel realms of the goddess who adorns the third heaven, and the rewards merited by honorable pursuits; in order that fortune, death, or time may not despoil great names and unique and eminent deeds.]

This struggle remains dominant throughout the poem[27] and, most significantly for our purposes, it affects the status of language. The word seems to strain toward the perpetuity of universal myth, the permanence of the myths sculpted outside Venus's palace. By offering a quintessence of European poetry, it reaches toward the repose of an eternalized history. From a certain perspective, it achieves this repose. Yet this achievement remains precarious, partly because the force of violent change obtrudes itself in the apocalyptic and truncated ending, partly because the integrity of the word depends on a tissue of fragments, partly because the status of the mythic itself has to be seen as anything but secure.

We can trace this insecurity in the copula of the *Stanze*. After taking in, along with the reader, the haunting and miraculous apparition of Simonetta, Julio addresses her:

O qual che tu ti sia, vergin sovrana,
o ninfa o dea, ma dea m'assembri certo . . . [1.49]

["Whatever you are, o sovereign virgin, nymph or goddess, but certainly you seem a goddess to me . . ."]

The reader may well echo this question: what in fact *is* she? The dramatic immediacy of the question is qualified by its Virgilian and Homeric associations, just as the long, exquisite portrait has interwoven phrases from Theocritus, Petrarch, Cavalcanti, Horace, Claudian, Dante, and Boccaccio. The very intricacy of allusion cannot fail to affect the ontological status of this figure, however fresh and distinct she emerges on the page. The young hunter has been led to her as he follows a chimerical stag fashioned by Amore; at the crucial moment the stag vanishes and the girl appears. Something of the magical does cling to her, despite her protests that she is simply a married woman, born in Genoa, who enjoys straying in the forest to gather flowers. Despite her disclaimers, Giuliano's address seems appropriate: there *is* something virginal, nymphlike, even immortal about her aura, something also of the Venus of the Virgilian subtext. The poet chooses not to resolve this tension between the extratextual Signora Vespucci and the prefiguration of that goddess whose person and palace he is shortly to evoke. History is in conflict with myth, and the conflict can be located precisely in that subjunctive copula: "qual che tu ti *sia.*" On which side of the conflict lies "reality"? The *Nutricia,* written much later, would assert that poetry lies at the origin of human development through time; poetry is the source of what man now *is.* But the *Stanze* transform what is into an artifice which insists on itself as artifice, as *literature,* and implicitly denies the process of becoming. There is a pressure on the copula not to let in too much. Thus one can speak of *vergin* as a "mistranslation" of Virgil's *virgo.*

At the culmination of book 1 this removal from the referential world is doubled by a second removal, in the long description of the mythographic bas-reliefs adorning the portals of Venus's palace. These represent first the birth of Venus and then other mythical stories of the loves of gods and men, descending gradually to the grotesque comedy of the clumsy Cyclops Polyphemus. Nothing is more true than these reliefs, writes the poet: "né 'l vero stesso ha piú del ver che questo" (119) (truth itself has not more truth than this). Yet it is striking that the cosmic vision of divine love and its descent has to be mediated by these immobile panels. The bourgeois earthly plane where the narrative began has yielded to the quasi-mythic Simonetta, who yields in turn to the fully mythic garden in its Lucretian vitality, which yields finally to the static mythography in stone. Each successive plane is rendered limpidly and impeccably, but we are left to ask whether their succession leads up toward a firmer Platonic truth, or simply and duplicitously away from that force of destruction which remains, scandalously, the ultimate actuality. If integration is the goal of the letter to Cortesi, the *Stanze* seem to function by a serial segregation.

Thus the stream of subtexts into the present of this surface text is diverted and broken up not only by its contaminative allusiveness but by its metaphysical insecurity. The imitative art of the *Stanze* does not, like the *Canzoniere,* act out a fall but rather a dispersal. Its great poetry does not yet rest on a robust intuition of cultural passage that would permit steady, completed etiological itineraries from past to present within the single text. Much less does it permit the courageous assumption of mutual, dialectical criticism. Humanist poetry would never be more exquisite, but it would become more open to the power of diachronic tides.

3

The theme of personal wholeness once assumed a ghastly vividness in Poliziano's experience, according to his own history of the Pazzi conspiracy. That account does not spare the reader the most atrocious details of the Florentine mob's revenge upon the conspirators, including the mutilation of their bodies both before and after death. Mutilation seems to have extended even to dismemberment, since in one grisly passage the head of a man is said to be carried on a pike to the Medici palace and on another pike a man's shoulder. The body of Jacopo de' Pazzi is subjected to the outrage of a double disinterment: first from the sacred ground where it had originally been buried and then later by a troop of children who dug it up again, dragged it through the city, and threw it finally in the Arno.[28] Thus the necromantic metaphor had a terrible reality for Poliziano during this pivotal series of events, as did the image of dismemberment, an image that would become obsessive and can be traced throughout his work.

It has been noted that the outrages of the conspiracy's aftermath reappear at the close of the *Orfeo*, probably written two years later.[29] There one of the Bacchantes urges her companions to rip Orpheus's heart from his breast, runs off stage, returns with the singer's head, and describes for the audience the circumstances of his death.

> Oh oh, oh oh, morto è lo scelerato!
> Eú oè, Bacco! Bacco, i' ti ringrazio.
> Per tutto 'l bosco l'abbiamo stracciato
> tal ch'ogni sterpo è del suo sangue sazio;
> l'abbiamo a membro a membro lacerato
> in molti pezi con crudele strazio:
> or vadi e biasmi la teda legitima!
> Eú oè, Bacco, accetta questa vittima. [ll. 365–72]
>
> [Oh oh, oh oh, the villain is dead. Eu oe, Bacchus! Bacchus, I thank you. We have mangled him throughout the wood, so that every bush is replete with his blood; we have torn him apart in many pieces, member by member, in cruel agony. Let anyone now reject the nuptial torch of legitimate marriage [as Orpheus had done]. Eu oe, Bacchus, accept this victim.]

The account of Orpheus's death in Ovid is longer but the details of his dismemberment less graphic; for these, Poliziano had to return to the Greek of Euripides' savage *Bacchae*. In the *Orfeo* the horror inflicted on Giuliano's murderers is displaced onto the archetypal poet, who confronted Death with courage and art. That confrontation repeats the perennial opposition of creation and destruction, civilization and violence, reenacted so often in Poliziano's imagination, and it is punished with the terrible *sparagmos* that denies wholeness even to the singer's corpse.

This repetition of history in the fate of Orfeo has been pointed out, but what to my knowledge has not been noticed is the vulnerability of the text as well as the creator to dismemberment. This common destiny is in fact the theme of the prefatory epistle to the *Orfeo*. There the author reports that this little drama was written hurriedly and that he would have preferred to destroy it after its composition, just as the ancient Spartans exposed a boy who was sickly or imperfectly formed. He would have preferred, he says, that this daughter immediately be torn up, just as Orfeo was himself (". . . fusse di subito, non altrimenti che esso Orfeo, lacerata.")[30] However, he explains, others prevailed upon him to let his offspring live. In another writer this analogy might be taken as merely a graceful witticism, but it cannot here because its obsessive character in the poet's canon is too patent. In the preface to the *Raccolta Aragonese*, written *before* the Pazzi rebellion, two prestigious texts are already said to have been once dismembered: namely the Homeric poems, which circulated only in fragments before their resurrection, reintegration, and reedition under Pisistratus. That ruler thus plays the metaphoric roles of both necromancer and Aesculapian healer.

> Né questo poeta . . . sarebbe in tanto onore e fama salito, se da uno clarissimo ateniese non fusse stato di terra in alto sublevato, anzi quasi da morte a sí lunga vita restituto. Imperocché, essendo la sacra opera di questo celebratissimo poeta dopo la sua morte per molti e vari luoghi della Grecia dissipata e quasi dimembrata, Pisistrato, ateniese principe, . . . proposti amplissimi premi a chi alcuni de' versi omerici gli apportassi, con somma diligenzia ed essamine tutto il corpo del santissimo poeta insieme raccolse, e sí come a quello dette perpetua vita, cosí lui a se stesso immortal gloria e clarissimo splendore acquistonne.[31]
>
> [This poet would not have risen to such veneration and fame, if an illustrious Athenian had not elevated him on high from the earth, as though restored to a long life from death. For since the divine work of this most renowned poet was scattered and so to speak dismembered after his death in many different parts of Greece, Pisistratus, the prince of Athens, . . . having promised generous rewards to anyone who would bring him lines by Homer, re-assembled the entire body of the sacred poet with extreme care and the closest scrutiny, thus at once giving him perpetual life and winning for himself immortal glory and supreme honor.]

By the end of this passage the body of the poet becomes indistinguishable from his work. Homer is restored to wholeness by the life-giving reintegration of his poems. He had suffered in death the *dispersal* that death imposes, the fate of Osiris, which is the common lot of poets and their poems. Both can be put together again only by the divine labor of the Isis-figure, the civilizer, the statesman, the philologist, the creator, who miraculously refits the mangled fragments into unity.

This passage from the preface ghostwritten by Poliziano to an anthology of other men's poems leads in several directions, into a network of narratives, images, and motifs forming together a personal myth, the inner drama of Poliziano's imagination, which will incidentally clarify what for him was subsumed by the act of imitation. The Pisistratus story leads most obviously to the figure of Lorenzo, supposed author of the preface, himself a civilizer, a creator, a gatherer of pieces as in the gathering of the *Raccolta*. In a Latin epigram, Poliziano represents the Florentine state as having been maimed, mutilated, a trunk without branches or a torso without a head, until Lorenzo completed it.

> Ante erat informis, Laurens, tua patria truncus,
>   Nunc habet ecce suum, te tribuente, caput.[32]

Thus the healing of a dismemberment is a political act, a response to the disper-
sions of mobocracy. But it is also a philological act, in the broadest Viconian sense
as well as the narrowest and most professional. Pisistratus was coping with the
heartbreak of textual mutilation by history as Poliziano while still an adolescent
wanted to cope. Here he is at eighteen, writing on the last page of his corrected
edition of Catullus.

> Catullum Veronensem librariorum inscitia corruptum, multo labore multisque
> vigiliis, quantum in me fuit, emendavi, cumque eius poete plurimos textus contulis-
> sem, in nullum profecto incidi, qui non itidem ut meus esset corruptissimus.
> [After much labor and many sleepless nights, I have corrected as best I could this work
> of Catullus Veronensis, corrupted by the incompetence of copyists; although I have
> collated a great many texts, I have found none which was less thoroughly corrupt than
> my own.] [33]

When all editions are faulty and divergently faulty, the *textus* lacks integrity and
the word lacks security, the acculturating word which is the fountainhead of all
civilization and all knowledge. (After the gift of poetry to men in the *Nutricia*, the
mind itself is finally restored to itself: "mens sibi tandem sic reddita mens est.")
Thus the philological act of healing is at once political and metaphysical, since it
repairs real substances against time the mutilator. This high function of
Pisistratus-Aesculapius is also assumed in Poliziano's lifetime by the book dealer
and copier Vespasiano da Bisticci.

> . . . deus veluti Cressis, Epidaurius herbis
>   Extintum patri reddidit Androgeon,
> Sic tu, quos rapuit nobis cariosa vetustas,
>   Restituis Latio, Vespasiane, viros;
> Per te Lethaeos iam spernit Graecia fluctus,
>   Nec metuit Stygium Romula lingua deum.
> Felix, cui liceat revocare in lumina vitae
>   Mortua priscorum tot monumenta virum,
> Felix, cui liceat sanctorum nomina vatum
>   Perdita flammatis eripuisse rogis.[34]
> [As the god of Epidaurus, by means of Cretan herbs, restored the dead Androgeon to his
> father, so you, Vespasian, restore to Latium those whom decrepit age has carried off.
> Because of you, Greece can now disdain the waters of Lethe, nor does the language of
> Romulus fear the god of the Styx. Happy the man who can recall to the light of the
> living so many dead monuments of the ancients; happy he who has been able to snatch
> from the flaming pyre the lost names of divine poets.]

In this early elegy the necromancer and the Epidaurian healer (Aesculapius) of the
mangled Hippolytus become the heroic defiers of consuming time on the pyre of
universal history.

The preface to the *Raccolta*, the epigram, and the elegy quoted all represent a
successful accomplishment of reintegration. In these texts the healing civilizer is
allowed to glimpse the goal that the *Manto* sets for Virgil: eternity. The whole

word and the whole creator endure forever; Orpheus overcomes Pluto. But in many other writings the outcome is less happy. In the Christian works of Poliziano, only Christ is able to survive dismemberment. For man without him, life is nothing but a swift race to death. Christ put on humanity by permitting his body to be torn: "tutto il corpo suo lacero, tutto flagellato, tutto piagato e sanguinoso" (his whole body lacerated, whipped everywhere, everywhere wounded and bloody).[35] But the ultimate mystery of Christ is the miracle whereby his body retains its wholeness in the dispersion of the Eucharist.

> Christo uno è tutto in uno tempo in diversi luoghi, . . . e persevera in sè stesso immutabile e invariabile sanza patire alcuna contaminazione o diminuzione nel partimento de l'ostia, anzi in ciascheduna delle parti tutto intero e perfetto, come lo specchio in sè stesso e nelle sue parti, si manifesta![36]
> [Christ is entire simultaneously in various places, . . . and remains immutable and invariable in himself without suffering any contamination or diminution in the division of the host; rather he reveals himself to be whole and perfect in each part, like a mirror in itself and its pieces.]

The infinite multiplication of the parts of Christ's body fails to diminish or contaminate it. In Christ there is no need for reintegration. But the apter image for men who suffer "questa nostra umana miseria che ha nome vita" (this human misery which is called life) [37] is the comic and hideous crufixion of the *Scabies*, the eczema celebrated in that brilliant, intolerable antihymn to the humiliation of the purulent body. At the culmination of his agony, as his body disintegrates in suppuration, the victim wears a grimacing mask almost akin to a repellent smile, but then breaks into a scream like the cries of a Bacchant: "euchyon eu oe!"[38] The dismemberer and dismembered fuse in this fantastic play with disgust.

The reliefs before Venus's palace in the *Stanze* begin with a Hesiodic Ur-dismemberment that sets in motion the action of the rest. Cronus's castration of his father Uranus leads to the birth of Venus, which then leads to the series of erotic legends arranged in a more or less descending order. Is there a paradox in this birth of the creative principle out of that violence the poet characteristically opposes to it? One resolution of this apparent paradox was suggested by Edgar Wind, who interpreted the birth of Venus both in Poliziano and Botticelli by means of Piconian philosophy.

> The unpleasant machinery of the myth, which is far remote from Botticelli, will seem less pedantic and far-fetched when it is understood that "dismemberment" is a regular figure of speech in the Neoplatonic dialectic. The castration of Uranus is of one type with the dismemberment of Osiris, Attis, Dionysus, all of which signify the same mystery to the neo-Orphic theologians: for whenever the supreme One descends to the Many, this act of creation is imagined as a sacrificial agony, as if the One were cut to pieces and scattered. Creation is conceived in this way as a cosmogonic death, by which the concentrated power of one deity is offered up and dispersed: but the descent and diffusion of the divine power are followed by its resurrection, when the many are "recollected" into the One.[39]

There are several reasons for doubting that this metaphysics holds the key to Poliziano's castration. The young poet of the *Stanze* had not yet fallen under the spell of Pico, nor indeed under the spell of any philosophy. It is also worth noting that the victim of dismemberment in the most accessible ancient sources (Plutarch and Macrobius)[40] was Dionysius, whose dismemberment Poliziano fails to represent anywhere. More tellingly, the first result of Uranus's castration in the *Stanze* is the birth of bloodthirsty Furies and Giants; this is only complemented subsequently by the birth of Venus.

> nell'una è insculta la 'nfelice sorte
> del vecchio Celio; e in vista irato pare
> suo figlio, e colla falce adunca sembra
> tagliar del padre le feconde membra.

> Ivi la Terra con distesi ammanti
> par ch'ogni goccia di quel sangue accoglia,
> onde nate le Furie e' fier Giganti
> di sparger sangue in vista mostron voglia. . . .   [1.97, 98]

[On one is sculpted the unhappy fate of old Celius; his son appears, angry in countenance, and with a curved scythe seems to cut away the fertile members of his father.

There the Earth with her outstretched mantles seems to gather up every drop of that blood, whence are born the Furies and fierce Giants, who show desire in their faces for bloodshed.]

Love and violence are born from this original mutilation, which thus cannot be read tendentiously as the transfiguration of flux by form. Venus cannot be regarded in any case as pure beauty or pure form; there is incipient violence in her own garden.

> E mughianti giovenchi a piè del colle
> fan vie piú cruda e dispietata guerra,
> col collo e il petto insanguinato e molle,
> spargendo al ciel co' piè l'erbosa terra.
> Pien di sanguigna schiuma el cinghial bolle
> le larghe zanne arruota e il grifo serra,
> e rugghia e raspa e, per piú armar sue forze,
> frega il calloso cuoio a dure scorze.   [1.86]

[At the foot of the hill, bellowing young bulls wage a much more brutal and pitiless war, with breast and neck wet and bloody, their hooves scattering the grassy earth to the sky. The boar boils with bloody foam, grinds his huge tusks, and shuts his snout; he roars and rasps, and, to arm himself further, he chafes his calloused hide against rough bark.]

The displacement of civilizing creativity on to Venerian fecundity involves a certain compromise with Mars. The descent into multiplicity is never creative for Poliziano; it is precisely that which terrifies him.

The image of dismemberment throughout his oeuvre is too protean and too suggestive to be reduced to a single version even by the seductive Neoplatonic metaphysics. If one looks for an intuitive conception of creation, it would tend to correspond to the second phase of the Neoplatonic cycle, to the recollection of the many into unity. The author of the *Stanze* may not have believed in the Macrobian or Ficinian One, but he seems to have believed instinctively in that spiritual innutrition which repairs patiently, endlessly, the immense mangled cadaver of the past. This is the great vocation of poetic imagination. Consciously or semiconsciously Poliziano believed in that assimilation which in the letter to Cortesi is the prerequisite for self-expression. If history begins with a divine maiming, then to match the furies and barbarians engendered the civilizer must become a lion or a bull, autonomous and proud guardians in this letter, solitary and whole.

It is the *horror fragmenti* that most truly illuminates Poliziano's contaminative imitation. The world left to itself would treat all texts as it treated the Homeric poems, as the Bacchantes treated Orpheus. It would undermine and disintegrate the word; it would produce the abominable manuscripts that defy all skill, or it would rend the text to pieces and drown it beyond the necromancer's power. Poetry in the face of this centrifugal power can only be a force of recollection. Imitative poetry is the supreme medium of the artistic vocation that receives by giving itself and fuses in receiving. Each circumstantial particularity of each verbal shard, of each broken subtext, is dissolved within the whole, even if for the philologist the apprehension of that particularity has required a career of labor. The assimilated word is dehistoricized and so protected; anachronism is smoothed away.

The portrait of Simonetta is a palimpsest of so many poems that their blurred cross-hatching serves to heighten her supratemporal reality.

Folgoron gli occhi d'un dolce sereno,
ove sue face tien Cupido ascose;
l'aier d'intorno si fa tutto ameno
ovunque gira le luce amorose.
Di celeste letizia il volto ha pieno,
dolce dipinto di ligustri e rose;
ogni aura tace al suo parlar divino,
e canta ogni augelletto in suo latino.   [1.44]
[From her eyes there flashes a honeyed calm in which Cupid hides his torch; wherever she turns those amorous eyes, the air about her becomes serene. Her face, sweetly painted with privet and roses, is filled with heavenly joy; every breeze is hushed before her divine speech, and every little bird sings out in its own language.]

This is only one of five stanzas that compose the portrait, yet for it alone the commentators [41] multiply subtexts so densely that the layers of allusion and topos require no simple archaeology. The first line in itself fuses Propertius, Ovid, Claudian, Horace, and Petrarch; the last line Cavalcanti, Salvini, Arnaut Daniel, and the anonymous author of *L'Intelligenza*. Petrarch, Dante, and Claudian haunt the intervening lines, and the itinerary of the topos in line 2 leads through too many texts to be counted. This integrating structure is Poliziano's artistic response to his own historical solitude. Simonetta exists as talismanic artifact against the demon of estrangement. To permit a true *rite de passage*, from a particular past to a distinct, modern present, would be to leave the poem in history and thus expose it to the force of disintegration. It offers instead incomparable artifices of eternity. The Aesculapian labor triumphs again and again at the level of the stanza, even if it fails at the level of the whole. If of the two major works that have lived, the *Orfeo* is termed by its author *lacerata*, one hardly wants to press the irony in the status of its greater companion as an episodic and mutilated segment.

The struggle played out in Poliziano's mind did not subside toward the end of his abbreviated life. If anything, each of the rival voices—the affirmation of wholeness and the intuition of decomposition—achieves a firmer statement. On the one hand there is the leonine letter to Cortesi; there is also the proudest and most personal assumption of the Aesculapian role, firmly arrogated to himself by the master philologist.

> Ciceronis liber secundus de deorum natura non minus lacer in omnibus novis, vetustis etiam exemplaribus reperitur quam olim fuerit Hippolytus turbatis distractus equis; cuius deinde avulsa passim membra, sicuti fabulae ferunt, Aesculapius ille collegit, reposuit, vitae reddidit; qui tamen deinde fulmine ictus ob invidiam deorum narratur.
>
> Me vero quae nam deterrebit invidia, quod fulmen, quo minus restituere ipsum sibi coner romanae vel linguae vel philosophiae parentem, nescio equidem a quo rursus Antonio truncatum capite et manibus? Fecimus idem antea in ipsius epistolis, eaque nostra quasi dixerim redintegratio iam recepta est, quantum intelligo, videlicet excusis passim voluminibus in eam formam quam nos de vetustis exemplaribus praescripseramus.[42]
>
> [The second book of Cicero's *De deorum natura* is just as mangled in all ancient and modern manuscripts as was Hippolytus once, pulled apart by frightened horses. The legends tell how Aesculapius later gathered the torn members, pieced them together and restored them to life, for which act he is said to have been struck by lightning as a result of the gods' jealousy.
>
> But what jealousy will deter me, what lightning bolt, from daring to restore the very father of the Roman language and philosophy, whose head and hands have been lopped off again by I know not what Antony? We did this before for his correspondence, and this restoration, so to speak, of ours has now been accepted, so far as I know, in that version, clearly printed at last, which we determined on the basis of the early manuscripts.]

So reads the opening of the first section, *De divinatione*, of the fragmentary *Miscellaneorum Centuria Seconda*, restored to life by two gifted scholars within the last decade. In that strong noun *redintegratio* lies the culmination of a career. But against this strength can be set the ambiguous testimony of the late *sylva*, *Nutricia*. It is true that the official theme of this long meditation on poetry is the harmony it bestows on an erstwhile savage humanity. Yet in the catalogue of poets that occupies the bulk of the work, it is the death of each which receives most attention, and not infrequently death by aggression. One after another—Linus, Hesiod, Ovid, Lucretius, Empedocles, Gallus, Lucan, Sappho, Archilochus—all fall by the violence of their own hand or another's. And even when no violence is involved, it is the mode of death, not of poetic harmony, which most commonly appears as paramount: it is *all* we learn, for example, about the three great Athenian tragedians. Perhaps the only authentic if meager affirmation emerges from the exemplary story of Orpheus, whose head and lyre, floating down the Hebrus, continue their music after his limbs have been strewn through the fields of Thrace. This minimal continuity survives dismemberment.

But another mangled body appears in the sequel. The epigone Neanthus steals Orpheus's lyre from the temple wall where it has been laid to rest, and his inept performance draws a pack of dogs who dispatch him. The incompetent imitator parodies the master even in death. Is this an allegory to frighten Cortesi's Ciceronians? It must not in any case be applied to Cortesi's correspondent. If one looks for an emblem of his destiny, it might be found in the letter recounting the death of Lorenzo, a calamity which, says the poet, has killed any desire of his to write again. Among the portents occurring on the night of the great man's end was noted the death struggle of two great-hearted lions enclosed in a public pen, who tore at each other so fiercely that one was nearly done for and the other altogether expired.

Nine • *Sixteenth-Century Quarrels: Classicism and the Scandal of History*

The first half of the sixteenth century produced the most vigorous and sustained debate over the proper modes and goals of imitation ever witnessed on the European continent. The topic became a kind of storm center drawing into its vortex debates over the ancients and the moderns, over the *questione della lingua*, over the psychology of literary creation, over the propriety of rules, over the value of a single classic as a model rather than many, over the relation between the classics and "nature" as an object of imitative endeavor, and over the usefulness of imitative exercises as a pedagogic method. The turbulence of these debates was heightened by the fact that imitation could mean many things: the adoption of a given author's vocabulary, syntax, and stylistic mannerism, the adoption of his themes, his *sententiae*, his moral style, or the adoption of his characteristic genre with its associated topoi, or the specific adaptation of a single work. Imitation could be interpreted to refer primarily to *elocutio* or to *inventio* or to both and *dispositio* as well. At issue also were the proper power of literary tradition over artistic originality, the status of the approved canon of authors, the continuity of human genius, the relationship of signifiers to signifieds or of *verba* to *res*, and, not least, that problem of peculiar relevance, the significance of historical difference.

No study of less than book length could adequately organize all the pertinent materials; the survey that follows aims to be representative rather than complete. From our perspective the theory of imitation can be traced in its veerings toward or away from understanding the paradoxical status of the model, at once alien and accessible, separated from the imitator by a cultural divide and yet capable of partial contact through the invention of a constructed itinerary. As the sixteenth century wore on, of course, ancient culture was increasingly absorbed through the processes of education and imitation. Renaissance civilization throughout western Europe increasingly defined itself in terms of its filtered assimilation of antiquity. Even the popular, irreverent anticlassical and parodic modes have to be regarded against the background of official classicism. Thus the paradox of rupture and continuity was itself constantly altering the relation of its antithesis. Presently the threatening character of the alien would dwindle as the remote was domesticated; the risk of anachronism would shrink; the dynamism of the imitative leap would flag, and humanism would feel the hardening chill of academicism.

Two of the most interesting texts for our purposes were written near the beginning of this hardening process, during the second decade of the sixteenth century, that decade *mirabilis* which still stuns us with the titanic splendor of its greatness. The exchange of letters composed during these years between Giovanfrancesco Pico della Mirandola and Pietro Bembo on the modalities of literary imitation is rich in focal problems. Pico and Bembo frequented the same circles in Rome during the year 1512; it is likely that as a result Pico saw in manuscript an early, fragmentary version of Bembo's *Prose della volgar lingua*, that this led to conversation over the question of imitation prominent in the *Prose*, and that conversation led to Pico's essay in the form of a letter, *De imitatione*. Bembo wrote a reply to which Pico in his turn wrote a rejoinder, although this last letter was shortly forgotten.[1] In some respects this exchange can be regarded as a repetition of the Poliziano–Cortesi debate twenty years earlier, with Pico maintaining a position analogous to Poliziano's. But in fact Pico's contributions are far longer and more tightly argued than Poliziano's curt missive; they are also more firmly based in philosophical speculation. The argument against the imitation of a single master, Cicero, is now grounded in a Neoplatonic theory that would situate an Idea of absolute eloquence in each individual but would particularize this Idea according to the imperfect biases and affinities of the individual temperament. Every student, according to Pico, should expose himself to a wide spectrum of authors, subjecting each to a respectful scrutiny that recognizes his shortcomings as well as his unique strengths, and out of this eclectic reading the student should form that style congenial to his own makeup and to that particular idea of eloquence which is his own. (The question whether the Idea is innate or acquired is not fully resolved.) To choose a priori a single model is to violate this distinctive personal standard.

> Et si enim homo omnium maxime vim obtinet imitandi, . . . proprium tamen et congenitum instinctum et propensionem animi nactus est ab ipso ortu, quam frangere et aliorsum vertere est ipsam plane violare naturam. Itaque cum nostro in animo Idea quaedam et tanquam radix insit aliqua, cuius vi ad quodpiam muneris obeundum animamur, . . . colere illam potius quam incidere, amplecti quam abalienare operae-precium est. . . . [Natura] Ideam igitur ut aliarum virtutum, ita et recte loquendi subministrat, eiusque pulchritudinis affingit animo simulachrum: ad quod respicientes identidem et aliena iudicemus et nostra. Neque enim eam quisquam adhuc perfecte attigit, ut hac in re illud etiam possit dicier, nihil omni ex parte beatum; quandoquidem non uni tantum, sed omnibus et universis distribuit praeclara sua munera: ut ex ipsa varietate totius universi pulchritudo constituatur.[2]
> [Even if a man possesses a greater power of imitation than all other creatures, he is furnished from the very beginning with a certain native genius and spiritual propensity; to frustrate and turn this to some other object is simply to violate nature. Thus, since there is in our mind a certain pattern [Idea], or a root, so to speak, through whose energy we are led to take up any function in life, . . . it is more worthwhile to cultivate it than to destroy it and to embrace it than to reject it. . . . Nature supplies us with a pattern for speaking well, as for the other virtues, and creates in our minds a simulacrum of this beauty with reference to which we habitually judge both what is not ours and what is. But no one to this day has completely attained to this beauty, so that in this

regard it may rightly be said that nothing is well-favored in every respect. For this beauty distributes her splendid gifts not exclusively to one but universally to all, so that beauty may be bodied forth from the very diversity of the whole universe.]

Pico writes with something close to passion about the inseparable knot, the "nexus inseparabilis," binding "inventio" and "dispositio" and all the elements of discourse. Even assuming that the imitator shares his subject matter and all the attendant circumstances with his model, as soon as he shifts the outlines, changes one member of the period, alters the rhythm, he has destroyed that "integritas orationis" which makes the original work the unique, harmonious creation that it is.

Pico was alert to the danger of anachronism, that worm in the bud of classicism. Not only is each writer unique in his eyes; each age is different from every other; given the variety of times and individuals, it is futile to imitate a model religiously, since the product of this effort will either fall short of true resemblance or else reproduce the model mechanically. If Bembo were to find an ancient sandal buried at Rome and wear it, he could never persuade the critics it was ancient. Even if the sandal were admired and worn elegantly and fitted Cicero's footsteps, what about the rest of the body? Men aren't dressed only in sandals. Sooner or later, an anachronistic absurdity will betray the wearer.

> Amictus alii asciscendi sunt: sed quoniam eorum nomina verius quam rem tenemus: et figurae magna ex parte nobis compertae non sunt: periculum erit opinor ne paludamentum pro toga, ne lacernam pro abolla, ne tunicam etiam pro chlamyde capias: tanta est antiquarum vestium nostris temporibus ignoratio: puto etiam quandoque deligi inconsulto posse pro sago mastrucam et sarrabaram.[3]
> [Some other clothes have to be acquired; but since we possess their names rather than their substance, and their forms have not on the whole been discovered, there is a risk, I think, that you will seize on a soldier's coat for a toga, a raincoat for a trenchcoat, or even a tunic for a cloak of state; so great in our times is men's ignorance of ancient dress; I also think that at some point a doublet might be chosen by mistake for a sheepskin.]

Thus the appeal to historical distance and philological ignorance underlies the anti-Ciceronian position. Pico does not deny the need for long study of the ancients in the formation of literary judgment, but the stress falls on the inner experiencing of the ancient work. The superstitious mimicry of a single author induces excessive attention to "dispositio" and "elocutio," whereas the highest value in all serious writing lies in its "inventio." By allowing ourselves the freedom to recombine spontaneously the elements gleaned and internalized from our reading, we will not merely follow our masters, writes Pico; we will be able to surpass them.

Bembo's letter does not, somewhat surprisingly, reject this invitation to "aemulatio," which had appeared intermittently in the theory of imitation ever since its early discussion by Dionysius of Halicarnassus, Quintilian, and Longinus. Bembo's Ciceronianism is of a moderate sort; he does not proscribe the study of authors other than Cicero, nor even the occasional exercise of imitating them. But he professes to find the confluence of various literary manners in a single work absurd, as though an architect were to adopt several styles in a single palace. He professes to have sought in vain for his own innate idea of excellence.

> De meo quidem animo tantum tibi affirmare possum; nullam me in eo styli formam, nullum dictandi simulachrum antea inspexisse, quam mihi ipse mente et cogitatione legendis veterum libris, multorum annorum spatio, multis laboribus ac longo usu exercitationeque confecerim. . . . Ante autem, quam in iis, quas dico, cogitationibus magnopere essem versatus, inspiciebam quidem in animum meum nihilo sane minus, quaerebamque, tanquam a speculo, effigiem aliquam, a qua mihi sumerem conficeremque quod volebam. Sed nulla inerat in eo effigies.[4]
> [I can say this about my own mind: I observed in it no form of style and no simulacrum of speech before those which I made ready thoughtfully and reflectively through reading the books of the ancients across many years with great labor and long use and practice. . . . Before I was especially well versed in these mental exercises I was no less accustomed to look into my mind and to seek there, as if in a mirror, some image from which I could take and prepare what I wanted. But no image was there.]

If in fact we all possessed an idea of pure beauty and eloquence, then, argues Bembo, it would behoove us to pursue this idea in that work which most perfectly embodies it, the "perfectae formae simulachrum." In the case of prose, this work will be Cicero's and in poetry Virgil's. Emulation is possible only if the writer first forms his taste by studying as intimately as possible the works of this greatest master, secondly seeks to equal him, and finally dares to surpass him. Such a program is the privilege only of a few, but it is the sole path to excellence. Imitation must be founded on a total possession of one's model, his language, his turn of phrase and of thought, his very temperament. Imitation of an idea is a deformation of the concept.

> Imitatio . . . quia in exemplo tota versatur, ab exemplo petenda est: id si desit, iam imitatio esse ulla qui potest? Nihil est enim aliud totum hoc, quo de agimus, imitari; nisi alieni stili similitudinem transferre in tua scripta; et eadem quasi temperatione scribendi uti, qua is est usus, quem tibi ad imitandum proposuisti.[5]
> [Imitation, . . . since it is wholly concerned with a model, must be drawn from the model; if it ceases to do so, then how can there be any imitation? For the whole subject of our discussion, the activity of imitating, is nothing other than translating the likeness of some other's style into one's own writings and to cultivate that very temperament present in him whom you have chosen as a master.]

Bembo is not here concerned with the "borrowing" of specific themes and images, which he approves only when pursued sparingly, but rather the quest for a more diffused and formal resemblance. As Eugenio Battisti remarks, Bembo's theory implies a kind of emanation from the greater to the lesser figure; the imitator assimilates the essence of an otherness without offering any resistance, any criticism, or even any creative shaping of his own artistic selfhood. In the *Prose della volgar lingua*, published over a decade after the composition of this long letter,

Bembo substituted Boccaccio for Cicero and Petrarch, now the supreme model, for Virgil, but his theoretical outlook did not significantly change.

One might ask whether, interpreted strictly and narrowly, the theories of either Pico or Bembo permit the imitative process to occur at all. If the individual's affinities and tastes are governed by a dominant Idea, as Pico would have it, then it isn't clear how he acquires the flexibility to experience otherness and recognize it in himself—"experiat et agnoscat in sese." If, on the other hand, one assumes with Bembo that there is no set of affinities at all, if the self is absolutely neutral, then it isn't clear into what the otherness is assimilated. But perhaps these psychologistic questions are not in any case the most rewarding in this debate. Beneath the ostensible issue (a single versus multiple models), one can if one chooses locate a deeper, less parochial confrontation: between *inventio* and *elocutio*, or *res* and *verba*, or expressionism and formalism, between creativity as spontaneous nature and creativity as discipline, between impulse and method, or between beauty as variety and beauty as unity, between color and purity. From the perspective of this study, still another area of disagreement will appear crucial: the disagreement over the distance between model and imitator. The distance inherent for Pico in the unlikeness of two sensibilities is doubled by historical distance: eloquence varies with the taste of each age, "mutatur aetate mutata." In the thought of Bembo, this alienation collapses; the true Idea of beauty lies in the mind of God, which is equally accessible to all ages. Although in the *Prose* Bembo recognizes the fact of linguistic change, this does not problematize for him the recommendation to imitate the trecento masters. His stylistic purity remains essentially a synchronic purity; his classicism draws its absolute rigor from the atemporal. There is a revealing passage in the *Prose* that represents the visitor to Rome training his eye by sketching the monuments of antiquity. The extraordinary aspect of this little vignette is the failure to mention the ruinous state of the monuments. For Bembo they are still whole, integral, *present*. But for Pico the hypothetical sandal can only be unearthed from ruins. If one perceives Renaissance culture in terms of an interplay between the intuition of rupture and the intuition of continuity, then in the Ciceronian quarrels these two intuitions tend to polarize themselves. The Ciceronian, whether moderate like Bembo or fanatic like Erasmus's opponent Longueil, will tend to deny any effective discontinuity between himself and his master. The anti-Ciceronian, like Pico and Erasmus, will tend to found his case on some form of historicism.

If one looks for extraliterary reasons for the progressively narrowing formalism of the earlier cinquecento, they are not far to seek. The dominance of Ciceronian classicism and dogmatic imitation in Italy coincides with the period of foreign invasion—roughly from 1494 to 1559. The subtlety, elegance, and formal perfection of Bembo's writing attain their harmony at the cost of an exclusion: the refusal to respond to contemporary history. It would be an error to suppose that Italian formalism was produced by the invasion of Charles VIII; it was already well developed when in 1485 the elder Pico wrote his famous letter to Ermolao Barbaro defending the study of medieval philosophy and protesting against a thin, merely verbal humanism. But the shame and degradation of public events as perceived by Italian intellectuals clearly functioned to weaken the vestiges of a more robust cultural community. The first book of the *Prose* contains a significant incident: one of the speakers in the dialogue alludes bitterly to the military plight of Italy, whereupon the reply of his interlocutor quickly skitters away: "Ma lasciando le doglianze adietro, che sono per lo più senza frutto, se la volgar lingua ebbe incominciamento. . . ." (But leaving aside these laments, which are generally fruitless, if the vernacular language had its beginning. . . .)[6] Bembo chose to suppress the diachronic dimension of the word because his flawless classicism served as a shield against the misery of public history. The preoccupation with the signifier, with the *verbum*, did not serve to enlarge the potentialities of signification (as it did for example in Rabelais) but rather strictly to confine them. The many-sided complexity of Petrarch was smoothed over as the dynamic political activism of Cicero was muted, that human fullness of the historical Cicero which Ramus would later attempt to resurrect in his *Ciceronianus* (1556).

The eclecticism of Pico would receive support at a more wordly and pragmatic level in the *Libro del Cortegiano* (1528) of Castiglione, which combines arguments for a linguistic pluralism with the defense of each individual's mode of speech and conduct. Language changes from age to age, according to Ludovico da Canossa, the author's spokesman, and imitation, though admirable at best, is not absolutely necessary for the vernacular.

> Se 'l Petrarca e 'l Boccaccio fossero vivi a questo tempo, non usariano molte parole che vedemo ne' loro scritti: però non mi par bene che noi quelle imitiamo. Laudo ben sommamente coloro che sanno imitar quello che si dee imitare; nientedimeno non credo io già che sia impossibile scriver bene ancora senza imitare; e massimamente in questa nostra lingua.[7]
>
> [If Petrarch and Boccaccio were living today, they would not use many of the words we find in their writings: hence, it does not seem good to me that we should imitate them in those words. I do indeed praise highly those who can imitate what is to be imitated; nonetheless, I do not think it at all impossible to write well without imitation; and particularly in this language of ours.]

If one did choose to imitate, Italian literature provided other models than Petrarch and Boccaccio (the two approved by Bembo), just as contemporaneous painting provided a number of great masters whose manners were divergent and just as the styles of the great Greek and Latin poets were dissimilar even if their eloquence was equal. The *Cortegiano* itself of course represents an admirable heuristic imitation of Cicero, more subtle and convincing than the theoretical discussion in book 1.[8] But during the second quarter of the cinquecento, Italian opinion tended to veer away from what might be described as the latitudinarian position toward a more regulative, classicizing rigor sponsored under slightly shifting formulations by the formidable authority of Bembo, Giraldi, Vida, and (later) Julius Caesar Scaliger, among others. The supreme classic may have been Cicero for Cortesi, Cicero (with Virgil) and then Petrarch (with Boccaccio) for Bembo, Virgil for Vida and Scaliger, but the suppression of the diachronic and of creative choice tended to maintain itself. The bugaboo for this hardening academicism was the kind of capricious, syncretic, irreverent freewheeling of an Ariosto; the ideal example of appropriate imitation became the pallid Petrarchan sonnets of Bembo himself or Vida's marmoreal epic, the *Christiad*. As the position rigidified, it also expanded to encompass *mimesis*, the representation of so-called nature, since the inner truth of things was thought already to have been apprehended by the great ancients. Vida's *De arte poetica* (1527) demonstrates on page after page how the *example* of a Virgil is codified into a *rule* that knows no exception; this in fact appears to be Vida's understanding of the function of his versified treatise.[9] Praxis is reified into precept, and the living specificity of the model is drained off to authorize a bloodless, synchronic regulation. Vida's mechanical and ahistorical conception of the imitative act can be gauged by his repeated use of the term *furtus* (theft) and his advice to conceal too flagrant cases of larceny.

> Cum vero cultis moliris furta poetis,
> Cautius ingredere, et raptus memor occule versis
> Verborum indiciis, atque ordine falle legentes
> Mutato.[10]
> [But when you are attempting thefts from the polished poets, proceed with particular caution; remember to conceal what you have stolen by altering the forms of words and to escape detection by switching word order.]

But of course one should not conceal one's dependence so successfully as to appear to violate tradition.

The influence of Bembo and Vida ensured that fidelity to a single model, a focus on *elocutio*, and a concern with dissimulation dominated the doctrines of the following generation. In the formalism that resulted, the element of self-expression prominent in Petrarch's and Poliziano's conceptions declined, and the sense of historical distance, though by no means absent, coexisted uncomfortably with a classicizing will to wish it away.[11] The treatise *Della imitazione* by Giulio Camillo Delminio (composed around 1530, published 1544) exemplifies these developments. Camillo is interested only in *elocutio* and is chiefly at pains to show how far a given figurative or periphrastic expression needs to be from its source in order to escape the blame of unoriginality. He has a kind of arithmetic view of excellence; if, he writes, the perfect author (for example, Cicero) has profited from a thousand beauties and insights scattered among his predecessors, then he who imitates this perfect forerunner imitates the perfection of a thousand gathered into one. This agglutinative idea of merit leaves no place for a truly transformative imagination; Camillo remains a collector and arranger, as in his more famous *Teatro*. But despite the mechanical and fragmenting analysis, which formally recognizes no historical distance as an obstacle, the awareness of change is writ large in the treatise. Camillo begins with a cyclical theory of history to support his dependence on Cicero, who wrote at the high point of the Roman curve. He cites book 2 of the *De oratore* on the homogeneity of each imitative generation's distinctive style in order to discredit those works which, failing to imitate one model, could not be dated by the philologists of later generations. Thus one

glimpses a kind of reprehensible anachronistic modernity. Camillo's most revealing slip appears in a simile.

> Sia, per grazia di essempio, smarrita l'arte di far mattoni, i quali non si potessero aver se
> non negli edifici antichi, . . . e venga in desiderio ad un architetto de' nostri tempi di fare
> un bello edificio di mattoni secondo il disegno che avesse fabricato nella mente. . . .[12]
> [Suppose for example that the art of brickmaking had been lost, and bricks could only
> be obtained from ancient buildings . . . , and suppose that an architect of our era wanted
> to erect a graceful building made of bricks according to a design he had conceived. . . .]

One need not follow the convoluted analogy that ensues, likening the modern
writer to this architect. The admission of loss is eloquent and explains the
fragmentary character of the only imitation Camillo can imagine. His architect is
haunted like Alberti's mosaicist by the Terentian phrase "Nihil dictum quin prius
dictum." Camillo seems representative of a generation in Italy trapped between a
barren classicism and a humbling historicism.

The growth of the Ciceronian cult tended to make the perception of change
more painful and to heighten feelings of belatedness that are generally betrayed
indirectly. The more the usable past narrows to one or two supreme figures, the
more that past becomes, almost by definition, unattainable and unmatchable. But
for the Ciceronian position to be tenable, the inferiority of the present cannot be
unduly emphasized. Cicero simultaneously is and is not within reach. Either way,
history very nearly becomes a scandal. It is not surprising that Erasmus drew his
most powerful arguments from the evidence of change in his assault on the
Ciceronian position. In the largely pro-Ciceronian Italian treatises of the cinquecento, history remains an irrepressible embarrassment.

Thus in the letter by Celio Calcagnini entitled "Super imitatione commenta-
tio," replying to a briefer letter on the same subject by Giovambattista Giraldi
Cintio (both letters 1532), the discussion chiefly remains at a comfortably supratemporal plane. Nonetheless, not far from the opening of his epistolary essay
Calcagnini laments the corruption of pure Latinity due to the barbarian invasions, refers obliquely and slightingly to the stylistic crudity of vestigial medieval
traditions, and seems in fact to base his argument for imitation heavily on the
necessity of repairing these historical breaches. Without the discipline of imitation, one falls inevitably into solecisms.

> Hoc est, hoc scilicet quod efficit ut imitationis praesidio magis egeamus. Nam ante-
> quam maiestas imperii romani pessum iret et splendor latini nominis obsolesceret,
> quom caetera ad imitationem vocarentur, verba certe cum lacte nutricis hauriebamus.
> . . . Nunc autem in tam perdita tempora incidimus ut in verbis perquirendis etiam
> frustra laboremus; nisi ad veteres et receptos conditores perfugiamus, quorum authori-
> tate innitamur, quos imitemur, quorum exempla mutuemur. Nam protritae voces
> illae, quibus non dico vulgus et tabernarum mancipes utuntur, sed ipsi proceres qui
> rerum in Italia potiuntur, tantum abest ut praesidii aut commodi quicquam nobis ad
> eam rem afferre possent, ut multo maxime a via nos deducant et transversos agant.
> Decepti enim vicinitate et quasi vocum imagine, manifestos etiam soloecismos barba-
> rismosque incurrimus.[13]

[This, yes, this victory of barbarism is what augments our need for the support imitation provides. For before the majesty of the Roman Empire went to ruin and the splendor of the name "Latin" departed from fashion, we drank in words, at least, with the milk of our nurse. . . . But now we have fallen on such forsaken times that in seeking out words we will not even labor to any effect unless we retreat to their ancient and received stewards, sustaining ourselves with their authority, imitating them, and partaking of their examples. For those vulgar expressions which not merely the crowd and shop-servants, but also the nobles who rule Italy use, are so far from providing any support or assistance to us in this study that they lead us astray most of all and pervert all our progress. For, deceived by the proximity of different expressions and, as it were, by a likeness of the correct ones, we embrace even manifest solecisms and barbarisms.]

Imitation here is a form of repairing history. But as an alternative to drinking in words as children, it involves a substitution that later critics would have no trouble in showing to be loaded against the imitator. Later Cicero is named as the preferred model (in accordance with Giraldi's position) and Calcagnini will appear poised over the trap into which Camillo had preceded him. At the end of his letter however Calcagnini swerves abruptly into a vigorous encomium of *aemulatio*. Imitation, we now learn, is only for novices; the adult orator who can swim without a cork needs to see his ancient masters as antagonists. Unless he learns to struggle against his masters, he is doomed to remain *infans*—deprived of speech, an infant still at the nurse's breast. The frankness and explosive energy of Calcagnini's concluding exhortations to turn upon one's models far surpass those of other proponents of his position. The intensity of tone reflects the cruelty of the Ciceronian dilemma. But it also indirectly suggests a way out. Insofar as emulation is not merely a psychologistic term and has any formal significance, it can only mean weaker resemblance, a wider discrepancy between subtext and surface text, in short greater liberty. Calcagnini turns back upon the imitative discipline he has ostensibly been advocating. Imitation now appears as an elementary method for repairing history and banishing solecisms, a propedeutic method that yields to a more advanced program readmitting history as creativity, history now perceived as potentially productive. To be no longer *infans* is to grow beyond and away from one's masters.

A more moderate position is taken by Bartolomeo Ricci in his *De imitatione* of 1541. Ricci assumes a middle position between those who base their writing solely on imitating another, and those who seek to express only themselves, arguing for a collaboration between art and nature of the kind one finds in agriculture. One can best cultivate one's own genius through contact with a number of authors, especially those particularly fitted for its development. Nature alone is anarchic, but by training one's special gifts one can hope to equal or even surpass one's forerunners. Each branch and genre of writing has its exemplars, whom Ricci names and discusses at length. Invention and disposition as well as diction are appropriate for imitation—even something more than these, the intellectual or spiritual virtues ("animi virtutes") of one's masters. In several respects, Ricci seems to want to free himself from the most paralyzing extremes of the prevailing formalism. Yet his treatment of history is cautious. It is true that he defends

Seneca's refusal to obey Horace's ban against staging violence: "Another age has come, and writers have been given another mind." (Subsecuta est alia aetas, atque alius scriptoribus animus est datus.)[14] But Ricci is opposed to the coining of new Latin words where the old ones fail to fit, as in religious terminology. This unwillingness to adjust new *verba* to new *res*—for which Erasmus reserved his most withering scorn—returns the compromiser Ricci back again close to the Ciceronian dilemma. By raising the problem of altered *res*, altered institutions to which words may or may not be accommodated, Ricci is of course recognizing the existence of change. Once this recognition is recorded, he must confront helplessly the problem of linguistic anachronism.

The "Dialogo delle lingue" of Sperone Speroni, published as one of his *Dialoghi* in 1542, shows more flexibility but is primarily concerned, as its title suggests, with the development of the vernacular language and with the diffusion of knowledge rather than with strictly literary training. Nonetheless, Du Bellay would draw on it heavily. As the century wore on, the more interesting and problematic issues clustered around representation, mimetic rather than textual imitation. The renewed interest in mimetic imitation is already manifest in the *Della poetica* of Bernardino Daniello, published in 1536. In the *Poetices* of Julius Caesar Scaliger (1561), the imitation of Virgil permits the writer to represent the perfect beauty whose norms are inherent in nature without the local defects and eccentricities visible in any given natural object (*Poetices* 3.25). Scaliger was anticipated in this linking of the two types of imitation by Lodovico Dolce, who had written in *L'Aretino ovvero Dialogo della pittura* (1557) that a painter should partly imitate nature, partly ancient sculpture that corrects the defects in nature.[15] Antonio Minturno, writing in 1564, well after the Aristotelian revolution of the mid-cinquecento, reflects a little more sensitivity to the diachronic character of language in his *Arte poetica*,[16] but by this stage the imitation of texts had become a routine matter, merely a threadbare item among other topics any complete survey of poetry had to address. It is rare that discussions of intertextuality acquire any vitality in the enormous body of later cinquecento criticism. The historicism of Petrarch and Valla was largely repressed or exhausted. A spokesman for Bernardino Partenio in his dialogue *Dell'imitazione poetica* (1560) refers to the vogue of poetic imitation in the past tense and complains that contemporary poets who scorn models can only meet with frustration and confusion like seafarers in a tempest ignorant of what port to turn to.[17] In the essay on comedy by Bernardo Pino da Cagli (published 1578), the argument against anachronism is placed in the service of the Counter-Reform: since times and customs change, the manners represented by comedy must follow them, and modern comedy must suppress those swindles, seductions, and adulteries which are disappearing from the new, reformed society.[18] A convenient end point for the history of imitative theory in the Italian Renaissance is the *De gl'heroici furori* of Giordano Bruno (1585), which scorns all imitation along with all precepts as artificial constraints based on remote texts. The poems of Homer, Bruno charges, have been perversely misused as a standard for rules mechanically derived, binding not on true creators but on apes.[19] In this anticipation of Romantic individualism, historicism becomes an argument for pure originality; tradition withers as well as all generic conventions. Bruno brutally and courageously brings a chapter of a civilization to its close.

2

If one looks for a sustained analysis of cultural anachronism during the sixteenth century, one has to look outside Italy to the *Ciceronianus* of Erasmus (1528). Indeed, one can explain the degree of hostility it provoked only in terms of the offense to classicism inherent in a demonstration of cultural change. Erasmus's long dialogue opens with a playful caricature of the Ciceronian devotee, Nosoponus, so superstitious that for seven years he has avoided all books except those of his idol, has refused to take a wife, turned down all offers of employment, and concentrated his energy on enormous compilations of Ciceronian words, tropes, *sententiae*, and rhythms. This monk of philological piety is now devoting seven years to the imitation of the master, working only in the silence of the night on a light stomach, when the wind is quiet and the stars propitious. Erasmus assigns the cure of this unhappy dolt to one Bulephorus, who in effect becomes the authorial voice. Bulephorus's mind is fertile in arguments that finally do succeed in mitigating Nosoponus's mental deformation. Not all in Cicero, he argues, is equally worthy of imitation; Cicero himself absorbed his entire heritage and imitated no one closely; he flavored his writing with phrases drawn from many authors; his own style would not have been pleasing during all phases of Roman history, for example to the contemporaries of Cato the Censor; he himself felt free to coin many words, at the risk of offending his auditors; it is insufficient for an imitation only to reproduce the externals of its model; imitation that excludes emulation is likely to miss its mark, particularly in view of the inseparability of a great author's strengths and faults; each genre has its own exemplars; each writer is characterized by his own temperament, which leads him to write more effectively in one style than another; one should follow Cicero by attaching greater weight to matter rather than to words, allowing elocution to adapt itself to concepts and values.

Each of Bulephorus's arguments has its share of truth, but the whole is bound together by recurrent reference to cultural discontinuity, returning again and again to the comedy, if not the moral shame, of classicizing in a Christian society.[20] A certain dress is appropriate, states Bulephorus, to each nation, age, sex, and estate; Apelles today would not represent the Germans as Greeks or Christ as Apollo; to speak like Cicero one would have to restore all ancient Rome; we stand today on a new stage.

> Quid igitur frontis habeat ille, qui a nobis exigat, ut per omnia Ciceronis more dicamus? Reddat is nobis prius Romam illam, quae fuit olim, reddat senatum et curiam, patres conscriptos, equestrem ordinem, populum in tribus et centurias diges-

tum. . . . Porro quum undequaque tota rerum humanarum scena inversa sit, quis hodie potest apte dicere, nisi multum Ciceroni dissimilis? Adeo mihi videtur hoc quod agebamus in diversum exisse.

Tu negas quenquam bene dicere, nisi Ciceronem exprimat; at res ipsa clamitat, neminem posse bene dicere, nisi prudens recedat ab exemplo Ciceronis. Quocunque me verto, video mutata omnia, in alio sto proscenio, aliud conspicio theatrum, imo mundum alium.[21]

[What effrontery would he have then who required us always to speak in a Ciceronian style? Let him first restore to us the Rome which existed at that time; let him restore the senate and the senate house, the conscript fathers, the knights, the people in tribes and centuries. . . . Since then the entire arena of human affairs has been altered, who today can speak well unless he greatly diverges from Cicero? It seems to me that we are led to a different course.

You refuse eloquence to anyone who fails to copy Cicero. But the actual situation shows that no one is eloquent unless he avoids the Ciceronian model. Wherever I turn, I see everything changed; I stand on a different stage; I see a different theatre, yes, a different world.]

It is offensive to morals, continues Bulephorus, to seek out pagan substitutes for Christian expressions, to call God *Juppiter Optimus Maximus* and Christ Apollo or Aesculapius; Cicero were he alive today would not be a Ciceronian but would accept the sacred books of Christendom as he did his own; it would be absurd for a painter to represent an old man as young, simply because years ago Apelles painted him young; a modern writer is truly Ciceronian if he speaks aptly, with knowledge and passion, of his faith, drawing on the eloquence of Solomon, the Psalms, and the Gospels as well as the ancients. Is imitation of any sort worth pursuing? Yes, within limits.

A mediocri aemulandi studio te non revoco, modo qua est optimus, hac aemuleris, modo aemuleris potius quam sequaris, modo studeas aequalis esse verius quam similis, modo ne pugnes adversus genium tuum, modo ne sic affectes congruere Ciceroni tuam orationem, ut rei, de qua loqueris, non congruat.[22]

[I don't prohibit a moderate pursuit of imitation, but imitate only the best works of Cicero; emulate rather than follow; try rather to rival than to duplicate precisely; develop your natural capacities; don't attempt to harmonize your style with Cicero's to the degree that it fails to fit its subject.]

Cicero himself teaches us how best to imitate.

Illius exemplo pectus suppellectile rerum cognitu necessariarum expleamus, ac prima sit sententiarum cura, deinde verborum, et verba rebus aptemus, non contra: nec inter dicendum usquam oculos a decoro dimoveamus. Ita demum vivida fuerit oratio, si in corde nascatur, non in labiis natet. . . . Concoquendum est, quod varia diutinaque lectione devoraris, meditatione traiiciendum in vaenas animi, potius quam in memoriam aut indicem, ut omni pabulorum genere saginatum ingenium ex sese gignat orationem, quae non hunc aut illum florem, frondem gramen've redoleat, sed indolem affectusque pectoris tui, ut qui legit non agnoscat fragmenta e Cicerone decerpta, sed imaginem mentis omni genere doctrinarum expletae.[23]

[Let us after his example fill our hearts with a store of general knowledge; let us care first for thoughts, then for words; let us adapt the words to the subject, not subjects to words; and while speaking let us never move our eyes from that which is seemly. Thus, in short, will the oration be alive only when it is born in the heart and does not float on the lips. . . . That must be digested which you devour in your varied daily reading, must be made your own by meditation rather than memorized or put into a book, so that your mind crammed with every kind of food may give birth to a style which smells not of any flower, shrub, or grass but of your own native talent and feeling; so that he who reads may not recognize fragments culled from Cicero but the reflection of a well-stored mind. Cicero had read all his predecessors and weighed carefully what was worthy of sanction or censure in each; yet you would not recognize any one of them in particular in Cicero but the force of a mind animated by the thoughts of them all.]

The final section of the dialogue is devoted to capsule evaluations of ancient and modern Latin authors, whether or not Ciceronians.

The *Ciceronianus* suffers from its author's blindness to the growing importance of the vernaculars. As a major statement about cultural change, moreover, it betrays certain limitations. Erasmus is not fully sensitive to the problems of historical understanding posed by the changes he underscores so heavily. Given his profound assimilation of classical literature, he doubtless felt more cut off from the early Christian world than from the ancient. He certainly shows less awareness of distance than Du Bellay. Nonetheless his book makes a significant statement. Although it is evidently inspired by Poliziano, whom Erasmus defends at length, it contains a good deal which is fresh. It introduces to a wide European audience a new conception of decorum that measures the propriety of a work against its contemporary human context.[24] The most prominent offense to this decorum is a refusal to assign Christian words to Christian concepts, the refusal for example to write *fides* in place of *persuasio.* The style that refers to the Virgin as Diana and to God the Father as *Juppiter Optimus Maximus* is offensive to Erasmus on both literary and religious grounds, both for its spurious elegance and its creeping paganism. But the revulsion against classicistic anachronism extends beyond the individual word to the distortions and claustrations of a dessicating estheticism. Erasmus's history is not conventional humanist history because it values Christian revelation more than it deplores the loss of classical civilization and pure Latinity. It reverses Petrarch's historiographical reversal and views the Christian Era as the truly enlightened. "Tota Graecorum philosophia prae philosophia Christi somnium est ac nugamentum."[25] (All the philosophy of the Greeks compared to the philosophy of Christ is a dream and a bauble.) (It is true that although Erasmus professes to prefer scriptural eloquence to ancient, his own style derives from the latter.) In this revaluation of traditions, Erasmus is neomedieval.

This revaluation ensured a fundamental breach with his opponents that would be irreconcilable. In a second fundamental ground of disagreement, Erasmus magnified an idea preexistent in imitative theory but seldom foregrounded so starkly. Imitation for him depended on the individual bent, propensity, intellectual character, "natura."

Amplector imitationem, sed quae adiuvet naturam, non violet; quae corrigat illius dotes, non obruat: probo imitationem, sed ad exemplum ingenio tuo congruens, aut certe non repugnans.[26]
[I favor imitation but imitation that aids rather than hinders nature; that corrects rather than destroys nature's gifts. I approve of the imitation of a model agreeing with your genius or at least not antagonistic.]

This intellectual character of the individual is primary, and it determines the imitative road he follows.

Ingenium ac naturam Ciceronis optare possum nobis, dare non possum. Habent singula mortalium ingenia suum quiddam ac genuinum, quae res tantam habet vim, ut ad hoc aut illud dicendi genus natura compositus frustra nitatur ad diversum.[27]
[I can wish for the talent and natural ability of a Cicero; I cannot furnish it. Minds of men have individual bent, and this has such power that if they are adapted to one style of speaking by nature they may strive in vain for another.]

Thus Erasmus postulates after Pico that predisposition which Bembo claimed to have searched for in himself without success. "To distort one's nature is to go masked in public," he writes (A nativa specie in diversum refingere, quid aliud est, quam in publicum venire personatum?),[28] and elsewhere he dwells on the pleasure one takes in savoring the unique quiddity of a writer's moral style.

Quum tanta sit ingeniorum dissimilitudo, quanta vix est formarum aut vocum, mendax erit speculum, nisi nativam mentis imaginem referat, et hoc ipsum est, quod in primis delectat lectorem, ex oratione scriptoris affectus, indolem, sensum ingeniumque cognoscere, nihilo minus quam si complures annos cum illo consuetudinem egeris. Et hinc diversorum tam diversa erga librorum scriptores studia, prout quenque genius cognatus aut alienus vel conciliat vel abducit: haud aliter quam in formis corporum, alia species alium delectat offendit've.[29]
[There are as many kinds of minds as there are forms of voices and the mirror will be straightway deceptive unless it give back the real image of the mind, which is the very thing that delights the reader especially—to discover from the language the feelings, the characteristics, the judgment, and the ability of the writer as well as if one had known him for years. Out of this has grown the great variety of preference for books, according as the writer's genius is kindred or alien, as it wins or repels the reader; just as in form and feature different types delight or repel different men.]

Because each writer's voice is unique, each relationship between writer and reader is unique. Reading allows one to recognize "a certain secret affinity of minds" (geniorum arcanam quandam affinitatem). Each imitative initiative, by implication, is also unique and private. But Erasmus balances the potential subjectivity of this implication by emphasizing as well the need to know, possess information, have ideas, command wisdom, seek out res before verba. The digestive metaphor, which recurs several times, is Senecan in its syncretic interiority.

The Ciceronianus, tireless, prolix, repetitive, is not a particularly elegant model of dispositio. It does not instruct us by example; it does not even envision the dense imitative dialectic of The Praise of Folly, or the fascinating exfoliate "imitation" of the Adagia, where a miniscule verbal kernel becomes a kind of subtext in a ruminative essay spiraling progressively outward. But in an era of heresies it advanced its own: an alternative decorum, an alternative kind of anachronism, an alternative history, a fresh theory of reading, a revived theory of self-expression, a plea for moral style. It does not lack areas of myopia, but it has the great merit of bringing informed and demystifying irony to bear on a sacrosanct topic. The hostility it provoked followed its author to his death.

In the discussions of imitation that followed Erasmus's deliberate provocation north of Italy, one can watch writer after writer searching for a *tertium quid* between the Erasmian and Ciceronian extremes. This is true even of those who, like Dolet, assumed the defense of Cicero and of Erasmus's putative butt, Christophe de Longueil. One of the most reasonable treatments of the issue in the aftermath of the *Ciceronianus* can be found in the *De tradendis disciplinis* of the gifted Spanish humanist Juan Luis Vives, who will be discussed in the closing chapter. Another moderate voice in the controversial tempest was that of Philip Melanchthon, whose *Rhetoric* (1531) contains a chapter on the subject and whose lectures on Quintilian's tenth book (delivered 1534, published 1570) return to the same inflammatory issue. The argument in these two works is not easy to summarize, precisely because their author clearly wanted to avoid a polarizing stance. But one feels in the German reformer a revulsion from formalism weaker than but analogous to the Dutch polemicist's. Although he sees imitation partly as a process of learning words, phrases, figures, and arguments, he reveals intermittently an ulterior concern with understanding the essential spirit of one's model or models;[30] we learn more perfect expression by conversing with many. The ultimate value of this conversation is an "inward command" (hexin cognitionis) of another's words and arguments, not merely a cento of phrases, so that the imitator's speech takes on a certain coloring from his study of a forerunner. By diligent attention to the model's diction and arrangement, one acquires sharper judgment, keener prudence, and an appreciation of his particular charm. Immersion in linguistic detail produces sensitivity to moral style. Does history present an obstacle to this attainment? Melanchthon certainly recognizes temporal pressures on language. In the commentary on Quintilian he writes that real discussions ("veris causis") are based on some unchanging meaning in things, but that times and commonwealths alter the way they use names ("Christ," "sacrament," "church," "cross"). In the *Rhetoric*, he states that the corruptions of Latin by the barbarian invasions resulted in such an unfamiliar concurrence of words as to beget a new language. Men really need a mode of expression to be understood in all eras; thus it would be best to choose the Latinity of Cicero, Caesar, and Livy for universal use. Still, some accommodation is required. "We must serve the time and the context, just as Virgil prudently avoided whatever in Homer was not in accord with the customs of Rome." (Serviendum est enim temporibus ac locis, quemadmodum Virgilius, etsi ad imaginem Homeri se totum composuit, tamen illa prudenter vitavit, quae Romanis moribus non congruebant.)[31] Thus there is an Erasmian decorum of the contemporary for Melanchthon as well as a decorum of tradition. The purists ridiculed by Erasmus violate the former; Melanchthon, despite his loyalty to the Latin golden age, would rather violate *its* norms. His equanimity rests on his belief that one can internalize the essence of Cicero, "the order and whole constitution of his speech" (collocatio . . . et universum corpus orationis)[32] without offending the decorum of modern experience.

Etienne Dolet's abusive assault on the *Ciceronianus* and on the person of Erasmus, *De Imitatione Ciceroniana, adversus Desiderium Erasmum Roterodamum, pro Christophoro Longolio* (1535), diverges from Melanchthon in the shrillness of its tone, but it in fact manifests more agreement with both Melanchthon and Erasmus than its aggressive rhetoric leads the reader to expect. In this dialogue between Thomas More (Morus), the defender of Erasmus, and Simon de Neufville (Villanovanus), Dolet's former teacher at Padua and the defender of Longueil, a good deal of the purist Ciceronian position is given away. The Longueil defended here is a more supple figure than the historical man of letters Erasmus actually attacked. We should not, says Villanovanus, stitch together Cicero's phrases in our own writing, but simply learn from him what is elegant, polished, and so on. Cicero becomes a kind of ideal or spirit of eloquence that we can assimilate in such a way that the man, were he to return to life, would not have just cause to reclaim anything. The imitation of his works is not confined to verbal superstition ("verborum religione"), but is judged on its purity, gravity, and rhythmic effectiveness. As for the historical remoteness asserted by Erasmus, is there not a continuity of virtue and vice? Does our age lack its Milos and Catilines? What if a certain orator did avoid using Christian terminology in his discourse to prelates at Rome (an occasion Erasmus had singled out for especial scorn)? This speaker chose to observe the decorum appropriate to his learned and refined audience, since the age no longer permits civic debate like that of republican Rome. There is no senate today in which a Cicero might exercise his talents. If there were, Cicero might well have been equaled by many. All that is left is meager scope for the elitist Latin of closet oratory, clearly superior to the vulgar *lingua franca* that Erasmus would impose on everyday life. With the admission that public oratory in the ancient Roman sense is dead (a point Erasmus himself had made), Dolet's argument very nearly collapses, undone in this case again by the scandal of history. There may have been living Milos and Catilines, but the interplay of power had found new institutional channels. In a significant sense, the argument for continuity fails. Erasmus had fought for a Latin in touch with modern society, a linguistic alternative that would eventually fall before the rise of the vernaculars. Dolet's elitist alternative was damned by his own showing; even his modified and enlightened version of it was condemned to be the pastime of a parasitic subculture. The pursuit of a Ciceronian excellence that is not a political instrument exposes itself as anachronistic. The undeniable fertility and ingenuity of Dolet's polemic are insufficient to suppress the fatal inconsistency in his perceived relation to the past.

With the *De imitatione* of Johannes Sturm (probably composed during the fifties, published 1574), the diffused influence of Ramus (Pierre de la Ramée) begins to make itself felt on imitative theory. The study of imitation, traditionally a subdivision of rhetoric or poetics, is now partly taken over by logic, so that despite its title, Sturm's treatise does not confine itself to matters conventionally associated with its announced subject. In those sections that are not devoted to dialectic, Sturm describes an *imitatio* which becomes a form of self-assertion, emancipation, acquisition, even—recalling Calcagnini—emulative aggression. True imitators take what they admire in another's possession and "sow and reap that in their own field." Old authors are like arsenals from which we borrow arms or material for arms. Arguments and *sententiae* are common to all orators to be used like javelins; each becomes the private possession of a given orator to the degree that he is able individually to throw it in his own way and to wound his particular opponents. This making a public object private emerges as the central imitative act, which is simultaneously the central creative act. The ancient text, the "poetic ornament," and the logical commonplace tend to be lumped together in a common domain, any element of which becomes interesting as the individual appropriates it and makes it his own ("suum facit"). Sturm doubtless has in mind Horace's "publica materies privati iuris erit" (*Ars poetica* 131), but he does succeed himself in appropriating this commonplace effectively. He discusses for example the way a block of stone ceases to belong to nature and becomes the sculptor's as he works on it.

Sturm's main methodological innovation was his advice to compare in detail the process of imitation in ancient authors; we shall meet this sound idea again in his correspondent Ascham. Sturm offers many examples from classical literature and analyzes them carefully, arguing that rivalry with one's source can only be free ("libera") if one allows oneself to alter it greatly. The Ramist orientation leads Sturm generally away from history, but he does mingle Plato and Quintilian at one point by drawing a distinction between inventors, imitators, and emulators, each placed at successively greater removes from the first source of wisdom. Homer "invented" a sentiment; Herodotus imitated it, *faute de mieux*; others later could try to outdo it. This modest admission of history to the treatise once again becomes a threat to coherence, since it relegates to an epistemological periphery that activity which is elsewhere a means to self-defining freedom. Sturm's central metaphors of appropriation, arrogation, making one's own, sowing public seed in a private field—these are essentially hopeful, constructive figures that open up history to the future and outweigh the nostalgia for origination.

Sturm, like many others who wrote about imitation, was a pedagogue who might be accused of having a vested interest in perpetuating classical studies. The vernacular languages however did not lack defenders, such as the courtier and diplomat Castiglione. Whereas professional humanists tended to assume the availability of the model and its capacity for renewal in imitative praxis, defenders of the vernaculars tended to stress the separateness of each, its roots in modern life, and thus its dissimilarity to Latin and Greek. Translators also had good reason to point to the difficulties of their task. In France an early reference to the comedy of

anachronism can be found in the *Champ Fleury* (1529) of the humanist printer
Geoffroy Tory, a partisan of the vernacular whose argument for the uniqueness of
his language ran counter to the oecumenical *Concorde des deux langages* of Jean
Lemaire de Belges. Tory imagines a Frenchman dressed in the garb of a Lombard
so ill at ease that he is obliged to slash his gown and pull it out of shape in order to
regain his comfort. His comic metaphor for the imitation of the ancients is less
flattering to the cause of the vernacular he claims to be defending.

> Si nous voulons user de Grec ou de Latin. Usons en en allegations dautheurs seulle-
> ment. . . . Quant ie voy ung Francois escripre en Grec ou en Latin. Il me semble que ie
> voy ung masson vetu dhabits de Philosophe ou de Roy qui veult reciter une farce sus les
> chaufaux de la Basoche, ou en la Confrairie de la Trinite, & ne peut assez bien
> pronuncer, comme aiant la langue trop grace, ne ne peut faire bonne contenence, ne
> marcher a propos, en tant qu'il a les pieds & iambes inusitees a marcher en Philosophe
> ou en Roy.[33]

The sense of inferiority betrayed by Tory's image disappeared by the middle of the
century; there developed instead, in the defenses of the French vernacular, something like a sensitivity to the solitude of each *mundus significans*. Such a sensitivity can be found for example in the letters of the scholar and jurisconsult Estienne
Pasquier, who was in touch with Ronsard as a young man and who as early as
1552 was defending the French tongue in these terms.

> J'adjouste que les dignitez de nostre France, les instrumens militaires, les termes de
> nostre practique, brief la moitié des choses dont nous usons aujourd'huy sont changées
> & n'ont aucune communauté avec le langage de Romme. Et en ceste mutation, vouloir
> exposer en Latin ce qui ne fut jamais Latin, c'est en voulant faire le docte, n'estre pas
> beaucoup advisé.[34]

This keen sense of anachronism would remain with Pasquier throughout his
career; much later one finds him pointing out the gap between the linguistic
worlds of two eras.

> Les langages ne se rapportent les uns aux autres, en leurs manieres de parler; & . . . ce
> qui est bienseant en une langue, le voulant transplanter en l'autre, sera trouvé de
> mauvaise grace; tellement, que tout ainsi qu'il y a plusieurs choses au latin qui ne se
> peuvent de mesme naifveté representer en nostre françois. Aussi y en a il plusieurs au
> françois, que Ciceron mesmes s'il venoit à renaistre, seroit bien empesché de rendre avec
> mesme grace, en latin.[35]

Pasquier goes on to discuss the precise ways whereby a language is rooted in
political and cultural institutions. This enrootedness is a major theme of the
analysis of linguistic change in Louis Le Roy's *De la vicissitude des choses* (1576),
whose second book is entitled "De la vicissitude et variété des langues."[36] The
awareness of linguistic and cultural distance spanning the sixteenth century in
France is notable because it provides a counterweight to the classical synchronism
of Bembo, Vida, and Scaliger.

It was possible, of course, though not easy, to entertain both perspectives at once. Thus Dolet was capable of attacking the *Ciceronianus* and was capable of praising the universal practice of imitation in all things, while still pointing out in a separate work the enormous barriers between languages.[37] A similar tension can be felt in the *Art poëtique* of Jacques Peletier du Mans (1555), a treatise that would doubtless have found more readers over the centuries had it not been written in Peletier's "reformed" spelling. Peletier's attitude toward his contemporary literary situation partakes of what might be called wistful optimism, an attitude that was shared by many of his compatriots and that indeed helped to determine their situation. As a defender of the vernacular, Peletier is obliged to argue that another Homer or Virgil might appear to adorn the French language; elsewhere, less guarded, he confesses his fear that the ideal epic poem, a *Herculeïde*, will have to await another century and another language.[38] His chapter on imitation begins by arguing that imitation is universal and necessary, but goes on to admit that alone it never made anybody great. The resulting exhortations to resolute artistic independence, reminiscent of Quintilian, are then followed by praise for Virgil's courage in choosing three supreme models (Theocritus, Hesiod, Homer). Apparently one chooses one form of courage or the other or assumes both to some degree. The chapter ends in any case with images of peril.

> An sommę, nous prandrons les Ecriz des Poëtes pour unę Mer: an laquelę i à eskeus [écueils], sablęs mouuans, goufręs: quę lę bon Pilotę par instruccion e par bonne vigilancę s'eforcęra d'euiter: Ręgardant quelę part il veút tirer, combien ęt son vesseau capablę, e dę quel vant il ę aspirè.   [p.30]

When we reach this grim conclusion, imitation begins to look like a universal abyss. The chapter on translation that follows evokes the impossible ideal of a word-for-word rendering that would preserve the elegance and purity of both languages, only to conclude, again wistfully: "Mes, commę j'è dit, il nę sę peùt fęre" (p. 34). Given the distance between language and the imperative fidelity to the original masterwork, it isn't clear that Peletier leaves the translator space to do his work;[39] his task may prove at least as risky as the writer-imitator's. Peletier, like many of his contemporaries, is whipsawed between fidelity and solitude. One of the reasons why the *Deffence et Illustration de la Langue Francoyse* of Du Bellay remains so interesting and so problematic is that it brings an acute consciousness of linguistic difference to bear on an *imitatio* represented as creative and crucial.

3

The general stance of the *Deffence* is well known: rejection of most of the native tradition, rejection of the Neo-Latin alternative, rejection of vernacular translation of the classics (stigmatized probably by its association with the school of Marot), a professed faith in the promise of the French language without much specific justification for it, praise for the endowments of the French land and people, a call for modern emulation of the ancients whose achievement is nonetheless seen as immense, a strenuous sifting of genres and forms to exclude many (chiefly late medieval) and endorse others (chiefly classical or Italian), above all an exhortation to ennoble the vernacular by means of *imitation*, an intimate assimilation of the ancients comparable to the Roman assimilation of Greece. The imitative process as Du Bellay envisions it is not limited to a single master; he is not in fact deeply concerned here with the choice of models (assuming they are ancient), nor, beyond the conventional innutritive metaphor, is he very specific about the technique of imitative art. There is little of the regulative exactness of a Vida. Du Bellay is consciously iconoclastic, consciously the spokesman of a movement taking shape, inspirational and disheveled, withering and buoyant.

Du Bellay's imitation is an act of vast labor and high genius; in fact it is a kind of miracle. Like most miracles, its precise workings do not bear looking into. At the core of the treatise lies a brilliant creative act which is named but not really described. Everything hinges on it but it is allowed to remain a mystery, almost a void. Behind this brilliance lies darkness, and around it lie other activities which are not poetic imitation, not that supreme intuitive flash, and which define it negatively. The darkness is profound. The opening page introduces us to speech as "diversité & confusion [qui] se peut à bon droict appeller la Tour de Babel."[40] Babel stands as an emblematic edifice at the entrance to this meditation on language. *Las*! It would be far better if all men employed a single natural language, but they do not (p. 64). The classical past is in ruins, and those who would resurrect it in the obvious, unmiraculous ways (Neo-Latin verse, poetic translation) cannot succeed.

> Vous ne serez ja si bons massons (vous, qui estes si grands zelateurs des Langues Greque & Latine) que leur puissiez rendre celle forme que leur donnarent premierement ces bons & excellens architectes: & si vous esperez (comme fist Esculape des membres d'Hippolyte) que par ces fragmentz recuilliz elles puyssent estre resuscitées, vous vous abusez, ne pensant point qu'à la cheute de si superbes edifices conjointe à la ruyne fatale de ces deux puissantes monarchies, une partie devint poudre, & l'autre doit estre en beaucoup de pieces, les queles vouloir reduire en un seroit chose impossible: outre que beaucoup d'autres parties sont demeurées aux fondementz des vieilles murailles, ou egarées par le long cours des siecles ne se peuvent trouver d'aucun.
> [pp.79–80]

This pessimism, which Du Bellay first found in Speroni, accords well with his original thought. Humanist archaeology and Aesculapian resurrection defy simple performances. Too much is lost or turned to dust. The ruins of the ancient palace lie too deep or too scattered for the imagination to subread them accurately. The sense of privation and the sense of estrangement, the "diversité" of Babel, are very strong. Each language possesses its own unique character, its *naif*, its native specificity, "je ne scay quoy propre seulement a elle" (p. 36). Given this powerful individuating essence, the attempt merely to translate poetry is doomed. The individual is isolated in his inherited prison house of language, and in the case of the French vernacular, this house has generally been neglected rather than maintained by its keepers through the centuries. Greek and Latin authors surpass the moderns in learning and eloquence (p. 56). Civilizations themselves are doomed to pass. "Dieu . . . a donné pour loy inviolable à toute chose crée de ne durer perpetuellement, mais passer sans fin d'un etat en l'autre" (pp. 56–57). Flux is universal and language is not protected from it.

Nonetheless language is the one available instrument to mitigate historical solitude. Language bridges as well as divides.

> Les ecritures & langaiges ont eté trouvez, non pour la conservation de la Nature . . . mais seulement à nostre bien & utilité: affin que presens, absens, vyfz & mors, manifestans l'un à l'autre le secret de notz coeurs, plus facilement parvenions à notre propre felicité, qui gist en l'intelligence des Sciences.   [p. 64]

Roman civilization at its peak had no defense against the assault, "l'injure," of time, without the support of its language; for this only we admire and adore the men who wrote it.

> La plus haulte excellence de leur republique. voire du tens d'Auguste, n'etoit assez forte pour se deffendre contre l'injure du tens, par le moyen de son Capitole, de ses thermes & magnifiques palaiz, sans le benefice de leur Langue, pour la quele seulement nous les louons, nous les admirons, nous les adorons.   [pp. 183–84]

Thus language pierces a little the darkness of history; language can solace and relieve to a degree the solitude of a belated culture. Poetry can heighten this function of language. Achilles through Homer is remembered; those are forgotten who put their faith in marble, colossi, pyramids (pp.134–35). Language moreover—and here Du Bellay follows the orthodox humanist belief—is subject to training; languages respond to cultivation; they depend on the judgment and will of men. "Toute leur vertu est née au monde du vouloir & arbitre des mortelz" (p.12). Against historical darkness Du Bellay pits human talent and will; the whole treatise is intensely voluntaristic.

Poetry heightens the communicative power of language, but it paradoxically heightens the walls between peoples. Each individual poem has its own *naif*, its native quiddity, which isolates it from facile appropriation. The fallen edifice of each ancient work depends on a lost Idea, which must be found in order to reconstruct the work (pp. 80-81). Poets are possessed of a

> divinité d'invention qu'ilz ont plus que les autres, de ceste grandeur de style, magnificence de motz, gravité de sentences, audace & varieté de figures, & mil' autres lumieres de poësie: bref ceste energie, & ne scay quel esprit, qui est en leurs ecriz, que les Latins appelleroient *genius*.   [p.40]

To violate this aura, this *genius carminis*, by a blundering word-for-word translation, is to commit a sacrilege, "prophaner . . . les sacrées reliques de l'Antiquité" (p.41). Equally guilty are those who patch together *centos* of tags from a grab bag of authors with no regard for context. These fools, cultivators of dead languages, import outmoded terms into modern discourse; Ciceronians, *reblanchisseurs de murailles*, only re-whitewash walls (p.76). How then can a language be truly cultivated, dignified, and adorned with great poetry? It can be done through imitation. Thus the Romans imitated the Greeks,

> se transformant en eux, les devorant, & apres les avoir bien digerez, les convertissant en sang & nouriture, se proposant, chacun selon son naturel & l'argument qu'il vouloit elire, le meilleur aucteur, dont ilz observoint diligemment toutes les plus rares & exquises vertuz.   [p.42]

The imitator simultaneously and paradoxically becomes his model and makes the model part of himself by innutrition. This happens rarely, since Nature has made each creature unique. Many an imitator fails to attain the innermost secrets of his model, mistakes *verba* for *res*, "s'amusant a la beauté des motz, [perd] la force des choses." But when the imitator succeeds, then his isolation is truly breached; a civilization flowers through willed acculturation; from the corruption of one society, a new one is generated (p. 57). Few critics have reserved so privileged a place for the act of imitation.

For literary historians the publication of the *Deffence* has remained a celebrated event and a useful reference point. But it cannot be said to have enjoyed in our century a good press. Villey, who first discovered its deep indebtedness to Speroni and other Italians, charged it with a total lack of originality. Chamard thought the defense of the vernacular "médiocre" and the theory of imitation "dangereuse," the whole work produced by a mind "encombré de choses confuses et mal digérées." Saulnier was able to praise only the "ardeur" that compensated for the expository incoherence and derivative arguments. Dassonville alleged an "opportunisme . . . cynique." Michel Deguy, subtler than his predecessors, praises the treatise for a modernity inherent in its problematizing of its subject.

> Le texte de la Deffence-Illustration est "moderne" en ce qu'avec lui l'imitation est devenu problématique, devenue la question même, et arrive à l'expression de sa nature contradictoire: "comme elles (les littératures grécolatines)! Pas comme elles! Ne les imite pas, pour être comme elles; imite-les pour parvenir à la différence de l'égalité."

Terence Cave finds Du Bellay's theory of imitation similar to that of the *Ciceronianus*, but "less rich and penetrating."[41] The most helpful reading of the book is the brilliant deconstruction by Margaret Ferguson, which all future commentary will have to take into account.[42] Ferguson's essay demonstrates more precisely than before the strains at work on the coherence of the *Deffence*. On the other hand the tone of her analysis bespeaks a sympathetic comprehension that is in itself a new and important interpretive factor.

The term *deffence* for Ferguson reveals an ambivalence toward antiquity that is offensive and defensive at once.

> The psychoanalytic phrase "defense against " is perhaps the best characterization of a rhetorical movement that asserts independence from the past and demands subservience to it, that proclaims and denies the possibility of "invention," that sees history as

a progress and as a degeneration, and that, finally, sees language itself both as an essential weapon in the quest for poetic identity and as a hindrance in the search for literary power. *La Deffence . . .* does not offer a unified poetic theory at all; rather, it presents a significant pattern of contradictions.   [p. 276]

The contradictions are there because Du Bellay's imagination was "trapped between future and past." "The hope for an immediate accession to 'primacy' is transformed into a prospect of wandering, of exile, because the vision of the future passes through the crucible of the poet's ambivalence toward the ancients" (p. 278). Thus Du Bellay vacillates between images of the French language as a promising growth needing cultivation and a desiccated plant on the point of death (Chamard ed., pp. 24–25), between a concept of a *translatio studii* which is emulative and one which is degenerate, between advice to cultivate the ancient languages and resentment at the years required for this cultivation, between appropriation of the ancients' power and a call for native individuality, between humanist reverence and modernist iconoclasm, "the need to be like and unlike the great originals." The doctrine of imitation then becomes "a kind of sacred space, a space in which all the poet's conflicting attitudes toward the ancients wage battle" (p. 283). Thus "imitation is a relation between texts, an unstable relation in which the balance of power is always shifting" (p. 286). This instability and the vacillations it produces are interpreted in conclusion as tokens of the perennial dialogue in Du Bellay between "the poet of the future and the reader of the past."

Ferguson's reading leads one to ask whether Du Bellay's conflicts can ever be read as productive dialectic rather than unstable vacillations. That double vision of history Gilmore traced in Erasmus, assuming both the repeatability and the unrepeatability of the past,[43] was endemic to the entire humanist movement and preeminently notable in Du Bellay. Humanist culture had its mainspring, as I have tried to suggest, in the paired intuitions of rupture and continuity. It may be that in the *Deffence* these tensions all explode into that confusion of Babel which it opens by affirming. It may be that its opposed emotions confusedly cancel each other out under the pressure of a historical anxiety too self-deceiving to be seminal. "Its aggressions," in Cave's language, "may seem an oddly misplaced piece of shadow-boxing which proves the superiority of no one."[44] But it is arguable that in this *chronomachia* between a qualified Quintilian and a qualified Speroni, abusive vacillation gives way intermittently to generative paradox.

The last sentence of the treatise can serve as a test case. Ferguson points out perceptively the inconsistency between the earlier horror at profaning relics and the plunder to which the final chapter gleefully invites the modern writer. One might add that it cites as positive examples two episodes of ancient history from which the Gaulish nation does not really emerge with credit. The invitation to pillage urges the modern to enter the Delphic temple boldly without fearing the muted Apollo. Then it concludes: "Vous souvienne de votre ancienne Marseille, secondes Athenes, & de votre Hercule Gallique, tirant les peuples apres luy par leurs oreilles avecques une chesne attachée à sa langue." (p. 197) The Lucianic Hercule Gaulois was a common figure in the official and literary culture of the

French Renaissance. A deconstructive reading might argue that this figure with a chain on his tongue provides an ambivalent book with an ambivalent ending. The chain could easily be interpreted as a restriction or a gag, and the nations at the other end as the agents or the common victims of this Herculean plight. Perhaps Du Bellay in this image revealed more than he intended. Perhaps he did, but this reading in turn would leave itself open to the charge of reductiveness. A chain can be the instrument of a jailer but also of an engineer. A chain *binds,* and in this instance it may bind both restrictively and supportively. To be read responsively, the metaphor has to be seen to represent both the burden *and* the link with those "peuples" who in this context can only be the ancients. There is a will to mastery, an oblique betrayal of subservience, and sublating both the recognition of a connection, a *tie* that hobbles and permits communication. We cannot read the *Deffence* without respect for this sublation. The modern expresses his will to mastery over the ancients with an image that goes back to Lucian, thus ironically disclosing his dependence. But this is not a simple irony. Du Bellay is bound to Lucian by an etiological passage, but the bond does not prove subservience, does not preclude freedom; it proves a concrete relationship.

Undeniably there is an offense to logic in the figurative account of imitation; one becomes the *aucteur,* and one takes him into oneself as nourishment. The reversal can be interpreted in terms of a will to power and to profanation, or in terms of an exaggerated instance of that simultaneous surrender and assertion involved in all dialogue, here heightened in mutually exclusive metaphors to fit the near-impossible dialogue with the alien. Given the distance and authority of the estranged text, the specific energy of its idiom which is not one's own, then the strenuous participation in communication would require a heroism of which the antithetical transformations, illogically juxtaposed, might evoke the extremity. Valentin Voloshinov's theory of meaning is pertinent.

> To understand another person's utterance means to orient oneself with respect to it, to find the proper place for it in the corresponding context. For each word of the utterance that we are in the process of understanding, we, as it were, lay down a set of our own answering words. The greater their number and weight, the deeper and more substantial our understanding will be.
>
> Thus each of the distinguishable significative elements of an utterance and the entire utterance as a whole entity are translated in our minds into another, active and responsive, context. *Any true understanding is dialogic in nature.* Understanding strives to match the speaker's word with a *counter word.* One only understands a word in a foreign tongue by matching it with the "same" word in one's own language.[45] (Voloshinov's italics)

Du Bellay's essay measures the staggering effort to find this matching word across two civilizations in a dialogue fated to be incomplete, even as it insists with tenacity on the obligation so to create dialogic meaning. If in any true dialogue there is both self-subordination and self-aggrandizement, is it not conceivable that both if required could be extended to their extremes without incoherence in order to preserve the possibility of an exchange?

Any use we make of the past contains an irreducible ambivalence. The tribute of pure repetition is dead. The tribute of variation includes rejection. Any creative variation contains some element of refusal, contains cruelty, but forms of outward cruelty may also include a tacit tribute. By perpetuating the past, by reproducing ritualistically its external features, we are actually exposing its pastness, pointing to its anachronism, putting it from us. By ostensibly ridiculing the past, by exposing its inconsequence and parodying its rhetoric, we may be revealing how we depend on it, how necessary it is to us, how little free of it we are, how we really stem from it. Myths of continuity and myths of innovation can be equally abusive. The construct informed enough to skirt both abuses already deserves our regard.

Paul de Man, in an essay already quoted (see above, p. 41), traces the perennial cycle initiated by the avant-garde impulse to modernity, leading the writer toward a chimerical absolute beginning before he is forced to acknowledge the roots of his work in his inheritance. In the postmedieval era this cycle is skewed by an *anxiety of originality*. The art of a culture barely emergent from a ceremonial society is still threatened by the contingency of history against which ceremonial had served as a protection. True originality was and was felt to be an aspect of the contingent. Under the shadow of supremely authoritative texts, originality in the post-Romantic sense was not even a theoretical option. That is why it is anachronistic for twentieth-century scholars like Chamard to cheer those Renaissance critics who seem to be speaking for a modern liberty.[46] The naive modern reader misses the double bind controlling the Renaissance artist and he misses the unexpressed presuppositions of the critic. Matching the cycle de Man describes was a second cycle initiated by an impulse merely to reproduce, *not* to originate, to compose those translated "versions" of the ancients recommended by Sebillet a year before the *Deffence* as one of the highest forms of literary art. Sophistication was achieved—and with it, doubtless, ambivalence—when reproductive imitation was recognized to be inherently anachronistic.

> Qu'on me lyse un Demosthene & Homere Latins, un Ciceron & Vergile Francoys, pour voir s'ilz vous engendreront telles affections, voyre ainsi qu'un Prothée vous transformeront en diverses sortes, comme vous sentez, lysant ces aucteurs en leurs Langues. Il vous semblera passer de l'ardente montaigne d'Aethne sur le froid sommet de Caucase.   [*Deffence*, pp.36–37]

The naive restorer of the ancient palace is doomed to botch his reconstruction, to put the kitchen or the stables where the great hall once stood, since part of that palace has turned to dust. And so in this second, Renaissance cycle the artist is weaned from reproduction, thrown back into that incipient creativity, that grey area of contradiction where if he is gifted he will find his idiolect and his maturity. In Ariosto, Ronsard, and Jonson, the limits of this grey area are accepted with joy and the contingent is bravely faced, but the limits are nonetheless respected. The movement back and forth between a nourishing, overshadowing tradition and a groping, miraculous invention is precisely the movement of the *Deffence*, which needs to be read synecdochically as the fissured crystallization of an era. Coexistent with its generative insights an ambivalence not fully mastered is certainly present, a dialectic escaping sustained control. The masterpiece would come only when the limits of the humanist cycle became themselves Du Bellay's central theme, limits accepted not joyfully but clairvoyantly and tragically.

Ten • *Imitative Insinuations in the* Amours *of Ronsard*

The position of French humanism in 1550, as compared with its counterpart in later quattrocento Italy, betrays a certain unevenness. It had benefited from the immense labor of editing and publication bestowed on ancient texts in both countries (but especially Italy) over a period of three generations. It benefited from a large number of translations from the Greek and from the comparatively greater access to that language on the part of the individual student. It benefited from the royal patronage of the recently deceased François I, whose most visible token of support had been the institution of the *lecteurs royaux* in 1530. It was also enriched by the penetration of Italian culture, particularly at Lyon, as well as by the frequency of visits to Italy of Frenchmen of all estates. By 1550 France had produced a large body of Neo-Latin verse based on classical models, as well as impressive works of erudition such as Robert Estienne's *Thesaurus latinae linguae*, Etienne Dolet's *Commentarii linguae latinae*, and Guillaume Budé's commentary on the Pandects, his *De asse*, and his *Commentarii linguae Graecae*. Vernacular imitation in something like a proto-Renaissance spirit can be traced back to the prose and verse of Jean Lemaire de Belges (drawing on Ovid's *Heroides* and *Amores*, Lucretius, and Virgil's *Georgics*) at the beginning of the century. Interesting adaptations of Martial, Petronius, Ovid (the elegies *Ex Ponto* and the *Tristia*), Virgil's eclogues, and even the Psalms can also be found in the original verse of Marot (in addition to his translations of the Psalms and the first two books of the *Metamorphoses*). Yet the enormous shift in the character of French civilization between 1520 and 1550 inevitably revealed the strains of its rapid transformation. The elite of humanist teachers and humanistically trained students was far smaller than in Italy. The universities, so far as can be judged, were by no means won over as a bloc to the new learning, and in some cases seem to have assimilated it only sluggishly. The quality of French Neo-Latin verse did not approach the distinction of Pontano's, Poliziano's, or Sannazaro's, and vernacular poetry was just beginning to reflect the impact of classical models with something like maturity. Budé, the humanist who dominated learning during the first half century in France, was not himself an imaginative writer. The one great writer with deep classical learning, Rabelais, was not commonly perceived as a serious artist and had a weak influence on the mainstream of culture. Thus in 1550 France was still struggling to absorb the wealth of ancient culture and to define the true character of a native humanist spirit.

This meant that it was still groping for a satisfactory native version of literary imitation. Du Bellay's *Deffence et Illustration* provided a theoretical statement,

197

albeit controversial, which sketched certain directions imitative poetry in France might take. But the finest poetry of the Pléiade, and notably of its leaders Ronsard and Du Bellay, produced work whose exemplary power eclipses any theoretical formulations. These two men composed a large number of texts that are brilliant instances of imitative discovery. In their work one can trace that progressive achievement of a creative voice through interplay with the alien which Petrarch had begun to describe two centuries earlier.

Yet it must be admitted that in the case of Ronsard, his writing about poetry, in prose as in verse, reveals no powerful vision of intertextual drama. He makes no reference to that *genius* dwelling within each language which Du Bellay recognized, and although he is aware of his culture's particular situation as he writes, he never refers to any *necessary* division from other cultures, including antiquity. His poems themselves do contain dense intertextual drama. But this drama is never powerfully thematized. When he uses the necromantic metaphor, as he does in the preface to the first four books of odes and again in one of these odes:

> . . . imprimant ma trace
> Au champ Attiq' et Romain,
> Callimaq', Pindare, Horace
> Je déterray de ma main.[1]

or when he uses the image of an itinerary:

> Bien que . . . mille rimeurs
> Fussent aux champs en dispit des neuf Soeurs,
> Je passay outre, amenant de la Grece
> Leur trouppeau sainct.   [L 18:317]

there is no evidence that he saw the problematic aspects of these metaphors as Du Bellay saw them. For the talented poet, the great poet which he perceived himself to be, the appropriation of inherited texts requires wide reading and judgment but no labor of transformation. The innutrition metaphor does not appear. The status of the text as a diachronic object does not seem to have been very meaningful to Ronsard. This attitude does not change greatly over the course of his career. It appears in the early preface to the odes (1550):

> Ne voiant en nos Poëtes François, chose qui fust suffisante d'imiter: j'allai voir les étrangers, & me rendi familier d'Horace, contrefaisant sa naive douceur.   [L 1:44]

in the *Abbrégé de l'art poëtique françois* (1565):

> Tu n'oubliras les comparaisons, les descriptions des lieux . . . te façonnant en cecy à l'imitation d'Homere, que tu observeras comme un divin exemple, sur lequel tu tirera au vif les plus parfaictz lineamens de ton tableau.   [L 14:15]

and in the posthumous *Préface sur la Franciade* (1587):

Or, imitant ces deux lumieres de Poësie [Virgil and Homer], fondé & appuyé sur nos vieilles Annales, j'ay basti ma *Franciade*, sans me soucier si cela est vray ou non.

[L 16:340]

The context makes clear that the reference in the *Abbrégé* to the poet's modeling himself (*te façonnant*) on Homer suggests no strenuous act of self-cultivation, but rather a supposedly simple copying of an illustrious example. There is little in these passages to distinguish Ronsard's reflection on the imitative process from that of a critic he despised, Sebillet,[2] and less attention to the risks involved than was paid by the obscure Jacobus Omphalius in a treatise composed in 1537 entitled *De elocutionis imitatione.*[3] Ronsard's theory of poetry was in fact split between a Neoplatonic theory of *fureurs* stemming from Ficino and a craftsman-like, Horatian assumption of self-conscious artifice.[4] A theory of imitation that tallied more closely with his own creative practice might have helped to bridge this split, but the theory never evolved.

What did evolve was a new version of the apian simile, a version reducing or suppressing the element of transformation which for Seneca and Petrarch had been primary. This simile is elaborated at length in two poems ("Hylas," "Responce aux injures et calomnies") and more briefly in two others ("Epistre à Charles, Cardinal de Lorraine," "Sonnet à . . . M. des Caurres, sur son Livre de Miscellanées")[5]; it is in these, and especially in the two longer passages, that the conception of intertextuality reveals a personal imprint. The images evoke a kind of capricious errancy that leads the poet on an apparently irregular itinerary from meadow to meadow, text to text, but that permits him to appear finally as a master-painter, selecting and combining with the skill of nature.

Mon Passerat, je resemble à l'Abeille
Qui va cueillant tantost la fleur vermeille,
Tantost la jaune: errant de pré en pré
Volle en la part qui plus luy vient à gré,
Contre l'Hyver amassant force vivres.
Ainsy courant & feuilletant mes livres,
J'amasse, trie & choisis le plus beau,
Qu'en cent couleurs je peints en un tableau,
Tantost en l'autre: & maistre en ma peinture,
Sans me forcer j'imite la Nature.   [L 15:252]

The transformative process of mellification is absent from this simile; the poet-bee is rather collecting for his verbal palette colors that undergo no change. The artifice consists in the weighing and choosing of the most beautiful. What is most suggestive is the initial *random* thoughtlessness of the artist who refuses the straight line of conscious deliberation and achieves a higher mastery by yielding to his caprice. We will encounter this *vagabondage* in other contexts.

The paradox of the artifice inherent in the surrender of the artificer's will recurs in the other extended instance of the bee simile.

Les Poëtes gaillards ont artifice à part,
Ils ont un art caché qui ne semble pas art
Aux versificateurs, d'autant qu'il se promeine
D'une libre contrainte, où la Muse le meine. . . .
  As-tu point veu voller en la prime saison
L'Avette qui de fleurs enrichist sa maison!
Tantost le beau Narcisse, & tantost elle embrasse
Le vermeil Hyacinthe, & sans suivre une trasse
Erre de pré en pré, de jardin en jardin,
Portant un doux fardeau de Melisse ou de Thin.
Ainsi le bon esprit que la Muse espoinçonne,
Porté de sa fureur sur Pernasse moissonne
Les fleurs de toutes pars, errant de tous costés.

[L 11:160–61]

Here the poet is still more passive; he wanders where the Muse leads him or he is borne by the poetic fury to Parnassus; later Tibullus and Horace will be represented as guided in like manner through the fields of Rome. The conception of beauty looks purely decorative and additive, whereby the nectar of the narcissus merely supplements the hyacinth's. But in fact the act of addition is a little more mysterious. The poet follows no path ("sans suivre une trasse") and yet his idiosyncratic fantasy attains an art beyond art. The epithet "gaillards" suggests the opposite of pure passivity. The counsel of deliberate labor and prolonged reflection repeated in the prose works is left in shadow; nonetheless a certain conception of creativity fusing receptiveness and power begins to emerge.

To accept Ronsard's own account of his work in these passages would be to categorize his imitative art as essentially syncretic, as belonging to the second of the four types sketched in the third chapter. A glance at the footnotes in the Laumonier critical edition, with its vast range of attributed sources, would only confirm this conclusion. Laumonier if anything did not do justice to the syncretism of Ronsard's poetic practice, since he frequently referred to a single source what had become a conventional topos. Terence Cave has connected Ronsard's syncretism with the wide influence of Erasmus's *De copia*, which promoted syncretic imitation by its advocacy of the commonplace book and by its reliance on the whole canon of accepted authors for the acquisition of a technique of elegant variation.[6] Erasmus of course only provided fresh support for a pedagogical method that, as we have seen, has been traced back to the birth of Renaissance humanism under Manuel Chrysoloras.[7] The attempt by Ronsard and his circle to transform radically the *mundus significans* of their age implied of course the kind of wideranging exploitation of a large canon implied by Ronsard's bee similes. Yet having granted this, one must distinguish Ronsard's practice from the *contaminatio* of a Poliziano. As Weber has shown, each genre for the Pléiade group was associated with one or two original masters: Homer and Virgil for the epic, Petrarch for the love lyric, Anacreon for the light ode, Pindar and Horace for the graver ode, and so on.[8] For the idyll, Theocritus was joined by Virgil and Sannazaro. In each genre, the authority of the original master would tell more heavily, even if numerically more subtexts accrue in a given poem from other authors. My own reading of Ronsard would be still more restrictive. Despite the extraordinary spectrum of allusion, despite the dense contaminative orchestration, Ronsard seems to me to have been involved in a serious, profound intertextual dialogue with only three or four poets: Pindar, Horace, Petrarch, and in a somewhat different relation, Hesiod. These were the major presences who haunted Ronsard's imagination, even when apparently mediated by secondary figures, even when he was working in genres apparently unconnected with them. To note only the number of echoes and allusions is to be misled by a statistical simplification and to miss the intertextual tension of Ronsard's poetry. It is significant that each of these major presences wrote in a language other than French. Ronsard was of course immersed in the French tradition, but he seems truly to have recognized no native predecessor who played the role which Horace, Dante, Petrarch, and Chaucer played in their respective traditions. He may have been less burdened by an anxiety of Gallic influence; he was in any case consciously less rooted, freer to take his flight to those alien meadows that drew him. They were perhaps fewer than he admitted.

Even a restricted view of intertextuality in Ronsard might furnish matter for many books. The pages that follow cannot pretend to be thorough; they will at most suggest paradigms for reading Ronsard diachronically. They will focus primarily on the *Amours* of 1552-53, although the issues raised by that collection will lead necessarily beyond itself. Thus the major relationship at the outset will be that with Petrarch, which means we will be considering the interplay of two imaginations strangely and radically dissimilar.

2

Sonnet 159 of the *Amours* can serve as a starting point.

Voyci le bois, que ma sainte Angelette
   Sus le printemps anime de son chant.
   Voyci les fleurs que son pied va marchant,
   Lors que pensive elle s'esbat seullette.   4
Iö voici la prée verdelette,
   Qui prend vigueur de sa main la touchant,
   Quand pas à pas pillarde va cherchant
   Le bel esmail de l'herbe nouvelette.   8
Ici chanter, là pleurer je la vy,
   Ici soubrire, & là je fus ravy
   De ses beaulx yeulx par lesquelz je desvie:
Ici s'asseoir, là je la vi dancer: 12
   Sus le mestier d'un si vague penser
   Amour ourdit les trames de ma vie.   [W 102]

Weber cites subtexts from three Petrarchan sonnets—for Ronsard's octave the opening quatrain of *Canzoniere* 165:

Come 'l candido piè per l'erba fresca
i dolci passi onestamente move,

vertú che 'ntorno i fiori apra e rinove,
de le tenere piante sue par ch' esca.
[As her white foot through the green grass virtuously moves its sweet steps, a power
that all around her opens and renews the flowers seems to issue from her tender soles.]

and the opening quatrain of 162:

Lieti fiori e felici, e ben nate erbe
che madonna pensando premer sòle;
piaggia ch'ascolti sue dolci parole
e del bel piede alcun vestigio serbe. . . .
[Happy and fortunate flowers and well-born grass, whereon my lady is wont to walk in
thought, shore that listen to her sweet words and keep some print of her lovely foot. . . .]

for Ronsard's sestet, sonnet 112:

   Sennuccio, i' vo' che sappi in qual manera
trattato sono e qual vita è la mia:
ardomi e struggo ancor com' io solia,
l'aura mi volve, e son pur quel ch' i' m' era.   4
   Qui tutta umile e qui la vidi altera,
or aspra, or piana, or dispietata, or pia;
or vestirsi onestate, or leggiadria,
or mansueta, or disdegnosa e fera.   8
   Qui cantò dolcemente, e qui s' assise,
qui si rivolse, e qui rattene il passo,
qui co' begli occhi mi trafisse il core;
   qui disse una parola, e qui sorrise,   12
qui cangiò il viso. In questi pensier', lasso,
notte e dí tiemmi il signor nostro Amore.

[Sennuccio, I wish you to know how I am treated and what my life is like: I am burning
up and suffering still just as I used to, the breeze turns me about, and I am still just what
I was.
Here I saw her all humble and there haughty, now harsh, now gentle, now cruel, now
merciful; now clothed in virtue, now in gaiety, now tame, now disdainful and fierce.
Here she sang sweetly and here sat down; here she turned about and here held back her
step; here with her lovely eyes she transfixed my heart; here she said a word, here she
smiled, here she frowned. In these thoughts, alas, our lord Love keeps me night and
day.]

If one looks for a verbal clue to Ronsard's metamorphosis of these Petrarchan
materials, one might fasten on the epithet "vague" of line 13, which means
primarily "wandering" or "vagabond" but also carries a secondary meaning of
"insubstantial." The reverie of the lover yields to that vagabondage we have
already met on the part of the imitative poet, and of course we have followed it as
well in the opening image of the sonnet, the aimless straying of the girl Cassandre
through wood and stream. The phrase "vague penser" subtly identifies the speaker's consciousness with the girl's, whose reverie as she wanders through the
landscape has been foregrounded by the accentual prominence accorded the

adjective "pensive" in the expressive fourth line. This pleasurably melancholy errancy of the body and sensibility is much less marked in the subtexts. The "pensando" in Petrarch's 162 is more neutral; "pensive" in the French already possesses the overtones suggested by the correlative terms given in Robert's dictionary: *songeur, absent, méditatif, rêveur.* Thus "pensive" constitutes a significant "mistranslation." The surrender to an insubstantial mood which is a spiritual errancy is doubtless echoed in the ambiguity of the verb "desvie" (line 11), which would normally mean "die" but also suggests "dévier," to deviate. This negative capability of the lover, this willed and fecund passivity, mitigates the apparent determinism of love's meshes, "trames" (line 14), and forms the greatest possible contrast with the passivity of Petrarch's sterile cycle: "l'aura mi volve, e son pur quel ch' i' m' era." The imprisoning character of Petrarch's iterative action fades from the French. The reverie, which is also a diversion, "ébat," wherein both speaker and girl participate, violates the discrete separations of Petrarch's world.

This holds true for the relation of the girl to the landscape. The Christian dualism of Petrarch's imagination makes itself felt even in these evocations of Laura's entrance into the natural sphere. The motif of the woman whose steps produce an instant flowering derives from antiquity, but in the *Canzoniere* this motif functions to demonstrate the angelic, miraculous status of the woman above nature. The "vertú," the fecundating power (165, line 3) that emanates from her is the evidence of her *un*natural condition. Moreover the reader is left as usual to wonder if this power is not a projection of the speaker's fancy.

> ombrose selve, ove percote il sole,
> che vi fa co' suoi raggi alte e superbe . . .   [162, 7–8]
> [shady woods where strikes the sun who makes you with her rays tall and proud . . .]

The "sole" is Laura; is one to suppose that her presence has literally caused the trees to grow or rather, and more probably, that the poet privately and fancifully attributes to her this power? The objective appears to collapse characteristically into the subjective. The regularity of this collapse tends to call into question the dependability of the verb "vidi" and the accuracy of the speaker's reporting. "Qui tutta umile e qui la vidi altera." Perhaps Laura is only *l'aura.* In Ronsard an antithetical process occurs. The term "angelette" has lost all Christian supernatural meaning. Cassandre enters the landscape to become a part of it, to animate ("anime," line 2) a world already vital. Her culminating activity, dancing (line 12), is added by Ronsard and confirms one's impression of a less stately, more lithe, spirited, and volatile young woman, closer to the earth and the flowers she plucks. The rhythmic dynamism of the sestet, with the charming enjambment at line 10, heightens this volatility. The images of the girl's movement are not appropriated by the speaker's consciousness, but he rather gives himself up to them with that refusal of assertiveness, that adaptability to impressions, focused by the word "vague." The speaker of these love poems lacks the formidable emotional intensity of Petrarch's speaker; in fact the poems offer precisely an opening out of that relentless enclosing power.

This heuristic movement from subtext to surface text can be studied again in the
octave of a late imitation that makes use, among others, of one of Petrarch's best
known and most imitated sonnets.

D'un solitaire pas je ne marche en nul lieu,
Qu'Amour bon artisan ne m'imprime l'image
Au profond du penser de ton gentil visage,
Et des mots gracieux de ton dernier Adieu.   4
    Plus fermes qu'un rocher, engravez au milieu
De mon coeur je les porte: & s'il n'y a rivage,
Fleur, antre ny rocher, ny forests ny bocage,
A qui je ne le conte, à Nymphe, ny à Dieu.   [W 406]

These lines would have reminded the literate contemporary reader immediately of
Canzoniere 35:

Solo e pensoso i piú deserti campi
vo mesurando a passi tardi e lenti,
e gli occhi porto per fuggire intenti
ove vestigio uman l'arena stampi.   4
    Altro schermo non trovo che mi scampi
dal manifesto accorger de le genti,
perché negli atti d'alegrezza spenti
di fuor si legge com'io dentro avampi;   8
    sí ch'io mi credo omai che monti e piagge
e fiumi e selve sappian di che tempre
sia la mia vita, ch'è celata altrui.
    Ma pur sí aspre vie né sí selvagge   12
cercar non so, ch' Amor non venga sempre
ragionando con meco, ed io co lui.
[Alone and filled with care, I go measuring the most deserted fields with steps delaying
and slow, and I keep my eyes alert so as to flee from where any human footprint marks
the sand. No other shield do I find to protect me from people's open knowing, for in my
bearing, in which all happiness is extinguished, anyone can read from without how I
am aflame within. So that I believe by now that mountains and shores and rivers and
woods know the temper of my life, which is hidden from other persons; but still I
cannot seek paths so harsh or so savage that love does not always come along
discoursing with me and I with him.]

and doubtless of other poems from the same source.[9] This can truly be said even if
every motif in the Italian sonnet had become conventional. Here at this point on
their historical itinerary, these motifs function to open a *freedom of passage* that
had been closed. The solitude of Petrarch had not been proto-Romantic; it had not
involved an interchange with nature or an esemplastic re-creation of nature by the
transfiguring imagination. For him the primary virtue of the wilderness lay in the
absence of other human beings, and his compulsion to return to it was to be taken
as a measure of his suffering. The wilderness is a shield, "schermo" (line 5), against
others and a backdrop to the only true interchange, between the poet and his

internalized "Amor." The knowledge of his pain attributed to hill and forest does not reduce their alien wildness; a kind of incipient oxymoron—deaf auditors—begins to make itself felt. This Petrarchan discontinuity becomes in Ronsard a continuity, as the landscape loses its desolate severity and acquires a hospitable population of deities and nymphs. In certain poems, Ronsard's solitary pleasure anticipates the dilettante promenades of Théophile, Saint Amant, Milton, and Marvell. But his historical role in the evolving cult of solitude remains distinct. This solitary is a lover, and *Amour* acts here as a unifying or conflating agent, overcoming the absence of the beloved and reducing the separation between background and self. The figure of the nymph is itself both conflated and conflating; partly hidden within rock or tree and indistinguishable from it, partly objective, visible presence, partly an inspirational energy within the poet's imagination, the nymph in the poetry of the Pléiade ensures the breakdown of those hermetic enclosures inherited from the Petrarchan tradition.[10] The activity represented by the verb "conte" (line 8) constitutes a leisurely beginning of creativity. Thus the word "solitaire" reveals itself as a rich and suggestive mistranslation of the Italian "solo." The French text invites the reader to move easily between man and nature, internal and external, familiar and numinous, absence and presence, visible and invisible, indulgence and creativity. This movement from a frustration of passage to freedom is not only thematic but also rhetorical and semiotic; signifiers such as "Nymphe" and "Amour" function to blur denotation with a rich and shifting openness.

In those love poems where Ronsard's originality asserts itself most dynamically, as distinguished from the abundant corpus of failures and hackwork, one feels the radical trope to define itself through a process which to my knowledge has never received a rhetorical label. This process consists of a fusion of entities so as to destroy their boundaries, their distinctness, and ultimately their being. It may take the form of personification, metaphor, periphrasis, metonymy, or some other figure; the conventional category matters less than the pressure to conflate. The pressure may be expressed moderately, as a simile, or boldly, as a metamorphosis, but it seems to me to be virtually a constant within those love poems—and not only love poems—that are still capable of arresting the reader's sensibility.

One prominent instance is the tendency of a woman's body to become a landscape and conversely, of a landscape to become her body, a tendency so subtle and pervasive as almost to merit the term *Joycean*. This imagistic drift can even affect individual anatomical parts, as when the mistress's fingers begin to turn arboreal—"Tant leurs branchetes sont plenes / De mile rameuses venes" (L 5:236)—or when in the "Elegie à Janet peintre du roi," the mistress's knees are to be painted as two hillocks; her nose must descend "ainsi comme descent / Dans une pleine un petit mont qui pend" (W 160) and her forehead must appear

> . . . tel qu'est la pleine marine
> Quand tant soit peu le vent ne la mutine,
> Et que gisante en son lit elle dort
> Calmant ses flots sillés d'un somme mort.   [W 159]

This final metaphor of the sea stretched out in sleep interjected within the larger simile demonstrates with its rhetorical Chinese boxes how a landscape can be anthropomorphized or feminized just as a woman can be naturalized. Both metamorphic counterpressures are at work at once.[11] What is resemblance in the "Elegie" appears as a fantasy of metamorphosis in an early sonnet.

> Et que n'est elle une Nymphe native
> De quelque boys? par l'ombreuse froydeur
> Nouveau Sylvain m'allenteroys l'ardeur
> Du feu qui m'ard d'une flamme trop vive.   [W 94]

The conceit would be a little repellent if it were not informed with genuine visionary force: the mistress's coldness might serve to assuage the lover's flames once she haunted the wood as a nymph, once her cruelty were transformed into shadowy coolness. This fantasized transformation in fact makes the woman more than a nymph; she *becomes the forest* through which the lover moves. In another sonnet from the first volume of *Amours* one also frees the text from its superficial bad taste by taking the image seriously.

> Ces flotz jumeaulx de laict bien espoissi,
>   Vont & revont par leur blanche valée,
>   Comme à son bord la marine salée
>   Qui lente va, lente revient aussi.
> Une distance entre eulx se fait, ainsi
>   Qu'entre deux montz une sente esgalée,
>   En toutz endroitz de neige devalée,
>   Soubz un hyver doulcement adoulci.   [W 118]

Poems like this one begin to reach the reader only when he can conceive of the body as an actual landscape, on that border of the grotesque and the archetypal situated by Baudelaire's "La Géante."

The superficial structure of the rhetoric in the passages just cited—simile, metaphor, metamorphic conceit—clearly matters less than the conflationary force that hazily transmutes each image and whose linguistic expression should be regarded as an underlying deep trope. This holds true for those poems deriving from the Petrarchan motif of erotic illusion, whereby the lover sees features or aspects of his beloved imprinted on the trees, rocks, and grass around him. This is the organizing situation of one of Petrarch's most powerful and terrible poems, canzone 129 ("Di pensier in pensier"), and it reappears with modifications in several other poems, including canzone 127 ("In quella parte") and sonnets 96 and 176. In the *Canzoniere* the motif serves to dramatize the speaker's enclosing solipsism; in Ronsard it fosters the assimilation of the scene to the female body.

> . . . soit que j'erre au plus hault des montaignes,
> Ou dans un boys, loing de gens & de bruit,
> Soit dans des prez, ou parmi les compagnes,
> Tousjours à l'oeil ce beau portrait me suit.

Si j'apperçoy quelque champ qui blondoie
D'espicz frisez au travers des sillons,
Je pense ouyr sa voix dessus le bord,
Qui, se plaignant de ma triste misere,
M'apelle à soy pour me donner confort.   [W 244–45]

The last image in a series of eight illusions is the most loaded, in view of Ronsard's recurrent fantasy of transformation into water.[12] Water in its passivity and fluidity yields itself with a vague indeterminacy like the speaker's fantasy.

Voila comment pour estre fantastique
En cent façons ses beaultez j'apperçoy,
Et m'esjouys d'estre melancolique
Pour recevoir tant de formes en moy.   [W 245]

The appeal of the spring, whose gushing resembles the mistress's voice, might be a sexual invitation (". . . m'apelle à soy pour me donner confort") but it is also an appeal to the imagination to *liquify* itself by receiving and assuming so many forms. The alteration of ecstasy and shattering disillusion in canzone 129, where the pain at the lost mirage bespeaks the anguishing separation of vision and "reality," is transposed to a lower level of intensity where the fluid succession of forms constitutes a dreamy pleasure.

It is true that this ambiguity of shape can be found in the Mannerist taste for grottoes and gardens where the presence of human or divine figures, incompletely disengaged from the vegetation, gives the impression of creatures half vegetable and half anthropomorphic, haunting the place with a slowly emergent visibility.[13] The scene is peopled with mythical or fantastic forms without ceasing to be organic. The fluidity toward which Ronsard's imagination wants to move can be regarded as a feature of his contemporaneous *mundus significans,* shared by all the arts and by many other poets. Nonetheless there is a sense in which he makes this feature peculiarly his own. He thematizes the fluidity repeatedly in naturalistic Lucretian terms.

. . . rien ne peut estre
Longuement durable en son estre
Sans se changer incontinent.   [L 1:209]

La matiere demeure, & la forme se perd.   [L 18:147]

More significantly, he is able with unique force to infuse a divine vitalism into the merging of entities, so that his poetry seems to incarnate the dynamic process it evokes. Nymph and muse are both conflating personifications; the forest nymph is internalized imaginative *vertu* and the muse is a goddess of the countryside. Conflation tends toward apotheosis. Ronsard addressing Spring in the "Elegie du Printemps" states that the season will find a mirror in the young Isabeau: "Tous les deux n'estes qu'un, c'est une mesme chose" (W 381). This hyperbolic compliment acquires a kind of authenticity in the sexual brutality of the "Avantvenue du Printens," where the arrival of the season leads to an orgiastic celebration.

Ja le ciel s'enflame,
Et dans le sein de sa fame,
Ja se rue en s'elançant,
Et mellant sa force en elle,
De sa rousée eternelle
Va son ventre ensemanssant.[14]   [L 1:150]

The earth as woman becomes a source of cosmic potency, like the poem penetrated by a celestial impregnating force.

Perhaps the most interesting of the poems that make this conflation is the long *Chanson* 'Quand ce beau Printemps je voy," whose middle section catalogues a series of erotic illusions and shows how profound is the revision of the Petrarchan drama.

Quand je voy les grands rameaux
    Des ormeaux
Qui sont serrés de lierre
Je pense estre pris aux lacs
    De ses bras,
Quand sa belle main me serre.   [W 299]

The extended series ends with a revealing summary.

Bref je fais comparaison
    Par raison
Du Printemps & de ma mie:
Il donne aux fleurs la vigueur,
    Et mon cueur
D'elle prend vigueur & vie.

The referent of "elle" in the last line is "ma mie," but one would doubtless not be greatly mistaken if one understood it to refer to "comparaison," in other words if one assumed a continuity between the poetic visionary activity, which is also a metaphoric activity, and the vitality of the woman and the season. The "je pense..." has become an assertive poetic act without losing its liquid responsiveness. This becomes explicit in the following stanza, where the poetic will announces itself.

Je voudrois au bruit de l'eau
    D'un ruisseau
Desplier ses tresses blonds
Frizant en autant de neuds
    Ses cheveux
Que je verrois frizer d'ondes.

In this complex of organic sinuosity and curvilinear flow the poet aspires to participate; the poetry insinuates itself into the fluency. The will in fact claims still more.

Je voudrois pour la tenir

Devenir
Dieu de ces forests desertes. . . .   [W 300]

The sexual fantasy is also a creative fantasy and a metaphysical fantasy; the metaphoric capacity of the poet, who is both passive receiver and metamorphic agent, transforms *him* into a hamadryad or *genius loci.* The triple interpenetration of woman, forest, and vagabond sensibility corresponds at this moment to a kind of divinity. In Petrarch the erotic illusion had been quasi-pathological and the unreality of things a symptom; now the fantasy is an instrument of symbiosis.[15]

Poetry for Ronsard and his circle was precisely that privileged place where the sacred has its epiphany. Poetry is an initiation into the divine immanence dwelling within mortal things. There is no reason to doubt the remark of Guy Demerson: "Ronsard, à la différence des auteurs classiques et néo-classiques, et comme beaucoup de ses contemporains, devait croire à une intervention *réelle* de l'Esprit."[16] This pantheist vitalism Ronsard may have found in the hymns of Marullus, but he needed no text of cosmic energy. In one form or another, most of his poems can be said to reflect this intuition, to thematize or to embody the presence or absence of a numinous immanent power. It is this energy that erases the boundaries between the internal and the external, between the poem and its theme, between signifier and signified. In the process of sacred insinuation, observer and observed, sign and referent, are caught up in a fusion that is mystical and perhaps dangerous. Ronsard appears to have reconciled this intuition with his Christian faith by the poetic theology expressed in the *Abbrégé.*

Les Muses, Apollon, Mercure, Pallas & autres telles deitez ne nous representent autre chose que les puissances de Dieu, auxquelles premiers hommes avoyent donné plusieurs noms pour les divers effectz de son incompréhensible majesté.   [L 14:6]

The divinities which people the pages of his poetry would be the personified functions of a single transcendent deity. Less orthodox but truer to the implications of the work is the opening of "Le Chat."

Dieu est par tout, par tout se mesle Dieu,
Commencement, la fin et le milieu
De ce qui vit, et dont l'ame est enclose
Par tout, et tient en vigueur toute chose,
Comme nostre ame infuse dans nos corps.   [L 15:39]

God as agent in the corporeal world is the *anima mundi* of the Neoplatonists, Joyce's "Annyma," source of that energy ("vigueur") which charges things and charges above all the poet's invention.

Dieu est en nous, & par nous fait miracles,
Si que les vers d'un poëte ecrivant,
Ce sont des dieus les secrets & oracles,
Que par sa bouche ils poussent en avant.   [L 1:176]

Ronsard dramatized this faith more consistently than the author of his subtext, Ovid. His poetry aspires to be nothing less than hierophantic.

The superb sonnet 20 of the early *Amours* carries, it seems to me, this aspiration.

Je vouldroy bien richement jaunissant
  En pluye d'or goute à goute descendre
  Dans le beau sein de ma belle Cassandre,
  Lors qu'en ses yeulx le somme va glissant.   4
Je vouldroy bien en toreau blandissant
  Me transformer pour finement la prendre,
  Quand elle va par l'herbe la plus tendre
  Seule à l'escart mille fleurs ravissant.   8
Je vouldroy bien afin d'aiser ma peine
  Estre un Narcisse, & elle une fontaine
  Pour m'y plonger une nuict à sejour:
Et vouldroy bien que ceste nuict encore   12
  Durast tousjours sans que jamais l'Aurore
  D'un front nouveau nous r'allumast le jour.   [W 15]

Ronsard is one of the greatest erotic poets, and it would be wrong to deny the subtle eroticism of this poem. Yet the traditional reading, which regards it only in terms of sexual fantasy, is reductive. It can be read with equal propriety as a displaced poetic manifesto, the dream of a text that would overcome the distance to the signified by a mastery which was also a surrender to liquidity. The sonnet is immersed in the seductive appeal of the fluid, the golden rain falling drop by drop, the vagabond girl wandering in the field, the pool whose fatal invitation is irresistible, the enveloping night. No Narcissus image has ever been less narcissistic than this one; the myth is distorted to render this a plunge into a welcoming otherness. Mythography functions in Ronsard, as Terence Cave has well perceived,[17] as a threshold device. Here four images of sexual possession from myth are set down paratactically without interpretation, and no paraphrase can circumscribe all that can be intuited beyond this imagistic threshold. Perhaps of all Ronsard's poems, this provides us with an allegory of his profoundest poetic will. Sexuality might be said finally to be only a vehicle of "the profound desire to go beyond the limits of the individual self" (McFarlane)[18], a desire that is both existential and artistic. Narcissus plunges into a pool that is not himself, an object of desire always available, welcoming the surrender of identity, setting no resistance to divine energy more than the *estre* through which fantasy passes into fulfillment.

It is not too much to say that the fantasy of liquefaction, the will to endless metamorphosis, is among other things a willed *escape from Petrarch*. By changing or trying to change all Petrarchan discontinuities into continuities, a dualism into a monism, a radical oxymoron into a radical conflation, Ronsard associates Petrarch with a failure of penetration. The diachronic poems of the *Canzoniere* tend to act out a kind of fall from their subtexts; the *Stanze* of Poliziano act out a kind of dispersal; Ronsard's strongest Petrarchan poems act out heuristically a liberation, a movement from circular frustration to dynamic, undulating freedom. In the glow of that freedom, a certain critique of Petrarchan solipsism can be glimpsed. Yet the slackening of tension invites perhaps a countercriticism. The pool or the fountain tempting the speaker to plunge may conceal a risk, like the pool where Hylas drowns. Pure fluidity would be pure nonbeing. The Petrarchan sense of incompleteness, the consciousness of unfulfilled desire and unavailable divinity, may act to preserve in Ronsard a coherent creative ego that would otherwise flow away into an absolute *vague* of dissolution. Insofar as the voice of Petrarch remains audible (and in the love poetry as a corpus it is very audible indeed), insofar as the distinctness of a suffering human ego is maintained, a centripetal force remains to counter the centrifugal drift toward undifferentiated insinuations.

In the later love poetry, where the Petrarchan elements are thinned out by more numerous reworkings of the *Greek Anthology*, the Roman elegists, and Neo-Latin subtexts, the fantasized metamorphosis into water finds more explicit expression. Should it be read positively or negatively? In the "Voiage de Tours," Perrot the narrator sees Marion departing by boat and dreams of becoming the river (W 285). In the "Amours d'Eurymedon et de Calliree," the same wish recurs, supported by a translingual pun on Calliree (flowing pleasantly), which name designates Charles IX's mistress Anne d'Atri d'Acquaviva. Eurymedon invokes this lady ("Ah belle eau vivre, ah fille d'un rocher") to turn him also into a stream,

> Et d'eau pareille, et de pareille course
> Plongé dans toy, tousjours je te suivray.   [W 361]

Although this has anticipations in Hellenistic verse, its presence in Ronsard is peculiarly ambiguous, since for him the ultimate goal of erotic desire approximates uneasily the goal of absolute nonbeing. In other contexts, water is a Heraclitean symbol of flux.

> Mais, tout ainsi que l'onde aval des ruisseaux fuit
> Le pressant coulement de l'autre qui la suit,
> Ainsi le temps se coule, et le present fait place
> Au futur importun, qui les talons luy trace.
> Ce qui fut, se refait; tout coule, comme une eau,
> Et rien dessous le Ciel ne se voit de nouveau,
> Mais la forme se change en une autre nouvelle,
> Et ce changement-là, *Vivre*, au monde s'appelle,
> Et *Mourir*, quand la forme en une autre s'en va.   [L 8:178]

These lines adapted from Plutarch in the "Hymne de la Mort" seem to reduce the distinction between life and death by equating both to the flow of a stream emptied of any divine presence. The temptation of liquefaction can lead to self-annihilation as well as self-transcendence. It leads in either case away from the static loneliness of Petrarch, whose canzone "Chiare fresche e dolci acque" ad-

dresses a stream pathetically removed from the speaker because it has touched
Laura's limbs. In the last of Ronsard's major Petrarchan sequences, the *Sonnets
pour Hélène*, the progressively bitter clash of desire and anger is resolved by the
culminating image of another spring. The "Stances de la Fontaine d'Hélène"
begin:

> Ainsi que cest eau coule & s'enfuyt parmy l'herbe,
> Ainsi puisse couler en ceste eau le soucy.   [W 446]

The "fontaine," which flows away, *flees* into the meadow, is the symbol of a
homage that is also a flight and a renunciation, the final flight doubtless from the
Petrarchan into a Horatian cult that honors the spring as spring and dehumanizes
the woman.

> Les Nymphes de ces eaux & les Hamadryades,
> Que l'amoureux Satyre entre les bois poursuit,
> Se tenans main à main, de sauts & de gambades,
> Aux rayons du Croissant y dansent toute nuit.   (W 448]

The unity of love and death affirmed four sonnets later in the sequence's last line is
a unity of the frozen, the marmoreal, and the sterile, all that belongs to that poem's
dominant quality, *rigueur*. Before the double valediction, to mistress and dead
king, of this closing sonnet, the goal of the poetry has already been displaced to the
ceaselessly mobile.

   This mobility, it is worth repeating, is a property of the language itself. "Je suis
de cette opinion," wrote Ronsard in the preface to the odes of 1550, "que nulle
Poësie se doit louer pour acomplie, si elle ne ressemble la nature, laquelle ne fut
estimée belle des anciens, que pour estre inconstante, et variable en ses perfec-
tions." (L 1:47) Poetry—nature—antiquity—mobility: this tetrad seems to form a
cluster for Ronsard. If one were to ask how this mobility made itself felt in his
poetry, or how his language could be called in any meaningful sense liquid, an
answer might take the form of another opposition with the *Canzoniere*. The
heuristic itinerary that has been analyzed here primarily in ontological terms was
also semiotic. When Petrarch uses the laurel image, *il lauro*, ambiguously or puns
on *l'aura*, he is asserting indirectly the distinctive existence of the word as an object
in itself, more complex than any simple referent. This autonomy of the signifier
was asserted of course even more radically in the prose of Rabelais. Ronsard's
language moves in the other direction, toward a refusal of this autonomy. The
symbiosis toward which so many of his poems seem to strive also includes the
signifier itself, surrendering its independence to the swirl of the signified. There are
poems where the word seems to strain to become what it denotes.

> Vous triomphez de moy, & pource je vous donne
> Ce lhierre, qui coule & se glisse à l'entour
> Des arbres & des murs, lesquels tour dessus tour,
> Plis dessus plis il serre, embrasse & environne.   [W 474]

The ancient epithalamic image of ivy or vine encircling a tree invites the language itself to spiral, cling, and embrace. If one regards theme as primary, the language will appear to give itself up; if one regards language as primary, it will appear to be reaching out for thematic counterparts of its own sinuous modes of being. The primacy does not matter; in either case the signifier exchanges, or seems to exchange, its autonomy for a delicate interpenetration whose emblem might be the laurel of "La Guiterre."

> Son laurier preste l'oreille,
> Si qu'au premier vent qui vient,
> De ressifler s'appareille
> Ce que par cueur il retient.   [L 1:230]

This responsiveness to the first breath of a solicitation constitutes the linguistic meaning of fluidity.

3

Beneath the Petrarchan and post-Petrarchan rhetoric of so many of the *Amours* one can discern traces of a Greek poet who played a critical role in Ronsard's artistic evolution—Hesiod. This role is manifest in the privileged place accorded the myth of the theogony in Ronsard's poetry, in the particular centrality of the muses in his pantheon, in the direct imitation or pastiche of Hesiod in the hymns of the seasons, and in the representation of deities as inseparable from primeval, elemental forces. Ronsard seems to have seen in the poet of the *Theogony* the supreme artist of initiation and to have associated his own sacred initiation with the experience recounted at the beginning of that poem. In the "Hymne de l'Autonne," he writes that as an adolescent he entered the moonlit dances of nymphs and sylvans hoping that

> J'aurois incontinent l'ame plus genereuse,
> Ainsi que l'Ascrean qui gravement sonna,
> Quand l'une des neuf Soeurs du laurier luy donna.   [L 12:48]

Hesiod belonged, in Ronsard's categories, to the race of "divine" poets, along with Orpheus, Linus, and Homer; later figures, including Pindar, were merely human. In many of the *Amours*, structures of Hesiodic epiphanies, hierogamies, and theogonies can be made out at a level beneath the rhetoric stemming from wholly different traditions. The brutal and grandiose unions, conflicts, and manifestations of Hesiod's elemental universe may be reduced, even trivialized, by Renaissance love conventions, diminished by the very form of the sonnet, but it helps to catch the full resonance of the French poems if one strains to hear the archaic voice behind them.

We have already met a Hesiodic presence, of course, in those poems where a woman becomes the vehicle of a divinity dwelling within a physical element. In

Amours 42, this relationship grows directly out of an episode from the *Theogony* that had already attracted Poliziano—not to mention Botticelli.

Quand au matin ma Deesse s'abille
   D'un riche or crespe ombrageant ses talons,
   Et que les retz de ses beaulx cheveux blondz
   En cent façons ennonde et entortille: 4
Je l'accompare à l'escumiere fille
   Qui or peignant les siens jaunement longz,
   Or les ridant en mille crespillons
   Nageoyt abord dedans une coquille.   [W 28]

Ronsard found in Hesiod's account of the birth of Aphrodite the rationalization of her name: "born of foam." The goddess, "l'escumiere fille," is the incarnation of that liquidity caught by the waves of Cassandre's hair, for which the poet coins a verb: "ennonder." In the playful exchange of the epithets "Deesse" and "fille" there is the hint of an epiphany that is more than playful. By virtue of her undulating hair, Cassandre is also "escumiere." By the close of the sonnet, she is beginning to disappear into nature like a divinity concealed by rock, stream, or wood.

Rocz, eaux, ny boys, ne celent point en eulx
   Nymphe, qui ait si follastres cheveux. . . .[19]

This epiphanic character is muted in 42 by the tenderness of the tone. In *Amours* 65 it is unmistakable; Cassandre acquires a role in a universal dynamism.

Tant de couleurs le grand arc ne varie
   Contre le front du Soleil radieux,
   Lors que Junon, par un temps pluvieux,
   Renverse l'eau dont sa mere est nourrie: 4
Ne Juppiter armant sa main marrie
   En tant d'esclaire ne fait rougir les cieulx,
   Lors qu'il punist d'un fouldre audacieux
   Les montz d'Epire, ou l'orgeuil de Carie: 8
Ny le Soleil ne rayonne si beau,
   Quand au matin il nous monstre un flambeau,
   Pur, net, & clayr, comme je vy ma Dame
De cent couleurs son visage acoustrer,   12
   Flamber ses yeulx, & claire se monstrer,
   Le premier jour qu'elle ravit mon ame.   [W 42]

The Hesiodic vision of this sonnet can be measured by reference to the Petrarchan subtext, which opens:

Né cosí bello il sol giá mai levarsi
quando 'l ciel fosse piú de nebbia scarco,
né dopo pioggia vidi 'l celeste arco
per l'aere in color tanti variarsi. . . .   [*Canz.* 144]

[I never saw the sun rise so fair when the sky is most free of mist, nor after a rain the heavenly arc diversify itself through the air with so many colors. . . .]

The Petrarchan cosmos is essentially ornamental; Ronsard's is generative and agonistic.[20] The apparently irrelevant details in Ronsard's threefold comparison are in fact organic: Juno's pouring down rain to nourish the Hesiodic figure of her mother, Earth, Jupiter's hurling the lightning bolt, even the faint implication of contention in the preposition "contre" (line 2), all serve to create a cosmos of power, struggle, and growth that invests the lady with a vibrancy not restricted to the ostensible comparisons in the *rapportatio* of line 12–13. Laura in Petrarch's sonnet is outside the circle of generation. Nothing mortal could equal her face. (Nulla cosa mortal pote aguagliarsi.) This Petrarchan transcendence has not completely faded from the representation of Cassandre, but in this sonnet it is challenged and ultimately overcome by a Hellenic immanence.

In several of the early *Amours* a kind of conflict develops between the Petrarchan and the Hesiodic. This conflct is still clearer if later ancient poets, including Pindar, Lucretius, and the Virgil of the *Georgics*, are understood to be for this purpose avatars of Hesiod, perpetuators of a mythographic vision that had *hit* Ronsard most forcibly in its archaic expression. The poem thus becomes a small battleground, the locus of a struggle between cultural worlds, a *chronomachia*. Characteristically the Hesiodic voice is heard first and then appears to yield to the Petrarchan.

This is what happens in sonnet 161.

En ce pandant que tu frappes au but
  De la vertu, qui n'a point sa seconde,
  Et qu'à longz traitz tu t'enyvres de l'onde
  Que l'Ascrean entre les Muses but,					4
Ici, Bayf, où le mont de Sabut
  Charge de vins son espaulle féconde,
  Pensif je voy la fuite vagabonde
  Du Loyr qui traisne à la mer son tribut.					8
Ores un antre, or un desert sauvage,
  Ore me plaist le segret d'un rivage,
  Pour essayer de tromper mon ennuy:
Mais quelque horreur de forest qui me tienne,					12
  Faire ne puis qu'Amour tousjours ne vienne,
  Parlant à moy, & moy tousjours à luy.					[W 103]

The "Ascrean" (line 4) is of course Hesiod; "vertu" (line 2) is creative power, divinely derived; the image of the archer striking his mark contains a Pindaric echo,[21] although Ronsard's verb "frappes" is more vigorous than its subtext's. The closing tercet adapts the close of the familiar sonnet 35 of the *Canzoniere*, "Solo e pensoso," we already know. Ostensibly the sonnet contrasts the divine creative energy of Baif, inspired by the Hesiodic-Pindaric energy of the Hippocrene spring, with the unproductive *otium* of the speaker, cut off from inspiration and from society by the pain of love. The "desert sauvage" (line 9) appears to be the Petrarchan scene where significance is grounded in the absolute ego, whereas on Hesiod's Helicon, significance is grounded in the sacred breath of the nine goddesses, not yet lifeless fictions: "They breathed a divine voice into me to celebrate the story of future things and past things." (*Theogony*, 31–32) The conflict within the poem seems to accord a preference to the Hesiodic while leaving the speaker subject to the Petrarchan. Yet it seems to me that this is a poem where a *tertium quid* emerges from the *chronomachia*, allowing a distinct new consciousness and perhaps even a new semiotic to define themselves. The crucial hinge is the second quatrain, part of whose imagery (line 7) we are already in a position to interpret. This quatrain supplies an intermediate scene, expressively sketched.

> Ici . . . où le mont de Sabut
> Charge de vins son espaulle féconde.

The instant intoxication of the Hippocrene (line 3) finds a counterpart in the slow, gradual ripening of the Vendomois vineyards, just as the gushing of the spring has its counterpart in the slow, serpentine course of the Loire, and the Pindaric flight of the arrow to its mark is matched by the slow passage to the sea of its tribute (line 8). In the vagabond obliquity of the speaker's receptive melancholy, there is a gathering of power as fecund and still as the vine-bearing hillside. Thus the dialogue with Love at the close cannot be read as solipsistic but open and restorative; the pursuit of solitude cannot be read as a desperate flight but as a cultivation of random impressions: "Ore *me plaist* le segret d'un rivage." Significance now is grounded in an interchange which finds its fertility in imaginative inaction and meanders toward a power as vast and formless as the ocean's. Between a poetry of immediate access and a poetry of enclosure, a poetry of progressive access amasses strength. What is impressive is the organic flowering of this poetic disposition out of an explicit *chronomachia*, a staged anachronistic conflict.

Ronsard is not always so successful. Sonnet 9 of the *Bocage* opens with a Lucretian invocation:

> Ecumiere Venus, roine en Cypre puissante,
>   Mere des doux amours, à qui toujours se joint
>   Le plaisir, & le jeu, qui tout animal point
>   A toujours reparer sa race perissante,
> Sans toi, Nimfe aime-ris, la vie est languissante,
>   Sans toi rien n'est de beau, de vaillant ni de coint. . . .   [W 148]

imposing a hedonistic reduction on that goddess that drains off her power and is only intensified anachronistically by the vapid Petrarchan close. More interesting is the cultural conflict in *Amours* 155.

> Or que Juppin epoint de sa semence,
>   Hume, à longz traitz led feux accoustumez,
>   Et que du chault de ses rains allumez,
>   L'humide sein de Junon ensemence: 4

Or que la mer, or que la vehemence
   Des ventz fait place aux grandz vaisseaux armez,
   Et que l'oyseau parmy les boys ramez
   Du Thracien les tançons recommence: 8
Or que les prez, & ore que les fleurs,
   De mille & mille & de mille couleurs,
   Peignent le sein de la terre si gaye,
Seul, & pensif, aux rochers plus segretz,   12
   D'un cuoeur muét je conte mes regretz,
   Et par les boys je voys celant ma playe.   [W 100]

The opening image of Jupiter fecundating the goddess-landscape transposes in somewhat stronger language a subtext from the *Georgics*.

tum pater omnipotens fecundis imbribus Aether
coniugis in gremium laetae descendit, et omnis
magnus alit magno commixtus corpore fetus.   [2.325–27]
[Then Heaven, the Father almighty, comes down in fruitful showers into the lap of his joyous spouse, and his might, with her mighty frame commingling, nurtures all growths.][22]

Lines 5–6 may echo a subtext in the *Aeneid*.[23] In the closest analogue from the *Canzoniere*, sonnet 310, the natural world is filled with joy at the return of spring.

   Zefiro torna, e 'l bel tempo rimena
e i fiori e l'erbe, sua dolce famiglia,
e garrir Progne e pianger Filomena,
e primavera candida e vermiglia;   4
   ridono i prati, e 'l ciel si rasserena,
Giove s' allegra di mirar sua figlia;
l' aria e l' acqua e la terra è d' amor piena;
ogni animal d' amar si riconsiglia.   8
   Ma per me, lasso, tornano i più gravi
sospiri. . . .
[Zephyrus returns and leads back the fine weather and the flowers and the grass, his sweet family, and chattering Procne and weeping Philomena, and Spring, all white and vermilion; the meadows laugh and the sky becomes clear again, Jupiter is gladdened looking at his daughter, the air and the waters and the earth are full of love, every animal takes counsel again to love. But to me, alas, come back heavier sighs. . . .]

Petrarch's great sonnet reshaped a medieval convention and made it available for innumerable Renaissance variations. If one confronts it with an ancient description of spring like Virgil's (of which I have quoted only the opening lines), one is struck by the disjunctures that underlie the surface resemblances. The personifications in Petrarch (Zephyr, Jove, his daughter Proserpine) are weakly projected, but in Virgil as in Ronsard the personified natural forces help to suggest a rugged cosmic generative power. Nature is filled with love in the one poem but makes love in the others. The *chronomachia* pits a world centered on individual suffering against a world where individual incompleteness is dwarfed and justified by immense constructive forces in space and time, a world where strenuous physical activity has value. Ronsard moves from the widest possible perspective on that world in the first quatrain down through progressively narrower perspectives to the private figure of the lover at the close. Logically the effect here as in Petrarch is to isolate him. Yet I submit that in the vehement vitality of the Hesiodic-Virgilian universe, the lover cannot easily retain his centrality. The will to participation, the will to yield up a private selfhood has not entirely been exorcised from the poem. The only talisman against participation lies in the Petrarchan wound, the "playe," which may or may not be absorbed, according to one's reading, in the cosmic rush. Petrarchan pain is the one weak guarantee of distinct identity. This is a poem that seems narrowly balanced between the cultural forces it brings into play, tilting toward the ancient subtexts without permitting a definitive victory.

In relation to the Hesiodic-Lucretian-Georgic voices, the voice of Horace in Ronsard's work sounds a sharply different note, or rather several notes, not easily or quickly analyzed. At least one or two remarks can be made. Horace supplied Ronsard with images of vital decline and death that did not violate Hesiodic images of cosmic energy. Horace supplied an "Epicurean" acceptance of death, not without regret but without anguish, that could serve as an alternative to Christian judgment and Petrarch's anxiety of temporality. As Ronsard grew older, his creative power became more intermittent (as he confesses in "La Lyre") along with the corollary intuition of universal forces. Horace's serene contemplation of organic decline permitted Ronsard to deal with those cold failures of vitalist faith and verve that are found in the late poetry; it offered him moral and rhetorical stances of which the *carpe diem* syllogism was only the most visible and common.

Horace could do this the more easily because his own sense of a sacred presence in nature had faded without entirely disappearing. He perpetuated the cult of divinities, both universal and local, out of a love for the cult as much as out of deeply felt faith. When Horatian subtexts appear in early Ronsard, one commonly finds them revitalized. Thus in the early versions of the first "Fontaine Bellerie" ode, Ronsard anthropomorphises the spring in ways Horace had avoided in his "Fons Bandusiae." In the Latin ode, the poet pours wine, scatters garlands, sacrifices a kid to the spring as a numinous local presence but stops short of representing it as a divinity and thus blurring its distinctness as a spring. This as one would expect is what Ronsard does proceed to do.

O Déesse Bellerie . . .
Tu es la Nimphe eternelle
De ma terre paternelle.   [L 1:203]

The poet's verses mingle with the gurgling of the spring, but the Horatian subtext seems to withhold him from any closer symbiosis. In the marvelous closing stanza, the poet represents himself as celebrating the gush of water and as celebrator remains an acolyte, bound by devotional sympathy but nonetheless apart.

It is tempting to read the lines just quoted as Ronsard never intended and to see this nymph as a symbol of the imitative facility with which he appropriated the heritage of his poetic fathers, in this instance Horace. If Ronsard failed to understand the problematic character of creative imitation, the counterpart of that failure was the thoughtless capacity to elicit a historical flow within his poems. The intertextual play within his work was not of course unpremeditated, but the manipulation of anachronistic disjunctures seems to depend finally on artistic instinct rather than calculation. There are diachronic as well as ontological symbioses, and they produce a genuine experience of discovery. Writing too much and working too fast, caught between dedication and mendicity, he was still haunted by those dead spirits Longinus described as effluences, impregnating the writer as the divine vapor fills the Pythian priestess. "Je suis semblable," wrote Ronsard, "à la prestresse folle,"

> Qui bégue perd la voix & la parolle,
> Dessoubz le Dieu qu'elle fuit pour néant.   [W 19]

But as he knew well, the priestess loses her voice only to find it.

Eleven • Du Bellay and the Disinterment of Rome

Architecture is a kind of rhetoric of power.

—*Nietzsche*

The canon of Du Bellay's poetry contains many types and accents of imitative art, from the fragile versions of Horace in the *Vers lyriques,* just hovering this side of the brink of reproduction, to the eclecticism of *Olive,* with its refractions of Petrarch and Ariosto and its virtual translations of obscure contemporaneous Italian sonneteers—not genuine imitations at all in our sense—to the formal rewriting of 1 Kings in the "Monomachie de David et de Goliath," and finally the kind of sardonic parody of Ovid and Catullus represented by *Les Regrets* 103, a withering lament for the deceased catamite of Cardinal Caraffa, the future Paul IV.

> il te faut lamenter
> Le bel Ascaigne mesme, Ascaigne, ô quel dommage!
> Ascaigne que Caraffe aymoit plus que ses yeux . . .[1]

The range of imitative relationships between subtext and surface text in Du Bellay's oeuvre is vastly wider than the *Deffence* had appeared to envisage. Nonetheless I shall confine my discussion of intertextuality in his poetry to *Les Antiquitez de Rome,* a sequence of thirty-two sonnets (excluding the *Songe* that follows) that brings a special self-consciousness and even a special drama to the imitative act. It also brings a special complication. According to the distinction suggested above in chapter 3, the *Antiquitez* constitute a work of "complex" imitation, since history is the theme of the sequence as well as the basis of a major formal technique. This imitative technique is in fact obliquely thematized, so that the interplay between theme and art becomes so dense as to be inexhaustible. The antithetical impulses that in the *Deffence* produce vacillation and ambivalence are now controlled and foregrounded, so as to make humanist insecurity a focal element of the poetic drama. The sequence watches itself act out the conventional humanist rituals and sets ironic traps for its own performance, thus producing paradoxically a more truly coherent, if deeply skeptical, commentary on the humanist adventure.

Du Bellay lived in Rome from 1553 to 1557. He served there in the retinue of a kinsman who was a cardinal, and his duties seem to have included such ungrateful chores as putting off creditors and courting moneylenders. Morose, ill, homesick, and self-pitying, he was doubly uprooted. He had left his family's land in Anjou as a younger son of the petty nobility, a product of the late feudal society still extant in the French provinces, a *déclassé* for whom aristocratic assumptions and loyalties

220

were not yet outmoded. He had left that heritage and moved in a series of displacements to the Latin quarter of Paris, to the fringes of the Valois court, and then to Rome. He was exiled from France but more poignantly from his *terre* and the role that went with it, and this loss of *attachments* is of course the subject of his most famous sonnet. Now he lived with the dislocations of a vivid but sterile modern metropolis that existed for money and based its power on money rather than land tenure. Deracinated and discontent, involved in a fruitless intrigue with a married courtesan, his ambition, nostalgia, and libido equally ungratified, he composed in Rome his most arresting poetry: four collections in four years, three in French, one in Latin, all of them reflecting his Roman experience in varying degrees and tonalities. There are accents of weariness and lament, of touristic curiosity, of malice, failure, self-doubt, and loneliness, together with repeated gestures of friendship toward friends in Italy and France, as though to improvise a fragile, invisible community. There are also accents of puzzlement and wonder which betray cultural shock, shock which embraces both the ruins of antiquity and the modern city, a ruined Renaissance, in its *dépaysement*. In this expression of displacement from his medieval sources and exclusion from a crumbled classical myth, Du Bellay can stand with exemplary clarity as representative of a stage of Renaissance poetry. If the Renaissance began with the discovery of cultural distinctions, this poet's rueful and perplexed dealings with the alien face of Rome can epitomize that discovery. It was all the more painful in this instance because it revealed the conjunction of past and present as deeply problematic.

Du Bellay's experience as displaced poet is exemplary because he seems to have passed through what might be called the central humanist drama. This at least is the experience realized in the poems, the only experience that matters to us. He discovered in Rome the fragmented, deciduous majesty of the ancient past; he encountered the heartbreaking inscrutability of history; he measured the difficulty of calling the dead back to life and faced the subtle frustrations of artistic emulation. The sorrow and the irony of the Roman poems at their deepest stem from the dismay of a pilgrim who reaches his goal uncertain of its meaning and value, unsure of his own posture, at a loss for the connection he wants to make. Du Bellay was finally obliged to recognize only the disorderly contiguity between the past and an uncontrollable European future already actualized hatefully in the Roman present. In all these respects he might be said to have experienced most acutely a series of shocks and strains that had been incipient continuously in the humanist enterprise and would remain. The poems represent a man living out these strains with a self-consciousness that makes the Roman period an extended crisis, both artistic and existential, a knot of tensions within a cultural sensibility and a creative imagination. Because Du Bellay's situation became in so many ways exemplary, it is possible to speak of a larger crisis of the humanist movement precipitated in the life of one microcosmic individual.

The *Antiquitez de Rome* constitute a poem not so much about the Roman ruins as about an individual responding to ruins, trying in the already well-worn image to resurrect them. Thus it becomes a deliberate imitation of an imitation. Before the close, it becomes not only an inquisition of humanism but an inquisition of the very value and morality of civilization. It translates a will to penetrate a shattered landscape, a specific, situated, famous landscape, with the power of poetry. It also translates a will to imitate, and emulate, the poets who are somehow latent in the landscape, haunting it or buried beneath it. It is at once a homage, a challenge, a ritual of summoning, a gesture of disinterment, a reconstruction, and a demystifying reflection on all these aspects of itself. They are all tinged with the suspicion of failure, even the demystification.

Du Bellay's title links his poem with the vast effort of travelers, epigraphers, archaeologists, and collectors that developed in the earlier quattrocento, an endeavor best symbolized by that charming and indefatigable tourist, Ciriaco d'Ancona. It was the quattrocento that gave us the term and role of *antiquary*, a role that was at once learned, dilettantist, fanciful, sometimes commercial, and did not lack a touch of the necromantic.[2] Ciriaco described his occupation as "awakening the dead." But the *Antiquitez* are also deliberately oriented toward the future, toward an architecture to come as well as an antiquarianism of *temporis acti*. In fact the prefatory sonnet to the king situates the sequence within the framework of a rebuilding not yet begun.

> Ne vous pouvant donner ces ouvrages antiques
>   Pour vostre Sainct-Germain, ou pour Fontainebleau,
>   Je les vous donne (Sire) en ce petit tableau
>   Peint, le mieux que j'ay peu, de couleurs poëtiques.   4
> Qui mis sous vostre nom devant les yeux publiques,
>   Si vous le daignez voir en son jour le plus beau,
>   Se pourra bien vanter d'avoir hors du tumbeau
>   Tiré des vieux Romains les poudreuses reliques.   8
> Que vous puissent les Dieux un jour donner tant d'heur,
>   De rebastir en France une telle grandeur
>   Que je la voudrois bien peindre en vostre langage:
> Et peut estre, qu'à lors vostre grand' Majesté   12
>   Repensant à mes vers, diroit qu'ilz ont esté
>   De vostre Monarchie un bienheureux presage.

If these lines are to be seen as a presage once greatness has been rebuilt in France, then they in themselves already constitute a preliminary act toward this end. Political, architectural, and poetic activity is all parallel, covered by the single verb in line 10.[3] The antiquarian dust will be soil on which the edifice of a new culture is to be erected. Masonry begins with the exhumation of lines 7–8, the opening of a dusty tomb in order to reconstruct an imitative civilization.

This exhumation becomes in the opening sonnet proper a formal rite, performed according to the ancient ceremonial. It is the quintessential humanist rite, the calling up of the ancient dead in imitation of their own gestures and their own style.

> Divins Esprits, dont la poudreuse cendre
>   Gist sous le faix de tant de murs couvers,

Non vostre loz, qui vif par voz beaux vers
  Ne se verra sous la terre descendre,   4
Si des humains la voix se peult estendre
  Depuis icy jusqu'au fond des enfers,
  Soient à mon cry les abysmes ouvers,
  Tant que d'abas vous me puissiez entendre.   8
Trois fois cernant sous le voile des cieux
  De voz tumbeaus le tour devocieux,
  A haulte voix trois fois je vous appelle:
J'invoque icy vostre antique fureur,   12
  En ce pendant que d'une saincte horreur
  Je vays chantant vostre gloire plus belle.

The Virgilian religiosity of this sonnet is achieved in part by a Virgilian crafts-manship: the alliteration and internal rhyme in lines 3–4, the triple rhyme in line 11—"voix trois fois," the delay of the first sentence's main clause until line 7, the hypotactic structure, which is never allowed to obscure the firm and spacious syntax. This is the first in a series that will reveal Du Bellay as one of the great architects of the French sonnet. The lofty arch of entry opens upon an initiation, or at least the prayer for an initiation, binding speaker and reader, which may or may not come to pass. For the threefold circling of the ancients' tombs, Screech cites Erasmus citing Virgil's eighth eclogue; this eclogue with its rehearsal of magical spells is doubtless relevant, but surely the funeral of Misenus in *Aeneid* 6. 212ff. is the more significant text, and all the more because it precedes a prayer by the poet that he be allowed to open up the earth and visit the dead.

Di, quibus imperium est animarum, umbraeque silentes
et Chaos et Phlegethon, loca nocte tacentia late,
sit mihi fas audita loqui, sit numine vestro
pandere res alta terra et caligine mersas.   [6. 264–67]
[Gods whose dominion is over the Souls, Shades without sound, Void, and you,
Burning River, and you, broad Spaces voiceless beneath the Night, may I remain
sinless in telling what has been told to me, and, by your divine assent, reveal [literally,
throw open] truth sunk in depths of earth and gloom.][4]

Thus in Du Bellay's prayer the literary repetition is a religious repetition. The invocation "Soient à mon cry les abysmes ouvers" seeks to stage a *solemnity* in the Renaissance sense, a formal ceremony, in this case an awesome penetration of chthonic depths, in order to receive the inspirational fury, "fureur" (1. 12) that may still cling to the place. The speaker cannot yet claim the authority of the initiate that Virgil claimed; he cannot pretend to tell things heard ("audita loqui") that others have not heard. Compared to Virgil, he seems unsupported and isolated. He can only hope to be effective by the sympathetic magic of verbal imitation. The "tour devocieux" (1. 10; Latin *devotio*—magical charm) of the poetic follower and rebuilder is announced as an arcane mystery. Only the sonnet's closing words break the spell with the hint of secret emulation; if we ask, "more beautiful than what?" the only answer can be "than my own glory."

The first *explicit* imitation of ancient poetry appears in sonnet 6, which draws again on the sixth book of the *Aeneid.*

Telle que dans son char la Berecynthienne
  Couronnée de tours, & joyeuse d'avoir
  Enfanté tant de Dieux, telle se faisoit voir
  En ses jours plus heureux ceste ville ancienne: 4
Ceste ville, qui fut plus que la Phrygienne
  Foisonnante en enfans, & de qui le pouvoir
  Fut le pouvoir du monde, & ne se peut revoir
  Pareille à sa grandeur, grandeur sinon la sienne.   8
Rome seule pouvoit à Rome ressembler,
  Rome seule pouvoit Rome faire trembler:
  Aussi n'avoit permis l'ordonnance fatale
Qu'autre pouvoir humain, tant fust audacieux,   12
  Se vantast d'égaler celle qui fit égale
Sa puissance à la terre, & son courage aux cieux.

The opening and closing lines allude to the great Cybele simile with which Anchises' survey of Roman history opens. The worship of the Berecynthian, goddess of the earth, her turreted crown symbolizing the cities built upon the earth, had been brought from Phrygia to Rome as Aeneas was led. Virgil's image itself looks back to Lucretius (2. 600ff.) and more remotely to Euripides (*Helen*, 1319ff.)

En huius, nate, auspiciis illa incluta Roma
imperium terris, animos aequabit Olympo,
septemque una sibi muro circumdabit arces,
felix prole virum: qualis Berecyntia mater
invehitur curru Phrygias turrita per urbes
laeta deum partu, centum complexa nepotes,
omnis caelicolas, omnis supera alta tenentis.   [6. 781–87]
[See, my son! It will be through his inauguration that Rome shall become illustrious, and extend her authority to the breadth of the earth and her spirit to the height of Olympus. She shall build her single wall round seven citadels, and she shall be blessed in her manhood's increase; like the Mother of Berecyntus, who rides in her chariot through Phrygian cities wearing her towered crown, happy in the divine family which she has borne, and caressing her hundred grandsons, who are all dwellers in Heaven and have homes on high.]

Cybele appears at the climax of Aeneas's visit to Hades as an embodiment of fertility but also of maternal attachment, of bonds between generations, as she embraces her sons and grandsons. The horizontal embrace between continents and across the empire is also a vertical embrace across time. Her recall in the ruinous present can only produce a majestic and virile sorrow that is in its own way profoundly Virgilian. Thus the poetry attains a kind of continuity in the act of dramatizing rupture. Yet if we take its own assertions literally, this continuity is impossible; imitation is impossible.

Rome seule pouvoit à Rome ressembler:
Rome seule pouvoit Rome faire trembler.

There is something hieratic and terrible in this fourfold iteration of an insistent syllable, something almost of a death-knell, not for the city but for the delusion of rebuilding it. How fecund *was* the city in its children, "foisonnante en enfans"? How far across time does the goddess's embrace reach? Not apparently to the modern visitor who would like to claim descendance. The open prosodic structure of the octave, with its frequent enjambments, gives way to this end-stopped chant that seems to crush the latter-day emulator. To hope to equal Rome is to defy the "ordonnance fatale" that decreed Roman uniqueness. The verb "se vantast" in line 13 echoes the prefatory sonnet.

> ce petit tableau . . .
> Se pourra bien vanter d'avoir hors du tumbeau
> Tiré des vieux Romains les poudreuses reliques.

The self-referential irony of sonnet 6 is humbling. The ceremonial solemnity in sonnet 1 is damaged by a secularizing consciousness that doubts the humanist rituals it is performing.

This doubt will recur repeatedly in the *Antiquitez*, and not least in those poems that make the heaviest use of ancient Latin subtexts. Sonnet 28 adapts an extended simile from Lucan's *Pharsalia*.

Qui a veu quelquefois un grand chesne asseiché,	
Qui pour son ornement quelque trophée porte,	
Lever encor' au ciel sa vieille teste morte,	
Dont le pied fermement n'est en terre fiché,	4
Mais qui dessus le champ plus qu'à demy panché	
Monstre ses bras tous nuds, & sa racine torte,	
Et sans feuille umbrageux, de son poix se supporte	
Sur son tronc noüailleux en cent lieux esbranché;	8
Et bien qu'au premier vent il doive sa ruine,	
Et maint jeune à l'entour ait ferme la racine,	
Du devot populaire estre seul reveré.	
Qui tel chesne a peu voir, qu'il imagine encores	12
Comme entre les citez, qui plus florissent ores,	
Ce vieil honneur pouldreux est le plus honnoré.	

Lucan's image is applied to the aging Pompey, emptied in age of the valor that once distinguished him, standing in the shadow of his own great name.

> qualis frugifero quercus sublimis in agro
> exuvias veteris populi sacrataque gestans
> dona ducum nec iam validis radicibus haerens
> pondere fixa suo est, nudosque per aera ramos
> effundens trunco, non frondibus, efficit umbram,
> et quamvis primo nutet casura sub Euro,

tot circum silvae firmo se robore tollant,
sola tamen colitur.   [1. 136–43]
[It was as when an oak towering above a lush meadow—the repository of votive
offerings and enemy spoils hung on its branches by bygone tribal chieftains—ceases to
derive any support from the roots, but relies merely on its bulk to keep it upright.
Leafless boughs protrude into the sky, it throws no more than a skeletal shadow and
totters in the breeze: the first northeaster will send it crashing down. How strange that
though many near-by trees are still green and firmly rooted, this hollow oak alone is an
object of veneration!][5]

Du Bellay's additions to Lucan's powerful simile make the tree drier, knottier,
more twisted, angled more insecurely, and in one expressive and original line, the
third, closer to a hideous senility. There is of course a cluster of ironies in the choice
of this image from this poem, written to chronicle what its author saw as the end of
Roman heroism and written during a reign (Nero's) that could only parody
heroism. There is a brilliance in seizing on this image of a hollowed idol to
represent the destiny of the community he failed to defend. The bite of the sarcasm
here, close to the end of the sequence, in the contemptuous phrase "ce vieil
honneur pouldreux" would have been out of place near the opening. Does the
sarcasm touch the speaker himself, who had begun with veneration for the
"poudreuses reliques" of this senile city? It is hard to exclude the humanist from
the superstitious, misguided "devot populaire" of line 11, who continue perversely
to pay homage to a shell of the past. We remember it was the speaker who at the
outset made his "tour devocieux" about the tombs of the dead. Again the imitative
gesture appears to be used against itself, and the result is almost aporetic. The
demystifying power of the imitation justifies it in the face of demystification. Rome
after all retains some substance, some perpetuity, if its poetry and its history can be
manipulated to such effect. The secularizing drift away from the conventional
necromantic ritual is countered by the fact of an achieved revitalization. The
itinerary of an image across a millennium and a half may lead to the temptation of
despair, but a crossing nonetheless is made.

The attentive reader of the *Antiquitez* learns to catch the self-referential glances
almost lost in the meditations and invocations. The figure of the visitor, the
northerner, the idolator, or the predator who collects imperial shards returns in a
dozen various guises, always under suspicion. Is there not a hint of self-judgment
in the marvelous chiasmus of sonnet 7?

Las peu à peu cendre vous devenez,
Fable du peuple, & publiques rapines!

or in the image of the vindictive imperial captives now freed from their bonds?

Ainsi ceulx qui jadis souloient, à teste basse,
Du triomphe Romain la gloire accompagner,
Sur ces pouldreux tumbeaux exercent leur audace.   [14]

To assert the presence of a deliberate self-referential allusion in sonnet 21 is more
hazardous, but it too seems to adumbrate at some level of authorial consciousness a

drama of humanist failure. It moves from an opening that telescopes passages in Horace and Lucan on the decay of the empire[6] to an image of shipwreck at the end of a voyage.

Celle que Pyrrhe & le Mars de Libye
  N'ont sceu donter . . .
Tant que sa nef par tant d'ondes ravie
  Eut contre soy tout le monde incité,
  On n'a point veu le roc d'adversité
  Rompre sa course heureusement suivie: 8
Mais defaillant l'object de sa vertu,
  Son pouvoir s'est de luymesme abbatu,
  Comme celuy, que le cruel orage
A longuement gardé de faire abbord,   12
  Si trop grand vent le chasse sur le port,
  Dessus le port se void faire naufrage.

The ostensible subject is that civil discord which in several though not all the sonnets is cited as the cause of Rome's fall. But the image of the voyage in fact fits Roman history less well than it fits the traveler who, spiritually and physically, has made a pilgrimage to the goal of his endeavor and is oppressed, even annihilated, by what he finds. Whether or not Du Bellay recognized the full aptness of his simile, he composed a little allegory of the itinerary of the humanist, defeated only when he ends his quest.[7]

The extension of the Roman historical curve to a universal curve is of course authorized by these poems. If the city was unique, it was also exemplary: "le plan de Rome est la carte du monde" (26). No presage of the French future could be more accurate and terrible than the warning against "fraternelle rage." And no experience for the necromancer and rebuilder could be more crushing than the end of building. The *Antiquitez* offer alternative versions of the relation between the Roman past and the French future. The liminary sonnet seems to suggest that "In my (Roman) beginning is my (French) beginning": the return to the source is fecundating. Other sonnets hint that "In their end is our end": as civil violence destroyed them, so it might us. More directly threatening to the speaker is the thought that "In my beginning is my end": I recognize from these ruins the futility of poetry, of enterprise, of civilization. I recognize the limits, metaphysical and moral, of the humanist impulse. I understand that my port is my shipwreck.

It is the futility of poetry and all edification that the closing sonnet finally voices without ambiguity.

Esperez vous que la posterité
  Doive (mes vers) pour tout jamais vous lire?
  Esperez vous que l'oeuvre d'une lyre
  Puisse acquerir telle immortalité?   4
Si sous le ciel fust quelque eternité,
  Les monuments que je vous ay fait dire,
  Non en papier, mais en marbre & porphyre,
  Eussent gardé leur vive antiquité.   8

This would appear to be the final demystification. The monuments have not remained alive, *vives*; the ritual summoning of the dead has failed to recall them; the faith in imitative magic has proven naive. The crumbling of these stones awaits all building. But this caustic rhetorical question and reply are followed curiously by a concession and a conditional affirmative.

> Ne laisse pas toutefois de sonner
>> Luth, qu'Apollon m'a bien daigné donner:
>> Car si le temps ta gloire ne desrobbe,
> Vanter te peuls, quelque bas que tu sois,   12
>> D'avoir chanté le premier des François,
>> L'antique honneur du peuple à longue robbe.

"Vanter te peuls"—the verb has become discredited with repetition and yet it returns here with the decision to continue. The poet will not silence his lute despite the losses that make up history, despite his own demystifications, despite the ironies he perpetuates, perversely and admirably, to the last line. The phrase "peuple à longue robbe" renders Virgil's "gentemque togatam," the final subtext of the sequence (*Aeneid* 1. 282). One can do no better than to quote Screech: "Ce vers, très connu à l'époque, aurait rappelé au lecteur cultivé tout son contexte." It is worth quoting this context, Jupiter's famous prophecy of endless dominion.

> Hic ego nec metas rerum, nec tempora pono:
> Imperium sine fine dedi. Quin aspera Juno, . . .
> Consilia in melius referet, mecumque fovebit
> Romanos rerum dominos, gentemque togatam.
> [To Romans I set no boundary in space or time. I have granted them dominion, and it has no end. Yes, even the furious Juno shall amend her plans, and she and I will foster the nation which wears the toga, the Roman nation, masters of the world.]

This paean to Roman immortality was the only text necessary to complete Du Bellay's web of ironies. It frames his decision to continue composing poetry, his failed demystification, with the hollowness of its cultural hope.

His work has to be read as a labyrinth of ironies. There is the irony of Virgil's (apparent) ignorance, the irony of Horace's and Lucan's uselsss wisdom. There is the irony of poetry's helplessness against time. There is the irony of the artist who wants to construct with fragments and resurrect without authority. There is the irony that the descent into history apparently undermines the imagination rather than nourishing it. Undermines but educates. The etiological itinerary from subtext to surface text is a process of ironization. Yet the loss and the threat of failure thematized by these poems is qualified by the gain of lucidity implicit in the irony. Dialectical imitation has in the last analysis contributed to great poetry, has both produced and endured its own skepticism. The strongest defense against anachronism is the deliberate insistence on anachronism. "In my end is my beginning": the humanist poet is exposed and authenticated by his inquisition.

2

The prefatory sonnet of the *Antiquitez de Rome* contains three metaphors for the composition of the poems to follow: painting ("ce petit tableau peint . . . de couleurs poëtiques"), exhumation, construction. These metaphors recur in the twenty-fifth sonnet, where each again refers to the composition of poetry but now is associated with a prestigious figure of antiquity.

> Que n'ay-je encor la harpe Thracienne,
>   Pour réveiller de l'enfer paresseux
>   Ces vieux Cesars, & les Umbres de ceux
>   Qui ont basty ceste ville ancienne?   4
> Ou que je n'ay celle Amphionienne,
>   Pour animer d'un accord plus heureux
>   De ces vieux murs les ossemens pierreux,
>   Et restaurer la gloire Ausonienne?   8
> Peusse-je aumoins d'un pinceau plus agile
>   Sur le patron de quelque grand Virgile
>   De ces palais les portraits façonner:
> J'entreprendrois, veu l'ardeur qui m'allume,   12
>   De rebastir au compas de la plume
>   Ce que les mains ne peuvent maçonner.

In lines 1–4 poetry is accorded a potential power superior to the magic of the liminary sonnet, since it might awake the shades of the dead, not only the ruins of their city, just as the Thracian singer Orpheus moved the shades of the underworld to tears and attempted to lead Eurydice back to life. Poetry in the second quatrain is also a means of rebuilding, as Amphion once built the walls of Thebes. But the boundary between the two metaphors is blurred in both quatrains. In the second the reconstruction is presented as a resuscitation by means of the verb "animer" and by the figurative linking of ruins with bones ("ossemens pierreux"). In the first quatrain the Orphic conjuration is specifically aimed at those who first built Rome ("ceux qui ont basty ceste ville ancienne"), as though the conjuration were only the first step to the reconstruction. Thus each metaphoric function of the poetic act tends to fade into the other; Orpheus and Amphion begin to trade roles. The last of the three functions already familiar to us appears in the first tercet, which names Virgil as the ideal master of poetry considered as descriptive painting. Yet here again the major verb, "façonner," refers back to the masonic function, and it is this Amphionic art that dominates the closing tercet, with its dependence on the key verbs "rebastir" and "maçonner" which had been withheld until this conclusion.

   Thus sonnet 25 repeats the triadic figuration of poetic composition sketched at the outset. But Du Bellay's repetition in this sonnet of his art's necromantic, formative, and painterly power is heavily qualified by its syntactic articulation. Whatever the potency to which humanist poetry might attain, here it is not merely hypothetical; it is contrary to fact. The poet represents himself as an Orpheus, Amphion, or Virgil *manqué* who will *not* construct a grandeur to rival antiquity, despite the implication here as elsewhere that the true poet is fitter than a king for such an endeavor. This contrast in syntax and attitude corresponds to the shift of outlook from the opening of the sequence to its close which we have already observed. In view of this shift, the persistence of the metaphoric triad is the more notable.

The triad reappears again in the opening sonnet of *Les Regrets*, where its formulation is flatly and aggressively negative.

> Je ne veulx point fouiller au seing de la nature,
> > Je ne veulx point chercher l'esprit de l'univers,
> > Je ne veulx point sonder les abysmes couvers,
> > Ny desseigner du ciel la belle architecture.   4
> Je ne peins mes tableaux de si riche peinture,
> > Et si hauts argumens ne recherche à mes vers . . .

These lines seem to announce the poet's refusal to assume the traditional responsibilities of poetry written in the high style, and in a certain measure the responsibilities assumed by the school he had helped to form and publicize. His aspirations in *Les Regrets* will fall short of poetry's noblest and most proper goals; they rise no higher than a versified journal.

> Et de plus braves noms ne les veulx deguiser
> Que de papiers journaulx, ou bien de commentaires.   [1.13–14]

Even in the negative posture of this pseudorenunciation, one can measure the amplitude of Du Bellay's demands upon poetry. The Amphion theme is expanded in line 4, in a majestic, effortless expansion, to fit the supernal structure of the cosmos. The Orphic theme is now applied to the mysterious depths of the universe, which another's vision, if not the poet's, may sound and explore. The grandiose amplitude of the conception withstands the faint irony and the insistent anaphora of lines 1–3, is sustained in the lofty simplicity of line 4, and only shrinks a bit with the appearance of the painterly motif in line 5, which completes somewhat less forcibly the triad we have come to recognize. Of the three formulations of this triad, one has been hopeful, one regretful, one renunciative. The structures to be reared by Amphionic power have varied, as have the depths to be plumbed by Orphic audacity and the tableaus rendered by the neo-Virgilian palette. But each text has circumscribed the composition of humanist poetry within these three activities.

In each of the three sonnets, the activity of painting receives the weakest imagistic evocation. Suggested perhaps by a famous Horatian tag, it did not truly speak to Du Bellay's imagination. Occasional passages in his verse, most notably in the Roman volumes, bear witness to an intermittent concern for visual vivacity and precision, but with this concession the painterly motif can be dismissed from the analysis of his art and his reflection upon it. As we know, the remaining two activities are central. It remains to be shown to what degree they are interdependent. If in sonnet 25 of the *Antiquitez* each metaphor, the Orphic and the Amphionic, penetrates the other, it is notable that something like this happens in several sonnets of the sequence. It happens in 5, for example, one of the most visibly necromantic.

> Rome n'est plus, & si l'architecture
> Quelque umbre encor de Rome fait revoir,
> C'est comme un corps par magique sçavoir
> Tiré de nuict hors de sa sepulture.

Here it is the fallen buildings themselves rather than the poet which practice the necromantic art, aided by a faint play on the word "umbre," which means both "remote vestige" and "ghost." The ruinous architecture calls up the memory of its splendor the way a spirit is conjured from the tomb. The use of assonance or internal rhyme before the caesura ("encor" / "corps"), not uncommon in this work, may in this passage underscore faintly the perpetuation of something almost lost. At any rate, the Amphionic-architectonic image is again interwoven with the Orphic-necromantic. This happens once more in sonnet 15.

> Palles Esprits, & vous Umbres pouldreuses,
> Qui jouissant de la clarté du jour
> Fistes sortir cet orgueilleux sejour,
> Dont nous voyons les reliques cendreuses: 4
> Dictes Esprits (ainsi les tenebreuses
> Rives de Styx non passable au retour,
> Vous enlassant d'un trois fois triple tour,
> N'enferment point voz images umbreuses)   8
> Dictes moy donc. . . .

The spirits addressed, represented here not as entombed but as confined to Hades, are those who once in the light of day caused this proud dwelling place to rise up, *le firent sortir*, literally caused it to come out, as though it emerged from the earth under which they now languish. The force of the verb *sortir* cannot be dissociated from the parenthesis in lines 5–8, which envisages a potential liberation of the dead spirits. Thus the original act of building Rome, of erecting this proud city, is contaminated with a passage up from the subterranean. Humanist revocation would be a reenactment of the first architectural conjuration.

If these two metaphoric clusters are mingled so often, this is doubtless because Du Bellay seems to have conceived of the creative act as *always* involving this double gesture—first penetrating depths to bring up some one or something from them, and secondly restoring it to being and form, designing, shaping, and structuring a harmonious edifice. There is textual evidence for this hypothesis. Twice before the Roman period he had occasion to describe the primal creation of the universe, once in Neoplatonic and once in Christian terms, and in both passages the creation consists of this same double act.[8] One passage appears in a sonnet from *Olive*.

> Comme jadis l'ame de l'univers
> Enamourée en sa beaulté profonde,
> Pour façonner cete grand' forme ronde
> Et l'enrichir de ses thresors divers,   4
> Courbant sur nous son temple aux yeulx ouvers,
> Separa l'air, le feu, la terre & l'onde,
> Et pour tirer les semences du monde
> Sonda le creux des abismes couvers . . .[9]   8

It is significant that in this sonnet's so-called source by an obsure Italian Petrarchan, the act of separating the elements can be found, but not this bending the temple of the sky to form a sphere, nor this reaching down into the hollow abyss to withdraw the Ficinian seeds of the universe. The Christian formulation of the same primeval dyad appears in the "Hymne Chrestien," where the speaker is addressing God the Father.

> N'est-ce pas toy, qui forma la rondeur
> De l'univers, tesmoin de ta grandeur,
> Et qui fendis l'obscurité profonde,
> Pour en tirer la lumière du monde?

This version substitutes the light of Genesis 1 : 3 for the Neoplatonic "semences," but it adds to the Hebrew account the act of *piercing* the deep to bring forth light, and it uses skillfully the modifier "profonde" to suggest a spatial as well as visual depth of darkness. In both accounts of creation, the act of reaching into chaos follows the act of shaping, although in the sonnet at least it might reasonably have been expected to precede. It is clear from the Roman poems that even if the two acts are described sequentially, in the poet's imagination they were inextricable. In the *Deffence* he interrupts the elaboration of one to insert parenthetically the other.[10]

To my knowledge, no other writer of the Renaissance conceived of cosmic creation and artistic creation so repeatedly and predictably in terms of this double gesture as did Du Bellay. Ronsard has a similar description in a sonnet of the *Amours*, and something like an analogous process in his "Ode de la Paix"; in his posthumous preface to *La Franciade* he compares the writing of a major poem to the ornamentation of a gorgeous palace,[11] but essentially his images for creativity tended to be organic rather than architectonic. Du Bellay is alone in the prominence he assigns this dyad. Nevertheless in a larger sense the dyad can be recognized as a fundamental structure of humanist art, traceable in a hundred aspects throughout Renaissance culture. It is particularly visible in writing centered on Rome. It would seem that Du Bellay articulated with a special clarity a pattern repeated, varied, and diffused across a civilization. It is worth documenting, even if sketchily and impressionistically, the range and fertility of this fundamental pattern before returning to its final appearance in *Les Antiquitez de Rome*.

3

The double role of Orpheus and Amphion, of archaeological explorer and inspired architect, is omnipresent in the enormous literature on the Roman antiquities from which Du Bellay took his title. If we think of it not simply as a double metaphor but as two necessary phases of the response to ruins, then this dyad ceases to seem merely ornamental and external, and appears as crucial and pervasive. Perhaps this is not in itself very surprising: one first stoops, digs, gropes downward into the disorder of the past and then one rises and constructs upward by imitation. What is striking is the way these phases are explicitly, repeatedly articulated. In the famous letter to Leo X on Roman antiquities composed by Castiglione in consultation with Raphael, Rome is represented as a lacerated corpse, little more than a skeleton, which it is the obligation of modern men to restore and flesh out, even if this reanimated city were only a faint image, scarcely a shadow—"un poco della immagine, e quasi l'ombra"—of the original body.[12] The instinct to recreate the original whole out of the fragment seems to have been universal. Raphael wrote to Castiglione that Leo had chosen him to be the architect of Saint Peter's and that his first model had been well received, but he, Raphael, was dissatisfied: "In my mind I rise higher; I would like to realize the beautiful forms of ancient buildings; I don't know whether my flight will be like Icarus's."[13] Raphael speaks in this respect for most of the great architects of the Italian Renaissance. It is extraordinary how many of them devoted months and years to the ruins at Rome in what amounts to a collective obsession extending over several generations: Alberti, Bramante, the Sangalli, Peruzzi, Palladio, Pirro Ligorio. There is a story in Manetti's life of Brunelleschi that he too visited Rome as a young man and devoted a year to the ruins. It is not known whether this story is true, but if not, if it is a legend which circulated posthumously, then it is all the more significant. Vasari, who repeats it, adds that Brunelleschi "became capable of seeing Rome in his imagination as it stood before it fell."[14]

This is the prototypical response. Beyond whatever interest the ruins had in themselves, they inspired a will to form. The evidence suggests that the study of ruins was not simply a preliminary, propedeutic exercise before the productive activity of designing and building. It would seem that the second phase was already somehow implicit in the first, *in ovo*, that to see the fragments was already instinctively to see how they had been or might be made whole. This seems to be the meaning of Hegel, when he writes in the *Philosophy of History* that a positive, creative impulse is inherently complementary to the regret ruins elicit from us.

> The sight of the ruins of some ancient sovereignty directly leads us to contemplate the thought of change in its negative aspect. What traveller among the ruins of Carthage, of Palmyra, Persepolis, or Rome, has not been stimulated to reflections on the transiency of kingdoms and men, and to sadness at the thought of a vigorous and rich life now departed. . . . But the next consideration which allies itself with that of change, is that change, while it imports dissolution, involves at the same time the rise of a *new* life—that while death is the issue of life, life is also the issue of death.[15]

By this account, the experience of physical restoration upward may follow in time
the experience of archaeological probing downward, but this necessary sequen-
tiality obscures what is in fact a single, complex moment. The Renaissance texts
bear witness to a simultaneity, as in Vasari's story about Brunelleschi or in
Palladio's remarks on antiquities. The preface to Palladio's *Four Books of Architecture* begins by boasting of his prolonged study of antiquities, and he returns to
them often in the course of his treatise. His discussion of the design of churches in
the preface to book 4 is representative.

> I shall . . . in this book show the form and the ornaments of several ancient temples,
> whereof the ruins are yet to be seen, and of which I have made the designs; that every
> one may know in what form, and with what ornaments, churches ought to be built.
> And though of some of these temples but very little is to be seen above ground, yet from
> this little considered together with the foundations that could likewise be seen, I have
> made my conjecture what they must have been, when they were entire.[16]

Palladio shows no concern for any anachronistic disparity between ancient and
Christian worship: one simply learns from temples how churches *ought* to be
built, and one fashions by conjecture out of the classical remnants, however
meager, what they *must* have been. Palladio, like Petrarch and Brunelleschi,
subread the ruins. The conjecture is not accidental or subsequent; it is a constitutive function of the perception. It is as though the encounter with the fragmentary
and the formless automatically produced an answering movement toward form.
The frontispiece of one little booklet on the Roman antiquities shows a nude
geometer standing among the shattered stones holding aloft a sphere, the symbol
of perfect form.[17] Jean Lemaire de Belges seems to assume almost as a historical
law that a city built upon ruins will prosper the more briskly.

> Ainsi creut soudainement en merveilleuse hautesse la grand cité de Belges, par la ruïne
> de Treves: car comme dit le Philosophe, la corruption daucune chose est la generation
> dune autre.[18]

Since the crumbled city was so central an image for the humanist movement, it
was inevitable doubtless that it extend beyond the architectural sphere into all
aspects of the recovery of the past. Nothing could be more natural than to think of
a rediscovered text as disinterred, or to think of literary imitation as a rebuilding, a
reconstruction. This is the force of Alberti's beautiful simile applied to humanist
composition (see chapter 2, note 11). Here the ruined edifice becomes a symbol of a
larger entity, an entire civilization, and the double act of gathering stones and then
repiecing a design stands for the doomed modern effort of imitative revival. Yet of
course the double image need not lend itself to despair. One finds a splendidly
affirmative formulation in a letter from Poggio to Niccolò Niccoli, where the
double metaphor is first applied to the search for lost texts and then is widened to
the fullest creative and existential dimensions, the scope of an entire career.

> I am a little weary . . . of this exhausting quest for new books. Now it is time for me to
> wake up and put to some use these ways of life which we read about daily and reflect on.

For always to collect pieces of wood, stones, and mortar would seem very foolish if you built nothing with them. But this edifice which we must construct to live well is so arduous, difficult, and laborious, that it can scarcely be completed even if we begin young. I for my part have the will to try.[19]

Once again, the activity of exhuming and collecting is not enough; it includes the obligation to reconstruct painfully not merely a building in this case but a culture and an ethos.

At the core of humanism lies this instinct to reach out into chaos, oblivion, mystery, the alien, the subterranean, the dead, even the demonic, to reach out and in the act of reaching already to be reviving and restoring. It was an instinct that required courage, and if it is sometimes presented as productive, it could also be terrifying. Renaissance archaeology in all its aspects was not free from primitive feelings about the earth, atavistic terrors and superstitions. A chapter title of the twelfth-century *Mirabilia urbis Romae* leaves open the question whether Rome was founded by human labor or magical power ("Quae vel arte magica vel humano labore sunt condita"). The Typhoean, Joycean giant buried under the earth turns up in the *Antiquitez*, in Camden's *Britannia*, and in Drayton's *Polyolbion*. In a dungeon of Spenser's House of Pride languish Roman examples of pride, Tarquin, Scipio, Caesar, and others, "the antique ruines of the Romaines fall," writes Spenser, with an ambiguity leaving open the possibility that the dungeon contains antiquities as well as ghosts. The Florentine Neoplatonists' term for the realm of matter was "il mondo sotteraneo," and they habitually referred to the soul imprisoned in matter as "apud inferos." Aesculapius, symbol of the humanist reviver, was killed by a thunderbolt for restoring Hippolytus to life, a judgment not forgotten in the Renaissance. When Polifilo in the *Hypnerotomachia Poliphili* enters at his mistress's urging the ruins of a temple of Pluto, the visit ends in panic and flight. Yet in that same work so many of the colossal structures are surrounded with broken fragments of stone that the fragments almost seem necessary for the structures to achieve their effect. One overcomes the fear inherent in the downward archaeological thrust by conceiving some structure endowed with *concinnitas*, an arch of triumph over terror and death like the Tempio Malatestiano. If the new structure contains evidence of its struggle and triumph, that evidence can only heighten the marvel. The Tempio included tombs of those humanists who by their writing had triumphed over mortality. Serlio advocated incorporating the broken, ruinous, and anachronistic into a building to broaden its expressive range. He even suggested that the architect do the "breaking and spoiling" for himself if necessary. George Hersey comments that "these bits and pieces, incorporated into new contexts, add a past tense, a history, to the present time of Serlio's architectural grammar."[20] They also add an allegory of the victory of form over the misshapen.

Renaissance culture is full of the failures resulting from the double phases of imitation, failures that in a sense justify the fear it inspired. It would be possible to draw up a pathology of the double gesture, a pathology based on a range of anachronistic distortion. Cola di Rienzo must have been one of the first to expose himself to prolonged study of the Roman ruins, and we know what happened when he emerged, His effort to restore the Roman republic was carried out with an apocalyptic tone that strikes one alternately as noble and psychotic. The effort in any case was infected with an egoism that led to his own bloody personal apocalypse. The rebuilt Roman republic as Cola fashioned it was anachronistically out of place in trecento politics, and he paid with his life for the anachronism. That is a violent pathological instance; a milder case would be the odd career of Annius of Viterbo, the Dominican monk who devoted his life to publishing ancient inscriptions and died before it was recognized that they were all invented. It remains a mystery whether Annius realized his descriptions were faked or whether he was himself somehow taken in by his own hoax. Either way he was clearly the victim of an anachronistic imagination run wild. These thunderstruck Aesculapiuses are extreme cases; the more typical form of reconstructive distemper is the hypothetical rebuilder imagined by Speroni and Du Bellay, who figuratively makes a muddle of the ancient palace by putting the kitchen or stables where the great hall once stood. Our libraries are full of forgotten Renaissance books which make that mistake and produce uncontrolled anachronism.

To the pathology of failure must be added the pangs of guilt. One should not underestimate the religious character of humanist resuscitation, particularly in the phase of exhumation. The joy that greeted Poggio's discovery of Quintilian or the unearthing of the Laocoon had a devotional component. The resurrected object possessed a numinous halo. But the counterpart of this awe is the guilt at the profanation felt in the second phase, when the reconstruction may be accused of violation or parody. The blind exploitation of the Roman ruins for all purposes, even the grinding of marble statues into lime, was so systematic over the centuries that it was taxed by the Holy See, which is one reason it continued. There is naiveté or hypocrisy in the anguished report of this scandalous exploitation to Pope Leo by Castiglione and Raphael. Fra Giocondo's wish that at least inscriptions and statues be spared by the pillagers of stone went unheeded.[21] This is another aspect of the dark side of disinterment, an aspect which has robbed all of us.

Once the double gesture of the humanist imagination is felt as fundamental, one can study a given writer for his individual versions, his personal adaptations and distortions of the pattern. If the simultaneous process is projected upon a sequential narrative, one can study the peculiar plotted relationships of each projection and the symbolic interpretation assigned to each phase. Perhaps least idiosyncratic of the great humanist writers was Ben Jonson, whose masques repeatedly act out the two phases in the succession of masque to antimasque. The characteristic "discovery" of the Jonsonian setting, whereby a "wild" backdrop disappears to reveal a hierarchical structure behind it, corresponds to the transition from the first phase to the second. In *The Masque of Queenes*, the first backdrop, an "ougly Hell," gives way to "a glorious and magnificent Building figuring the House of Fame." In *Oberon*, Jonson begins with "all wildness that could be presented" followed by "a bright and glorious Palace." *Pleasure Reconciled to*

Vertue presents the same pattern, saturating the contrast with intricate symbols of metaphysical, moral, and social order. Although threats to this order can be glimpsed which are not fully exorcised, the masques as a set bear witness to Jonson's faith in the health and strength of humanist structuring.

Du Bellay's own "Musagnoeomachie" begins with a descent into the dark cave of Ignorance and ends after the defeat of her cohorts with an arch of triumph and the temple of the muse.[22] Rabelais's *Gargantua* begins with a literal excavation, the unearthing of a book from a tomb buried in the earth and bearing mysterious Etruscan characters. This book, "un gros, gras, grand, gris, joly, petit, moisy livret, plus, mais non mieulx sentent que roses," contains the life of Gargantua, that life which has been translated by Alcofribas Nasier and which one is about to read.[23] The entire book has been resurrected from subterranean obscurity, an obscurity that is then intensified by the chaos of the "Fanfreluches Antidotées," the bewildering, fragmentary, nonsensical poem the reader must cross in order to reach the narrative. At the opening stand the unearthing of the book and the "Fanfreluches"; at the end stands the institution of the Abbey of Thélème. Disinterment and construction frame the volume. Or rather they almost frame it. In Rabelais's version of the humanist pattern, the institution of the civilized community at Thélème is followed by a second, more terrifying chaos in the "Enigme en Prophétie," whose meaning is left ambiguous and whose images of universal disaster may or may not threaten the harmony of the abbey. A deeper skepticism pervades that infinitely deceptive poem, *The Faerie Queene*, whose most engaging heroine, Britomart, begins her quest in the cave of Merlin, "in a deep delve, farre from the vew of day," and who finds herself at the end of her book in the gleaming prison of Busirane's palace. Perhaps the ultimate parody organizes book 1 of *Paradise Lost*, which begins with a passive fall into the nethermost depths and ends with a magic construction "Built like a Temple, where Pilasters round / Were set, and Doric pillars overlaid / With Gold'n Architrave."[24] Pandaemonium with its round pilasters and gilt Doric is only an intensification of the formless darkness; this second chaotic phase is also implicit in the first, the antiarchaeology of the opening fall.

It is significant that when Montaigne visited Rome, he chose to see the paltry ruins still standing as insignificant remnants of Roman civilization, asserting that the true ruins must be buried so deep that no modern could survey them. It would be hopeless, he thought, to try to locate them and bring them to light. Rome, he remarked (echoing Du Bellay and doubtless others), had become its own tomb. But even this tomb, Montaigne insisted (and here he was original), was buried beyond reach. The fractured corpse of the empire had become an offense to its executioners and had to remain permanently hidden.

Ceux qui disoint qu'on y voyoit au moins les ruines de Rome en disoint trop; car les ruines d'une si espouvantable machine rapporteroint plus d'honneur et de reverence à sa mémoire; ce n'estoit rien que son sépulcre. Le monde, ennemi de sa longue domination, avoit premierement brisé et fracassé toutes les pieces de ce corps admirable; et, parce qu'encore tout mort, ranversé et défiguré, il lui faisait horreur, il en avait enseveli la ruine mesme. . . . Encore craignoit-il . . . que la sépulture ne fût elle mesme pour la plupart ensevelie.

By studying old maps and going over the terrain on foot, Montaigne decided that all modern conjectures about the ancient city's topography were confused to the point of uselessness. "A la verité, plusieurs qu'on prent de la peinture de ceste ville antienne n'ont guiere de verisimilitude, son plant mesme estant infiniment change de forme."[25] Nobody actually could know, let alone reconstruct, what the depths of the earth withheld. With this refusal to conjecture, to subread, to see in the mind's eye like Brunelleschi and Palladio and so many others, we come to a turning point. With the visible ruins meaningless and the substantial inheritance unreachable, incapable of disinterment, the humanist Renaissance on the Continent reached a kind of conclusion. Creation in two phases would continue but its status would be more vulnerable to baroque parody.

But how finally had the double gesture been represented in *Les Antiquitez de Rome*? We have seen how the Orphic and Amphionic images of the twenty-fifth sonnet express a consciousness of lack: "Que n'ay-je encor la harpe Thracienne. . . ." What is slightly less explicit and more surprising is a sense of guilt blighting both ancient and modern city, both native and visitor, perhaps blighting civilization itself. In sonnet 24 an oblique allusion to the killing of Remus by Romulus ("quelque vieil peché") hints at a theory of Roman original sin. In sonnet 12, one of the collection's richest, the building of imperial Rome is compared to the revolt of the giants against the Olympians.

> Telz que lon vid jadis les enfans de la Terre
>   Plantez dessus les monts pour escheller les cieux,
>   Combattre main à main la puissancer des Cieux,
>   Et Juppiter contre eux qui ses fouldres desserre: 4
> Puis tout soudainement renversez du tonnerre
>   Tumber deça dela ces squadrons furieux,
>   La Terre gemissante, & le Ciel glorieux
>   D'avoir a son honneur achevé ceste guerre: 8
> Tel encor' on a veu par dessus les humains
>   Le front audacieux des sept costaux Romains
>   Lever contre le ciel son orgueilleuse face:
> Et telz ores on void ces champs deshonnorez   12
>   Regretter leur ruine, & les Dieux asseurez
>   Ne craindre plus là hault si effroyable audace.

This mythopoeic reading of history reflects back on the turreted crown of Cybele, goddess of the earth adorned with cities. The Roman building of grandiose edifices in its hubristic overreaching polluted the earth that supported them and that now lies, venerable and dishonored, beneath their blasted pieces. The earth here is not the radiant matriarch of a divine race but the complicitous mother of criminal rebels. Rome *raised* its proud face against heaven—"[leva] contre le ciel son orgueilleuse face"—by raising its colossal monuments on the seven hills, monuments that stand synecdochically for all the arrogance required to create an empire.

The very act of constructing, of extending a civilization upward from the ground, would seem to be suspect. It is this initial pride that will lead to the senile gesture of modern Rome, perceived to "lever encor' au ciel sa vieille teste morte" (28).

In sonnet 19, the dishonored earth of the contemporary scene remains polluted and perhaps polluting, by a conflation of the myths of Astraea and Pandora.[26] The ancient city brought together all good and all misery, sealed within its limits as in a box or urn.

> Tout le malheur qui nostre age dedore,
>   Tout le bonheur des siecles les plus vieux,
>   Rome du temps de ses premiers ayeux
>   Le tenoit clos, ainsi qu'une Pandore.   8
> Mais le destin debrouillant ce Caos,
>   Où tout le bien & le mal fut enclos,
>   A fait depuis que les vertus divines
> Volant au ciel ont laissé les pechez,   12
>   Qui jusq'icy se sont tenus cachez
>   Sous les monceaux de ces vieilles ruines.

The spirits of the divine dead, earlier pictured as covered by the ruins, are replaced by a diffused evil tainting the stones. The poet who wants to summon the divine spirits may find himself conjuring more sinister powers. This at least may be the implication of the loaded but slightly mysterious phrase "jusq'icy" (line 13), which seems to suggest a possible imminent emergence of the vices from their concealment. Why now? The only event calculated to disturb them would seem to be the invasion by the poet and others like him. He may be playing unwittingly the role of Pandora himself, loosing evil upon the world by his naive and ill-advised rituals. Or is the reference rather to the pillage of the ruins by modern builders? Perhaps to both of these latter-day intruders. In either case the modern imitator seems doomed to repeat the misfortune of the ancients without their redeeming success, their *hubris* without their *virtus*. The willed itinerary back to the source is a passage into its incipient corruption stripped of nobility.

The roles of the poet and the pillaging builder converge further in sonnet 27, which moralizes on the new reconstruction of the city out of the debris of the old and provides Du Bellay's most powerful version of the double humanist gesture.

> Toy qui de Rome emerveillé contemples
>   L'antique orgueil, qui menassoit les cieux,
>   Ces vieux palais, ces monts audacieux,
>   Ces murs, ces arcs, ces thermes, & ces temples,   4
> Juge, en voyant ces ruines si amples,
>   Ce qu'a rongé le temps injurieux,
>   Puis qu'aux ouvriers les plus industrieux
>   Ces vieux fragmens encor servent d'exemples.   8

The builders of the new city must stoop to the fragments of the old to find models of architectural style. This of course was literally the case. But the fragments are vestiges of structures whose magnificence was guilty; the judgmental terms "orgueil" and "audacieux" are those already employed by 12 in exposing Rome's Titanic defiance of heaven. The contemporary repetition of this suspect raising is anything but assured; it may be an endeavor willed by the *genius loci*, but its very derivative dependence on earlier brilliance leaves open the question of its success.

> Regarde apres, comme de jour en jour
>   Rome fouillant son antique sejour,
>   Se rebatist de tant d'oeuvres divines:
> Tu jugeras, que le demon Romain   12
>   S'efforce encor d'une fatale main
>   Ressusciter ces pouldreuses ruines.

Modern guilt stems less from pride than from profanation, but in this fated reenactment of the ancient tragedy the morally equivocal clings to the site. The term *fatal* in sixteenth-century French did not normally carry the senses of "mortal" and "sinister" it later acquired. But this context unmistakably carries the suggestion of an unworthy as well as predetermined repetition. Once again a self-referential glance can be glimpsed. The poet himself with his array of Latin quotations, shards from the ancient slagheap, is one of those who repeat the fatal double gesture, groping, *fouillant*, and robbing in order to pile up stones again. But the attempt seems only an attempt; the phrasing seems to leave the effort permanently incomplete, perhaps because the demon endeavors, "s'efforce," to resurrect the ruins without the divine audacity of their first shapers. It is not only Rome that is judged. "Rome fut tout le monde, & tout le monde est Rome" (26). The shift in verb tenses universalizes the guilt. The act of building a civilization, both the downward movement of pillage and the upward movement of imitative, mediocre piecework, is tainted with ethical shabbiness. Nowhere surely did a Renaissance artist face with more courage the anxiety of influence, without shrinking and without paralysis. Du Bellay saw about him the literal pillage of antiquities, that pillage which as a metaphor he had closed the *Deffence* by advocating; he looked and found in that literal violation, that actual double gesture, an image of his own imitative act, his own predistined, dubious, incomplete ritual. By the courage of that analogy he saved himself from the various forms of anachronistic pathology.

Before the close of the *Antiquitez* he includes one more image of stooping.

> Comme le champ semé en verdure foisonne,
>   De verdure se haulse en tuyau verdissant,
>   Du tuyau se herisse en epic florissant,
>   D'epic jaunit en grain que le chauld assaisonne;   4
> Et comme en la saison le rustique moissonne
>   Les undoyans cheveux du sillon blondissant,
>   Les met d'ordre en javelle, & du blé jaunissant
>   Sur le champ despouillé mille gerbes façonne: 8
> Ainsi de peu à peu creut l'Empire Romain,
>   Tant qu'il fut despouillé par la Barbare main,
>   Qui ne laissa de luy que ces marques antiques,

Que chacun va pillant: comme on void le gleneur   12
   Cheminant pas à pas recueillir les reliques
   De ce qui va tumbant apres le moissonneur.   [30]

Empires rise and fall with the steady rhythm of natural growth, and the harvester, the barbarian destroyer, can be interpreted as a regular, necessary participant in this rhythm. The extraneous figure, irrevelant to the rhythm, is the pillager/ gleaner. His irrelevance is enforced by the expressive "rejet" and break in line 12. The gleaner in this bleakly serene simile is most immediately the contemporary mason, collecting broken statuary for the foundations of a modern palazzo. But in the fullest meaning, it is the poet; it is ruined Renaissance man, stooping to pick up stones from the floor of the ancient temple. This gleaner, however, will sow no new seed, make no new design; the second phase of true creation is denied him. In the calm of this humility, the resignation of this sorrow, humanism found the strength to comprehend its tragedy and its solitude.

Twelve • Wyatt: Erosion and Stabilization

One way to trace the development of early English humanism is to follow the growth of its historical consciousness. This consciousness passes through a number of serial phases, sometimes in the work of a single author. It will be convenient to distinguish four of these, each of them bearing the possibility of progressively sophisticated etiological retrospects.

The first phase can be represented by William Caxton, the fifteenth-century printer and translator. Caxton's prologue to the *Polychronicom*, a work translated into English by John Trevisa from the fourteenth-century Latin original of Ranulph Higdon with a continuation by the printer, might be said to reflect a minimal awareness of historical change. Caxton speaks of the wisdom gained from travel "by the experyment of jeopardyes and peryllys, whiche have growen of folye in dyverse partyes and contrayes." He goes on to say that the same wisdom can be gained with less risk "by the readyng of historyes conteynyng dyverse customes, condycyons, lawes and actes of sondry nacions."[1] Here a dim conception of cultural difference seems to take shape, though one is obliged to note that the otherness of alien societies is virtually reduced to folly. At any rate Caxton was following in this very passage Diodorus Siculus or a French translation of Diodorus. Elsewhere he shows little evidence even of the limited awareness visible in this prologue. His *Eneydos* (ca. 1490) is an English prose rendering of a French version of an Italian version of Virgil; it excludes large parts of the *Aeneid*, including the last six books, and greatly expands book 4, so that essentially we are given a romance centering on the Dido story. Caxton's prologue speaks of the original author as "that noble poete and grete clerke Vyrgyle," and his (Caxton's) intended audience as "clerkys and very gentylmen that understande gentylnes and scyence."[2] Although his book represents literally the endpoint of a complicated itinerary, the language of the prologue collapses the itinerary by identifying Virgil as a noble clerk like the clerks and the elite who will be reading him. The brevity of the historical itinerary Caxton apprehended is revealed both by the anachronism of the prologue and the freedom of his revision, which attributed to the Aeneas story an absolute presence and thus an absolute flexibility.

This freedom was bitterly attacked by Gavin Douglas in the verse prologue to his vibrant translation of the *Aeneid* into Scots verse (1513). Caxton's feeble story, Douglas charges, has nothing to do with Virgil's.

> It has na thing ado therwith, God wait,
> Ne na mair lyke than the devill and Sanct Austyne.[3]

In this perceived unlikeness lies a seed of historical consciousness that can be regarded as marking a second phase of English (or British) humanism. Caxton's version offends Douglas because it cuts and expands irresponsibly, because it gets names wrong (confusing the "Tovyr," or Danube, with the "Tibir"), gets the story wrong, and misses the truth concealed by the poetic fable. Douglas is conscious of an enormous gap not only between Virgil's poetic gifts and his own (some of this can be dismissed as a modesty ritual) but between Virgil's language and his own "bad, harsk spech and lewit barbour tong," a contrast that doubtless stood synecdochically at some level of Douglas's consciousness for a larger cultural contrast. In the prologue to the thirteenth book, Douglas justifies his decision to translate this epilogue from the Latin of the quattrocento poet Mapheus Vegius even though his style diverges from Virgil's: "Thocht hys stile be nocht to Virgill lyke" (l. 189). This sensitivity to the distance between Renaissance Neo-Latin and Augustan poetry opens up another perceived gap of sorts that Caxton doubtless would have failed to recognize. Yet Douglas's own version is itself full of anachronisms, consistently presenting Virgil's characters as late medieval knights and ladies. When Aeneas arrives at Carthage, workmen are busy constructing a castle. We hear of "Sir Diomed" and "nuns of Bacchus"; *duces* is rendered "douchty chiftanys full of chevalry." The translation may well owe part of its charm, as its editor David Coldwell suggests, to its anachronistic naiveté.[4] Anachronism can be considered a blemish only when a text demonstrates a greater degree of historical consciousness than Douglas's ever does. Where the cultural gap is so dimly perceived, there is no clumsiness in the failure to bridge it. Anachronism becomes a problem to the degree that history is a problem to the writer. This has not yet happened in the *Aeneis*. Only, in the poet's sense of responsibility to a master felt as remote, unlike, hard of linguistic access, his naiveté is qualified by the faint beginnings of a humanist outlook.

A third stage in the growth of English historicism can be discerned in the mind of Sir Thomas More, who touches the subject of literary imitation most closely in his polemics with a certain French humanist named Brixius (Germain de Brie). The origins of the quarrel need not occupy us; what matters is that two of More's Latin epigrams (1520) responding to Brixius's *Chordigerae navis conflagratio* deal sarcastically with the Frenchman's inept use of classical phrases.[5] In the more interesting of the epigrams, Brixius is alleged to be guilty of stealing passages from the ancients without attention to the art required for mingling old and new, in other words without regard for the risk of anachronism. More praises his opponent ironically for reanimating what otherwise might perish from neglect.

Ars O beata, quisquis arte isthac tamen
   Vetusta novitati dabit,
Is arte nulla (quamlibet sudet diu),
   Novis vetustatem dabit.[6]
[O blessed art! And yet whoever, employing your artistic method, shall insert his antique borrowings in a new context, will by no effort of art, however long he sweats about it, succeed in imparting their antiquity to his new verses.]

More's prose *Letter to Brixius* (1520) renews the criticism by ridiculing Brixius's *Antimorus* for its "purple patches plucked from various authors and inserted quite out of place in your own crude woolen cloak."[7] By quoting Horace on linguistic change in this letter, More demonstrates his own perception of the difficulties attendant on true imitation as well as the embarrassments attendant on its perversion. His stress on the imitator's obligation to consider context and concrete historicity[8] studied with philological precision can serve to represent a newly enlightened stage of British humanism. More would have been incapable of the flagrant, engaging, anachronistic violence of Douglas upon his source.

More however did not himself produce any major imitations. If one looks for a fourth phase, heuristic imitation in the full Renaissance sense, one must turn to the translations and adaptations of Sir Thomas Wyatt and, to a weaker degree, those of his younger contemporary, Henry Howard, earl of Surrey. These texts breathe an atmosphere incapable of producing Douglas's Bacchic sisters. But this does not mean that the effort to deal with cultural distance is everywhere definitively fulfilled. In a weaker poem like Wyatt's translation of Petrarch in poulter's measure, entitled "In Spain," one must admit that the effort has failed. Petrarch writes:

> Il tempo passa, e l'ore son sí pronte
> a fornire il viaggio,
> ch'assai spacio non aggio
> pur a pensar com'io corro a la morte.   [*Canz.* 37.17–20]
> [Time passes and the hours are so swift to complete their journey that I have not enough time even to think how I run to death.]

Wyatt's version runs:

> The tyme doth flete and I perceyve thowrs how thei bend
> So fast that I have skant the space to marke my comyng end.[9]

That couplet, like the poem as a whole, fails to do anything with Petrarch's anguish of temporality; there is no equivalent anguish, no equivalent sense of time in Wyatt, nor is there any transformation into something else; there is simply a deadening of Petrarch's pathos. There is a clash of cultures not under artistic control.

Thus one can trace a continuing effort in Wyatt and Surrey to open up a historical space. But they seem always to show at least a rudimentary alertness to cultural context. Thus in Wyatt's rendering of three passages in Boethius, beginning "If thou wilt mighty be," he writes, "see thou kepe thee free / From the foule yoke of sensuall bondage." This corresponds to Boethius's "Nec victus libidine colla, / foedis submittat habenis." This appears in Chaucer's prose translation as "[he should] ne putte nat his necke overcomen under the foule raynes of lechery."[10] Chaucer's "lechery" in its context cannot fail to evoke the anachronistic framework of the seven deadly sins, whereas Wyatt's "sensuall bondage" in its context does not.[11] Wyatt's poem, although it freely condenses and omits, clearly constitutes an attempt to find a diction, imagery, and moral style appropriate to the late classical subtext. It respects the mode of being of Boethius's meters without attempting to reproduce them mechanically. The attention to context More implicitly required is reflected to varying degrees in the poetry of both Wyatt and Surrey. Both moreover must have been aware of themselves as attempting something new, as filling a vacuum. (This is the way they were perceived during the remainder of the century and for that matter today.) Given this self-awareness, they must have seen the intertextual itineraries contained in their poems as crossings of a cultural rupture. To the extent that these crossings were effected, they did achieve at least a weak degree of heuristic creativity.

But in the finest imitations by Wyatt, of which there are more than a few, historical consciousness goes still further. Imitation becomes fully heuristic and frequently dialectical; it takes the full responsibility for its cultural moment and location, "in Kent and Christendome," with the vulnerability as well as the strength these involve. To demonstrate this degree of consciousness, one need only cite the superb little version of Seneca, doubtless written after the execution of Wyatt's patron Cromwell.[12]

Stond who so list upon the Slipper toppe
  Of courtes estates, and lett me heare rejoyce;
And use me quyet without lett or stoppe,
    Unknowen in courte, that hath suche brackishe joyes: 4
      In hidden place, so lett my dayes forthe passe,
  That when my yeares be done, withouten noyse,
    I may dye aged after the common trace.
For hym death greep'the right hard by the croppe   8
    That is moche knowen of other; and of him self alas,
    Doth dye unknowen, dazed with dreadfull face.   [176]

This derives from a chorus of Seneca's *Thyestes* (391ff.)

Stet quicunque volet potens
aulae culmine lubrico:
me dulcis saturet quies:
obscuro positus loco   4
leni perfruar otio.
Nullis nota Quiritibus
aetas per tacitum fluat.
Sic cum transierint mei   8
nullo cum strepitu dies,
plebeius moriar senex.
Illi mors gravis incubat
qui, notus nimis omnibus,   12
ignotus moritur sibi.

Wyatt Englishes this by suppressing the Latin "leni... otio" (l. 5), the easy leisure that despite the Thyestes legend calls up an aristocratic Roman villa. Wyatt's language identifies him as an Anglo-Saxon countryman whose quietude will not be voluptuous, "dulcis," and whose death will not simply go unremarked, "nullo cum strepitu" (l. 9), but will in its obscurity adhere to the perennial manner of ordinary folk, "after the common trace" (l. 7). "Trace" is itself one of those rustic words that help to situate the speaker. Wyatt omits the hint of sensual satisfaction in Seneca's "saturet" (1. 3), adds the powerful modifier "brackishe" (salty, nauseating) in his fourth line, plays the force of "rejoyce" against the sobriety of "quyet" (ll. 2-3), with its echo of the poet's translation of Plutarch, *The Quyete of Mynde*. Above all Wyatt rewrites the closing lines, roughening Seneca's neat antithesis in lines 12-13 and suppressing his sinister image of suffocation ("incubat" [l. 11]— settles down upon, broods on like a bird) for the more violent clutch of Death's abrupt hand: "hym death greep'the right hard by the croppe." The five stressed monosyllables in unbroken sequence violate the rhythmic pattern with a wrench that corresponds to the action, and the harsh Anglo-Saxon folk words maintain the identity of a speaker hidden in the countryside outside a Latinate court. The control of verse movement, expert throughout, culminates in the majestic rallentando of the last line and a half, its terrible subsiding intensified by the pitiless alliteration. Brilliantly, Wyatt chooses not to explain why the lack of self-knowledge renders death's grip so much harder, nor to explain the brilliant concluding phrase, his own addition—"dazed with dreadfull face." The great man is "dazed"—stupefied, bewildered, numbed—because death's assault has been so sudden, because its numbing physiological effect has already begun or is completed, because we can assume the dying man has fallen from the slipper top of eminence, and perhaps because in his naive egoism he had thought of himself as immune from mortality. He is "dreadfull"—inspiring reverence, awe, or fear— because as a power at court he has always inspired these, because he is suffering the humiliation of death after so much sway, because conceivably he has been publicly executed like Cromwell, and because, most profoundly, he is suffering this death in the limelight without the redeeming possession or acquisition of self-knowledge; he remains "of him self . . . unknown." Wyatt's use of the Latin chorus only serves to help him find an idiom that is radically anti-Latinate and calls attention to its own parochial rusticity; his use of the somewhat facile Stoic morality helps him to adumbrate a drama of his own time and place. By insisting on its English provincialism the text assumes a vulnerability toward the elegant classicism of its subtext, and only by accepting this vulnerability can it implicitly criticize the subtext's facility. This is an intensely Tudor poem and conscious of itself as such, awake to the diacritical distinctions it has created. By achieving this degree of control over potential anachronism, Wyatt made it possible for the first time to speak of mature English imitation.

2

The richest body of Wyatt's imitative poetry draws not on antiquity but on Petrarch. It is true that the *Penitential Psalms* paraphrase the Old Testament psalmist mediated by Aretino, Campensis, and others, that the first satire follows Alamanni, the third Horace somewhat more distantly, that the second satire might have drawn on Horace, Caxton, Pynson, Henryson, or any combination of these for its version of Aesop, that Seneca is again put to use elsewhere, that Serafino of

Aquila along with lesser known Italians provided subtexts for several poems, that one rondeau adapts Jean Marot, and that the presence of Chaucer makes itself felt repeatedly on Wyatt's pages. Nonetheless the deepest involvement is unmistakably with Petrarch, most particularly with twenty-five specific poems from the *Canzoniere*, and in a single chapter devoted to Wyatt as imitator the stress must fall primarily on this relationship. The involvement has to be sure already profited from a good deal of critical attention, including one book,[13] but from the perspective of this study, a few things remain to be said. It has to be stated at the outset that the body of Petrarchan imitations contains both distinguished and mediocre poetry, work highly characteristic of Wyatt's idiolect and work that is close to colorless. The interest here will be directed to those versions where the idiolect is most distinctly heard, the historical consciousness most active, and where patterns of distancing can be most coherently described.

The gap between the two poets begins with the poetic means available to each. Measured from the early Tudor perspective, the *mundus significans* on which Petrarch could draw as vernacular love poet reveals its wealth and firm definition. The verse forms he inherited—the sonnet, canzone, sestina, madrigal, and *ballata*—were already securely established at the opening of his career; the poetic tradition they collectively circumscribed contained a large number of stock images, motifs, conceits, tropes, myths, and commonplaces whose resonance was far from exhausted. Petrarch would refine the psychologistic analysis and would thicken the rhetorical impasto to produce his *cantar soave*; he would alter his *mundus* in various subtle and profound ways, but both before and during this alteration, the poetic vocabulary at hand possessed range, dignity, elegance, and expressiveness.

This needs to be pointed out again only because the poetic vocabulary available to Wyatt was seriously shrunken. Most of the verse forms and styles of the fifteenth century in England were losing their appeal or had lost it as he began writing: the ballade, the carol, the "broken-backed" alliterative line, the aureate style were fading rapidly, and the inspired doggerel of Skelton was not to find any followers. The alliance of verse with music had produced lyrics without obtrusive rhetorical features. A drift had already begun that would lead the poem away from performance and occasion. Wyatt in certain respects intensified this reduction of poetic means. He suppressed classical mythology; he avoided descriptions of nature and of women; and he led the English lyric a few steps further toward its eventual parting from music. He seems deliberately to have muted whatever imagistic brilliance he found in the *Canzoniere*. What rhetorical equipment remained at his disposal tended to be somewhat stiff and narrow. Given this inherited poverty and willed asceticism of the poetic word, we may ask what kind of passage from the one *mundus* to the other an imitation of Wyatt's could dramatize. What kind of genuine passage was possible other than an impoverishment?

One immediate answer to this question concerns the reality of the woman, the addressee of the love poetry. If in the *Canzoniere* the poetic consciousness repeatedly fails to make authentic contact with an external presence, if it constitutes a closed, circular system, in Wyatt our sense of an external presence in any given poem, an object of desire and of trust, is very strong, even though paradoxically this presence lacks *enargeia*, descriptive vividness. The poetic consciousness as a system is no longer closed. We are aware of the woman through the mediating mind of the speaker, but we know that she is there; we know that interaction between individuals is occurring, partly because the outcome of the interaction in so many poems is problematic.

> Madame, withouten many wordes
>   Ons I ame sure ye will or no;
> And if ye will, then leve your bordes,
>   And use your wit and shew it so.[14]   [34]

Within the poetic fiction, the speaker is truly responding to a second person who is responding to him, and the guarantee of this mutuality is the uncertainty. Frequently we don't know with assurance what will be the issue of the relationship, as we do know in reading Petrarch that one phase of the oxymoronic cycle is about to yield or is already yielding to its antithesis. Thus the etiological passage from the Italian text to the English can be described as an *engagement* of the closed system with its human surrounding, an opening up to the nonself, an involvement, a contextualization. This involvement does not, as in Ronsard, lead beyond the woman to a universal force. It may lead at most to a dangerous or debasing involvement with a given social circle. Most commonly it stops short of any circle wider than the tense, unsentimental interplay between the isolated couple.

The passage into engagement inevitably affects the oxymoronic iteration that dominates Petrarch's rhetoric. The oxymoron in English love poetry goes back at least to Chaucer, whose "Complaint to his Lady" addresses her as "my swete fo" and "best beloved fo." It is possible that a statistical count would find as many oxymorons in Wyatt as in Petrarch. Hietsch states that Wyatt added more to those he found in his subtexts.[15] Yet in those poems of Wyatt where an original voice is heard most distinctly, the oxymoron has to be regarded as superficial; it does not as in Petrarch determine the sensibility where speech and feeling are grounded; it is not as in Petrarch absolutely fundamental to the imagination, the voice, and the experience evoked by the voice. The involvement of the speaker's consciousness with an unpredictable human being outside itself weakens the oxymoronic linguistic structure because the oxymoron in Petrarch imposes a predictable linguistic and experiential course. The endlessly spinning Petrarchan cycle with its corollary, the iterative present verb tense, tends to be interrupted in Wyatt's most characteristic imitations.

When in Wyatt we do know the issue of the involvement with a woman, we are led to see it as irreversible. It tends to grow from a deliberate commitment to which the speaker deliberately binds himself.

> It was my choyse, yt was no chaunce
>   That browght my hart in others holde.   [121]

This commitment by the speaker may or may not be matched by the woman in whom he has placed his trust, and if it is matched, this trust may or may not be betrayed. If it is betrayed, he will perceive the betrayal and make known his perception. Thus the two crucial acts on the speaker's part are first, commitment, and the second, when it is called for, perception of inauthenticity. Most of the original love poems by Wyatt tend to depend on one or both of these two acts. In comparing the speaker's experience with that of the speaker of the *Canzoniere*, we may note that what matters is that these two actions do not allow for circularity. Within a given personal relationship, they cannot be reversed or repeated; they are definitive. Thus the dramatic situation characteristic of Wyatt will not be oxymoronic in the radical Petrarchan sense; it will depend rather on crises—a crisis of fidelity or a crisis of discovery.

This distance between the two poets is less marked in Wyatt's versions of Petrarch, but we can frequently watch him in these poems pulling away in his own direction. The first poem in the Egerton manuscript, "Behold, love" (1), which adapts a graceful but slender Petrarchan madrigal (*Canz.* 121), attributes a betrayal to the woman that would have shattered its subtext.

> The holy oth, wherof she taketh no cure,
> Broken she hath.

There is nothing in the Italian of this incipient crisis of discovery. Another imitation, "The lyvely sperkes that issue from those Iyes" (47), transforms the sestet of a Petrarchan sonnet to dramatize a stunned allegiance that is rejected.

> L' alma nudrita sempre in doglia e 'n pene
> (quanto è 'l poder d' una prescritta usanza!)
> contra 'l doppio piacer sì 'nferma fue,
>   ch' al gusto sol del disusato bene,
> tremando or di paura or di speranza,
> d' abandonarme fu spesso entra due.   [*Canz.* 258]
> [My soul, nourished always in sorrow and pain (how great is the power of an established habit!) was so weak against the double pleasure that at the mere taste of the unaccustomed good, trembling now with fear, now with hope, it was often on the point of abandoning me.]

> Dased ame I muche like unto the gyse
> Of one istricken with dynt of lightening,
>   Blynded with the stroke, erryng here and there,
>   So call I for helpe, I not when ne where,
> The pain of my falt patiently bering:
>   For after the blase, as is no wounder,
>   Of dedly *nay* here I the ferefull thounder.

The lightning of the lady's eyes leaves the speaker like one blinded, patiently bearing his pain. Beneath the patience, the unshaken acceptance of an altered condition, we subread the restless divisions of Petrarch's vacillating speaker, "tremando or di paura or di speranza," his very life in suspense: "d' abandonarme fu spesso entra due." This last phrase "entra due" would normally mean the speaker's life was in doubt (Durling's reading), but in the *Canzoniere* and in this context it also means inescapably "with a divided mind." (Patricia Thomson cites the sixteenth-century Petrarchan commentator Vellutello: "cio è fu spesse volte tra 'l si e 'l no," implying that the lady keeps the lover in suspense.) The cycle of hope and fear in the Italian sets off the steadiness of the shaken but patient Wyatt, dazedly, loyally surveying the effect of a fall that is definitive.

Thus the heuristic passage from the subtext to the surface text can be described as a process of *linearization* as well as of engagement. This linearization is clearly present in Muir 29, another free imitation from Petrarch's Italian.

    Mirando 'l sol de' begli occhi sereno,
ov' è chi spesso i miei depinge e bagna,
dal cor l' anima stanca si scompagna
per gir nel paradiso suo terreno.   4
    Poi trovandol di dolce e d' amar pieno,
quant' al mondo si tesse, opra d' aragna
vede, onde seco e con Amor si lagna
ch' a sí caldi gli spron, sí duro 'l freno.   8
    Per questi estremi duo contrari e misti,
or con voglie gelate or con accese,
stassi cosí fra misera e felice.
    Ma pochi lieti e molti penser' tristi,   12
e 'l piú si pente de l' ardite imprese:
tal frutto nasce di cotal radice.   [*Canz.* 173]

[Gazing at the clear sun of her lovely eyes, where there is one who often makes mine red and wet, my weary soul leaves my heart for its earthly paradise;

    then, finding it so full of sweetness and bitterness, it sees that whatever is woven in the world is cobwebs, and it complains to Love, whose spurs are so hot, whose bit is so hard.

    Between these two extremes so contrary and so mixed, now with frozen desires, now with kindled, it stays thus half miserable and half happy;

    but few happy thoughts and many sad ones: mostly it repents of its bold enterprise, such fruit is born from such a root.]

Avysing the bright bemes of these fayer Iyes,
   Where he is that myn oft moisteth and wassheth,
   The werid mynde streght from the hert departeth
   For to rest in his woroldly paradise,   4
And fynde the swete bitter under this gyse.
   What webbes he hath wrought well he perceveth,
   Whereby with himself on love he playneth;
   That spurreth with fyer, and bridilleth with Ise.   8
Thus is it in suche extremitie brought:
   In frossen thought nowe and nowe it stondeth in flame;
   Twyst misery and welth, twist ernest and game;

But few glad, and many a dyvers thought;   12
   With sore repentaunce of his hardines:
   Of suche a rote commeth ffruyte fruytles.

Wyatt's version seems about to forsake linearity and to introduce iterative action with the adverb "oft" in his second line, corresponding to Petrarch's "spesso." But in fact his version pulls away from iteration by the close to establish its own pattern; it presents again a crisis of discovery, not of betrayal in this case but of sterility. The crucial breakaway appears in line 9. Petrarch's line "Per questi estremi duo contrari e misti" and what follows contain an almost classic expression of an oxymoronic sensibility. Wyatt alters the entire drama with brilliant economy by altering the number of the noun: no longer extremes—"estremi"— but an "extremitie," the drastic moment when the futility of living between extremes is recognized.[16] The perception of Love's webs in line 6 is critical here as it never is in Petrarch; it means that the experience of "paradise" won't contain equal measures of sweet and bitter, "di dolce e d' amar pieno," but rather that the sweet is perceived as essentially, definitively bitter. Thus in retrospect "woroldly paradise" in line 4 has to be read ironically, as an instance of the subdued sarcasm that is characteristic of Wyatt's voice but that is altogether missing from the Italian "paradiso suo terreno." Wyatt follows a single, linear progression into lucidity, which culminates in the finality of the last line and even the last word, "fruytles," for which the subtext has no basis. Petrarch's speaker repents his audacity; Wyatt's repents the entire relationship and is already detaching himself irreversibly in the act of articulating his discovery. The sentimental poles of misery and wealth are yielding to the stable recognition of vanity.

This process of linearization, transforming a circular plot to a unique, unrepeatable plot, occurs in the *Penitential Psalms,* where it can be related to a shift from the Roman to the Protestant theology of justification. Here is the account of R. A. Rebholz:

> Wyatt departs from Aretino in order, I think, to create a shape for the whole work that presents a Reformed Christian's view of the individual's experience of redemption rather than a Roman Catholic's. Aretino's David vacillates between hope and a fear bordering on despair throughout the work; he thereby creates the impression that, even though he is seeking forgiveness for his sins against Uriah and Bathsheba, he is in fact caught up in the continuing cycle of sin and forgiveness and sin typical of much Roman Catholic spirituality: as he says in the last psalm, his soul dies to grace as often as it sins and therefore must be reborn each time with new acts of contrition and divine forgiveness. Wyatt, on the other hand, is trying, I think, to make David the type of the Reformed Christian who experiences the genuinely profound, almost despairing sense of his sinfulness only once before the critical act of believing that God forgives him, justifies him by imputing righteousness to him, loves him, and will make him holy.[17]

This interpretation of the Psalms is supported in my view not only by the somewhat unwieldy text but also by the movement away from vacillation in so many of the imitative love poems. The abrupt, alert, impatient temper of the lover in these poems, endowed with moral intelligence, resistant to self-pity, unsparing of inauthenticity, quick to sarcasm toward others and himself—this lover is not given to vacillation. It would be an error to conflate his voice with that of the Psalms, but the parallel diachronic passage in two such contrasting modes is all the more notable.

The linearizing force of the lover's temper is nowhere clearer than in "The longe love, that in my thought doeth harbar," a sonnet that has become a touchstone if not a warhorse of Wyatt criticism. One change in the Petrarchan original that has not been adequately weighed is the simple suppression of an adverb in the first quatrain.

> Amor, che nel penser mio vive e regna
> e 'l suo seggio maggior nel mio cor tene,
> talor armato ne la fronte vene;
> ivi si loca' ed ivi pon sua insegna.   4 [*Canz.* 140]
> [Love, who lives and reigns in my thought and keeps his principal seat in my heart, sometimes comes forth all in armor into my forehead, there camps, and there sets up his banner.]

> The longe love, that in my thought doeth harbar
>   And in myn hert doeth kepe his residence,
>   Into my face preseth with bolde pretence,
>   And therein campeth, spreding his baner.   [4]

Petrarch's "talor" (sometimes—l. 3) is the signal that the little drama he recounts is played out an indefinite number of times. Because of this repetition not much is riding on any given reenactment and no moral decision is called for. The lover and his master Love act the way they have to act and the lady responds the way she must. No one can break out of the ritual. This situation is perpetuated in Surrey's translation, which contains the adverb "oft." But Wyatt drops the adverb, and the singleness of the event in his version helps to explain the tauter dramatic intensity. Thus the progression from "harbar" (lodge, encamp, conceal one's self) to "preseth with bolde pretence" carries a real risk missing in the Italian as it calls for a moral judgment that cannot be fully approving. The captain's audacity may well be ill-advised, and in the light of this suspicion the act of spreading a banner looks like a further provocation. The rest of the sonnet justifies the suspicion.

> Quella ch' amare e sofferir ne 'nsegna,
> e vol che 'l gran desio, l' accesa spene,
> ragion, vergogna e reverenza affrene,
> di nostro ardir fra se stessa si sdegna.   8
>   Onde Amor paventoso fugge al core,
> lasciando ogni sua impresa, e piange e trema;
> ivi s'asconde e non appar piú fore.
>   Che poss' io, temendo il mio signore,   12
> se non star seco infin a l' ora estrema?
> ché bel fin fa chi ben amando more.

[She who teaches us to love and to be patient, and wishes my great desire, my kindled hope, to be reined in by reason, shame, and reverence, at our boldness is angry within herself.

Wherefore Love flees terrified to my heart, abandoning his every enterprise, and weeps and trembles; there he hides and no more appears outside.

What can I do, when my lord is afraid, except stay with him until the last hour? For he makes a good end who dies loving well.]

She that me lerneth to love and suffre,
  And willes that my trust and lustes negligence
  Be rayned by reason, shame and reverence,
  With his hardines taketh displeasur.   8
Wherewithall, unto the hertes forrest he fleith,
  Leving his enterprise with payn and cry;
  And ther him hideth, and not appereth.
What may I do when my maister fereth   12
  But in the feld with him to lyve and dye?
  For goode is the liff, ending faithfully.

Wyatt splits up the association between lover and master implied by "us" (ne—l. 5) and "our" (nostro—l. 8), reassigning the roles so that the lover is the one who learns restraint and his master the one who violates it. The captain Love remains morally ambiguous to the end: Wyatt's omission of the Italian qualifier "paven-toso" (terrified) and his addition of the expressive phrase "lustes negligence" (logically applicable to either but attracted to Love by the context) recast the character of the chief actor, distinguished throughout for his "hardines," his erotic overreaching. This moral ambivalence is what makes the lover's moral decision at the end difficult and interesting. The master has returned, not to his comfortable main residence as in Petrarch, but to the "hertes forrest," a tangled, dark region of seclusion, obscurity, and confusion. So we have at the end another crisis of commitment; the speaker is left out there in the cold, bivouacking with his liege lord, vulnerable to an exposure and a finality that are new.[18] The aphoristic last line, talking about life and faith rather than death and love, makes its feudal fealty against the grain, against the knowledge of cost and moral ambivalence. It repudiates in advance, with its hard-bitten clairvoyance and its throwaway feminine ending, the handsome pose struck by Surrey's aphorism: "Sweet is the death that taketh end by love."

3

The study of mistranslations is particularly rewarding in the case of Wyatt, since meanings in his heuristic imitations tend to shift with unusual mobility under the pressure of context. The clash of cultures and sensibilities is focused microcosmi-cally in the passage from "estremi" to "extremitie," or in the sonnet "Such vain thought..." the passage from Petrarch's narcissistic "a me stesso m'involo" to the cool withdrawal "from compayne to live alone," or in the sonnet just discussed

from "'l gran desio, l' accesa spene" to "my trust and lustes negligence," a coupling
that complicates the moral and sentimental relationship while replacing the story
of deferred desire with one of a divided will. Most significant is the mistranslation
elsewhere (in the sonnet "Though I my self be bridilled of my mynde") of
Petrarch's "vertute" by the key term "trouth," the Chaucerian word that organizes
Wyatt's moral code. ("Sotto quell' arme / che gli dà il tempo, amor, vertute e 'l
sangue" becomes "under the defence / Of tyme, trouth and love.") In the rondeau
"Goo burnyng sighes" Wyatt replaces

> che 'l nostro stato è inquieto e fosco,
> sí come 'l suo pacifico e sereno.   [*Canz.* 153]
>
> [Our state is as unquiet and dark as hers is peaceful and bright.]

with

> I must goo worke, I se, by craft and art,
> For trueth and faith in her is laide apart.   [20]

Each of these mistranslations, kernels of diachronic interplay, focuses a conflict
between cultures and moral styles; each is a key to the specificity of Wyatt's art.

Many of his lyrics could be gathered under a rubric taken from the refrain of a
rondeau: "What vaileth trouth?" (2), a question which the canon of his poetry
poses not as a rhetorical or cynical but serious and open question. The word *trouth*
gathers into itself most of the various values which in Wyatt are repeatedly
threatened with debasement. Its richness of accumulated but beleaguered signification serves to illustrate the ways moral ambiguities turn out to be semiotic
ambiguities. As it appears in Wyatt's poems, it is already a shrunken thing, leaking
the ethical and spiritual certitudes that inform Chaucer's "Balade de Bon Conseyl"
with the refrain "And trouthe shal delivere, it is no drede." Wyatt's poems
demonstrate a shrinking of the values whose resonance was still full even when
Chaucer (in another ballade, "Lak of Steadfastnes") accused his society of violating them.

> Trouthe is put doun, resoun is holden fable;
> Vertu hath now no dominacioun . . .
> The world hath mad a permutacion
> Fro right to wrong, fro trouthe to fikelnesse.[19]

The ethical centrality of "trewthe" is also the supreme message of Langland's
Holy Church.

> Whan alle tresores aren tried, quod she, trewthe is the best; . . .
> It is as derworth a drewery as dere god hym-selven.[20]

It is the word from which our modern words *truth* and *troth* are both descended,
having split apart at some point during the sixteenth century. In a philosophical
context *trouth* meant "reality"; in a social context it meant a covenant, the kind of
engagement on which the medieval system of fealty rested; ethically, it meant

"integrity," a recognized continuity in word and act that renders a man authentic, which is to say real; psychologically, *trouth* meant "faith" or "trust," a disposition to credit realities, including the supreme Reality; in this sense, it was one of the three theological virtues. It also meant, as early as 1380, "a true statement, a true doctrine, an established principle" (*OED*). In Wyatt's first letter to his son, he ends the list of his own father's virtues by praising "trougth above all the rest."[21]

Many of Wyatt's poems use the perceived leakage in this word as a focus of their moral disorientation. The woman's lack of *trouth*, her betrayal or her "dyversite," seems to stand synecdochically for some larger absence.

What vaileth trouth? or, by it, to take payn?
To stryve by stedfastnes for to attayne?   [2]

Ffor fansy at his lust
    Doeth rule all but by gesse;
Whereto should I then trust
    In trouth or stedfastnes?   [43]

And of this grief ye shalbe quitte
    In helping trowth steadfast to goo;
The time is longe that [he] doth sitt
    Feble and weike and suffreth woo.   [93]

Light in the wynde
    Doth fle all my delight;
Where trouth and faithfull mynd
    Are put to flyght.   [84]

Ago, long synnys, that she hathe truly made
    Dysdayne for trowght, sett lyght yn stedfastnes,
I have cause goode to syng this song.   [88]

Most wretched hart most myserable,
    Syns the comforte is from the fled,
Syns all the trouthe is turned to fable,
    Most wretched harte why arte thow nott ded?   [91]

There is no Petrarchan equivalent for the term *trouth*. In Petrarch the threat to the word lies in cyclical contradiction and in the tendency of apparently objective reference to betray its subjective character, to collapse into purely solipsistic reference. This perpetual Petrarchan threat of collapsing reference yields in Wyatt to a different semiotic threat, the collapse of traditional, principled relationships on which a coherent society has depended and in which language has been grounded. In the satires as in the lyrics, the word is in danger of losing its *trouth*, its basis in common practice, and the poet records the ungrounding of *trouth*, a property of human relations that is also a property of language.

Wyatt's poetry, like Du Bellay's *Les Regrets*, is postfeudal; it reflects the moral, social, and linguistic disarray caused by the disappearance of medieval ethical-political norms. The satires spell out what many lyrics suggest indirectly: that the

moral problem posed when money and intrigue replace the feudal hierarchy is a
verbal problem, a problem of signifying. "I perceive I lacked discretion / To
fasshion faith to wordes mutable," writes Wyatt (19). This predicament of the lover
is also the maker's. One of his solutions was to build his poems consciously around
words whose meanings are pointedly eroded or debased, like the word *trouth* itself.

> There was never ffile half so well filed,
>> To file a file for every smythes intent,
>> As I was made a filing instrument
>> To frame othres, while I was begiled.   [16]

Among Wyatt's editors Daalder supplies the widest range of glosses for the central
term, *file*: as a noun he gives "1) the instrument for polishing, 2) deceiver"; as a
verb "1) to polish, 2) deceive, 3) defile."[22] But surely the medieval meaning of
"whore" is also relevant to the noun, and the following meanings of the verb: "to
charge with a crime, accuse"; "to violate the chastity of, to deflower"; "to taint with
disease, infect." The poem sketches an obscure plot of courtly erotic manipulation
and passes judgment on it by letting the seamiest implications show through the
language. But "file" as used by a smith is at least a morally neutral word; in the
sestet a more "noble" word is subtly devalued.

> Yet this trust I have of full great apearaunce:
>> Syns that decept is ay retourneable,
>> Of very force it is aggreable
> That therewithall be done the recompence.   12
>> Then gile begiled plained should be never,
>> And the reward litle trust for ever.[23]

The "trust" of the last line is the central act of commitment, here as so often
betrayed; thus the trust that remains in line 9 is merely the bleak belief in the justice
of deceiving deceivers. That moment typical of the poet when scales fall from his
eyes means a rearrangement of assigned meanings: no longer a superannuated,
naive trust, the earnest belief in steadfastness, but a hollow reliance on the
workings of the world. The poem records and hinges on these verbal readjust-
ments. Its irony stems from the fluctuations of its referents.
   The drabness of Wyatt's language is of course essential to his moral style. He
systematically reduced the tones of Petrarch's highly ornamented surface. He
refused the Petrarchan *cantar soave*, and when in his version of the long canzone
that refers to this suavity (*Canz.* 360), he reached the relevant passage, he took an
inhabitual liberty and skipped the entire section. This suppression of ornament
and Petrarchan decorative richness, this imagistic asceticism, is essential to Wyatt's
language because it strips the word of its esthetic pretentiousness and leaves it as a
naked gauge of integrity. He seems almost to have invested with value the
impoverished formal poetic means available to him. When integrity is revealed as
inauthentic, then the semiotic crisis is not infrequently thematized. The last line of
"They fle from me"—"I would fain knowe what she hath deserved"—means

among other things "I would fain know what language is appropriate," even "what poem I ought to write."

Perhaps the one service one can perform for this much-worried poem is to show how its linguistic texture helps to answer this question through a calculated series of redefinitions and devaluations.

> They fle from me that sometyme did me seke
>   With naked foot stalking in my chambre.
> I have sene theim gentill tame and meke
>   That nowe are wyld and do not remembre   4
>   That sometyme they put theimself in daunger
> To take bred at my hand; and nowe they raunge
> Besely seking with a continuell chaunge.
>
> Thancked be fortune, it hath ben otherwise   8
>   Twenty tymes better; but ons in speciall,
> In thyn arraye after a pleasaunt gyse,
>   When her lose gowne from her shoulders did fall,
>   And she me caught in her arms long and small;   12
> Therwithall swetely did me kysse,
> And softely saide, *dere hart, howe like you this?*
>
> It was no dreme: I lay brode waking.
>   But all is torned thorough my gentilnes   16
> Into a straunge fasshion of forsaking;
>   And I have leve to goo of her goodenes,
>   And she also to use new fangilnes.
> But syns that I so kyndely ame served,   20
> I would fain knowe what she hath deserved.   [37]

"Stalking" (l. 2) at first appears to mean "walking cautiously" and "walking with high stiff steps like a bird"; only on rereading does it reveal itself to mean "approaching an animal stealthily in order to kill it." This ambiguity of hunter and hunted affects several words. "Caught" (l. 12) first seems to mean "embraced" and only later is seen to mean "trapped," as "hart" (l. 14) first seems to mean "heart" and later "prey." "Straunge" (l. 17) first seems to mean "unfamiliar," then "cold, unfriendly," then is seen to possess its Tudor meaning of "prostituted." "Kindly" (l. 20), which is understood to be sarcastic immediately, fluctuates between "generously," "affectionately," "aristocratically," "characteristically," and "naturally"—this last implication suggesting the natural law of the jungle. Other wobbly words are "daunger" (l. 5), "gyse" (l. 10), and "fasshion" (l. 17). The wobbliest and richest of all is "gentill" (l. 3), which means first "tame" and "grateful" and then is set off ironically by "gentilnes" (l. 16), which draws with varying degrees of subversion on a range of meanings: "inner nobility," "innocence," "naiveté," "adherence to a traditional code of the well-born," "lack of ruthlessness." In the background lies another Chaucerian poem, "Gentilesse."

> The firste stok, fader of gentilesse—
> What man that claymeth gentil for to be

Must folowe his trace, and alle his wittes dresse
Vertu to serve, and vyces for to flee. . . .
This firste stok was full of rightwisnesse,
Trewe of his word, sobre, pitous, and free.

The semiotic inconsistency of Wyatt's great poem, wherein signifiers keep trading
in meanings for new, often uglier ones is a constitutive structural element in the
poem. It helps to define the plight of the nobleman who has thought he knew the
rules of the games that were dirtying his hands, only to discover that the games are
dirtier than he realized, have no fixed rules and thus no reliable vocabulary. The
reader's progressive semiotic discovery of eroded signifieds corresponds to the
speaker's own existential discovery of moral groundlessness. He has to deal with
linguistic as well as political and sexual "new fangilnes"; words as well as men
slide from their slipper top. This use of the Chaucerian stanza, rhyme royal, which
initially serves to place the speaker, only turns further the ironic screw of his
isolation at the end between two social and verbal worlds.

Recent editions of Wyatt, especially Daalder's, have contributed to our awareness of the density of proverbs in the texture of his verse. They seem to form one
solution to the problem how to keep one's language stable. Thus the third satire.

These proverbes yet do last.
Reason hath set theim in so sure a place
That lenght of yeres their force can never wast.   [198]

As the verbal "stedfastnes" leaks away, the postfeudal social extremity is seen as a
linguistic extremity. The poet cannot, so he says, frame his tongue to feign; he
can't or won't frame it to adorn; the proverb supplies a certain stiffening but it
scarcely suffices. What essentially keeps the language of these poems from being
"wasted"?

Doubtless many things, but one solution we have already met is particularly
distinctive and needs more analysis. It seems to surface obliquely in the lyric
beginning "Ys yt possyble?" That question, repeated eight times in the opening
four stanzas, registers the stunned disbelief that accompanies a crisis of discovery.
Is it possible, asks the poet, to find so diverse, so changeable a mind that turns "as
wether and wynd"?

Is it possible
To spye yt in an Iye
That tornys as oft as chance on dy?
The trothe whereoff can eny try?
Is it possible?   [111]

Rebholz glosses "to spye yt" as "to discern the real attitude." The eye apparently
turns even faster than the mind, turns with the speed of a die and with the same
random result. Whoso list can try its "trothe," since the eye will dally with "eny"
and betray its own diversity. Without that guarantee of authenticity, there are no
limits to the credible, so that the last stanza concludes sarcastically, "All ys

possyble." With "trothe" spinning like a die, the only other option seems to be total credulity; since no real knowledge is possible, one can only close one's eyes and propose.

      All ys possyble,
     Who so lyst beleve;
   Trust therfore fyrst, and after preve:
  As men wedd ladyes by lycence and leve,
      All ys possyble.

The whole erotic or matrimonial ritual is turned to scorn, but so presumably is the use of language. Characteristically the sexual dilemma seems to adumbrate a larger uncertainty. Any social act or any speech act would seem to require a modicum of trust, a shared agreement, a common expectation. Wyatt's own response to the uncertainty is not formulated but it is illustrated here as elsewhere: it is that irony we have already come to know and whose relation to *trouth* is a mainspring of his moral style.

Irony is appropriate because it makes use of the duplicity which does always remain possible in language but which irony can manipulate and control. It introduces two or more voices into a single word but in so doing it imposes a hierarchy on these voices; it valorizes one at the expense of the other or others. When Wyatt writes, "all ys possyble, / Who so lyst beleve," we hear both the voice of the dupe and the voice of the skeptic, who is capable of moral criticism. When he writes "As men wedd ladyes by lycence and leve," in the single word "ladyes" we discern the tramp who puts on chastity and the disenchanted poet whose curt intelligence invests the sarcasm with its power. Classical irony of this kind establishes a hierarchy of moral voices within the "diversity" of language; it loads the dice on which "trothe" is spinning; it polarizes and stabilizes the play of inauthenticities by distinguishing perspectives. Thus to the question "I would fain knowe what she hath deserved," one answer would be: she deserves to have it said of her, "I have leve to goo of her goodenes." Because one voice is valorized at the expense of others, ironic statement seems to acquire a certain stability that resists the attrition of conventional meanings. Beset by debasements and erosions, overcommitments and pseudocommitments, betrayals of principle and betrayals of the word, it maintains a certain continuity and affirms the integrity of the isolated moral observer.

   ... On my faith me thinck it goode reason
  To chaunge propose like after the season,
  Ffor in every cas to kepe still oon gyse
  Ys mytt for theim that would be taken wyse;
  And I ame not of suche maner condition.   [10]

The knowing duplicity that so cunningly advertises its surrender of one guise has found a means to remove itself from the play of guises and preserve its own equilibrium.

Thus when we read a Wyatt poem that requires us to subread a Petrarchan poem, we experience the passage between them as a process of *stabilization*. The English tends to settle the restlessness of the Italian as it linearizes the cycle and arrests the iteration. This is observable even in the contrast of copulas. Consider again two passages we have already examined.

> L'alma nudrita sempre in doglia e 'n pene
> (quanto è 'l poder d' una prescritta usanza!)
> contra 'l doppio piacer sí 'nferma fue,
>   ch' al gusto sol del disusato bene,   12
> tremando or di paura or di speranza,
> d' abandonarme fu spesso entra due.

The instances of the verb "to be" in lines 11 and 14, both in the past definite tense, illustrate well the insecurity of Petrarch's oxymoronic copula. The verb "fue" in line 11 is employed to affirm the weakness of one emotive pole weighed against the other; the copula "fu" in the last line also carries, as we have seen, the sense of division between antithetical extremes. Even the copula in the parenthetical line 10 only serves to weigh the power of one pole against the other. Wyatt's corresponding "dazed ame I" conveys no comparable division. The speaker may wander "here and there" but he continues to bear a pain that is continuous and whole. Wyatt's affirmations are beset by overcommitments, debasements, betrayals, exposure to changefulness, but they do typically tend to maintain their meaning with a stubborn endurance that shores up the copula's predications.

> For goode is the liff, ending faithfully.   [4]

> Was I never yet of your love greved,
> Nor never shall while that my liff doeth last.   [9]

> But ye, my birdes, I swear by all your belles,
> Ye be my fryndes, and so be but few elles.   [170]

> It is not tyme that can were owt
>   With me that once ys fermly sett . . .
> Yet am I hyrs, she may be sure,
> And shallbe whyle that lyff doth dure.   [114]

As a conductor for metaphor, Wyatt's copula (explicit or implicit) tends to be conservative, and probably more conservative when there is no significant subtext. It functions most responsively as a vehicle for shades of assertion, and its stubborn toughness remains when the thematic statement expresses doubt or is exposed to ironic skepticism.

> It may be good, like it who list,
>   But I do doubt; who can me blame?   [21]

> *Noli me tangere*, for Cesars I ame.   [7]

> I have her hert in my possession,

And of it self there cannot, perdy,
  By no meanes love an herteles body;
And on my faith, good is the reason,
    If it be so.   [18]

Through out the world, if it wer sought,
Faire wordes ynough a man shall finde:
They be good chepe, they cost right nought.
Their substance is but onely winde:
    But well to say and so to mene,
    That swete accord is seldom sene.   [192]

It was no dreme: I lay brode waking.   [37]

It was no dream; the experience was real if misleading; it was valid, in a world the context reveals to be lacking in validity. Wyatt's copula measures out degrees of validity; it tends to support a lonely, existential steadfastness always exposed to attrition and always lacking metaphysical underpinning. It is beleaguered but it endures.

An openness to skepticism seems to provide a certain resistance to attrition. It anticipates the debasement of language and norms by retaining a double focus on the earlier, uncorrupted stage and the modern degradation. This diachronic interplay of codes can be facilitated by imitation. In the well-known sonnet "Who so list to hount . . . ," the irony debases the emblematic and visionary subtext but confers a certain repose of lucidity on the Petrarchan play of presence and absence not untouched at the close with hysteria.

    Una candida cerva sopra l' erba
  verde m' apparve, con duo corna d' oro,
  fra due riviere, all' ombra d' un alloro,
  levando 'l sole a la stagione acerba.   [Canz. 190]

[A white doe on the green grass appeared to me, with two golden horns, between two rivers, in the shade of a laurel, when the sun was rising in the unripe season.]

Who so list to hount, I knowe where is an hynde,
  But as for me, helas, I may no more:
  The vayne travaill hath weried me so sore.
  I ame of theim that farthest commeth behinde.   [7]

Doubtless it is possible to feel in Wyatt's brutal rewriting (and the brutality is not really affected by the possible mediation of Petrarchan commentators)[24] a certain nostalgia for the visionary spirituality of the Italian, the purity of the white, green, and gold in medieval illuminations, as well as nostalgia for the hunt as a noble sport of kings. A good deal of the speaker's self-referential irony is aimed at this irrational performance in an outmoded exercise. Once the allusion to Petrarch has been made from the perspective of a parodic hunt, the nostalgia is hard to suppress. "Hynde" becomes a savage mistranslation of "cerva," anticipating the double debasement below in *"Noli me tangere,"* with its introduction of a second, supremely privileged subtext.

Who list her hount, I put him owte of dowbte,
  As well as I may spend his tyme in vain:
  And, graven with Diamonds, in letters plain
There is written her faier neck rounde abowte: 12
  Noli me tangere, for Cesars I ame;
  And wylde for to hold, though I seme tame.

But in the dismissal of the visionary, in the refusal of illusions about the woman, about the ineffectual speaker or the duped Caesar who wants to hold a wild creature, there lies a tranquility of the intelligence to counterbalance nostalgia. The devaluation of Petrarchan symbols implies a criticism of the phantasm as it reveals the poverty of its own alternatives. This is a dialectical imitation that points to a rupture broader than humanism could traditionally tolerate; having exposed two antagonistic vulnerabilities, it bases its own claim to integrity on the steadiness of its controlled indirection.[25]

In the satires, where the irony is not self-referential, we find in the speaker's representation of himself the most successful English assimilation of Roman classicism before Jonson. The speaking voice belongs to a civilized critic capable of friendship, anger, discrimination, and wisdom, a well-traveled man *in situ*, located in a social, historical, geographical context, synthesizing in his firm moral style the native tradition with the ancient, confident of his unblinking estimates, registering depravity, hypocrisy, and suffering without hysteria, strong in his independence—"wrappid within my cloke"—which is a token of dignity and poise. This temper is neither quite Horatian nor Senecan nor Juvenalian nor Chaucerian, though all four voices have been absorbed. In the first and third satires, the erosion of signification is thematized as it had seldom been in comparable Roman poetry. The third satire is framed by proverbs because, as the passage already quoted has it, "their force can never wast." By introducing the threat of verbal "wasting," Wyatt adds a level of linguistic self-consciousness missing in the principal subtext, the fifth satire of Horace's second book. Both poems consist mainly of cynical advice for worldly success which the reader is meant to reject, but in Wyatt the interest lies as well in the manipulation of language to dispense with *trouth*.

  Thou knowst well first who so can seke to plese
  Shall pourchase frendes where trowght shall but offend.
  Ffle therefore trueth: it is boeth welth and ese.   [198, ll. 32–34]

The body of the poem amounts to a textbook example of the flight from *trouth*, and nowhere in Wyatt are the linguistic and moral components of the term more densely interfused.

  In this also se you be not Idell:
  Thy nece, they cosyn, thy sister or thy doghter,
  If she be faire, if handsom be her myddell,
  Yf thy better hath her love besoght her,

Avaunce his cause and he shall help thy nede.
It is but love: turne it to a lawghter.   [ll. 67–72]

The corresponding passage in Horace[26] leads us to think about the ethical but not
the rhetorical violations; fine as the Latin poem is, it has nothing quite so
brilliantly self-damning as the last line quoted. Thus the passage from Horace to
Wyatt moves toward a complication of rhetorical awareness, a functioning perception of the inextricability of word and act. To keep one's language clean in Wyatt
literally *costs*.

Nay then, farewell! And if thou care for shame,
Content the then with honest povertie,
With fre tong what the myslikes to blame,
And for thy trouth sumtyme adversitie.   [ll. 85–88]

In the shorter poems, the unassailable poise of the satires tends to be attenuated
and the irony, because it is diffused, more original. It is not the classical irony of
Jonson and Pope, because it is capable of including the ironist himself in its
referential field. But it is not on the other hand the irony of Du Bellay because the
primary act that essentially defines the speaker—in Wyatt's case, the exercise of
critical intelligence—is exempted from subversion. One can speak of the imitative
itineraries in both Du Bellay and Wyatt as processes of ironization, but the end
points of this process diverge: Wyatt in his most characteristic poems keeps an
equilibrium the speaker of the *Antiquitez* is still unsure of. The shadings in
Wyatt's play with subtexts, like the shadings of self-presentation, are curiously,
hauntingly modern. Standing at the opening of the mature humanist endeavor in
England, Wyatt at his ablest demonstrated the potential force of diachronic poetry
with a subtle power only a few of his successors would surpass.

Thirteen • Accommodations of Mobility in the Poetry of Ben Jonson

It is appropriate to begin a discussion of Jonson in his English context with some attention to Juan Luis Vives, a Christianized Spanish Jew who spent his mature life in northern Europe, made several extended visits to England, lectured at Oxford, was in touch with the major English humanists, and enjoyed the patronage of a discriminating queen, Catherine of Aragon. Vives's interest to students of English literature transcends his presence on certain crucial pages of Jonson's *Discoveries*, or even his formative role in the development of Tudor pedagogy.[1] For our purposes he is most significant because many dominant features of English humanism can be traced back to his thought. He deserves to be regarded as one of the finest educational thinkers of his century, finer surely than his friend Erasmus, whose influence he only gradually shook off.

Although Vives's educational and intellectual program was essentially constructive, hardheaded, forward-looking, and "sensible," it needs to be read against a background of negativity. This negativity is not stressed and is never milked for pathos; in fact it is repeatedly invoked to justify a positive moral or intellectual imperative. Nevertheless it recurs and must be recognized. No humanist for example faced more lucidly than Vives the fact of fundamental and continuous cultural mutability. But this perception is balanced by assertions of the continuity of human nature.

> Negare nemo potest omnia illa esse mutata, et mutari quotidie, nempe quae sunt voluntatis nostrae atque industriae; sed illa tamen nunquam mutantur quae natura continentur, nempe causae affectuum animi, eorumque actiones et effecta.[2]
> [No one can deny that everything has changed, and continues to change, every day, because these changes spring from our volition and industry. But similar changes do not ever take place in the essential nature of human beings, i.e. in the foundations of the affections of the human mind, and the results which they produce on actions and volitions.]

Some argue, writes Vives, that the knowledge of antiquity is of no value, because "the method of living all over the world has changed" (mutata sit universa ratio) (232; 6:389) But this argument does not coincide with the judgment of wise men. Nothing from the past is so useless that it cannot be adopted to the present.

> Illa ipsa, quae mutata esse constat, quanta emolumenta suppeditant, vel ut aliquid in tuum usum revoces, vel ut causam intelligas cur quidquam tum sic agebatur, quo eandem ipsam aut similem rationem ad actiones tuas, quum res feret, applices? *nihil est enim veterum adeo desuetum et abolitum, quod nostris vivendi moribus accomo-*

264

dari quadam tenus non queat; nam etsi forma iam alia, usus tamen idem manet.
[6:390]

[Even knowledge of that which has been changed is useful; whether you recall something of the past to guide you in what would be useful in your own case, or whether you apply something, which formerly was managed in such and such a way, and so adapt the same or a similar method, to your own actions, as the case may fit. *Indeed, there is nothing of the ancients so worn out by age and so decayed, that it may not in some measure be accommodated to our modes of life.* For although now we may employ a different form, the usefulness yet remains.]   [233]

The italicized sentence formulates that perceived coexistence of rupture and continuity which is latent in so many Renaissance texts, and here the continuity is not simply biological, inherent in the nature of man, but precariously, hortatively cultural. It leaves a channel open for the strenuous, compensating task of accommodating a withered legacy, and in this concept of accommodation, adaptation, application, lies the possibility of a cross-cultural itinerary. The emphasis falls not on the difficulty, the intellectual heroism of restoring vitality to an exhausted institution, but rather on the creative opportunity. Form finally is less significant that *usus*, praxis, utility, discovered relevance.

This movement from a negative assumption to a positive endeavor can be followed again in the realm of historical epistemology. No author and no era has a monopoly on truth, according to Vives; certainly the ancients did not; history is a sporadic, undependable, but progressive accumulation of learning, which must remain finite and imperfect.[3] Classical authorities require skepticism as well as respect. In Jonson's version:

> To all the observations of the Ancients, wee have our owne experience: which, if wee will use, and apply, wee have better meanes to pronounce. It is true they open'd the gates, and made the way, that went before us; but as Guides, not Commanders: *Non Domini nostri, sed Duces fuêre.* Truth lyes open to all; it is no mans severall.[4]

This fallibility of authority and finitude of knowledge can again be turned to a positive challenge, as this quotation demonstrates. Each investigator can make his contribution, provided that he remains modest and dispassionate. The challenge extends particularly to the interpretation of the past and the writing of history, which must avoid anachronism and mythologizing at all costs and must aim at the understanding of every text in its diachronic context. "How is it possible to grasp the meanings of authors if they are isolated and unsupported by [the knowledge of] those who preceded and those who followed?" (Qui possunt auctorum sensus percipi, deserti et destituti suis velut fulcimentis, nempe iis quae antecedunt, quaeque subsequuntur?)[5] This is not very far from the principle of Tynjanov and Jakobson concerning the constitutive presence in every system (and thus every text) of each element's past and future. For Vives, this grasp of the text's diachronic dimension has to remain incomplete, but the limitation is not allowed to become a disincentive.

It is in the light of these attitudes toward history that Vives's comments on imitation need to be studied. They reflect the influence of Quintilian but never betray a mechanical acceptance, a failure of that respectful reassessment which is always evident. The treatment of imitation, as presented in book 4, chapter 4 of the *De tradendis disciplinis* (1531), begins again with a negative: man is born utterly devoid of skills, even hostile to "art." Because of this hostility, his innate bent for imitation has to be cultivated if he is to be civilized. "Children are naturally apes," Vives wrote elsewhere. "They always imitate everything." (Sunt pueri naturaliter simii, imitantur omnia et semper—6:280.) Imitation is essential, but no school-master and no writer is excellent in all aspects. Cicero may be the finest, but he is not perfect, and insofar as he is excellent, he is inimitable. In any case, more significantly, the imitator will always fall short of any single master. In Jonson's words (following Seneca and Vives): "Never no Imitator, ever grew up to his Author; likenesse is alwayes on this side Truth" (8.590). In the case of writing Latin and Greek, moreover, the true art has been lost.

> Sunt . . . ex humanis inventis nonnulla, quorum vel ars omnino periit, vel usus, haec aegre perfeceris, qualia ii, qui tum vixerunt quum ars aut usus vigeret, quemadmo-dum in linguis Latina et Graeca, quarum quoniam populum amisimus, mutuanda sunt semper ex veteribus vocabula, nec nos ulla, aut certe perpauca, possumus novare.
> [6:366–67]
>
> [There are some human inventions, of which either the art or the practice has altogether perished; with these you will have but poor success. Of this kind are the writings of those authors who lived when the art or practice was flourishing. So it is in the Latin and Greek tongues, since the people who spoke those languages are no longer in existence, we have to ring the changes on the words they left behind; we cannot make new terms or, at any rate, new terms must be very few.]   [197]

This negation is transformed once again into an invitation to cultivate the vernacular languages, since it is risky to emulate the ancients' elegance in their own medium. Each potential source of failure becomes the ground of a fresh task which is feasible and incumbent upon the student even if destined to be incomplete. Imitation is "the fashioning of a certain thing in accordance with a proposed model" (Imitatio porro effictio est rei alicuius ad exemplar propositum) (189; 6:362), and by its means the student learns to express himself. Speech cannot in fact fail to reflect the mind behind it, the parent whose image it is: "oratio . . . imago est animi parentis sui" (2:130). Vives seems to see *imitatio* as a technique for achieving in writing a deliberate, controlled expression of the parental mind rather than a passive disclosure. His account of the means to this achievement contains familiar advice. In selecting models, one must have regard for the masters of the various genres and modes, imitating *per diversa genera dicendi*. One must recognize the particular excellence of each master, choosing as Zeuxis did at Crotona. The teacher must guide the student to the model and genre best suited to the student's inclination; on this subject Vives adds the more original notion that a well-chosen model of a dissimilar character can also work as a counterinfluence to correct an inclination carried to excess. He remarks sensibly that if a young man's inclination leads him astray, he should be allowed to strike out on his own "so that he may be true to himself when another's example will not suit his purpose" (ut sit suus, qui alienus non potest) (194–95; 6:365). As he progresses, "he will imitate truly, that is to say, he will fashion what he wishes to express according to his model" (. . . vere imitabitur, id est, ad exemplar affinget quae volet) (194–95; 6:365). At a still later stage, the mature student begins to emulate rather than follow, comparing the model's shortcomings with his own and correcting these, until at the end of this arduous work, the cyclical interplay with the other text becomes second nature. "For fixed habit in any direction passes over into a state of one's own nature" (nam consuetudo in naturae conditionem transit) (198; 6:367).

The strength of this program—and not only in Vives—lies in the unity of the critical act with the act of original composition, especially when composition is not regarded as an exercise of shallow stylistic facility. This trivial and purely verbal conception is most emphatically rejected by Vives, who is notable among his contemporaries for his subordination of *verbum* to *res*. The unity of the critical and creative acts is doubled by the simultaneous understanding of a concrete past and of the concrete present seen in relation to it. This double understanding is bound up in the crucial act of accommodation. After the most rigorous and detailed analysis of, say, a speech by Cicero (Vives supplies the bases for the analysis), "we do not make use of the same material, but adopt those which stand in the same position to us, as they did to the author" (non quo nos utamur eorundem, sed ut eorum, qui nobis loco eodem sunt, quo illi erant auctori nostro) (196; 6:366). A sentence from Cicero is quoted as an example, followed by a poor imitation (too reproductive, insufficiently accommodated) and an approved imitation which changes more and enlarges the Christian elements. The approved version opens a distance, sketches a significant itinerary, as the disapproved version does not.

In practice, Vives was worried more than most humanist educators before the Reform by the risk of exposing the immature to the beguilements of pagan literature. The Puritanism of his pedagogic taste led him to want to substitute second-rate Christian poets like Prudentius, Sidonius, and Juvencus for Lucian and Tibullus. But these failures of judgment count for less than the weight Vives threw, along with Erasmus and Colet, behind a pedagogy of concrete usage as opposed to the pedagogy of rules enshrined in the standard grammatical textbook of the later Middle Ages, the *Doctrinale* by Alexander of Villedieu. His enlightened independence also appears in his battle to teach women and the poor, in his eagerness to use sense impressions for learning, and in his insistence on extending the curriculum to the sciences. His pragmatic, demystifying mind, leaning toward Pelagius rather than Augustine, indisposed to idolize, resistant to doctrinal final-ity, courageous in the face of loss, sympathetic to the vernacular, trustful in the continuity of genius, would give comfort for all its piety to the secularizing tendencies of the next century and a half. It would also abet the transition from a sense of exclusion, inferiority, and crudity to a progressively secure independence in the development of English humanism.

A representative native work of the following generation which played a role in this transition is *The Schoolmaster* of Roger Ascham, published posthumously in 1570. Ascham is perhaps the closest thing England produced to an influential Ciceronian, although one has to begin qualifying that statement as soon as one has made it. The standard accusation of Ascham running from Bacon to C. S. Lewis, namely that he cared only for style narrowly defined at the expense of values and of judgment, is quite simply wrong and is refuted by an unprejudiced reading of his book. Doubtless he is vulnerable, but not along the oversimplified lines of his critics. Ascham believed in quite the opposite of the line commonly attributed to him; he believed in the intimate penetration of *verbum* and *res*, language and praxis, and he protested against their "divorce." The following is a characteristic remark. "All such authors as be fullest of good matter and right judgment in doctrine be likewise always most proper in words, most apt in sentence, most plain and pure in uttering the same."[6] The humanist belief that language and judgment are inextricable constitutes Ascham's naiveté, if that is what it is. Jonson would reflect it when he wrote, following Vives: "Language most shews a man: speake that I may see thee. It springs out of the most retired, and inmost parts of us, and is the Image of the Parent of it, the mind" (8. 625). Or again, following Seneca: "If the mind be staid, grave, and compos'd, the wit is so; that vitiated, the other is blowne, and deflowr'd. Doe wee not see, if the mind languish, the members are dull? . . . Wheresoever, manners and fashions are corrupted, Language is. It imitates the publicke riot" (8. 592–93). Ascham takes this faith one step further in assuming that training in "pure" linguistic expression is likely to produce an upright character. It is this faith that would be demystified in Montaigne's "Institution des enfans." Bacon, failing to understand it, pummeled something else. It needs to be apprehended in order to see the goal of Ascham's educational program, which consists in the early stage of what he called "double translation" and in the later stages of "*imitatio*."

Although the fragmentary *Schoolmaster* breaks off before reaching its culmination in Cicero, it is clear enough that "Tully" was to be the supreme imitative model for the young as for the mature. Ascham has kind words for Cortesi answering Poliziano and for Bembo answering Pico, but nothing to say for their correspondents. Still, once Ascham has aligned himself with that school, his deviations from it are at least as striking as his orthodoxy. His own downright, perspicuous, somewhat conversational style, enlivened with homely similes, has little of the Ciceronian about it. Like Vives and many others, he distinguishes the outstanding exemplars of each genre; for the writing of history, "Caesar and Livy . . . are perfect examples of imitation."[7] Moreover he extends his key term beyond pedagogy and composition to a technique of analysis by no means limited to Cicero. He is interested by imitative passages from the ancients when both subtext and surface text are extant, and he sees the detailed comparison of these as a means of isolating the quiddity of each writer's art.[8] Whether or not Ascham received this method as he claims from Johannes Sturm and Sir John Cheke, it remains a fruitful approach to literary criticism, a more promising bridge to the past than the imposition of quantitative meters on English verse, which Ascham also advocates. The comparative method does not necessarily privilege Cicero at the outset over his model Demosthenes or over anybody else.

Imitation is particularly needful in Ascham's eyes for a rude nation still recovering from Gothic barbarity. "If ye would speak as the best and wisest do, ye must be conversant where the best and wisest are, but if you be born or brought up in a rude country, ye shall not choose but speak rudely. The rudest man knoweth this to be true" (p. 114). We can take this as Ascham's indirect but unmistakable expression of his own awareness of cultural distance, all the more typical in that opposition of the wise and the rude of speech which interweaves prudential and linguistic aptitude. "Rude" was one of the commonest words used by Tudor translators in describing the impoverished language into which they were obliged to turn foreign masterpieces. Imitation then becomes a means of compensation for native crudity, a restoration of a loss. Speaking of his teacher, Cheke, and his friend Watson, Ascham writes:

> They wished, as Virgil and Horace were not wedded to follow the faults of former fathers (a shrewd marriage in greater matters) but by right imitation of the perfect Grecians had brought poetry to perfectness also in the Latin tongue, that we Englishmen likewise would acknowledge and understand rightfully our rude, beggarly rhyming.   [p. 145]

The immediate issue, rhyme, is subsidiary to the larger issue, a linkage with the past through an activity analogous with the past's. The past is both the desired object of knowledge and the source of a means to gratify the desire. That Ascham saw this gratification as taking place, that in fact his consciousness of rudeness was qualified with native pride, we learn from a charming address to Cicero, who had once mocked England for its lack of both silver and learning.

> But now, Master Cicero, blessed be God and his son Jesu Christ whom you never knew, except it were as it pleased him to lighten you by some shadow . . . blessed be God, I say, that sixteen hundred year after you were dead and gone it may truly be said that for silver there is more comely plate in one city of England than is in four of the proudest cities in all Italy, and take Rome for one of them. And for learning, beside the knowledge of all learned tongues and liberal sciences, even your own books, Cicero, be as well read, and your excellent eloquence is as well liked and loved and as truly followed in England at this day, as it is now, or ever was since your own time, in any place of Italy.   [pp. 150–51]

Here indirectly is Ascham's reply to his own indirect accusation, a manifesto of that native assertiveness which would become the characteristic English response to loss.

Imitation as Ascham typically describes it is less a matter of bridging distance than a matter of precise calculations and sensitivity to shadings; it is learning to distinguish the sublime (*sublime*) from the pompous (*tumidum*) or the dry (*siccum*) from the arid (*aridum*). Imitative learning depends upon making these subtle distinctions in another's text or in one's own. The valorization of precision, clarity, directness, hitting the mark in the center, was Ascham's contribution to the English Renaissance. A far more slender figure than Vives, a man of limited but accurate discriminations, his imitative doctrine and example can be said to have brought a sober and healthy ordering to the writing of English before the dark, symbolic elaborations of Spenser and Sidney.

During the crowded thirty years that followed the publication of *The School-master*, what is striking is the relative weakness of his program's impact on the actual production of English literature. It is true that the imitative method was firmly implanted in the Tudor grammar school, and that the teaching of rhetoric in particular was centered upon it.[9] The third quarter of the century saw the growing popularity of the "formulary rhetoric," a volume containing models of orations and epistles to be imitated, systematically chosen to cover a variety of topics and situations.[10] But in the actual poems, plays, and prose fiction of the mature Renaissance, the response to classical literature tended to be diffused rather than specific, and particularly so at the levels of highest quality. Sidney was basically accurate when he wrote:

> Yet confesse I alwayes, that as the firtilest ground must bee manured, so must the highest flying wit, have a Dedalus to guide him. That Dedalus, they say, both in this, and in other, hath three wings, to beare it selfe up into the ayre of due commendation: that is, Arte, Imitation, and Exercise. But these, neyther artificiall rules, nor imitative patternes, we much cumber our selves withall.[11]

George Puttenham, in the major critical work of the nineties, the *Arte of English Poesie*, cumbered himself very little with the question of imitation in this meaning. Spenser's brilliant "Epithalamion," a triumph of diachronic poetry, must be weighed against *The Faerie Queene*, where the historical self-consciousness seems sporadic and dim, and where the use of Homer, to take a single example, in the twelfth canto of book 2 lacks etiological firmness. Classical genres such as verse satire, eclogue, elegy, verse epistle, and pastoral romance, to say nothing of tragedy, were progressively naturalized, but the naturalization lacked—perhaps salutarily—the close imitative reference of so many continental texts. Continental conventions and modes were themselves naturalized, most visibly the novella and the Petrarchan sonnet, but the former yielded little first-rate work, and the latter, at its richest, quickly achieved a relative independence. If one considers simply the legacy of antiquity, and if one remembers the necessary limits on Wyatt's reading, then Douglas Bush's tribute to Ben Jonson remains valid: "the first great English theorist and practitioner of neoclassicism, the first really direct, learned, deliberate, and single-hearted heir of antiquity."[12]

Would it be reasonable to inquire into the causes of this gradual, *filtered* reception of Elizabethan neoclassicism? One answer might be the circumstance that the efflorescence of the literary Renaissance coincided with the earliest wave of Ramism in England. Ramus and his disciples, who challenged so much, challenged in effect the systematic use of imitation in the teaching of rhetoric. This becomes clear in the Ramist treatment of practice (*exercitatio*), which since Plato's *Phaedrus* and the *Rhetorica ad Herennium* had been regarded as the third requirement for oratorical achievement, following ability (*natura*) and rules (*doctrina*). Imitation falls of course under *exercitatio*. (This organization is maintained at the close of Jonson's *Discoveries*.) But in the Ramist scheme, practice, now shifted from rhetoric to dialectic, subordinates imitation to two other activities. The first is "analysis," the reduction of a given text to its basic syllogistic and figural elements. The second is "genesis," which reverses analysis and is sometimes called "synthesis"; it consists of putting together the elements that the student has already learned to isolate. Although Ramus theoretically countenanced "imitation," in practice his method excluded a sensitivity to moral style, excluded the effort of the historical imagination, the effort of self-knowledge, and the profound assimilation of an alien voice. Composition as genesis was a more cerebral, mechanical operation.

> Now in writing, the first and easiest way is imitation. Hence we must look carefully to whom we imitate. . . . But next we must strike out for ourselves, and take our independent arguments from popular daily affairs close to ordinary life; then draw the causes, effects, and other genera of the available arguments from the sources of invention; and finally, make use of all the ways of disposition with equal care, concluding now this way, now that.[13]

Ramus's *exercitatio* in effect reduces the relation of past text and fresh composition to a purely synchronic table. One might accuse it, as Derrida accuses structuralism, of a decadent hostility to the force of history. Ramus's critic Jacques Charpentier alleges that he has ruined "exercise" because, in Father Ong's paraphrase, "Ramus annihilates one author after another and leaves nobody to imitate."[14]

Ramism doubtless played a role in checking the deliberate pace of English classicism, especially in the case of the metaphysicals.[15] But one must note that it reached England too late to affect the training of the great Elizabethans,[16] and that the greatest English Ramist, John Milton, was by no means closed to imitation either in theory or practice. Another continental current that might be cited in this context is the so-called anti-Ciceronian movement, first identified by Morris Croll fifty years ago and subsequently redefined by a series of scholars.[17] According to Croll, Marc-Antoine Muret, Justus Lipsius, Montaigne, and Bacon led a movement away from Cicero and the Augustans as imitative models toward the terser, choppier, less orotund authors of the Roman silver age: Tacitus, Seneca, Pliny the Younger, Lucan, and Juvenal, among others. Croll saw this swing as filling a gap left by Erasmus's *Ciceronianus* and also as corresponding to more "libertine" currents of thought. But however seminal the work of Croll and his school has been, it must be pointed out that in England only Bacon really fits his major categories, and that if "anti-Ciceronian" passages can be found in the first version of the *Advancement of Learning*, a later version includes a passage describable as anti-anti-Ciceronian.[18] The original attack at any rate is based upon a misrepresentation of Bacon's principal whipping boy, Ascham. The magnificent literature of the late Renaissance and baroque era in England is in fact too diverse to be reducible to any set of models or any formula, even one as elastic as Croll's has proven to be.

The deepest causes for the gradual filtering of classical influence into England are doubtless domestic rather than foreign, and like most "causes" in literary history, defy illumination. The only appropriate job for the historian is to record the slow, progressive emergence of something like a cultural consensus. Prominent in this consensus is the refusal to repudiate the native medieval tradition with the same vigor we have met in France. Wimsatt and Brooks, after citing Vida and Du Bellay on plundering the ancients, noted the important distinction.

> In the next generation, however, the distinguishing feature of an English defense of vernacular, E. K. 's Epistle prefixed to the *Shepheardes Calender*, is a reversal of Du Bellay's thesis in that E. K. applauds the Spenserian enrichment of the language from native, if rustic, dialect sources, rather than from the "inkhorns" of humanistic pedants who were practising the theory of Du Bellay with all too great a will.[19]

Despite the expression of loss in "The Teares of the Muses," "The Ruines of Time," and his translations of Du Bellay, Spenser did not choose to respond to this loss by taking the paths of Vida, Du Bellay, or Ascham. Campion's tentative, experimental essay on the possible value of quantitative prosody for English verse was demolished by Daniel's powerful "Defence of Ryme" (1603), which, following Vives, affirms the continuity of genius in all ages. It also decries the superstition of classical idolatry and denounces the deprecation of the Middle Ages. Every age is rich, according to Daniel, although some are too obscure to be valued as they deserve.

> We must not looke upon the immense course of times past, as men overlooke spacious and wide countries, from off high Mountaines and are never the neer to judge of the true Nature of the soyle, or the particular syte and face of those territories they see. Nor must we thinke, viewing the superficiall figure of a region in a Mappe that wee know strait the fashion and place as it is. Or reading an Historie (which is but a Mappe of men, and dooth no otherwise acquaint us with the true Substance of Circumstances, than a superficiall Card dooth the Sea-man with a coast never seene, which always prooves other to the eye than the imagination forecast it) that presently wee know all the world, and can distinctly judge of times, men and maners, just as they were.[20]

The perpetual revolution of all things defines our historical solitude, but this has never justified violent innovation or creative paralysis. The awareness that produced humanist pathos elsewhere is acutely present in Daniel, but in him it produces instead an acceptance, independence, bravery, pride, which would enter into his community's response to pathos. Jonson claimed to have written a reply to both Campion and Daniel, "especially this last" (1.132). It has not survived, but his entire canon might be considered a kind of reply. Jonson's work however was as determined as much as any other writer's by his *mundus significans*. And on the precise issue of rude, beggarly rhymes, Ascham's and Campion's issue, it is worth recording at the outset that no one has ever produced more loving pastiches than Jonson of John Skelton's tatterdemalion chiming.[21]

2

Jonson occupies his preeminent place in the history of English classicism because in a real sense he invented a classical idiom for his language, just as more broadly he invented a classical temper, a moral style or set of styles, both recognizably native and recognizably derivative from Latin. Once the thing was done, the achievement became transparent, but it was nonetheless momentous. How does one English a Latin text so that the transformation is radical and, so to speak, *free*, not the laborious wordbound deciphering of a trot but a deliberate exercise of poetic manner, a form of play that does not exclude respect? The result has to give the impression that a choice has been made along a range of available solutions, the impression of careless preference made by a master of flexible artistry. How might Catullus sound in the easy play of an English sensibility? Nobody really knew until it was done.

> Kisse me, sweet: The warie lover
> Can your favours keepe, and cover,
> When the common courting jay
> All your bounties will betray.
> Kisse again: no creature comes.
> Kisse, and score up wealthy summes
> On my lips, thus hardly sundred,
> While you breath. First give a hundred,
> Then a thousand . . .
> Till you equall with the store,
> All the grasse that Rumney yeelds,
> Or the sands in Chelsey fields,
> Or the drops in silver Thames,
> Or the starres, that guild his streames,
> In the silent sommer-nights,
> When youths ply their stolne delights.   [8.103]

It is slender, but in its quickness, jauntiness, control of pause and movement, its modulations of tone, its willingness to Anglicize, it bespeaks a maturity that became a permanent acquisition of the language. The individual maturity of Wyatt did not have behind it a culture so rich in available choices. Jonson had the advantage of a keener historical consciousness growing progressively if unevenly around him,[22] but he contributed to this consciousness more than he took. His achievement has to be measured not only against the clumsier and slower adaptations of earlier English humanism, but also against so fine a version as the beautiful Lucretian hymn in Spenser.

> Great Venus, Queene of beautie and of grace,
> The joy of Gods and men, that under skie
> Doest fayrest shine, and most adorne thy place,
> That with thy smyling looke does pacifie
> The raging seas, and makst the stormes to flie . . .   [*FQ* 4.10.44]

Spenser shares the breadth of Lucretius's metaphysical vision and is able to make the hymn his own. But from the particular perspective of this study, he appears in the hymn as a poet whose loyalty to his own medieval roots limits his room for poetic maneuver, as one unconcerned with the exercise of bridging a rupture and playing with the differences between the separated worlds. Jonson, no greater a poet, altered English literary history more radically. To be an English poet after he wrote was to command a finer, more various and sophisticated power. Jonson is one of the noblest examples of the creative force available in an imitative program. The sophistication he left as an endowment bears witness to the widening scope of a diachronic consciousness. He justifies in himself the goals of the humanist enterprise, and if he is often presented in his genetic role as a father, he can also be understood as a culmination. He truly played the transitive role valorized by humanism: he passed on a discipline.

Yet his own remarks in the *Discoveries* on the specific topic of imitation are strikingly ambivalent. This ambivalence cannot be explained simply by the fact that this work constitutes for the most part a kind of commonplace book. Too much discrimination as well as rewriting clearly went into its compilations, and not all entries have as yet been traced to a source. Nor, I think, can the ambivalence be explained by the sort of intimidation felt by the young Du Bellay before the ancient masters. Intimidation would scarcely ever seem to be a word appropriate to Ben Jonson. Yet the ambivalence is there. One can dismiss perhaps his criticism of those, allegedly like Montaigne, who reproduce undigested the last books they have read and contradict themselves unconsciously by their thoughtless copying (8.586). This censure is aimed only at an abuse. This is not the case of the remark already quoted, derived from Seneca and Vives, about the necessary inferiority of the imitator to his "author" (8.590), likeness always being on this side truth. It is true that the remark occurs in a context where Jonson is criticizing the choice of a single model: "One, though he be excellent, and the chief, is not to be imitated alone." Perhaps likeness might overtake truth if the choice of models were dispersed and the resemblance diffused. There is no easy way, however, to dismiss the following paragraph, brief but highly suggestive, for which no source has as yet been identified.

> I have considered, our whole life is like a Play: wherein every man, forgetfull of himselfe, is in travaile with expression of another. Nay, wee so insist in imitating others, as wee cannot (when it is necessary) returne to our selves: like Children, that imitate the vices of Stammerers so long, till at last they become such: and make the habit to another nature, as it is never forgotten.   [8.597]

This is all the more powerful because it reflects two recurrent themes of Jonson's moral reflection: the close correspondence between speech and character, and the strength of the autonomous personality as distinguished from the changeable. If this travail to express another is also merely the perversion of a good, it is a perversion that lies close to the heart of Jonson's ethics.

Opposed to these negative remarks in the *Discoveries*, one finds strong formulations of Jonson's belief in imitation, as in the following adaptation of Quintilian.

> As it is fit for grown and able Writers to stand of themselves, and worke with their owne strength, to trust and endeavour by their owne faculties: so it is fit for the beginner, and learner, to study others, and the best. For the mind, and memory are more sharpely exercis'd in comprehending an other mans things, then our owne; and such as accustome themselves, and are familiar with the best Authors, shall ever and anon find somewhat of them in themselves, and in the expression of their minds, even when they feele it not, be able to utter something like theirs, which hath an Authority above their owne. Nay, sometimes it is the reward of a mans study, the praise of quoting an other man fitly: And though a man be more prone, and able for one kind of writing, then another, yet hee must exercise all. For as in an Instrument, so in style, there must be a Harmonie, and concent of parts.   [8. 616–17]

This may begin with a pedagogic concern with learners, but the child presently grows to be a man, and the harmony at the end constitutes the goal of a lifetime. The harmony derives from reading a spectrum of authors, so that the adult independence of the opening sentence has to be reinterpreted to include a poly-semous enrichment from outside. In this working back of the end upon the beginning there is already the hint of a tension, if not a conflict. The beginning of the paragraph asserts the value of the fully independent, centered self, but what follows suggests the possible transcendence of the isolated self in the exhilarating contact with external greatness. Are there limits to the wisdom of autonomy? This would seem to be the implication of another allusion to Quintilian.

> The reading of Homer and Virgil is counsell'd by Quintilian, as the best way of informing youth, and confirming man. For besides, that the mind is rais'd with the height, and sublimity of such a verse, it takes spirit from the greatnesse of the matter, and is tincted with the best things.   [8. 618]

The grown man is *confirmed*, made more himself, by the tincture of otherness. (Quintilian's phrasing is less sweeping: ". . . ad intellegendas eorum virtutes firmiore iudicio opus est"—1.8). The paradoxicality of all these comments, taken together, is not quite absent from the last of them, even if it appears unambiguous and frankly positive.

> The third requisite in our Poet, or Maker, is Imitation, to bee able to convert the substance, or Riches of an other Poet, to his owne use. To make choise of one excellent man above the rest, and so to follow him, till he grow very Hee: or, so like him, as the Copie may be mistaken for the Principall. Not, as a Creature, that swallowes, what it takes in, crude, raw, or indigested; but, that feedes with an Appetite, and hath a Stomacke to concoct, divide, and turne all into nourishment. Not, to imitate servilely, as Horace saith, and catch at vices, for vertue: but, to draw forth out of the best, and choisest flowers, with the Bee, and turne all into Honey, worke it into one relish, and savour: make our Imitation sweet: observe, how the best writers have imitated, and follow them.   [8. 638–39]

The contradiction between total self-surrender to the other ("so to follow him, till he grow very Hee") and total assimilation of the other ("feedes with an Appetite, and hath a Stomacke to . . . turne all into nourishment") is less marked in the supposed source, Johannes Buchler, who writes only of an effort to resemble ("unus . . . cui nos similes esse studeamus"), not an absolute identity. One can speak only of a putative source, since every statement in this passage was long worn with repetition. The stress on a particular moral style ("one relish, and savour") is nonetheless characteristically Jonsonian, as is the intensification of resemblance into fusion, a shift that introduces this paragraph directly into the dialectic of selfhood at work in the preceding quotation. If rhetoric and ethos are so closely bound up in Jonson's mind, this homology between literary interaction and moral interaction strengthens the knot. Language most shows a man indeed. To speak of intertextuality is to speak of *paideia*. But to speak about all this is also, it would seem from our array of quotations, to end up unpredictably on various sides of the issue.

Because this homology lies so deep in Jonson's mind, something will have to be said about the dialectic of selfhood throughout his work. The ostensible human ideal in the plays and poems is the figure so strong in its moral center of gravity as to be unshakable by fortune or temptation, a figure carrying with it that equilibrium of dwelling which Penshurst is said to confer upon its master.[23] This is a figure like William Roe, "that good Aeneas, past through fire,/Through seas, stormes, tempests: and imbarqu'd for hell,/Came back untouch'd" (8.81) or like Sir Ralph Sheldon, who

Dar'st breath in any ayre; and with safe skill,
    Till thou canst finde the best, choose the least ill.
That to the vulgar canst thy selfe apply,
    Treading a better path, not contrary;
And, in their errors maze, thine owne way know.   [8. 76]

or like the poet "high and aloofe, / Safe from the wolves black jaw, and the dull Asses hoofe" (8.175). The long Jonsonian poem seems to provide typically such an image of human stability toward the end. The negative example in the poems as in the plays is the absolutely protean figure who changes roles, places, masks, attitudes, flatteries, lovers, and vices as the times decide. In Jonson's imagination autonomy aligns itself with the inner as against the outer, the "natural" as against the contrived, integrity against imposture, soul against sense, poetry as expression or self-revelation against poetry as affective persuasion, moving a reader or an audience. Thus virtue tends to be represented with substantives and adjectives evoking an unassailable stability, vice by verbs and adverbs evoking ugly, driven, deceitful, destabilizing passion. The highest virtue is that like Roe's and Sheldon's, which preserves its substantiality despite exposure to the hostile variety of the uncentered. Jonas Barish has pushed this distinction to its absolute poles.

> Somewhere in Jonson there lurks a puritanical uneasiness about pleasure itself, and also a distrust of movement, which connects with . . . an ideal of stasis in the moral and ontological realm. But whatever exists in time, and unfolds in time, and utilizes human actors, must also involve motion as one of its mainsprings.[24]

Because the polarization of static and kinetic is so sharp, many of Jonson's texts can be read as contests between the substantive (generally positive) and the verbal (generally negative), and when approved activity *is* presented, it is likely to be capped by a substantive. This can be an actual name ("Nothing perfect done, but as a Cary, or a Morison"—8.247) or an exemplum ("that good Aeneas") or a static image.

> Yet we must more then move still, or goe on,
> We must accomplish; 'Tis the last Key-stone
> That makes the Arch.   [8.157]

Here movement becomes accomplishment which becomes the fixed keystone. The artistic problem in most of Jonson's ethical poems, which is to say the central, major poems in this canon, might be described as the problem of redeeming the necessary dynamism of existence.[25]

The problem is all the more pressing because in the opposition originality/imitation, it is obviously imitation that has to be aligned with the negative poles, with the threat of alteration, dilution, tincturing, destabilization of the internal man. In imitation one becomes a very Another. This disposition of the imitative process emerges from all the relevant comments in the *Discoveries*. Imitation raises a man above himself, leads him to self-forgetfulness and prevents his return to his basic selfhood, discolors his native purity by an osmosis of otherness. The ultimate destructiveness of imitation, which Jonson never portrays, would presumably be the series of endless transformations catalogued seductively and wickedly by Volpone as the final enticement of Celia, the dream or nightmare of the perfectly protean.[26] The rhetorical equivalent of this infinite translatability is the trope called translation, or metaphor. Jonson's comments on metaphor in the *Discoveries* seem to argue for a mean between insipid plainness and "farfet" contrivance, but in fact he is true to his Latin forerunners in feeling the latter abuse as the more insidious. Thus, speaking of the best words:

> They are to be chose according to the persons wee make speake, or the things wee speak of. . . . And herein is seene their Elegance, and Propriety, when wee use them fitly, and draw them forth to their just strength and nature, by way of Translation, or Metaphore. But in this Translation wee must only serve necessity (*nam temerè nihil transfertur à Prudenti* [a wise man uses no metaphor at random]) or commodity, which is a kind of necessity. . . . Metaphors farfet hinder to be understood, and affected, lose their grace.   [8.621]

Deformed language (the wretched contrivances of metaphysical metaphor?) corresponds to the charlatans, boasters, nimble changelings, moral transvestites of the comedies. The farfet metaphor is the *alazon* of rhetoric.[27] Unbridled metaphor like unlimited imitation carries the threat of ethical and social blight; it corresponds to "the publicke riot." The artistic problem of redeeming existential dynamism would seem to be paralleled by the rhetorical problem of containing "translations," those forms of transformation indigenous in Renaissance poetry.

Beneath the official attitudes and orthodoxies, of course, preferences are not so sharp-edged. Jonson could not have created his Subtles and Brainworms and Moscas without a latent sympathy. He could not have written Volpone's great speech of metamorphoses, or created the puppet show at Bartholomew Fair, or made a living legend of himself, without a furtive attraction to imposture.[28] "Alongside the well-articulated antitheatricalism," writes Barish," "... there ... lurks a less acknowledged but nonetheless potent theatricalism."

> It is precisely the uneasy synthesis between a formal antitheatricalism, which condemns the arts of show and illusion on the one hand, and a subversive hankering after them on the other, that lends to Jonson's comic masterpieces much of their unique high tension and precarious equilibrium.[29]

Add to this division in Jonson a complementary ambivalence about withdrawal to the centered home-base. Posterity, he writes after Quintilian, will come to appreciate the true artificer, "How he doth raigne in mens affections; how invade, and breake in upon them; and makes their minds like the thing he writes" (8.588). The will to withdraw is opposed by the will to invade and acquire. Cutting across these divisions or tensions or, in Barish's more hopeful term, syntheses, lies the problematic decorum of the imitative act, a kind of diachronic metaphorizing, an intertextual translation, which in practice compelled Jonson the poet repeatedly "to enlarge, and veere out all sayle" or "to take it in, and contract it" (8.623). It will be worthwhile examining the techniques of this navigational prudence which allow the poet, like Roe, to travel well without really leaving home, or resemble Selden, "you that have beene ever at home: yet, have all Countries seene" (8.159).

3

Epigram 101, "Inviting a Friend to Supper," can serve to introduce Jonson as imitator. It might be described crudely as a versified menu; it derives clearly from three menu-poems by one of Jonson's favorite Romans, Martial. The following is representative.

> Cenabis belle, Iuli Cerialis, apud me;
>   condicio est melior si tibi nulla, veni.
> octavam poteris servare; lavabimur una:
>   scis quam sint Stephani balnea iuncta mihi.
> prima tibi dabitur ventri lactuca movendo
>   utilis, et porris fila resecta suis,
> mox vetus et tenui maior cordyla lacerto,
>   sed quam cum rutae frondibus ova tegant;
> altera non derunt tenui versata favilla,
>   et Velabrensi massa coacta foco,
> et quae Picenum senserunt frigus olivae.
>   haec satis in gustu. cetera nosse cupis?
> mentiar, ut venias: pisces, conchylia, sumen,
>   et chortis saturas atque paludis aves,

quae nec Stella solet rara nisi ponere cena.
   plus ego polliceor: nil recitabo tibi,
ipse tuos nobis relegas licet usque Gigantas,
   rura vel aeterno proxima Vergilio.[30]
[You will dine nicely, Julius Cerialis, at my house; if you have no better engagement,
come. You will be able to observe the eighth hour; we will bathe together: you know
how near Stephanus' baths are to me. First, there will be given you lettuce useful for
relaxing the bowels, and shoots cut from their parent leeks; then tunny salted and
bigger than a small lizard-fish, and one too which eggs will garnish in leaves of rue.
Other eggs will not be wanting, roasted in embers of moderate heat, and a lump of
cheese ripened over a Velabran hearth, and olives that have felt the Picenian frost.
These are enough for a whet: do you want to know the rest? I will deceive you to make
you come: fish, mussels, sow's paps, and fat birds of the poultry-yard and the marsh,
which even Stella is not used to serve except at a special dinner. More I promise you: I
will recite nothing to you, even although you yourself read again your "Giants"
straight through, or your "Pastorals" that rank next to immortal Virgil.]

The interest of a poem like this one lies in its proximity to conversational prose:
how close can the plain style edge toward the unbuttoned chat of familiar
conversation—the neighborhood bathing establishment, Stella the cook, the laxa-
tive lettuce—while still remaining in some modest way a poem? Martial knows
how to cut this calculation very fine, and his success at it provides a kind of
unpretentious satisfaction. His poem indirectly defines a certain degree of acquaintance between two literary men and a certain degree of pleasure they might
share, neither very intense, both mildly agreeable. Another invitation promises
blameless conversation.

. . . accedent sine felle ioci nec mane timenda
   libertas et nil quod tacuisse velis:
de prasino conviva meus venetoque loquatur,
   nec faciunt quemquam pocula nostra reum.   [10.48.21–24]
[To crown these shall be jests without gall, and a freedom not to be dreaded the next
morning, and no word you would wish unsaid; let my guest converse of the Green and
the Blue [factions of charioteers]: my cups do not make any man a defendant.]

and a third describes the sort of pleasure included and excluded.

parva est cenula (quis potest negare?)
sed finges nihil audiesve fictum
et voltu placidus tuo recumbes;
nec crassum dominus leget volumen,
nec de Gadibus inprobis puellae
vibrabunt sine fine prurientes
lascivos docili tremore lumbos;
sed quod nec grave sit nec infacetum,
Parvi tibia Condyli sonabit.
haec est cenula. Claudiam sequeris.
quam nobis cupis esse tu priorem?   [5.78.22–32]
[My poor dinner is a small one—who can deny it?—but you will say no word insincere

nor hear one, and, wearing your natural face, will recline at ease; nor will your host
read a bulky volume, nor will girls from wanton Gades with endless prurience swing
lascivious loins in practice writhings; but the pipe of little Condylus shall play
something not too solemn nor unlively. Such is your little dinner. You will follow
Claudia. What girl do you desire to meet before me?]

I have omitted the opening menu. Until the close, the poem seems to be promising
a middling meal: undistinguished wine but choice ("nobiles") olives, neither
boring poetry nor the titillations of belly dancers. The last line seems to surprise
the potential guest, Toranius, with the offer of a girl before the first course. (Is there
a touch of vulgarity in the way this surprise is sprung? "You will follow Claudia."
Not a graceful wording.) Despite the abrupt concluding swerve into carnality, the
key phrase for this and the other invitation poems is the phrase "voltu placidus
tuo"—keeping a relaxed face. It is an apt formula for all three poems, offering
moderately good food and unpretentious fellowship with a cool, unforced demean-
or. Jonson's poem is quite a different thing.

> To night, grave sir, both my poore house, and I
>   Doe equally desire your companie:
> Not that we thinke us worthy such a ghest,
>   But that your worth will dignifie our feast,
> With those that come; whose grace may make that seeme   5
>   Something, which, else, could hope for no esteeme.
> It is the faire acceptance, Sir, creates
>   The entertaynment perfect: not the cates.
> Yet shall you have, to rectifie your palate,
>   An olive, capers, or some better sallade   10
> Ushring the mutton; with a short-leg'd hen,
>   If we can get her, full of egs, and then,
> Limons, and wine for sauce: to these, a coney
>   Is not to be despair'd of, for our money;
> And, though fowle, now, be scarce, yet there are clarkes,   15
>   The skie not falling, thinke we may have larkes.
> Ile tell you of more, and lye, so you will come:
>   Of partrich, pheasant, wood-cock, of which some
> May yet be there; and godwit, if we can:
>   Knat, raile, and ruffe too.   [8.64–65]

As in Martial's epigrams, the body of Jonson's ostensibly consists of a list of nouns,
related metonymically. But in Jonson the real subject has nothing to do with the
accumulation of dishes; it lies in the spirit of the voice ordering this series, subtly
modulated from line to line but never crossing the limits of smiling respect and
courteous banter. This spirit has no name in the poem, although toward the end a
few words emerge that help to circumscribe it. It might be located grossly by the
phrase "civilized urbanity." Martial's poems are raised to the level of an exercise or
demonstration of a certain quality of "entertaynment" whose special character it is

the poem's function to define by performance. The performance is a rendering of the substantive which is never supplied but whose stability is never threatened.

The play with tone is already present in the opening vocative, "grave sir," a phrase which is truly deferential to the unnamed guest, evidently of a higher social position than the speaker, but which is tinged with a smiling archness diffusing any awkwardness the social gap might have imposed. Although all three of Martial's invitation poems name their guests (and all of Jonson's complimentary epigrams their dedicatees), Jonson avoids naming his, thus leaving open the possibility that the reader is the grave personage being welcomed into the poem. The smiling qualification of gravity and solemnity of the first line anticipates the teasing of the menu list, which tantalizes with its conditional and hypothetical delicacies. The poem shows us how to be humble without servility, how to promise without promising, how to mingle playfulness with deference, how, possibly, to deflate the reverend gravity of an important acquaintance without offense to good breeding. The cardinal, double-edged statement appears in lines 7–8: "It is the faire acceptance, Sir, creates / The entertaynment perfect." Acceptance in this context refers to the guest's tolerant willingness to enjoy a professedly simple meal, but "acceptance" is also a description of what the host is doing. The real criterion and real subject at issue are the mutual acceptance of guest and host together. The guest is invited to bring his "grace" (l. 5), but the poet is offering his in the performance of the poem.

> How so ere, my man   20
> Shall reade a piece of Virgil, Tacitus,
>   Livie, or of some better booke to us,
> Of which wee'll speake our minds, amidst our meate;
>   And Ile professe no verses to repeate:
> To this, if ought appeare, which I not know of,   25
>   That will the pastrie, not my paper, show of.
> Digestive cheese, and fruit there sure will bee;
>   But that, which most doth take my Muse, and mee,
> Is a pure cup of rich Canary-wine,
>   Which is the Mermaids now, but shall be mine: 30
> Of which had Horace, or Anacreon tasted,
>   Their lives, as doe their lines, till now had lasted.
> Tabacco, Nectar, or the Thespian spring,
>   Are all but Luthers beere, to this I sing.
> Of this we will sup free, but moderately,   35
>   And we will have no Pooly', or Parrot by;
> Nor shall our cups make any guiltie men:
>   But, at our parting, we will be, as when
> We innocently met. No simple word,
>   That shall be utter'd at our mirthfull boord,   40
> Shall make us sad next morning: or affright
>   The libertie, that wee'll enjoy to night.   [*Epigrams* 101]

Martial's suggestion that his guest read his own eternal works aloud is replaced by a trio of approved authors to be heard, with the whimsical addition "or of some better booke," which sustains the tantalizing half-promising; *were* there better books for Jonson? With the mention of the wine, another modulation of tone replaces the half-promise with the hyperbolic promise, a more difficult exercise in good taste that was beyond the reach of Martial—"parva est cenula (quis potest negare?)"—but managed with brio before another modulation at line 35 leads to a soberer prediction beginning to delimit the actual subject of the poem with a series of thematizing words: "free," "moderately," "innocently," "simple," "mirthfull." These adverbs and adjectives yield finally to the substantive "libertie," which will do duty as the culminating thematic term, vitalized, redefined, and expanded by the entire preceding poem. "Libertie," set off by its leading position in the last line and the comma following, substantivizes the verb "enjoy" without emptying it of its own thematic contribution. Martial's poems are really about a series of fictive enjoyments in time; their passage into Jonson's text involves a substantivization of their sequence, since he has been presenting throughout that refinement of pleasure, that mingling of the senses, the intelligence, and the sociable which he finally chooses to call "libertie." He has been taking liberties with his guest, his reader, his subtexts, and the truth ("their lives, as doe their lines . . .") to enrich that concluding noun, which thus becomes a mistranslation of Martial's *libertas* (10.48.22), a mere reference to wit unblemished by conversational malice. Jonson's *libertie*, reaching back retrospectively to gather together his poem, points to its drift toward autoreferentiality and focuses its festive refinement.

The passage from Martial to Jonson constitutes a movement toward a richer, more hospitable *receptivity*. If all four poems are about "entertaynment," Jonson's is distinguished by its fuller evocation of the receptive complex—not only the host as he defines himself in speech, nor the list of dishes, but the agent, place, offering, spirit, "grace" together, the particular set of interfused pleasures into which the guest is asked to make his way. The potential experience awaiting the guest in Martial's little epigrams is a shallower affair; there is less to penetrate. This thickening of a denser receptivity in Jonson is worth noting because I should like to argue that this activity of reception is a focal process in his art and a means of reconciling stability with mobility. In Jonson's canon as a whole, drawing or admitting people into one's establishment is a morally loaded act, as is the contrary gesture of excluding them. The comedies offer a range of manipulative receptions, as in Volpone's beguilement of his visitors or the gulling of clients by Subtle and Face or the manipulation of the marks enticed into the booths of Bartholomew Fair. These offenses against "entertaynment" are counterparts to the doors locked against the world by Morose and the nervous husband, Corvino. In the poems, various types of reception are repeatedly at issue, often as an enrichment of the closing image of stability. The epistle to Sackville (Underwood 13), prompted by that nobleman's generosity to the poet, is about the morality of giving and accepting; the "Epistle answering to one that asked to be Sealed of the

Tribe of Ben" (Underwood 47) admits the unnamed candidate into a select fellowship; the epistle to the countess of Rutland (Forrest 12) is concerned with his gift and her "acceptance" of a poem ("With you, I know, my offring will find grace"); "An Epistle to a Friend" (Underwood 37) is about a gift of a book from the dedicatee; the "Epistle Mendicant to the ... Lord High Treasurer of England" asks for a gift to relieve the old poet's destitution (Underwood 71); the "Epistle to Selden" praises its dedicatee for *his* choice of a dedicatee ("He thou hast given it to, / Thy learned Chamber-fellow, knowes to doe / It true respects"— Underwood 14, 71–73); in a broader, metaphorical sense, the song to Celia asks her to score up wealthy sums on the poet's lips. The ode "To Sir William Sydney," like "To Penshurst" and "To Sir Robert Wroth" (Forrest 14, 2, 3), evokes the festive receptivity of a country house. Jonson's own appreciation of another individual's excellence is sometimes presented as the reception of an impression ("I yeeld, I yeeld, the matter of your praise / Flowes in upon me, and I cannot raise / A banke against it"—Underwood 14.61–63). The morality of grief in the epigram on his son's death centers on the need to repay a loan, and in the epigram on his daughter's death, on the repayment of a gift.[31] In another metaphorical domain, the poor "reception" of the poet's play can be represented as a failure of acceptance.

> Say that thou pour'st'hem wheat,
>   And they would Akornes eat:
> 'Twere simple fury, still thy selfe to wast
>   On such as have no taste:
> To offer them a surfeit of pure bread,
>   Whose appetites are dead.   [6.492]

Is it excessively ingenious to point out that most of the epigrams, as well as many other poems, are written and entitled "To" somebody and so constitute a kind of sweet or poisoned gift? In one way or another, the ethics of receptivity forms a constant preoccupation of Jonson's art.

This preoccupation is not, of course, unrelated to his relationship to his subtexts. The temptation to turn the reception of the unnamed guest in Epigram 101 into a crude allegory of the reception of Martial's invitation poems should be resisted. But it would be a mirror perversity to ignore the duality of the poem's involvement with *conversation*. Just as it acts out proleptically an entertainment in which the speaker is active while remaining fixed at home, it engages Martial in an exchange that "confirms" the speaker's selfhood while extending his range of accents and his mastery of echoes. The speaker, "Ben Jonson," can translate himself by hosting a Roman guest. He demonstrates in fact the monumental weight of his own personality by accepting the alien subgenre, the witty, brittle, worldly voice of the subtext into his own bluff elegance without condescension and without strain. The Latin we subread has been mobilized, shifted, transferred, so that the reader experiences something of that pleasure Aristotle attributed to metaphor, the pleasure of perceiving likeness in difference. Jonson has given himself up to Martial only to show that he gives up nothing. He has converted Martial's "riches" to his own use with a magnanimity that profits the original owner. The theme of reception lends itself to the intertextual interplay because in both dimensions the receiving element is so dense and so capacious.

The capacity for receptivity, acceptance, entertainment, is subtly attributed to Penshurst Place by the structure of the poem that describes it. There the perspective of speaker and reader is that of the guest rather than host, and the poem artfully leads from periphery to center in a progressive penetration. After the first eight introductory lines, a spiraling movement begins around the outer reaches of the estate's park, which corresponds to the most distant imaginative realm from the actual daily life of the house. On the "Mount" (l. 10), the highest ground of the park, satyrs, fauns, and divinities can be introduced who would be out of place in the hall but who are allowed to resort in this outlying land, not simply dropped into it, to be sure, as in the subtext from Martial (9.61), but associated in various ways with specific trees and places intimately enrooted in the property. The spiraling promenade leads on to "the lower land" (l. 22) by the Medway and then almost unobtrusively to the "middle grounds" (l. 24), where the house itself is set. The reader, barely conscious that the promenade is more than random, encounters the ponds (l. 32) (where a milder degree of fanciful fiction is appropriate in 32ff.), which lie still closer to the house, then to the orchard and garden (l. 39), which he presently learns (l. 44) abut the walls of the dwelling itself. The movement is especially skillful from orchard to wall to entrance to the interior hall, where stand the master and mistress to receive.

> The blushing apricot, and woolly peach
>   Hang on thy walls, that every child may reach.
> And though thy walls be of the countrey stone,
>   They'are rear'd with no mans ruine, no mans grone,
> There's none, that dwell about them, wish them downe;
>   But all come in, the farmer, and the clowne:
> And no one empty-handed, to salute
>   Thy lord, and lady, though they have no sute.   [8.94–95.43–50]

The reader is led inside almost unawares at the midpoint of the poem, and once himself received, is initiated in the following forty-eight lines into the house's art of entertainment—extended toward the tenants, toward the bourgeois guest of middle station like the poet, and climactically toward royalty. But the concluding lines (89ff.) lead still further within, to the more intimate virtues of the mistress's chastity, the family's religious piety, and ultimately the last penetralia, the "mysteries of manners, armes, and arts." The mysteries offer a further density to penetrate at the core of the estate, a final substance which the poem names but does not dissect. It is only after having brought us so far within that the poem arrests our penetration with the definitive affirmation of stability in the very last words: "thy lord dwells." Even this stability is active rather than static, but it marks the close of the outsider's progress inward by focusing on the insider's rooted strength. To dwell, in contrast to the parvenu, showy building of others, apparently means precisely this enjoyment of a dense, irradiating human and natural reality that presents no hard repellent surfaces to the visitor but rather a network of relationships and mysteries that require a progressive, sympathetic, moral, and imaginative cognizance.

Receiving in "To Penshurst" as in "Inviting a Friend" possesses that ambiguity we have already observed clinging to the word *acceptance*. In any act of hospitality, the host receives in one sense and the guest in another. In "To Penshurst" the peasants are accepted into the hall but the owners accept gifts from them. The estate "yields" game and fruit but has to receive the seeds that produce its fertility. The poet, who is the active penetrator of the house, is also the passive recipient of its warmth, and will bestow a poem on those who have bestowed friendship (and patronage?) on him. This dialectic of acceptance, with its two-sided version of receiving, provides a useful emblem for Jonson's relationship with the authors of his subtexts, Martial and Juvenal. The acquisitive, aggressive Jonson caricatured by Edmund Wilson, the man who invades the rooms of others and makes their things his own—this authorial presence can be traced in the poems but is softened, acculturized, ennobled by the dramatic speaker's participation in an exchange of intertextual "acceptance." The imagery of plunder employed by Carew addressing Jonson (see chapter 3, note 27) remains a vulgar oversimplification when applied, as Carew intended, to the nondramatic poetry. If this imagery corresponded to something real in Jonson's makeup, it fails to describe the gentler and subtler exchanges of his actual imitative practice. In the stronger poems, the subtext is "entertained," received into a wealthy human complex that invests it with a kernel of signifying potential it might otherwise have appeared to lack. Has anyone ever *given* more to Martial, enhanced his achievement more, than Jonson in his imitations? Martial's villa of Faustinus (3.58) is a swarming, messy establishment, overrun with poultry, pigs, and slaves in a healthy, productive disorder where exchanges of rural goods are also possible.

> nec venit inanis rusticus salutator:
> fert ille ceris cana cum suis mella
> metamque lactis Sassinate de silva;
> somniculosos ille porrigit glires,
> hic vagientem matris hispidae fetum,
> alius coactos non amare capones.
> et dona matrum vimine offerunt texto
> grandes proborum virgines colonorum.
> facto vocatur laetus opere vicinus;
> nec avara servat crastinas dapes mensa,
> vescuntur omnes ebrioque non novit
> satur minister invidere convivae.   [ll. 33–44]

[The country visitor does not come empty handed: that one brings pale honey in its comb, and a pyramid of cheese from Sassina's woodland; that one offers sleepy dormice; this one the bleating offspring of a shaggy mother; another capons debarred from love. And the strapping daughters of honest farmers offer in a wicker basket their mothers' gifts. When work is done a cheerful neighbor is asked to dine; no niggard table reserves a feast for the morrow; all take the meal, and the full-fed attendant need not envy the well-drunken guest.]

Martial communicates the cheery, ruddy exchanges with plain vigor. When it is subread in Jonson's poem, the richer human possibilities of these homely barterings are both a tribute to the Latin and an over-going. Not only is the hospitable density of the estate dignified and extended sociologically, but the *kinds* of exchanges it offers are rendered finer, more "mysterious." The potential suggestiveness of the Latin text has been allowed to penetrate the speaker's receptive sensibility and the thicker texture of his verse until it appears transfused in his dynamic equilibrium. Thus the Latin text follows an itinerary into a profounder dialectic of acceptance, both Penshurst's and Ben Jonson's.

This is poetry which exhibits a notable paucity of metaphors, farfet or otherwise. The apricot on the wall may blush, but that freedom of trope seems to mark the limit beyond which, apparently, poetic tribute would risk the charge of public riot. The polemical heat of the ode to himself may justify the somewhat more sustained metaphors of wheat, acorn, and bread. But Jonson's major poems, the ethical tributes, odes, and satires of middle length, seem only rarely to attain that privileged level of secondary discourse Ricoeur designates as the realm of metaphor. They might be understood to reach this level only if we remember Jonson's pairing of the terms "Metaphore" and "Translation" (see p. 277). He uses this latter term of course in its original Latin sense (*translatio*—trope, specifically metaphor). Yet it may not violate too harshly the spirit of his work if we reverse this pair of terms and conceive of heuristic imitation as presenting a kind of metaphor, a transferal not of imagistic fields but of voices. *Alazon* and puritan, Subtle and Cicero at once, the poet translates codes, eras, *mundi significantes*, reconciles riot and perspicuity, authorizes a mobility he knows he can dominate.

4

The act of receiving, simultaneously dynamic and still, can be seen as a technique of redeeming mobility. I should like to suggest more briefly two other techniques. For the first, the poems already considered can serve as illustrations, but so can almost all the others Jonson ever wrote. This technique is based on his way of turning poems into performances. It would help to read them if each were regarded as a performative speech and enclosed by inverted commas. Sometimes the poet helps us to notice this character by beginning with a kind of prologue that prefaces the performance proper. Thus line 17 of the poem to Shakespeare: "I therefore will begin. Soule of the Age!" This is not an ode about Shakespeare; it is about Ben Jonson addressing him. The voice that is so carefully elaborated, in all its varied wealth of tone and accent, the voice that draws on what everybody knows of the historical Jonson and mythologizes it with witty self-taunts ("Cupids Statue with a Beard"; "My mountaine belly, and my rockie face") and by subtle stylization—this voice confers a dramatic register upon any given poem so that it becomes an exercise of wit and judgment. The epigram "On something, that walkes some-where" (11), which opens

> At court I met it, in clothes brave enough
>   To be a courtier; and lookes grave enough,
> To seeme a statesman . . .   [8.30]

and which closes with awful solemnity, "Good Lord, walke dead still"—this epigram is not about the stuffed shirt at Saint James's, but about his *meeting* in the first line with the imposing observer and performer, who takes him in, measures him, and disposes of him in a kind of theatrical vignette. The epigram would be flat without the performance of a "Ben Jonson" who lives up to the role he has led us to expect him to play. All the poems depend upon a felt weight of personality, the plain, candid, blunt, but discriminating man, quick to size up, contemptuous of the ignorant and fraudulent, not given to fancy or sentimental expansiveness, alert, brusque, a famous character. Each poem modulates a recognizable moral style, what Leavis described as "the Latin judicial poise and conscious civilization . . . curiously inseparable from a weighty and assertive personal assurance."[32]

When the poems of compliment succeed, as they not infrequently do, it is because the performance of a moral tribute by such a speaker is made inherently, consistently interesting and credible. It is necessary at every point for the speaker to keep up the impression of his own fine moral discrimination. If he loses our belief, the performance fails. Here is a failure.

> I Sing the just, and uncontrol'd Descent
>   Of Dame Venetia Digby, styl'd The Faire:
> For Mind, and Body, the most excellent
>   That ever Nature, or the later Ayre
> Gave two such Houses as Northumberland,
>   And Stanley, to the which shee was Co-heire.
> Speake it, you bold Penates, you that stand
>   At either Stemme, and know the veines of good
> Run from your rootes; Tell, testifie the grand
>   Meeting of Graces, that so swell'd the flood
> Of vertues in her, as in short, shee grew
>   The wonder of her Sexe, and of your Blood.   [8.274; Underwood 84.2.1–12]

This offers no evidence of an alert moral sensibility; the flattery is crude, the voice flattens, and our faith drains away. "To Penshurst" makes its way line by line on the confidence it induces of a sophisticated gift for appreciation, separating out the authentic from the ethical second-rate. Both the poems of praise and the poems of insult are lubricated by the poet's faith-inducing performative skill as an honest confidence man. This permits another resolution to the tension between integrity and imposture, the stasis and mobility of the self. The poems of compliment and insult are not quite dramatic monologues composed for a totally fabricated persona. We know this because all the poems, however different and however variously successful, are referable to a recognizable, individual moral style that could not merely be invented. It clearly draws some of its vitality from the continuous sensibility of a specific imagination. The historical self behind the poems is stylized, *mobilized*, theatricalized, mythified by the performative character of the poems.

In this theatricalization, the allusive propensity of the speaking voice lends a certain authority. The actual erudition of Jonson is made to work as a trait of a learned and judicious "Ben Jonson." The poem is a prosopopoeia spoken by a figure saturated not only in the themes and topoi of Latin poetry but in the verse movement, the structures of expression, the modes of feeling, the idioms and moral styles of his Roman forerunners. The transformative contradiction in the *Discoveries*, whereby the writer surrenders his selfhood to assimilate otherness into the self, finds a kind of resolution in the quasi-fictive experience of the poetic speaker. Thus the passage from a text by Martial to a text by Jonson can be read as a passage into a more self-conscious and skillful performance, a process of histrionization.

To the means of reconciliation I have been trying to distinguish, reception and performance, I want to add a third, which might be called exfoliation, and whose illustrative text will be the Pindaric ode "To the Immortall Memorie, and Friendship of that Noble Paire, Sir Lucius Cary, and Sir H. Morison," a poem only lately coming to be recognized as one of Jonson's most triumphant achievements.[33] It has now been so well read that it requires no full-dress interpretation. But certain aspects of its imitative conduct can use some underscoring. They lead us back again to the pull between rhetorical withdrawal and promiscuity, the motionless and the protean. This pull seems particularly acute in the ode, which thematizes the superiority of upright being to fruitless business. Its negative example is a troublemaker, a "Stirrer," who after a promising youth lived to be eighty, vexing time and provoking needlessly the state. What is notable in the account of his career is the intensification of metaphor at its unfortunate turning point.

> Hee entred well, by vertuous parts,
> Got up and thriv'd with honest arts:
> He purchas'd friends, and fame, and honours then,
> And had his noble name advanc'd with men:
> But weary of that flight,
> Hee stoop'd in all mens sight
> To sordid flatteries, acts of strife,
> And sunke in that dead sea of life
> So deep, as he did then death's waters sup;
> But that the Corke of Title boy'd him up.   [8.244; Underwood 70, ll. 33–42]

The Stirrer plummeted ("stoop'd") like a predatory bird only to be figuratively drowned in a sea of futile and self-destructive action, a "dead sea of life." The rhetorical swallowing of violent activity, carried by a verb, in an immobilizing and paralyzing nominal phrase not only corresponds to Jonson's contempt for meaningless motion; it also reflects the particular hostility to all mobility in this poem, including the linguistic mobility of metaphor tarred by negative applications. Earlier Hannibal "did crowne his rage" by rasing Saguntum, and the frightened infant which refused to be born "mad'st thy Mother's wombe thine urne." Since the ode's main thrust is celebratory, the rhetorical problem facing the poet was to find poetic language that saved the friendship to be praised from both dead immobility and fruitless business, from a flat list of virtues and a demeaning abuse of analogy. Here the kind of dynamism provided by imitation may have appeared to Jonson insufficient. There is however a major subtext in the poem, Seneca's ninety-third moral epistle, posing the perennial problem of combining "Newnesse of Sense, Antiquitie of voyce" (Underwood 14, l. 60).

Jonson solves both problems in the ode as elsewhere by a typical, personal trope, a quiet, progressive enrichment of nouns with accumulative extensions and fields of reference, a multiplication of referential direction that is not quite metaphor, not quite pun, not quite etymological throwback (though all these may be suggested) but rather a kind of gradually heightened verbal luminosity of exfoliation. This means for the imitative relationship the emergence of mistranslations that become so densely charged as to overpower the original Latin expression without ever parodying it. Thus the poetic texture acquires a liveliness without becoming uncentered.

We have already met this verbal exfoliation in the culminating allusion of "To Penshurst" to "the mysteries of manners, armes, and arts," where "mysteries" suggests at once the activity of a rite and a number of stable continuities: mystery as a skill or art, an office, a body of private wisdom, a quasi-secret set of virtuous practices, an inherited knowledge of hidden truths that ground the praxis of daily life and public achievement. This quiet expansion of the irradiating noun is more pronounced in the Cary-Morison ode (8.242–47) and more directly linked to Latin roots. The ode's main thematic statement is the insignificance for right judgment and for friendship of a human life's brevity, if that life, like Morison's, has been virtuous and fulfilled. This essentially is the burden of Seneca's epistle to Lucilius, who had supposedly lamented the injustice of a certain Metronax's early death.

> Non ut diu vivamus curandum est, sed ut satis; nam ut diu vivas, fato opus est, ut satis, animo. Longa est vita, si plena est; impletur autem, cum animus sibi bonum suum reddidit et ad se potestatem sui transtulit. Quid illum octoginta anni iuvant per inertiam exacti? Non vixit iste, sed in vita moratus est, nec sero mortuus est, sed diu. Octoginta annis vixit. Interest, mortem eius ex quo die numeres. At ille obiit viridis. Sed officia boni civis, boni amici, boni filii executus est; in nulla parte cessavit. Licet aetas eius imperfecta sit, vita perfecta est. . . . Obsecro te, Lucili, hoc agamus, ut quemadmodum pretiosa rerum sic vita nostra non multum pateat, sed multum pendeat. Actu illam metiamur, non tempore.[34]
>
> [We should strive, not to live long, but to live rightly; for to achieve long life you have need of Fate only, but for right living you need the soul. A life is really long if it is a full

life; but fulness is not attained until the soul has rendered to itself its proper Good, that is, until it has assumed control over itself. What benefit does this older man derive from the eighty years he has spent in idleness? A person like him has not lived; he has merely tarried awhile in life. Nor has he died late in life; he has simply been a long time dying. He has lived eighty years, has he? That depends upon the date from which you reckon his death! Your other friend, however, departed in the bloom of his manhood. But he had fulfilled all the duties of a good citizen, a good friend, a good son; in no respect had he fallen short. His age may have been incomplete, but his life was complete. . . . Pray, let us see to it, my dear Lucilius, that our lives, like jewels of great price, be noteworthy not because of their width but because of their weight. Let us measure them by their performance, not by their duration.]

Jonson's version of this last sentence turns it into a question to which the rest of the poem forms a kind of answer: "For what is life, if measur'd by the space, / Not by the act?" "Measur'd" corresponds to the Latin verb *metiri*, but as the poem develops, the English word in its substantive cognate attracts more and more derivative meanings, multiplies fields of reference and areas of experience, until it becomes a mistranslation so saturated with accrued weight that it exposes the univocality of the subtext.

The word reappears first as a substantive under the shadow of another Senecan (and Ciceronian) word that is also led to exfoliate by its context.

All Offices were done
By him, so ample, full, and round,
In weight, in measure, number, sound,
As though his age imperfect might appeare,
His life was of Humanitie the Spheare.   [ll.48–52]

Officia in the Latin seems to refer to a checklist of dutiful acts required of the citizen, friend, and son; Metronax had discharged them all. Jonson's phrasing suggests a more creative, moral-esthetic whole whose elements hover on the border of metaphor. "Sound" has to be read not only in terms of fame but also in terms of music and poetry, and thus reinvests "measure" and "number" retrospectively with a double reference. The musical field might suggest that Morison's completeness as a person included the fine arts, or rather that his life possessed the ordered perfection of a musical composition. The very concept of "offices" in any case has become a less rigid and perfunctory, more open, "mysterious," lively praxis, the shaping of a life whose completeness is of a more humane and life-affirming temper than the Stoic moral imagination could glimpse. The metaphor of the sphere, almost a signature of Jonson's, was acceptable to the wary rhetorician because it doesn't appear to fragment or alienate; it substantivizes activity ("All Offices were done . . . ") without freezing it.

The word "measures" reappears twice more, to suggest the kind of decorum appropriate for judging a life like Morison's.

Life doth her great actions spell,
By what was done and wrought

In season, and so brought
To light: her measures are, how well
Each syllab'e answer'd, and was form'd, how faire;
These make the lines of life, and that's her ayre.   [ll.59–64]

In small proportions, we just beautie see:
And in short measures, life may perfect bee.   [ll.73–74]

Before its conclusion, the poem will provide economic, arithmetic, poetic, musical, ethical, agricultural, and legal fields through which the single word can acquire more realms of meaning. Other words exfoliate in the same way: "light," "lines," "ayre," "portion," "copy."[35] The effect is rather the reverse of the polysemous wordplay in Wyatt, since here it implies enhancement, not erosion. It is also unlike the wordplay in Donne, since it is not brilliant, ingenious, or cerebral. Jonson allows the borders between the divided meanings of words to blur, so that no punning leap is required of the reader but rather a progressively energetic alertness to the thickening foliation. Thus again mobility of language is contained and redeemed. What begins as moral enlargement ends as rhetorical and even semiotic transformation. The passage from *officia* to offices, from *metuamur* to "measure," begins as the invigoration and amplification of a certain view of life; it ends as the alteration of a univocal signifier into a thickly cadenced mistranslation.

Not a word of this ode, perhaps not a word of Jonson's verse, would be as it is without the nourishing exchange with Latinity. This exchange was definitive; it lies as close to the artistic principles at the core of these texts as any intertextual relation can. But the achievement of Jonson as a humanist artist was to hierarchize, in his most assured work, the voices and codes he mingled. The etiological itinerary from Martial or Seneca to Jonson was not simply a horizontal passage from culture to culture; it was also a vertical progression from a cruder plane of conversation to a more truly refined and polysemous magnanimity. If Jonson's imitations cannot quite be called dialectical, it is not because they fail to criticize obliquely their subtexts. This they do, without perceptible anxiety of influence. But it is difficult, in analyzing their receptivity, to see this as in any way an exposure of vulnerabilities. The reception, performance, exfoliation are too poised to involve a risk; the consciousness of an achieved equilibrium feels no threat from its acknowledged historicity.

5

We noticed in chapter 11 (pp. 236–37) how the action of Jonson's masques conforms to the double gesture of the humanist imagination. The same dyad structures two poems. In the epistle to Selden (Underwood 14), Jonson praises that scholar for having "sought out the Fountaines, Sources, Creekes, paths, wayes, /And noted the beginnings and decayes" of "Antiquities"; he then goes on to praise the "richnesse" and the "workmanship" of Selden's finished book (8.160). And in Jonson's poem for the frontispiece of Raleigh's *History of the World*

(Underwood 24), a frontispiece depicting a temple or loggia with allegorical
figures, tribute is paid to

> . . . the beamie hand
> Of Truth that searcheth the most hidden Springs,
> And guided by Experience, whose straite wand
> Doth mete, whose lyne doth sound the depth of things . . .

a tribute to the archaeological courage of the historian which is succeeded by a
tribute to the edifice constructed by History, who "chearfully supporteth what she
reares" (8.176). Both poems honor the intrepid explorer of history's dark backward
and abysm, incidentally bearing witness to an informed sensitivity to historical
distance. This keener historicism is of course evident in the work of Selden, who
laid stress on contextualism and made advanced use of philological tools. The
growing seventeenth-century awareness of anachronism can also be illustrated by
the methodology of Sir Henry Spelman.[36] Jonson takes his place with these men in
sharing an enlightened historicism. If the preface for Raleigh's book chiefly looks
backward to a Ciceronian–humanist historiography, the epistle to Selden breathes
an air of the more rigorous, protoscientific discipline to come. Both poems reflect a
consciousness of estrangement while praising its challengers.

 Yet elsewhere in his work Jonson seems to move away from this consciousness,
under the pressure of a given purpose or occasion. In the printed text of *The
Masque of Queenes*, he asks if it is proper to "bring Persons, of so different Ages, to
appeare, properly, together? Or, Why (which is more unnaturall) with Virgil's
Mezentius, I joyne the living with the dead? I answere to both these, at once,
Nothing is more proper; Nothing more naturall: For these all live; and together, in
theyr Fame; And so I present them" (7.313). If the first of Jonson's two prefatory
poems honoring Clement Edmondes's *Observations on Caesar* praises the author
for restoring Caesar to life, the second underscores the Roman's contemporaneity.

> Who Edmonds, reades thy booke, and doth not see
> What th'antique souldiers were, the moderne bee?
> Wherein thou shew'st, how much the latter are
> Beholding, to this master of the warre;
> And that, in action, there is nothing new,
> More, then to varie what our elders knew.   [8.72]

These gestures of contemporaneization are notable because they correspond to a
countermovement mitigating the sense of estrangement, a movement operating
almost imperceptibly in Jonson's culture and indeed in his own mind. Leavis's
remark about his historical posture is pertinent. "Jonson's effort was to feel
Catullus, and the others he cultivated, as contemporary with himself; or rather, to
achieve an English mode that should express a sense of contemporaneity with
them. . . . In [this mode] the English poet, who remains not the less English and of
his own time, enters into an ideal community."[37] This interplay between the
timeless community and the poet's "own time," between the community of the
masque and the remoteness of "the most hidden Springs," must be read as another

form of the tension between fixity and mobility in Jonson's mind. From a later perspective it is clear that of the two pulls, it was the tendency toward contemporaneization that would gradually acquire more momentum in the generations to follow. Indeed this momentum gathered strength all the more easily because Jonson had written.

In the long run the achievements of *imitatio* would ensure its decay in the form analyzed by this study. After the age of Jonson, ancient culture acquired in England that straddling status it already possessed on the Continent: it was foreign but at the same time it *belonged*. It had undergone its process of reception, and now it was progressively a native possession. It lent itself to the play of parody and travesty without imposing the threat—or allowing the thrill—of sacrilege. It merged with postclassical continental literature as a kind of penumbra or extension of the domestic tradition. After the Restoration, as Bate has shown, it was the Elizabethan–Jacobean past that represented the heaviest burden upon the English imagination. The shock of anachronism became dulled, in part because it had already been dramatized, manipulated, and tamed. In the composition of *Paradise Lost*, Milton would need deliberately to push away his subtexts, lengthen their distance artificially, to achieve something like that shock. One can watch him doing it, among other places, in his prologues. Marx's dictum that "violence is the midwife of history" can doubtless be applied to literary history, but after the Restoration this violence was no longer of that kind harnessed to produce imitative discovery.

Thus after the turn of the seventeenth century on the Continent, a generation later in England, a history of imitation would require different assumptions, perhaps different terms, than those employed in this book. The movement was past when, in Croll's terms, men wanted to Hellenize or Romanize themselves. If one were to address like Petrarch missives to the age of light, if one were to honor Plato with banquets like the Florentine Academy's, these would have lost their reverential seriousness. Partly through the activity of imitation in all its forms and usages, the classics were domesticated, *apprivoisés*. The superb formal imitations of Pope, Swift, and Doctor Johnson adjust the idiom of familiars who have lost their numinous ghostliness. Imitation becomes an updating, a progress report on the perennial. Our easy contemporary way of acculturating the remote, appropriating the shards of all eras, costs us that shock of confrontation which might assist us to situate ourselves more knowingly in time, might help us uncover the vulnerabilities of our own specific historicity. "Reading is indispensable," wrote Seneca, "primarily to keep me from being satisfied with myself alone."[38] It may be that in history as in the Dublin of Leopold Bloom, the longest way round is the shortest way home. The light in Troy is no longer ravenous, dying, desperately paideic; it is steady, comfortable, and artificial. Perhaps it could become an urgent heuristic force once again only if we stopped appropriating, allowed our fragments to withdraw into their proper strangeness, if the natural glow of alien embers were scanned as before in their tragic, spectral dimness.

Notes

Chapter 1. Introduction

1 Franco Simone "La coscienza della rinascita negli umanisti francesi," *Rivista di lettera-*
ture moderne 2 (1947): 236.

Chapter 2. Historical Solitude

1 Quotations from the *Divina Commedia* are taken from the edition by Natalino
Sapegno (Florence: La Nuova Italia, 1957). English translations are from John D.
Sinclair, *Dante's Purgatorio* and *Dante's Paradiso* (New York: Oxford University Press,
1961).
2 Adam's phrasing of the shift of the name for the godhead from "I" to "El" faintly recalls
a passage in the *Purgatorio* evoking another shift equally the result of the vagaries of
fashion. This is the discourse by Oderisi da Gubbio on the mutability of artistic fame, a
discourse which, despite its apparent moral superiority, does not lack a certain inex-
pungible pathos. "In painting Cimabue thought to hold the field and now Giotto has
the cry" (*Purg.* 11.94–95). This discourse is framed by images of natural decay which
anticipate Adam's blossom that falls and is replaced:

Oh vana gloria dell'umane posse!
  com' poco verde in su la cima dura!   [11.91–92]
[O empty glory of human powers, how briefly lasts the green on its top!]

La vostra nominanza è color d'erba,
  che viene e va, e quei la discolora
  per cui ella esce della terra acerba.   [11.115–17]
[Your renown is the color of grass which comes and goes, and that withers it by
which it springs green from the ground.]

The term "nominanza" anchors the concept of fame in the act of speech; the parallel
terms and metaphors also insist on this basis in the voicing of the spoken word:

Non è il mondan romore altro ch'un fiato
  di vento, ch'or vien quinci e or vien quindi,
  e muta nome perché muta lato.
Che voce avrai tu più . . . ?   [11.100–03]
[The world's noise is but a breath of wind which comes now this way and now
that and changes name because it changes quarter. What more fame shalt thou
have . . . ?]

Line 102 points directly ahead to the discourse of Adam. At a certain level of abstraction
both discourses would seem to be about the same thing, about the pathos of the

wandering word, the fragile and decentered homelessness of the "voce," the "nome," the "lingua."

3 See Richard Foster Jones, *The Triumph of the English Language* (Stanford, Cal.: Stanford University Press, 1953), pp. 263ff.

4 Samuel Daniel, "A Defence of Ryme," in *Elizabethan Critical Essays*, ed. G. Gregory Smith (Oxford: Oxford University Press, 1959), 2:384.

5 "Il [notre langage] escoule tous les jours de nos mains." Michel de Montaigne, *Essais*, ed. A. Thibaudet (Paris: Pléiade, 1940), p. 953.

6 See Claude-Gilbert Dubois, *Mythe et langage au XVIe siècle* (Bordeaux: Ducroz, 1970), pp. 67–81.

7 Dante Alighieri, *De vulgari eloquentia*, ed. B. Panvini (Palermo: Ando' Editori, n.d.), 1.9, p. 72. English version from *The Literary Criticism of Dante Alighieri*, ed. and trans. Robert S. Haller (Lincoln: University of Nebraska Press, 1975), p. 14.

8 Dante had already used the term *opus* in this architectural sense earlier within this treatise, following common ancient usage.

9 It is clear that Dante distinguished period styles both at the microcultural level (his distance from Bonagiunta da Lucca, for example) and at the macrocultural (his distance from antiquity). Bonagiunta's most famous phrase ("dolce stil *novo*") bears witness to a change in period style, as does his acceptance of the formulation defining the new school's novelty:

> Io veggio ben come le vostre penne
>   di retro al dittator sen vanno strette
>   che delle nostre certo non avvenne.   [*Purg.* 24.58–60]
>
> [I see well how your pens follow close behind the dictator, which assuredly did not happen with ours, and he that sets himself to examine further sees nothing else between the one style and the other.]

It is impossible moreover to exclude this awareness of stylistic succession from Oderisi's speech thirteen cantos earlier. When Oderisi says "So has the one Guido taken from the other the glory of our tongue" (*Purg.* 11.97–98), he means by this *taking* that supersession of a poetic idiom by another which is more than just the eclipsing of a personality. Dante was by no means the only man of his age sensitive to microcultural shifts like this one, but to my knowledge he was the only man to extend his awareness into so imposing a grasp of broad historical process. He saw the coming and going of generational change, the succession of Guidos ("erba, che viene e va"—*Purg.* 11.115–16) as a minor case of major millennial change ("come fronda in ramo, che sen va e altra vene"—see above).

10 Morris Bishop, ed. and trans., *Letters from Petrarch* (Bloomington: Indiana University Press, 1966), p. 68. In his "Letter to Posterity," Petrarch wrote: "I devoted myself, though not exclusively, to the study of ancient times, since I always disliked our own period; so that, if it hadn't been for the love of those dear to me, I should have preferred being born in any other age, forgetting this one; and I always tried to transport myself mentally to other times."

11 Leonardo Bruni, comparing the moderns to the ancients, wrote: "We people of today are clearly dwarfs ["homunculi"], and even if we were not dwarfs in spirit, our lives have not the stuff needed for lasting glory." Quoted by Hans Baron, *The Crisis of the Early Italian Renaissance*, rev. ed. (Princeton: Princeton University Press, 1966), p. 282. For Alberti, see the prologue to his *Della pittura*. Elsewhere he evokes some great temple

visited by an ancient architect who admired its magnificent walls, columns, and ceilings, but found only fragments of marble underfoot and went on to make a beautiful pavement from these fragments. Then Alberti compares antiquity to this temple and pictures modern writers as stealing fragments from it to piece together their own pitiful structures, as though nothing truly new could be said: in Terence's phrase, "Nihil dictum quin prius dictum" (nothing said which has not already been said). *Opere volgari,* ed. Cecil Grayson, 2:160–62.

12 Quoted by Emilio Bigi, *La cultura del Poliziano* (Pisa: Nistri-Lischi, 1967), p. 81. (My translation)

13 Angelo Poliziano, *Miscellaneorum centuria seconda,* ed. V. Branca and M. P. Stocchi (Florence: Alinari, 1972), 1:53.

14 "Siquidem multis iam saeculis non modo nemo latino locutus est, sed ne latina quidem legens intellexit." E. Garin, ed., *Prosatori latini del Quattrocento* (Milan and Naples: Ricciardi, n.d.), p. 598.

15 Angelo Fabroni, *Laurentii Medicis Magnifici vita* (Pisa: Gratiolius, 1784), 2:279. (My translation)

16 Quoted by Martin Heidegger in *On the Way to Language,* trans. Peter D. Hertz (New York: Harper and Row, 1959), p. 129. Another version can be found in W. von Humboldt, *Linguistic Variability and Intellectual Development,* trans. G. C. Buck and F. A. Raven (Coral Gables: University of Miami Press, 1971), p. 65.

17 Jacques Derrida, *Marges de la philosophie* (Paris: Minuit, 1972), p. 376.

18 Derrida, *Marges,* p. 378.

19 Horace, *Satires, Epistles, and Ars poetica,* trans. H. R. Fairclough (Cambridge, Mass.: Harvard University Press, 1966).

20 Dante alludes to this Horatian passage in the *Convivio* 2.13.10.

21 My colleague Edward Stankiewicz informs me that to be precise it would be more accurate to speak of a common root than a derivation.

22 Emile Benveniste, "Subjectivity in Language," in *Problems in General Linguistics,* trans. M. E. Meek (Coral Gables: University of Miami Press, 1971), pp. 223–30.

23 Humboldt, *Linguistic Variability,* p. 28.

24 "Le synchronisme pur se trouve être maintenant une illusion: chaque système synchronique contient son passé et son avenir qui sont des éléments structuraux inséparables du système." J. Tynjanov and R. Jakobson, "Les Problèmes des études littéraires et linguistiques," in *Théorie de la littérature,* ed. T. Todorov (Paris: Seuil, 1965), p. 139.

25 An analogy can be found in Vico's analysis of Roman law. The challenge to all jurisprudence, for Vico, was the reconciliation of authority and liberty. Authority was maintained in Sparta by Lycurgus's insistence that laws not be written down, but with the passing of eight centuries and the attendant changes in the language, the laws proved rigid and anachronistic, lacking the flexibility to ensure personal liberty. In Athens, on the other hand, laws were rewritten every year; liberty was ensured but authority was lost. In Rome, both dangers were avoided. The law of the Twelve Tablets guaranteed liberty but the patrician class retained the power of interpretation, and since the language kept changing, this power guaranteed the maintenance of authority. In time, further to protect the rights and liberties of the people, the office of praetor was established, and its holder was charged with the responsibility of conserving intact the force of the Twelve Tablets as times and language altered. The praetor accomplished this, according to Vico, by having recourse to fictions (*fictiones*). As a shield against the rigidity of law in a changing society, the praetor pretended that certain things had

occurred which in fact had not occurred, and vice versa, This accommodation of the legal text to retrospective constructions helped to ensure the endurance of the Roman state for so many centuries because it permitted the text to adjust to social and verbal variability. See Jules Chaix-Ruy, *Vico* (Paris: Seghers, 1967), pp. 50–52: also Vico's *De uno universi iuris principio et fine uno*, chaps. 166, 182, 184.

26 Derrida, *Marges*, p. 389.

27 Ibid., p. 381.

28 Both Freud and Erik Erikson considered the capacity for retrospective reshaping to be a mark of maturity. To be an adult Erikson requires precisely the ability to create a strong personal etiology. "To be an adult means among other things to see one's life in continuous perspective, both in retrospect and in prospect. By accepting some definition as to who he is, . . . the adult is able to selectively reconstruct his past in such a way that step for step, it seems to have planned him, or better, he seems to have planned *it*. In this sense, we *do* choose our parents." *Young Man Luther* (New York: Norton, 1958), pp. 111–12. Freud, in his study of Leonardo, draws an extended analogy between the developing organization of the past in individuals and in societies. The mature individual, like the developed society, "elicits" memories and interprets them to create a constructed story. Even though the memories are heavily edited, they do have value. "In spite of all the distortions and misunderstandings, they still represent the reality of the past." Sigmund Freud, *Leonardo da Vinci and a Memory of his Childhood*, trans. A. Tyson (New York: Norton, 1964), p. 34.

29 Claude Lévi-Strauss, *La Pensée sauvage* (Paris: Plon, 1962), pp. 309–10).

30 Jonathan Culler, *Structuralist Poetics* (Ithaca, N.Y.: Cornell University Press 1975), p. 130.

31 Benjamin Lee Whorf, *Language, Thought, and Reality* (Cambridge, Mass.: M.I.T. Press, 1956), p. 252.

32 "C'est tout un découpage du monde que le langage impose, à travers ces figures de rhétorique. Cela relève-t-il du style? de la langue? Ni de l'un ni de l'autre; il s'agit en vérité d'une institution véritable, d'une *forme* du monde, aussi importante que la représentation historique de l'espace chez les peintres." Roland Barthes, *Sur Racine* (Paris: Seuil, 1963), p. 155.

　　　Fredric Jameson suggests a Hegelian-Marxist version of a *mundus significans*: "One might imagine a dialectical *Rhetoric*, in which the various mental operations are understood not absolutely, but as moments and figures, tropes, syntactical paradigms, of our relationship to the real itself, as, altering irrevocably in time, it nonetheless obeys a logic that like the logic of language can never be fully distinguished from its object." *Marxism and Form* (Princeton: Princeton University Press, 1971), p. 374.

33 An outline of my own view of reading and interpretation can be found in "Anti-hermeneutics: The Case of Shakespeare's Sonnet 129," in *Poetic Traditions of the English Renaissance*, ed. Maynard Mack and George deForest Lord (New Haven and London: Yale University Press, 1982).

34 On the special character of the copula in metaphors, see Paul Ricoeur, *La métaphore vive* (Paris: Seuil, 1975), pp. 311ff.

35 Phillip Damon, *Modes of Analogy in Ancient and Medieval Verse* (Berkeley: University of California Press, 1961), pp. 265–66.

36 Is the sexual implication of this adjective extraneous here? In the passage from the *Ars poetica* quoted above, the principal parts of Horace's first verb are *coeo, coire, coii,*

coitus. On the broader relationship between language and sexuality, see George Steiner, *After Babel,* pp. 38–45.

37 See however the suggested revisions in rhetorical taxonomy by Gérard Genette, *Figures I* (Paris: Seuil, 1966), pp. 251–52.

Since the traditional taxonomy still stands, in spite of suggestions like Genette's, and since no alternative rhetorical vocabulary exists, I shall continue to refer to "metaphors" and other conventional tropes in this study while attempting whenever feasible to underscore the specificity of each individual instance.

38 *The Philosophy of Rhetoric* (London: Oxford University Press, 1971). p. 125.

39 It may be true, as Joseph Mazzeo has stressed, that we no longer regularly allegorize past texts to defend received dogma against their alterity. "We are no longer required to translate everything that time or distance has rendered strange to us into our own preferred mythology." *Varieties of Interpretation* (Notre Dame, Ind.: University of Notre Dame Press, 1978), p. 69. It is true that allegoresis is no longer so popular a defense, although it lingers still in the school of D. W. Robertson. The preferred modern defense is irony. We no longer allegorize to salvage most texts that threaten us; we ironize them. Swift could not possibly have admired the Houyhnhnms, nor More his Utopia, nor Rabelais his abbey. The modern intelligence is easily disposed to find out the lapses, which is to say the divergences of a past moral ideal from its own, and when it succeeds, it has at hand the interpretive ironization that will nullify the lapse—at the risk of anachronism. We shall soon have an ironized reading of that unbearable windbag and bluestocking, Beatrice. Mazzeo's confidence in the detachment of the sophisticated modern interpreter is reassuring but unjustified.

Chapter 3. Imitation and Anachronism

1 Speaking of vernacular poets, Dante writes:

Differunt tamen a magnis poetis, hoc est regularibus, quia magni sermone et arte regulari poetati sunt, hii vero casu, ut dictum est. Idcirco accidit ut, quantum illos proximius imitemur, tantum rectius poetemur. Unde nos doctrine operi intendentes, doctrinatas eorum poetrias emulari oportet (*De vulgari eloquentia,* 2.4.2). [These poets, however, differ from the great poets, those who follow the rules, in that the great ones have written poems in a language and with an art which follows rules, while these, as I said, do so intuitively. For this reason it happens that the more closely we imitate those great poets, the more correctly we write poetry. And therefore, where we intend to write works in a learned manner, we should follow their learned poetic (*The Literary Criticism of Dante Alighieri,* ed. and trans. Robert S. Haller [Lincoln: University of Nebraska Press, 1975], p. 38).

2 Charles Trinkaus, *The Poet as Philosopher: Petrarch and the Formation of Renaissance Consciousness* (New Haven and London: Yale University Press, 1979), p. 91.

3 Cassirer's discussion of the use of period terms remains pertinent. He points out that "Middle Ages" and "Renaissance" are not strictly speaking the names of historical periods but of ideal types, and that there can be no clear division between periods. "Nevertheless the distinction itself has a real meaning. What we can express by it . . . is that from the beginning of the fifteenth century onward the *balance* between the particular forces—society, state, religion, church, art, science—begins to shift slowly. . . .

And the character of every culture rests on the equilibrium between the forces that give it form. Whenever therefore we make any comparison between the Middle Ages and the Renaissance, it is never enough to single out particular ideas or concepts. What we want to know is not the particular idea as such, but the importance it possesses, and the strength with which it is acting in the whole structure," Ernst Cassirer, "Some Remarks on the Question of the Originality of the Renaissance," *Journal of the History of Ideas* 4 (1943): 55.

4   *Petrarch's Letters to Classical Authors*, ed. and trans. Mario Emilio Cosenza (Chicago: University of Chicago Press, 1910), pp. 102–03. I have altered slightly Cosenza's version. The original Latin can be found in *Fam.* 24.8.

5   *Epistola metrica* 2.1. My translation.

6   The passages from Virgil and Propertius appear at *Georgics* 3.10ff. and *Elegies* 3.1.1ff., respectively. Compare the somewhat different itinerary in Lucretius, *De rerum natura*, 4.1ff. "Avia Pieridum peragro loca nullius ante trita solo . . ." (I am blazing a trail through pathless tracts of the Muses' Pierian realm, where no foot has ever trod before . . .—trans. R. Latham). See also Horace, *Satires* 1.19.21ff. The passage in the *Africa* appears at 9.456–57: "Poterunt discussis forte tenebris / Ad purum priscumque iubar remeare nepotes" (Perhaps some day our descendants, the shadows dispelled, will be able to turn back in triumph to the pure radiance of the past).

7   Franco Simone, *La coscienza della rinascita negli umanisti francesi* (Rome: Storia e Letteratura, 1949), p. 160. My translation. Compare Etienne Gilson: "Pour nous, le moyen age s'oppose à l'Antiquité dont la Renaissance fut la redécouverte; pour eux, leur propre temps continuait l'Antiquité sans que, historiquement parlant, rien ne les en séparat. Nulle part la continuité des deux ages ne leur semblait plus évidente que sur le terrain de la culture intellectuelle." *La Philosophie au XIIe siècle* (Paris: Payot, 1944), p. 325.

8   For the source of this example and for the shift from medieval to Renaissance perceptions of anachronism, see Peter Burke, *The Renaissance Sense of the Past* (London: Arnold, 1969), chap. 1.

9   "E sentenzia de' buoni filosofi la corruzione d'una cosa essere creazione d'un'altra . . . e questo di necessità avviene, perché, essendo la forma e spezie . . . immortale, di necessità si conviene sempre si muova dalla materia, e di questo perpetuo moto necessariamente nasce una continua generazione di cose nuove . . . E, secondo Aristotile, la privazione è principio delle cose create." Lorenzo de' Medici, *Opere*, ed. A. Simioni (Bari: Laterza, 1913), 1:24.

10 "The identity of past and present is at one with the essential identity of all objects. This is Milton's 'universe of death' and with it poetry cannot live, for poetry must leap, it must locate itself in a discontinuous universe, and it must make that universe (as Blake did) if it cannot find one. Discontinuity is freedom." *The Anxiety of Influence* (New York: Oxford University Press, 1973), p. 39.

11 *Scienza nuova*, #211, 699, 819. See also *De nostri temporis studiorum ratione*, chaps. 3, 8; *De antiquissima Italorum sapientia*, 7.3.

12 "De faict, l'on luy enseigna un grand docteur sophiste nommé Maistre Thubal Holoferne, qui lui aprint sa charte si bien qu'il la disoit par cueur au rebours; et y fut cinq ans et troys mois. . . . Puis luy leugt *De modis significandis*. . . . Et le sceut si bien que, au coupeland, il le rendoit par cueur à revers." *Gargantua*, chap. 14.

13 Erasmus, *Declamatio de pueris statim ac liberaliter instituendis*, ed. and trans. J.-C. Margolin (Geneva: Droz, 1966), p. 58.

14 Ibid., pp. 59–60.

15 Nancy S. Struever, *The Language of History in the Renaissance* (Princeton: Princeton University Press, 1970), p. 193.

16 Ibid., pp. 150–51.

17 For the relation of these developments to the growth of humanist rhetoric, see Struever, passim. See also Hanna Gray, "Renaissance Humanism: The Pursuit of Eloquence," *Journal of the History of Ideas* 24 (1963); 497–514.

18 Bernard Weinberg, ed., *Critical Prefaces of the French Renaissance* (Evanston, Ill.: Northwestern University Press, 1950), p. 164.

19 Pierre de Ronsard, *Oeuvres complètes*, ed. P. Laumonier (Paris: Didier, 1914), 1:43–50. Ronsard speaks of his pleasure in seeing "par mon moien les vieus liriques si heureusement resuscités" (p. 45), and again of his friend Du Bellay's "ardant desir de reveiller la poësie Françoise" (p. 46). In the last paragraph, he writes: "Et ferai encores revenir . . . l'usage de la lire [lyre] aujourdui resuscitée en Italie" (p. 48).

20 *Ruines of Time*, ll. 169–72.

21 *De dignitate et augmentis scientiarum*, 2.4. Francis Bacon, *Essays, Advancement of Learning, . . . and Other Pieces*, ed. R. F. Jones (New York: Odyssey Press, 1937), p. 388. This image does not appear in the English version of the *Advancement*. The Latin text can be found in the Spedding, Ellis, and Heath edition of Bacon's *Works*, 14 vols (London: Longmans, 1857–74), 1:504.

22 Lines 117–19. See also Underwood 24, "The mind of the Frontispiece to a Booke," on Raleigh's *History of the World*, and Underwood 14, "An Epistle to Master John Selden," where Selden's friend Hayward is praised because "he can approve / And estimate thy Paines; as having wrought / In the same Mines of knowledge" (ll. 74–76).

23 Alexander Neville, in the dedication to his translation of Seneca's *Oedipus* (1563), quoted by Jones, *Triumph of the English Language*, p. 17.

24 See Jones, *Triumph of the English Language*, chaps. 1–4 passim.

25 Desiderius Erasmus, *Ciceronianus*, trans. Izora Scott (New York: Teachers College, Columbia University, 1908), pp. 61–62.

26 Weinberg, *Critical Prefaces*, p. 277.

27 For Donne and Jonson, see below, pp. 44–45. Carew praises Donne for having freed English poetry from imitation:

> The Muses garden with Pedantique weedes
> O'rspred, was purg'd by thee; The lazie seeds
> Of servile imitation throwne away;
> And fresh invention planted, Thou didst pay
> The debts of our penurious bankrupt age;
> Licentious thefts, that make poëtique rage
> A Mimique fury, when our soules must bee
> Possest, or with Anacreons Extasie,
> Or Pindars, not their owne.
>
> ["Elegie upon the death of Donne," ll. 25–33]

but encourages Jonson to continue:

> . . . if thou overcome
> A knottie writer, bring the bootie home;
> Nor thinke it theft, if the rich spoyles so torne
> From conquered Authors, be as Trophies worne.

["To Ben Jonson," ll. 39–42]

28 Erikson, *Young Man Luther*, p. 254.
29 Reinhold Niebuhr, *The Nature and Destiny of Man*, one vol. ed. (New York: Scribner's, 1951), 2:304–05.
30 Friedrich Nietzsche, *The Use and Abuse of History*, trans. A. Collins (Indianapolis: Bobbs-Merrill, 1957), p. 21.
31 Italian text in E. Garin, ed., *L'educazione umanistica in Italia* (Bari: Laterza, 1949), p. 119.
32 Pierre de Nolhac, *Petrarque et l'Humanisme* (Paris: Champion, 1907), 1:145–48.
33 On the epistles' anachronistic style, Petrarch writes:

> From beginning to end in both, the style is so crude and so different from that of the ancients that they seem to have been dictated recently by some ignorant writer, who, wanting childishly to ape their language in every word, falls continuously into solecisms and blunders which would reveal even to the eyes of a blind man the absolute inauthenticity of these monstrous writings. The language reveals itself to be so different from that which it tries to be, namely, the style of our Roman fathers and Caesars, that a credulous old woman or a peasant born and bred in the mountains might possibly be taken in by these letters, but certainly anyone who had two ounces of brains could never be duped by them. (my translation)

This denunciation of anachronistic style seems to me not to have received the attention its historical importance deserves.
34 Gérard Genette, *Figures III* (Paris: Seuil, 1972), p. 17.
35 Horace, *Odes* 3.13. Ronsard's "A la fontaine Bellerie" appeared in the 1550 edition of his odes, 2.9.
36 These phrases appear in Valla's preface to his *Elegantiae*, reprinted in Garin, *Prosatori latini*, p. 596.
37 Geoffrey Hartman, "The Interpreter: A Self-Analysis," in his *The Fate of Reading* (Chicago: University of Chicago Press, 1975), pp. 16–17.
38 Paul de Man, "Literary History and Literary Modernity," in his *Blindness and Insight* (New York: Oxford University Press, 1971), pp. 162, 149.
39 There is a kind of homology between the contrast of sacramental and heuristic imitation and Freud's contrast of neurotic repetition and therapeutic remembering. According to Freud, the patient is at first condemned to repeat repressed experience even after the analyst has reconstructed it for him; in fact, through the process of transference, this repetition may even be intensified.

> The patient cannot remember the whole of what is repressed in him, and what he cannot remember may be precisely the essential part of it. Thus he acquires no sense of conviction of the correctness of the construction that has been communicated to him. He is obliged to *repeat* the repressed material as a contemporary

experience instead of, as the physician would prefer to see, *remembering* it as something belonging to the past. (Freud's italics)

The analyst's goal is to transform this repetition into a recollection that leaves a space between past and present. He must lead the patient

> to re-experience some portion of his forgotten life, but must see to it . . . that the patient retains some degree of aloofness, which will enable him, in spite of everything, to recognize that what appears to be reality is in fact only a reflection of a forgotten past.

Beyond the Pleasure Principle, in vol. 18 of the Standard Edition, ed. James Strachey (London: Hogarth Press, 1955), pp. 18–19. See also Freud's essay "Recollecting, Repeating and Working Through," 12:147–56. Creative imitation opens up a comparable experience of removal from its own point of departure, although this latter is not dismissed as irrelevant once recognized. But like the movement from Freud's repetition to healthy retrospection, the movement from reproductive to heuristic imitation confers a gain of freedom. This is why Bloom's account of neurotic influence seems to me inapplicable to the great humanist texts. Repetition and reproduction are narrowly, obsessively exclusive; recollection and successful imitation are tolerantly inclusive.

40 Erwin Panofsky, *Studies in Iconology: Humanistic Themes in the Art of the Renaissance* (New York: Harper & Row, 1962), pp. 70–71.

41 Walter Benjamin, *Illuminations*, trans. H. Zohn, ed. H. Arendt (New York: Schocken Books, 1969), p. 188.

42 *Seniles* 2.3 to Francesco Bruni. Translation in Bishop, *Letters from Petrarch*, pp. 228–29.

43 "Mai nessuno debbe imitare la maniera de l'altro, perche sarà detto nipote e non figliolo della Natura, inquanto l'arte." Leonardo da Vinci, *On Painting*, ed. C. Pedretti (Berkeley: University of California Press, 1964), p. 32.

44 Berni's attack appears in his *Dialogo contra i poeti* (1527). As its title suggests, a dialogue by Niccolo Franco, *Il Petrarchista* (1539), is directed chiefly against the imitation of Petrarch.

45 Montaigne, *Essais*, 1.26, p. 162.

46 *Love's Labor's Lost*, 4.2.

47 *Ben Jonson*, ed. C. H. Herford, Percy and Evelyn Simpson (Oxford: Oxford University Press, 1947), 8:590, 597.

48 John Donne, "Satyre II," ll. 25–28.

49 The dark and demonic elements in Renaissance "archaeology" are discussed by Erikson: "The devil and his home, and feces and the recesses of their origin, are all associated in a common underground of magic danger. To this common underground, then, we may assign both the bowels of the earth, where dirt can become precious metal (by means of a magic process which the alchemists tried to repeat experimentally . . .) and also that hidden self, that hidden 'soul ground' (*Seelengrund*) where a mystical transformation of base passions can be effected." *Young Man Luther*, p. 62.

50 Quoted by Walter Jackson Bate, *The Burden of the Past and the English Poet* (Cambridge, Mass.: Harvard University Press, 1970), p. 85.

51 Prefatory Epistle to "The Progresse of the Soule."

52 *Essais*, 2.32, p. 700.

53 Margaret W. Ferguson, "The Exile's Defense: Du Bellay's *La Defence et illustration de la langue françoyse*," *PMLA* 93 (1978): 283.

54 *Longinus on the Sublime*, trans. W. Rhys Roberts (Cambridge: Cambridge University Press, 1907), p. 81.

55 "Adeo non foret causa posterioribus scribendi quodammodo, si nihil esset in quo superioribus adversaremur." Quoted by Linda Gardiner Janik, "Lorenzo Valla: The Primacy of Rhetoric and the De-moralization of History," *History and Theory* 12 (1973): 402.

56 J. G. A. Pocock, *Politics, Language, and Time* (New York: Atheneum, 1971), pp. 255-56, 254.

57 Hayden White would argue that the refusal of pure repetition and pure continuity is inherent in the writing of history. "The historian serves no one well by constructing a specious continuity between the present world and that which preceded it. On the contrary, we require a history that will educate us to discontinuity more than ever before; for discontinuity, disruption, and chaos is our lot. If, as Nietzsche said, 'we have art in order not to die of the truth,' we also have truth in order to escape the seduction of a world which is nothing but the creation of our longings." "The Burden of History," *History and Theory* 5 (1966): 134.

58 Marvin Becker is perhaps the historian who has analyzed most sensitively the rise of historical awareness in terms of declining ceremonial roles. "At a time when ceremonial identity, ritual ties, and sacramental bonds were cast in doubt, early humanism and Florentine burgher culture were colonizing the . . . mind with a novel mode of historical consciousness." "An essay on the quest for identity in the early Italian Renaissance," in *Florilegium Historiale: Essays Presented to Wallace K. Ferguson*, ed. J. G. Rowe and W. H. Stockdale (Toronto: University of Toronto Press, 1971), p. 303.

59 Edward W. Saïd, *Beginnings: Intention and Method* (New York: Basic Books, 1975), p. 350.

60 Ibid., p. 353.

61   The whole image of human authority and its history to which Florentines were supposed to look was being drastically reconstructed, deprived of its continuity and . . . increasingly secularized. . . . Affiliation with the empire . . . was affiliation with the timeless. . . . The republic was not timeless, because it did not reflect by simple correspondence the eternal order of nature. . . . To assert the particularity of the republic . . . was to assert that it existed in time, not eternity, and was therefore transitory and doomed to impermanence, for this was the condition of particular being. . . .

      To affirm the republic, then, was to break up the timeless continuity of the hierarchic universe into particular moments: those periods of history at which republics had existed and which were worthy of attention. . . . The particularity and historicity of the republic involved then the particularization of history and its secularization (J. G. A. Pocock, *The Machiavellian Moment* [Princeton: Princeton University Press, 1975], pp. 53-54).

62 Ibid., pp. 61-62.

63 For the anthologies edited by Gabriel Giolito, see the *Avertissement* by Henri Chamard to his edition of Du Bellay's *Oeuvres poètiques* (Paris: Cornély, 1908), 1:xiii.

64 Rosalie L. Colie, *The Resources of Kind: Genre-Theory in the Renaissance* (Berkeley: University of California Press, 1973).

65 For the pedagogical distinctions, see James Hutton, *The Greek Anthology in France* (Ithaca, N.Y.: Cornell University Press, 1946), pp. 29ff.

66 Dryden's distinctions are contained in his "Preface to the Translation of Ovid's Epistles," in *Essays of John Dryden*, ed. W. P. Ker (Oxford: Clarendon, 1900), 1:237-43.

67 A German scholar, Arno Reiff, has argued that ancient Roman theorists made the threefold distinction indicated by the title of his doctoral dissertation: "Interpretatio, imitatio, aemulatio: Begriff und Vorstellung literarischer Abhängigkeit bei den Römern" (diss., Cologne, 1959). However, G. W. Pigman III, in an important and richly documented essay, maintains that *aemulatio* was not a technical literary term before Erasmus, while admitting that the general concept of emulation was current in antiquity as well as during the Renaissance. A short discussion of this concept will be found in chapter 4 below. Pigman points to the triad *sequi, imitari, aemulari* in Erasmus's *Ciceronianus*, where however the triad does not yet attain the doctrinal status it achieves in the *De imitatione* of Bartolomeo Ricci (1541). See Pigman's "Versions of Imitation in the Renaissance," *Renaissance Quarterly* 33 (1980): 1-32.

68 "Alle Poesie eigentlich in Anachronismen verkehre." Goethe goes on: "The *Iliad* as well as the *Odyssey*, all the writers of tragedy, and all that has remained of true poetry, lives and breathes only in anachronisms." He refers not only to commerce between texts; he is thinking primarily of the writer's tendency to sublimate a past, literary or historical, which will always be more brutal, less close to the refined, evolved present than we want it to be. The writer deliberately modernizes the past in order to render its traits vivid or bearable. "Theilnahme Goethes an Manzoni," in Johann Wolfgang von Goethe, *Schriften zur Literatur*, ed. Johanna Salomon (Berlin: Akademia Verlag, 1971), p. 202.

Chapter 4. Themes of Ancient Theory

1 On imitation in ancient theory, I have found the following studies to be particularly useful: G. M. A. Grube, *The Greek and Latin Critics* (London: Methuen, 1965); George Kennedy, *The Art of Rhetoric in the Modern World* (Princeton: Princeton University Press, 1972); Gordon Williams, *Change and Decline: Roman Literature in the Early Empire* (Berkeley: University of California Press, 1978); Arno Reiff, "Interpretatio, imitatio, aemulatio: Begriff und Vorstellung literarischer Abhängigkeit bei den Römern" (diss., Cologne, 1959); W. K. Wimsatt, Jr., and Cleanth Brooks, *Literary Criticism: A Short History* (New York: Vintage Books, 1957); Folco Martinazzoli, *Sapphica et Vergiliana: Su alcuni temi letterari della tradizione poetica classica* (Bari: Adriatica, 1958); Richard McKeon, "Literary Criticism and the Concept of Imitation in Antiquity," *Modern Philology* 34 (1936-37): 1-35; Donald Lemen Clark, *Rhetoric in Greco-Roman Education* (New York: Columbia University Press, 1957); George Pigman, "Versions of Imitation in the Renaissance" (see chap. 3, n. 67); A. Guillemain, "L'imitation dans la littérature latine," *Revue des Etudes Latines* 2 (1924): 35ff. Less useful is H. Koller, *Die Mimesis in der Antike: Nachahmung, Darstellung, Ausdrücke* (Bern: Francke, 1954). I have been unable to procure the collection of essays edited by David West and Tony Woodman, *Creative Imitation and Latin Poetry* (Cambridge: Cambridge University Press, 1979). See also notes 22, 30, 31, and 35.

2 *Poetics* 1448b. English translation by Ingram Bywater in *The Basic Works of Aristotle,* ed. R. McKeon (New York: Random House, 1941), p. 1457.

3 Quintilian, *Institutio oratoria,* 4 vols., trans. H. E. Butler (Cambridge, Mass.: Harvard University Press, 1979), 4:74-75. All quotations from Quintilian will be taken from this edition.

4 *Isocrates,* trans. G. Norlin (London: Heinemann, 1928), 2:175, 301-03.

5 It would appear that Theophrastus advocated the imitation of models as a means of achieving *hellenismos,* stylistic purity, one of the goals of all good writing.

6 Philodemos, *Über die Gedichte,* ed. and trans. Christian Jensen (Berlin: Weidmannsche Buchhandlung, 1923), pp. 67-69.

7 Ibid., p. 75.

8 Dionysius of Halicarnassus, *The Critical Essays,* trans. S. Usher (Cambridge, Mass.: Harvard University Press, 1974), 1:7.

9 Ibid., 1. 13.

10 This appears in the long quotation from the treatise *On Imitation* contained in the letter to Pompeius. See Dionysius of Halicarnassus, *The Three Literary Letters,* trans. W. Rhys Roberts (Cambridge: Cambridge University Press, 1901), p. 105ff.

11 Dionysius of Halicarnassus, *Critical Essays,* 1:9.

12 Kennedy, *Art of Rhetoric,* p. 348.

13 Aristotle praised emulation in the *Rhetoric* as "a good feeling felt by good persons," as distinguished from envy, "a bad feeling felt by bad persons." "Emulation makes us take steps to secure the good things in question, envy makes us take steps to stop our neighbor from having them." *Rhetoric* 1388a, 29ff. *Basic Works,* p. 1402, trans. W. Rhys Roberts. The Stoics would attach a negative valuation to the term which appears to have influenced Cicero and Horace. For a brief history of the term in antiquity, see Giorgio Pasquali, *Orazio lirico* (Florence: Le Monnier, 1920), pp. 119ff.

14 Quoted by Grube, *Greek and Latin Critics,* pp. 211-12. Greek text in *Dionysii Halicarnasei quae extant,* ed. H. Usener and L. Radermacher (Stuttgart: Teubner, 1965), 1.307.7.

15 Grube, *Greek and Latin Critics,* p. 153.

16 *Rhetorica ad Herennium,* trans. H. Caplan (Cambridge, Mass.: Harvard University Press, 1954), pp. 8-9.

17 A note by the Loeb translator, Harry Caplan (p. 242, n. c), indicates that precedents existed for both practices.

18 *Rhetorica ad Herennium,* pp. 250-51. The quotation above from 4.6.9 appears on pp. 248-49.

19 Cicero, *De inventione. De optimo genere oratorum. Topica,* trans. H. M. Hubbell (Cambridge, Mass.: Harvard University Press, 1949), pp. 168-71.

20 Cicero, *De oratore,* trans. E. W. Sutton and H. Rackham (Cambridge, Mass.: Harvard University Press, 1942), 1:264-65.

21 Ibid., 1:266-69.

22 The discussion that follows is indebted to the article by Elaine Fantham, "Imitation and Evolution: The Discussion of Rhetorical Imitation in Cicero *De oratore* II, 87-97 and some Related Problems of Ciceronian Theory," *Classical Philology* 73 (1978): 1-16. See also her companion article, "Imitation and Decline: Rhetorical Theory and Practice in the First Century after Christ," same volume, 102-16.

23 Fantham, "Imitation and Evolution," p. 8.

24 Cicero cites an imaginary critic asserting that his versions are inferior to the Greek. He replies by asking whether the Greeks could do better in Latin. (Unum hoc: "Verum melius Graeci." A quo quaeratur exquid possint ipsi melius Latine.) *De optimo genere oratorum* (18), pp. 368–69.

25 Cicero, *Orator*, trans. H. M. Hubbell (Cambridge, Mass.: Harvard University Press, 1939), pp. 312–13.

26 Friedrich Nietzsche, *The Use and Abuse of History*, trans. A. Collins (Indianapolis: Bobbs-Merrill, 1957), pp. 51, 72.

27 Nietzsche, *Twilight of the Idols*, trans. R. J. Hollingdale (Baltimore: Penquin Books, 1968), p. 106.

28 Horace, *Satires, Epistles, and Ars Poetica*, trans. H. R. Fairclough (Cambridge, Mass.: Harvard University Press, 1966). All quotations from these works will be taken from this edition.

29 This is Fraenkel's interpretation. Eduard Fraenkel, *Horace* (Oxford: Clarendon, 1966), p. 341, n. 1.

30 By contrast Horace refers to the "muddy (*lutulentus*) stream" of Lucilius in Satire 1.4.11 and again at 1.10.50. On the metaphor of the stream in Horace, see C. O. Brink, *Horace on Poetry: Prolegomena to the Literary Epistles* (Cambridge: Cambridge University Press, 1963), p. 159, n. 3.

31 Horace, *The Odes and Epodes*, trans. C. E. Bennett (Cambridge, Mass.: Harvard University Press, 1964). The standard history of the apian analogy is Jürgen von Stackelberg, "Das Bienengleichnis," *Romanische Forschungen* 68 (1956): 271–93.

32 I have made a few alterations in Fairclough's version. Line 28 contains a well-known crux which is not easy to resolve. I take the *Musam* to be Archilochus's, not Sappho's.

33 For Lucretius, see above, chap. 3, n. 6. However the passage from *De rerum natura*, 4.1ff quoted there should be compared to 3.1ff., where the poet's itinerary is guided by Epicurus.

> Te sequor, O Graiae gentis decus, inque tuis nunc
> ficta pedum pono pressis vestigia signis. [3–4]
> [You are my guide, o glory of the Grecian race. In your well-marked footprints now
> I plant my resolute steps.]
>
> [Latham translation]

The apian image, which Lucretius appears to have originated, appears a few lines below.

> . . . tuisque ex, inclute, chartis,
> floriferis ut apes in saltibus omnia libant,
> omnia nos itidem depascimur aurea dicta. [10–12]
> [From your pages, as bees in flowery glades sip every blossom, so do I crop all your
> golden sayings.]

Lucretius discusses the difficulty of expressing Greek ideas in Latin at 1.136–45. Propertius presents his imitation of Callimachus and Philetas as a pioneering expedition at *Elegies* 3. 1.1–4. Other references to his use of these poets appear at 2. 34.31–32 and 4. 6.3–4.

34 An apparent allusion to Callimachus (Epigram 28) in lines 131–32 is mingled here with legalistic language distinguishing public property from private. The same imagistic field underlies terms like *vacuum* and *aliena* in the epistle to Maecenas. However this *metaphoric* legality in the *Ars poetica* is succeeded by the literal body of laws or rules governing genre—"operis lex," where legality appears not as a benign object of manipulation but a potential agent of claustration. For the legal language, see Brink, *Horace on Poetry: Prolegomena*, pp. 181–82, p. 109, n. 2.

35 Brink, following Augusto Rostagni, glosses "pudor" as "timidity, lack of confidence," and comments on "operis lex": "An unnecessary and unwholesome limitation is imposed by the work that the imitator has undertaken." On "in artum": "The imitator imprisons himself and cannot escape." *Horace on Poetry: The "Ars Poetica"* (Cambridge: Cambridge University Press, 1971), pp. 211–12.

36 "The main thing assumed in the criticism of Horace is the normative value of the literary 'species,' the genre, kind, or type, and of the companion principle designated by the term 'propriety'—*to prepon* in Aristotelian criticism, *decorum* in Latin." Wimsatt and Brooks, *Literary Criticism*, p. 80.

37 D. A. Russell and M. Winterbottom, eds., *Ancient Literary Criticism: The Principal Texts in New Translations* (Oxford: Clarendon, 1972), pp. 359–60.

38 The Latin and English texts of this quotation and those following from Seneca are taken from *Ad Lucilium epistulae morales*, trans. R. M. Gummere, 3 vols. (Cambridge, Mass.: Harvard University Press, 1970).

39 "Erit haec . . . laus eorum, ut priores superasse, posteros docuisse dicantur" (10.2.28). Quintilian, *Institutio oratoria*, 4: 90–91.

40 "Curae et diligentiae vel ideo in hoc plus est, quod ei fuit magis laborandum" (10.1.86).

41 *Aemulatio* (with its cognate forms) in Rome seems to have become nearly synonymous with *imitatio* by the time of Pliny the Younger (early second century). Pliny himself at least tends to use the term in contexts where the sense of rivalry seems weak. Pigman ("Versions of Imitation," p. 23, n. 32) cites many usages by Pliny in support of his argument that *aemulatio* never became a "fixed critical term" during antiquity. Pliny of course also speaks of *imitatio*, as in 7.9.2, where he writes that imitation of the best models leads to an aptitude for original composition. Longinus pairs *mimesis* and *zelos*, but there can be no doubt that a spirit of healthy contention is essential to his reflection on intertextuality.

42 *Longinus on the Sublime*, trans. W. Rhys Roberts (Cambridge: Cambridge University Press, 1907), p. 81.

43 Ibid.

Chapter 5. Petrarch and the Humanist Hermeneutic

1 *De doctrina christiana*, 4.12. Latin text edited by William M. Green (Vienna: Hoelder—Pichler—Pinsky, 1963), p. 120. English text from *Works*, ed. Dods (Edinburgh: Clark, 1873), 9.123.

2 Latin text from Macrobe, *Les Saturnales*, vol. 1 (1–3), ed. and trans. H. Bornecque; vol. 2 (4–7), ed. and trans. F. Richard (Paris: Garnier, 1937), 1.24.18; 6.1.6. English text from Macrobius, *The Saturnalia*, trans. P. V. Davies (New York: Columbia University Press, 1969), pp. 157, 386.

3 Richard, 6.1.2. Davies, p. 385.

4 *Ben Jonson*, ed. C. H. Herford and Percy and Evelyn Simpson (Oxford: Clarendon, 1947), 8:616–17.

5 Richard, 5.15.16. Davies, p. 352.

6 See Jacques Flamant, *Macrobe et le néo-platonisme latin, à la fin du IVe siècle* (Leyden: Brill, 1977), pp. 297–304; Pierre Courcelle, *Les lettres grecques en occident de Macrobe à Cassiodore* (Paris: Boccard, 1943), pp. 9–16.

7 *The Rhetoric of Alcuin and Charlemagne*, ed. and trans. W. S. Howell (New York: Russell and Russell, 1965), pp. 132–33.

8 "Solebant querere quem quisque imitetur, quem quisque auctor omittat." Bernard of Utrecht, Commentary on the Eclogue of Theodulus, ed. R. B. C. Huygens in *Accessus ad Auctores* (Leyden: Brill, 1970), pp. 64–65. I owe this reference to Professor Michel-André Bossy.

9 Peter of Blois from his *Epistolae* in J.-P. Migne, ed., *Patrologia Latina*, 207, 289–90. My translation. The use of the verb *aemulari* by Macrobius (p. 82) adds strength to the argument that *aemulatio* and *imitatio* were virtually synonymous in antiquity (see chap. 4, n. 41); its use by Pierre suggests that this quasi-synonymy continued into the High Middle Ages.

10 The history of this familiar topos is chronicled by Robert K. Merton in his whimsical survey, *On the Shoulders of Giants: A Shandean Postscript* (New York: Free Press, 1965).

11 The student of medieval historiography must learn to do without perspective in historical presentation. A medieval writer could distinguish stages in the history of salvation, but they were religious stages. He did not discern change or development in temporal history. He saw continuity in customs and institutions, where we see diversity. Roman emperors are made to talk and behave like medieval rulers. Alternatively, a writer learned in the Latin classics tended to make medieval rulers talk and behave like the Caesars. The historian did not only look back to the Old and New Testaments for parallels and precedents; he lived in an expanding Bible. . . . Past and present interlock; ancient precedents imposed themselves on the present; the past resembled the present as the historian saw it. He had no sense of anachronism (Beryl Smalley, *Historians in the Middle Ages* [London: Thames and Hudson, 1974], p. 63).

12 Latin text from Migne, *Patrologia Latina*, 199, 855. English text from John of Salisbury, *The Metalogicon*, trans. D. D. McGarry (Berkeley: University of California Press, 1962), pp. 68–69.

13 Chrétien, *Cligès*, ed. A. Micha (Paris: Champion, 1968), ll. 39–42. English translation from Chrétien, *Arthurian Romances*, trans. W. W. Comfort (London: Dent, 1970).

14 Gerald L. Bruns, "The Originality of Texts in a Manuscript Culture," *Comparative Literature* 32 (1980): 126.

15 Bruns, "Originality of Texts," p. 125. On medieval intertextuality, see also Douglas Kelly, "*Translatio studii* in Medieval French Literature," *Philological Quarterly* 57 (1958): 287–310. Still useful is the older study by G. Paré, A. Brunet, and P. Tremblay, *La renaissance du XIIe siècle* (Paris: Vrin, 1933).

16 In England the poetry of Chaucer seems in a few passages to reveal a dawning awareness of historical mutability, even an awareness that changes in language and in culture go hand in hand. Just as Dante's expression "l'uso de' mortali" expands its reference

from linguistics to social history, so Chaucer expands a discussion of word change into a
meditation on "usages."

> Ye knowe eek that in forme of speeche is chaunge
> Within a thousand yeer, and wordes tho
> That hadden pris now wonder nice and straunge
> Us thenketh hem, and yit they spake hem so,
> And spedde as wel in love as men now do;
> Eek for to winnen love in sondry ages
> In sondry landes sondry been usages.
> . . . .
> For every wight which that to Rome went
> Halt not oo path or alway oo manere;
> Eek in som land were al the game shent
> If that they ferde in love as men doon here,
> As thus: in open doing, or in cheere,
> In visiting, in forme, or saide hir sawes
> Forthy men sayn, "Each contree hath his lawes."
>
> [*Troilus and Criseide*, 2.22–28, 36–42]

Chaucer moves from "wordes" to "usages" to "manere" and finally the synecdochic
"lawes." Yet this express acknowledgment of mutability is accompanied by a kind of
passive resignation not to know the original forms and usages now obscured by
oblivion. The proverbial character of the last line quoted suggests a folk wisdom,
content with that which is presently ascertainable. Even if Horace and Dante can be
subread beneath the surface of Chaucer's deceptively plain manner, the contentment
with partial knowledge, the refusal truly to pursue the path to Rome, are dominant. A
few lines after the passage quoted Chaucer refers to the legendary Greek priest "Amphi-
orax," one of the seven against Thebes, as a "bishop." (2.105) Perhaps he was aware of
the anachronism. But the historical consciousness he does display would be distorted by
the term *humanist*. The distinction is felt if one compares a letter of 1439 written by
Duke Humphrey of Gloucester to Pier Candido Decembrio: "You have renewed for this
age the eloquence and power of speech, ancient and worthy of the ancients, which had
all but perished." Chaucer, perhaps fortunately, was not interested in this kind of
renewal.

17 For the changes in late medieval humanism leading up to Petrarch, the standard studies
are Roberto Weiss, *The Dawn of Humanism* (New York: Haskell House, 1970) and *Il
primo secolo dell' umanesimo* (Rome: Storia e Letteratura, 1949), and Giuseppe Billa-
novich, "Petrarch and the Textual Tradition of Livy," *Journal of the Warburg and
Courtauld Institutes* 14 (1951): 137–208.

18 "In place of the harmonious circularity of the myth of the eternal return, Dante asserts
the discovery of the linear, open-ended translation of history." Giuseppe Mazzotta,
Dante, Poet of the Desert (Princeton: Princeton University Press, 1979), p. 102. Mazzotta's entire book is an extended meditation on Dante's conception of history. For Dante's
classicism, see Charles T. Davis, *Dante and the Idea of Rome* (Oxford: Clarendon, 1957),
and Augustin Renaudet, *Dante Humaniste* (Paris: Les Belles Lettres, 1952).

19 All quotations from Petrarch's correspondence, unless otherwise identified, are taken from *Le familiare*, ed. Vittorio Rossi and Umberto Bosco, 4 vols. (Florence: Sansoni, 1933–42). Letters will be identified by volume and number according to Petrarch's original division. Translations of the correspondence, unless otherwise identified, are taken from *Letters from Petrarch*, trans. Morris Bishop (Bloomington and London: Indiana Universtiy Press, 1966).

20 Mario Emilio Cosenza, ed. and trans., *Petrarch's Letters to Classical Authors* (Chicago: University of Chicago Press, 1910), pp. 138–39 (slightly altered).

21 Among the many discussions of Petrarch's perception of history, a few of particular interest can be cited: Theodor Mommsen, "Petrarch's Concept of the Dark Ages," *Speculum* 17 (1942): 226ff.; Erwin Panofsky, *Renaissance and Renascences in Western Art* (Stockholm: Almqvist and Wiksell, 1960), pp. 8ff.; Beryl Smalley, *English Friars and Antiquity in the Early Fourteenth Century* (New York: Barnes and Noble, 1960), pp. 292–98; Peter Burke, *The Renaissance Sense of the Past* (London: Arnold, 1969), pp. 21ff.; Roberto Weiss, *The Spread of Italian Humanism* (London: Hutchinson, 1964), pp. 23–28.

22 Burke, *Renaissance Sense of the Past*, p. 2.

23 Translations of the *Aeneid* are those of W. F. Jackson Knight, *Virgil: The Aeneid* (Baltimore: Penguin Books, 1956).

24 "Inter humanarum inventionum tot ruinas, letterae sacrae stant. . . . Reliquarum nobilissimae pereunt, et iam magna ex parte periere." (Among so many ruins of things made by man, the sacred writings survive. . . . The noblest of the remaining works are perishing, and the greater part has already perished.) *Francisci Petrarchae Opera* (Basel: Sebastian Henricpetri, 1581), 1:43.

25 See for example the tribute by Francesco Florido: "Immo et plurimum laudis inter eos meruit Petrarcha qui primus apud Italos (nisi fallor) latinam linguam diu sepultam ex ruderibus et vetustate in lucem afferre adortus est." (Petrarch deserves the greatest praise among [the early humanists] since unless I'm mistaken he was the first Italian who tried to restore to light the Latin language from the ruins of time after its long burial.) *Apologia in linguae latinae calumniatores* (Basel, 1540), fol. 106. Quoted by Franco Simone, *La coscienza della rinascita negli umanisti francesi* (Rome: Storia e Letteratura, 1949), p. 65.

26 Cited by B. L. Ullman, *Studies in the Italian Renaissance* (Rome: Storia e Letteratura, 1955), p. 13.

27 On Dante: "Per costui la morta poesia meritamente si può dire suscitata." (He can truly be said to have resuscitated dead poetry.) *Vita di Dante*, ed. Carlo Muscetta (Rome: Edizioni dell'Ateneo, 1963), p. 7. On Giotto: ". . . avendo egli quella arte ritornata in luce che molti secoli . . . era stata sepulta." (. . . he having restored to light that art which had been buried for so many centuries.) *Decameron*, fifth story of the sixth day. On Petrarch: "Poeticum diffundit nomen a se in lucem et latebra revocatum." (He alone propagated the dignity of poetry, recalled from shadow into light.) Letter to Jacopo Pizzinghe, *Lettere edite e inedite*, ed. F. Corazzini (Florence: Sansoni, 1877), p. 196.

28 *Liber de origine civitatis Florentiae et eiusdem famosis civibus*, quoted in J. von Schlosser, *Quellenbuch zur Kunstgeschichte des Abendländischen Mittelalters* (Vienna: Graeser, 1896), p. 370.

29 In the *De vita solitaria*, Petrarch writes of demonstrating gratitude to the ancients by "nomina illorum vel ignota vulgare, vel obsolefacta renovare, *vel senio obruta eruere*."

(... either by making their obscure names well known, or by renewing what has been corrupted, or by digging up what has been buried by time.) *Francisci Petrarchae Opera* 1:240. Imagery of revival recurs frequently in the *Hortatio* to Cola di Rienzo. One example: "Italia, quae cum capite aegrotante languebat, sese iam nunc erexit in cubitum." (Italy, which until recently lay inert, her head bowed to the ground, now has risen to her elbow.) *Opera,* 1:538. In *Familiares* 2.9, Rome is seen as a "desertam effigiem" (abandoned effigy). Compare the metrical epistle to Clement VI (2.5), where Rome is represented as a widow weeping: "Quot sunt mihi templa, quot arces / Vulnera sunt totidem: crebris confusa ruinis / Moenia relliquias immensae et flebilis urbis / Ostentant, lachrymasque movent spectantibus." (My wounds are as numerous as my churches and fortified palaces; my walls, thickly strewn with ruins, reveal but the remnants of a stately and lamentable city, and move all spectators to tears.) *Opera,* 3:92.

30 See Valla's *Scritti filosofici e religiosi,* ed. and trans. G. Radetti (Florence: Sansoni, 1953), p. 445, n. 1.

31 Sir Kenneth Clark, *The Nude* (New York: Pantheon Books, 1956), pp. 96–97.

32 Anthony Blunt, *Art and Architecture in France 1500 to 1700* (Baltimore: Penguin Books, 1957), p. 46.

33 On the subject of "poetice narrationis archana," the Augustinus of the *Secretum* wonders whether in fact Virgil thought of them as he wrote or whether he was not totally remote from any such thought: "sive enim id Virgilius ipse sensit, dum scriberet, sive ab omni tali consideratione remotissimus." Francesco Petrarca, *Prose,* ed. G. Martellotti et al. (Milan and Naples: Ricciardi, 1955), p. 124.

34 The secondary literature on Renaissance theories of imitation is very large. Studies that treat primarily a single author will be cited on pages dealing with that author. Of the general studies on this subject, I have found the following most useful: F. Ulivi, *L'imitazione nella poetica del Rinascimento* (Milan: Marzorati, 1959); H. Gmelin, "Das Prinzip der Imitatio in den romanischen Literaturen," in *Romanische Forschungen* 46 (1932): 83–360; Bernard Weinberg, *A History of Literary Criticism in the Italian Renaissance,* 2 vols. (Chicago: University of Chicago Press, 1961); Terence Cave, *The Cornucopian Text: Problems of Writing in the French Renaissance* (Oxford: Clarendon 1979); G. W. Pigman III, "Versions of Imitation in the Renaissance," *Renaissance Quarterly* 33 (1980): 1–32, and "Imitation and the Renaissance Sense of the Past: The Reception of Erasmus' *Ciceronianus,*" *Journal of Medieval and Renaissance Studies* 9 (1979): 155–77; Izora Scott, *Controversies over the Imitation of Cicero* (New York: Teachers College, Columbia University, 1910); Nancy Struever, *The Language of History in the Renaissance* (Princeton: Princeton University Press, 1970); Cesare Vasoli, "L'estetica dell' Umanesimo e del Rinascimento," in *Momenti e problemi di storia dell' estetica* (Milan: Marzorati, 1959), 1:325–423; Ezio Raimondi, *Rinascimento inquieto* (Palermo: Manfredi, 1965); Robert J. Clements, *Critical Theory and Practice of the Pléiade* (Cambridge, Mass.: Harvard University Press, 1942); Eugenio Battisti, "Il concetto d'imitazione nel cinquecento da Raffaelo a Michelangelo," *Commentari* 7 (1956): 86–104; Paolo Portoghesi, *Rome of the Renaissance,* trans. P. Sanders (London: Phaidon Press, 1972); G. Castor, *Pléiade Poetics* (Cambridge: Cambridge University Press, 1964); Harold White, *Plagiarism and Imitation during the English Renaissance* (Cambridge, Mass.: Harvard University Press, 1935); Haskell M. Block, "The Concept of Imitation in Modern Criticism," *Proceedings of the Fourth Congress of the International Comparative Literature Association,* ed. François Jost (The Hague: Mouton,

1966), pp. 704–20; A. J. Smith, "Theory and Practice in Renaissance Theory: Two Kinds of Imitation," *Bulletin of the John Rylands Library* 47 (1964): 212–43; Jerome Mazzaro, *Transformations in the Renaissance English Lyric* (Ithaca, N.Y.: Cornell University Press, 1970), pp. 73–107.

35 "Quel che scrive non si riveste solo di cultura, ma nasce di cultura: la letteratura . . . è il tramite attraverso il quale l'esperienza gli si tramuta in sentimento." Umberto Bosco, *Petrarca* (Turin: U.T.E.T., 1946), p. 149.

36 The same implication seems to emerge briefly in a passage of the *De vita solitaria* (1.3), exhorting each man to consider what nature has made him and what he has made of himself: "qualem eum natura, qualem ipse se fecerit." *Prose*, p. 330.

Compare Struever: "Under the rubric of imitation the Humanist forms a notion of identity; nor is this a theoretical discussion only: if freedom is the foundation of his achievement, his rhetorical-critical activity fills this concept of freedom with concrete activity, and exercises his convictions in quotidian employment." *The Language of History*, p. 150.

37 Maurice Merleau-Ponty, *Signes* (Paris: Gallimard, 1960), p. 93.

38 W. H. Draper, trans., *Petrarch's Secret* (London: Chatto and Windus, 1911), p. 96. The Latin original appears in Francesco Petrarca, *Opere*, ed. Emilio Bigi (Milan: Mursia, 1968), p. 602.

39 Quoted by Bosco, *Petrarca*, p. 85.

40 "Ad quos enim nostri copia et convictus nunquam forte venturus est, sermo perveniet. Iam vero quantum posteris collaturi simus, optime metiemur, si quantum nobis contulerint maiorum nostrorum inventa meminerimus." Bigi ed., p. 706. (Such study permits us to be useful to those living in distant regions with whom we will never be permitted to socialize but to whom our words may perhaps come. And indeed how much good we will do to our posterity can very well be judged when we consider how much our greater predecessors have left to us—English version from Aldo S. Bernardo, trans., *Rerum familiarum libri I–VIII* [Albany: State University of New York Press, 1975], p. 49).

41 "Si vero forsan studii mei labor expectationis tue sitim ulla ex parte sedaverit, nullum a te aliud premii genus efflagito, nisi ut diligar, licet incognitus, licet sepulcro conditus, licet versus in cineres, sicut ego multos, quorum me vigiliis adiutum senseram, non modo defunctos sed diu ante consumptos post annum millesimum dilexi." (If then my research and labor satisfy your thirst to some degree, then I ask no other reward from you than to be cherished, even if I am unknown, even if buried in the grave, even if turned to ashes, just as I have cherished those whose studies succored me after a thousand years, although they were not only dead but long ago consumed.) (Preface to the *De Viris illustribus*). Author's translation. Latin text in *Prose*, ed. G. Martellotti et al., p. 226. See also *Fam.* 6.4 and the passage from the *De vita solitaria* in *Prose*, pp. 356–58.

42 Quotations of Petrarch's vernacular poems are taken from the Bigi edition. The English translations are from Robert M. Durling, trans., *Petrarch's Lyric Poems* (Cambridge, Mass.: Harvard University Press, 1976).

Chapter 6. Petrarch: The Ontology of the Self

1 See the discussion in Hans Baron, *From Petrarch to Leonardo Bruni* (Chicago: University of Chicago Press, 1968), pp. 19ff. The most helpful discussions of this famous letter I

am familiar with are those by Arnaud Tripet, *Petrarque, ou la connaissance de soi* (Geneva: Droz, 1967), pp. 65–73, and Robert M. Durling, "The Ascent of Mont Ventoux and the Crisis of Allegory," *Italian Quarterly* 18 (1974): 7–28.

2 Francesco Petrarca, "The Ascent of Mont Ventoux," in *The Renaissance Philosophy of Man*, ed. Ernst Cassirer, Paul Oskar Kristeller, and John Randall, Jr. (Chicago: University of Chicago Press, 1971), pp. 36–37. The translator of the Petrarch selections in this anthology is Hans Nachod. The Latin text of the letter can be found in Francesco Petrarca, *Opere*, ed. Emilio Bigi (Milan: Mursia, 1968), pp. 730–42. The Latin original of the passage quoted appears on p. 730. References following each quotation will indicate first the page of the English translation and second the corresponding page of the Bigi edition.

3 Umberto Bosco, *Francesco Petrarca*, 2d ed. (Bari: Laterza, 1961), pp. 113–14.

4 ". . . iandudum in campis cogitationum mearum de utriusque hominis imperio laboriosissima et anceps etiam nunc pugna conseritur." (A stubborn and still undecided battle has been long raging on the field of my thoughts for the supremacy of one of the two men within me.) (43; 738)

5 *Georgics* 2.490–92.

6 Natalino Sapego speaks of "l'illusione tenace, ma sempre vana, di poter alfine evadere dalla sua solitudine e raggiungere una concezione unitaria e comprensiva di tutta la realtà." *Il Trecento* (Milan: Garzanti, 1965), p. 280.

7 ". . . immobile, nella sua perplessità." Bosco, *Petrarca*, p. 10. The formula is still applicable to the experience of the speaker of the *Canzoniere*, despite the fact that more recent scholarship has succeeded in distinguishing relatively distinct phases of the spiritual and artistic development of Petrarch the man. See the opening essay of Baron, *Petrarch to Bruni*.

8 "Augustine's attitude toward secular history is essentially no different from that of the Romans . . . : history remains a storehouse of examples. . . . Secular history repeats itself, and the only story in which unique and unrepeatable events take place begins with Adam and ends with the birth and death of Christ. Thereafter secular powers rise and fall as in the past and will rise and fall until the world's end, but no fundamentally new truth will ever again be revealed by such mundane events." Hannah Arendt, *Between Past and Future* (New York: Viking Press, 1961), p. 66.

9 "Et levis inpulsos retro dabat aura capillos" (And her hair streamed behind her in the light breeze), *Metamorphoses*, 1.529. Giuseppe Mazzotta discusses this and other Ovidian subtexts he finds at work in the sonnet, along with echoes of Dante and Guinizelli, in his fine essay "The *Canzoniere* and the Language of the Self," *Studies in Philology* 75 (1978): 271–96. Mazzotta analyzes well the failure of the self to express itself into coherence; I would disagree, however, with his contention that this effort is not central.

10 The subjectivity of the lover's perceptions is already present in the Sicilian origins of the Italian love lyric. Giacomo da Lentini writes: "Avendo gran disio, / dipinsi una pintura, / bella, voi simigliante, / e quando voi non vio, / guardo 'n quella figura, / e par ch'eo v'aggia avante." (Filled with great desire / I painted a picture / O Beautiful, it was your likeness; / and when I do not see you / I look upon that image, / and then it seems I have you before me.—trans. Frederick Goldin, *German and Italian Lyrics of the Middle Ages* [Garden City, N.Y.: Doubleday, 1973], p. 211.) In Cavalcanti's doctrinal canzone "Donna me prega," the process of subjectivization receives a more technical formulation in terms deriving from Averroistic psychology. Love is born when the

sensory perception of the woman is abstracted and becomes a form located in the possible intellect as in a subject where ideal forms are located. "Vèn da veduta forma che s'intende, / che prende—nel possibile intelletto, / come in subietto,—loco e dimoranza." (It comes forth from a form perceived and understood, / which takes its dwelling / in the possible intellect, as in its subject—ibid., p. 325). Once the lover is enamored of this form, he becomes incapable of perceiving it ("forma non si vede") and must content himself with its image in his memory. But this distinction between woman, form, and image is by no means constant in Cavalcanti's poetry, and the less rigorous formulation by Dante in the canzone "Amor, che movi tua vertù dal cielo" approximates more closely the assumptions that underlie most of his school's poetry. "Quanto è ne l'esser suo bella, e gentile / ne glie atti ed amorosa, / tanto lo imaginar, che non si posa, / l'adorna ne la mente ov'io la porto." (As she is beautiful in her essence, and noble and loving in her actions, just so my ceaseless imaginative faculty adorns her in my memory where I bear her with me.) This presumes a distinction between the actual woman's reality and her image within the lover's mind, but it asserts a correspondence between her actual and her remembered or envisioned beauty.

11 Robert M. Durling, "Petrarch's 'Giovene donna sotto un verde lauro,' " *Modern Language Notes* 86 (1971): 1–20, and John Freccero, "The Fig Tree and the Laurel," *Diacritics* 5 (1975): 34–40.

12 Freccero, "Fig Tree," p. 37.

13 Ibid., p. 38.

14 Ibid., p. 39.

15 "Una manus vobis vulnus opemque feret" (A single hand both wounds and strengthens you), *Remedia amoris*, 44. Bernart writes "Cent vetz mor lo jorn de dolor—e reviu de joi autras cen" in his lyric beginning "Non es meravelha s'eu chan," ll. 27–28.

16 I do not myself see in Petrarch's poetry, with rare exceptions, the processes of resolution and harmonization that Emilio Bigi finds as balances to the use of antithesis. See his "Alcuni aspetti dello stile del *Canzoniere* petrarchesco," in *Dal Petrarca al Leopardi* (Milan: Ricciardi, 1954), pp. 1–22.

17 Dámaso Alonso grounds Petrarch's "bimembering" rhetoric in the poet's mind. "Le profonde necessità estetiche che cercavano una forma nello spirito del Petrarca miravano ad esprimersi, a modellarsi, secondo un sistema equilibrato da un movimento bilanciato, un movimento binario, che sorge, potremmo dire, da una bimembrazione del pensiero poetico." "La poesia del Petrarca e il Petrarchismo," *Lettere italiane* 11 (1959): 287. Alonso argues that this "bimembrazione" is absent from the poetry of Petrarch's forerunners and notably from the *dolce stil nuovo* (p. 283).

18 The entire canzone is packed with images reflecting Petrarch's close familiarity with Virgil. The opening of the stanza quoted recalls *Aeneid* 5.836–37: "placida laxabant membra quiete / sub remis per dura sedilia nautae" (the crews, who lay stretched on their oars, were relaxed in sweet repose). Lines 49–53 recall the passage from *Aeneid* 4 quoted above on p. 116. Compare also *Purgatorio* 8.1ff. and 4.137–37.

19 The major antithesis of the canzone is reserved for the very close. Addressing his poem in the *commiato*, the speaker says ". . . assai ti fia pensar di poggio in poggio / come m'à concio 'l foco / di questa viva petra ov' io m'appoggio." (It will be enough for you to think from hill to hill how I am reduced by the fire from this living stone on which I lean)—ll. 76–78. He is consumed by flames emanating from the rock which paradoxically supports him.

20 Dino's commentary is discussed and quoted by John Charles Nelson, *Renaissance Theory of Love: The Context of Giordano Bruno's "Eroici Furori"* (New York: Columbia University Press, 1958), pp. 36–39.

21 Pietro Bembo, *Opere in volgare*, ed. M. Marti (Florence: Sansoni, 1961), p. 30.

22 G. G. Ferrero, *Petrarca e i trovatori* (Turin: Gheroni, 1958), p. 32.

23 *Virgil*, ed. and trans. H. R. Fairclough (Cambridge, Mass.: Harvard University Press), vol. 1.

24 *Opere*, ed. Bigi, p. 580.

25 *De remediis utriusque fortune*, 1.1

26 Ce qui demeure toujours dans l'univers représentatif de Pétrarque, c'est, beaucoup plus que l'idée d'évolution et de résolution, celle d'antithèse et d'incompatibilité. Il y a toujours contre ce qu'il èst, et jusqu'en lui-même, quelque chose qui n'est pas ce qu'il est. Son esprit butte en quelque sorte contre la réalité extérieure, contre son corps qui pactise avec celle-ci. C'est pourquoi il se saisit avec tant de ferveur des images à travers lesquelles il voit l'âme echapper à l'espace, soit qu'elle s'ouvre sur l'infini du ciel au sommet de la montagne, soit qu'elle se réduise a l'infiniment petit de la profondeur intime. Il fuit aussi, dans un rêve de solitude spirituelle, l'affrontement avec l'altérité du monde extérieur qui se déroule sur le terrain commun de l'espace. Refus stoïcien des passions, indifférence, détachement, tout cela est encore l'expression d'une fin de non-recevoir (Arnaud Tripet, *Pétrarque, ou la connaissance de soi* [Geneva: Droz, 1967], p. 73).

Chapter 7. Petrarch: Falling into Shadow

1 Two interesting and provocative recent readings of this poem are those by John Brenkman, "Writing, Desire, Dialectic in Petrarch's '*Rime* 23,' " *Pacific Coast Philology* 9 (1974): 12–19, and Marguerite Waller, *Petrarch's Poetics and Literary History* (Amherst: University of Massachusetts Press, 1980), pp. 84–104.

2 Terence C. Cave, "Ronsard as Apollo: Myth, Poetry, and Experience in a Renaissance Sonnet-cycle," *Yale French Studies* 47, *Image and Symbol in the Renaissance*, p. 86.

3 *The Confessions of Saint Augustine*, trans. J. K. Ryan (Garden City, N. Y.: Doubleday, 1960), 8.12, p. 202.

4 Leo Spitzer, "The Problem of Latin Renaissance Poetry," *Studies in the Renaissance* 2 (1955): 130. Erich Auerbach writes: "With Petrarch lyrical subjectivism achieved perfection for the first time since antiquity, not impaired but, quite on the contrary, enriched by the motif of Christian anguish that always accompanies it. For it was this motif that gave lyrical subjectivism its dialectical character and the poignancy of its emotional appeal." *Literary Language and its Public in Late Latin Antiquity and in the Middle Ages*, trans. Ralph Manheim, Bollingen Series, 74 (New York: Pantheon, 1965), p. 318.

5 Francesco Petrarca, *Opere*, ed. Emilio Bigi (Milan: Mursia, 1968), p. 556. The translation is from W. H. Draper, trans., *Petrarch's Secret* (London: Chatto and Windus, 1911), p. 43.

6 *De vera religione*, 1.3.

7 *Familiares* 4.12. English version from Francesco Petrarca, *Rerum familiarium libri I-VIII*, trans. Aldo S. Bernardo (Albany: State University of New York Press, 1975), p. 207.

8 Adelia Noferi remarks on how the word *ombra* was for Petrarch "ricca di sostanza spirituale, di un suo mistero conturbante, appena addolcita la violenza delle 'tenebre'

agostiniane, conservate, esse, alla loro assoluta drammaticità." *L'esperienza poetica del Petrarca* (Florence: Le Monnier, 1962), p. 179. See also p. 146.

9   "Pulvis et umbra sumus." *Carmina*, 4.7.16.

10   The final stanza, which follows immediately that from which the quotations are taken, describes a renewed effort to achieve inner clarity. It opens: "Ove d' altra montagna ombra non tocchi / ... tirar mi suol un desiderio intenso." (Where the shadow of some other mountain does not reach ... an intense desire is wont to draw me.)

11   This quotation is taken from the English translation of the Coronation oration contained in Ernest Hatch Wilkins, *Studies in the Life and Works of Petrarch* (Cambridge, Mass.: Mediaeval Academy of America, 1955), p. 307.

12   Saint Augustine, *Soliloquiorum libri duo*, 2.33.

13   Some of the phonic effects in this sonnet are discussed by Cesare Segre, "La critica strutturalistica," in *I metodi attuali della critica in Italia*, ed. Maria Corti and Cesare Segre (Turin: ERI, 1973), pp. 328–30.

14   Francesco Petrarca, *Prose*, ed. G. Martellotti et al. (Milan and Naples: Ricciardi, 1955), p. 228.

15   Ricardo Quinones writes of this sonnet: "Here as he is speaking, time, premonitory of death, steals the wonder that Laura promises, and gives precocious instruction in her own unreliability as a source of being." *The Renaissance Discovery of Time* (Cambridge, Mass.: Harvard University Press, 1972), p. 127.

16   "L'amore per Laura è un amore che nasce e cresce al cospetto della morte, come lotta assidua del principio di gratuità assoluta contro le leggi della ragione naturale e soprannaturale." Fausto Montanari, *Studi sul Canzoniere del Petrarca* (Rome: Studium, 1958), p. 175.

17   Ovid, *Amores*, 1.11.15, and Horace, *Carmina*, 1.11.7–8. In the *Secretum*, Franciscus cites some lines of verse composed during his youth that have not been preserved elsewhere: "Loquimur dum talia, forsan / innumeris properata viis, in limine mors est." (Even while we speak, along a thousand ways with stealthy steps up to our very door Death creeps.) Bigi ed., p. 554; Draper, *Petrarch's Secret*, p. 40.

18   Ovid, *Remedia amoris*, 85–88. *The Art of Love*, trans. R. Humphries (Bloomington: Indiana University Press, 1966), p. 184.

19   Bigi ed., p. 678; Draper, *Petrarch's Secret*, p. 185.

20   There may be an echo of this line in the passage quoted on pp. 107–08 from the account of the ascent of Mont Ventoux.

21   ". . . discende / dagli altissimi monti maggior l'ombra" (the shadows descend more widely from the highest mountains)—ll. 16–17.

22   *Familiares*, 2.5. Bernardo trans., p. 87.

23   Bigi ed., p. 554; Draper, *Petrarch's Secret*, p. 42.

24   Mikhail Bakhtin, *Problems of Dostoevsky's Poetics*, trans. R. W. Rotsel (n.p.: Ardis, 1973).

25   Ibid., p. 167.

Chapter 8. Poliziano: The Past Dismembered

1   The use of notebooks for collecting aphorisms, idioms, proverbs, memorable and difficult passages, and terms applicable to various subjects or aspects of daily life from the ancient languages appears to have been introduced into Italy by the Byzantine scholar Manuel Chrysoloras at the turn of the fifteenth century. This became a peda-

gogic tool of prime importance which would eventually spread throughout western Europe. A valuable discussion of this method, stressing its culmination in Erasmus's *De copia*, can be found in R. R. Bolgar, *The Classical Heritage and its Beneficiaries* (Cambridge: Cambridge University Press, 1954), pp. 265–75. Useful and pertinent as Bolgar's discussion is, he seems to me to claim too much for this method in implying that through it, students "learned to think in the categories [of the past] and . . . [to] adopt its sensibility and its standards." (p. 268) The work of cataloguing and of rote memory required by this method could not in itself produce sensitive understanding and creative imitation. That imitation was also understood at the end of the trecento to refer to patterning one's style on a single model is demonstrated by a letter written in 1396 from Pier Paolo Vergerio to Lodovico Buzzacarino, arguing for the choice of Cicero for prose and Virgil for poetry. "Deligendus est autem nobis unus quem imitemur; quod in omni genere rerum efficacissimum adiumentum est." Pier Paolo Vergerio, *Epistolario*, ed. L. Smith (Rome: Tipografia del Senato, 1934), p. 177.

2   Charles Trinkaus, "The Unknown Quattrocento Poetics of Bartolommeo della Fonte," *Studies in the Renaissance* 13 (1966): 40–122. This monograph contains the first published text of the *De poetice ad Laurentium Medicem libri III*. The short discussion of imitation appears on p. 112.

3   For an edited typescript copy based on the available manuscripts of Barzizza's treatise, I am indebted to George W. Pigman III, who is, at this writing, preparing an edition of it.

4   These appear to correspond to Quintilian's four types of transformation—*adiectio*, *detractio*, *transmutatio*, and *immutatio* (1.5.38). The terms applied to these four operations by Barzizza and the explanations assigned to each are not identical in the four manuscripts.

5   See J. von Stackelberg, "Das Bienengleichnis," *Romanische Forschungen* 68 (1956): 271–93, and G. W. Pigman, "Versions of Imitation in the Renaissance," *Renaissance Quarterly* 33 (1980): n. 13.

6   *Prosatori Latini del Quattrocento*, ed. Eugenio Garin (Milan: Ricciardi, 1953), p. 878.

7   See chap. 2, n. 13.

8   Quoted by Emilio Bigi, *La cultura del Poliziano* (Pisa: Nistri-Lischi, 1967), p. 105, n. 10.

9   Quoted by Eugenio Garin, "L'ambiente del Poliziano," in *Il Poliziano e il suo tempo*. Atti del quarto convegno internazionale di studi sul rinascimento (Florence: Sansoni, 1957), p. 36.

10 Angelo Ambrogini Poliziano, *Prose volgari inedite e poesie latine e greche edite e inedite*, ed. Isidoro del Lungo (Florence: Sansoni, 1957), p. 36. (Henceforth referred to as "del Lungo.")

11 See the fuller quotation below, p. 165, and n. 34.

12 The history of these debates by Izora Scott remains useful, although her translations of selected texts are not always reliable: *Controversies over the Imitation of Cicero* (New York: Teachers College, Columbia University, 1910).

13 Remitto epistolas diligentia tua collectas, in quibus legendis, ut libere dicam, pudet bonas horas male collocasse. Nam praeter omnino paucas, minime dignae sunt quae vel a docto aliquo lectae vel a te collectae dicantur. Quas probem, quas rursus improbem, non explico. Nolo sibi quisquam vel placeat in his, auctore me, vel displiceat. Est in quo tamen a te dissentiam de stylo nonnihil. Non enim probare soles, ut accepi, nisi qui lineamenta Ciceronis effingat. Mihi vero longe honestior tauri facies aut item leonis quam simiae videtur, quae tamen homini similior est.

Nec ii, qui principatum tenuisse creduntur eloquentiae, similes inter se, quod Seneca prodidit. Ridentur a Quintiliano qui se germanos Ciceronis putabant esse, quod his verbis periodum clauderent: *esse videatur.* Inclamat Horatius imitatores, ac nihil aliud quam imitatores. Mihi certe quicumque tantum componunt ex imitatione, similes esse vel psittaco vel picae videntur, proferentibus quae nec intelligunt. Carent enim quae scribunt isti viribus et vita; carent actu, carent affectu, carent indole, iacent, dormiunt, stertunt. Nihil ibi verum, nihil solidum, nihil efficax. Non exprimis, inquit aliquis, Ciceronem. Quid tum? non enim sum Cicero; me tamen, ut opinor, exprimo.

Sunt quidam praeterea, mi Paule, qui stylum quasi panem frustillatim mendicant, nec ex die solum vivunt, sed et in diem; tum nisi liber ille praesto sit, ex quo quid excerpant, colligere tria verba non possunt, sed haec ipsa quoque vel indocta iunctura vel barbaria inhonesta contaminant. Horum semper igitur oratio tremula, vacillans, infirma, videlicet male curata, male pasta, quos ferre profecto non possum; iudicare quoque de doctis impudenter audentes, hoc est de illis quorum stylum recondita eruditio, multiplex lectio, longissimus usus diu quasi fermentavit. Sed ut ad te redeam, Paule, quem penitus amo, cui multum debeo, cuius ingenio plurimum tribuo, quaeso, ne superstitione ista te alliges, ut nihil delectet quod tuum plane sit et ut oculos a Cicerone nunquam deicias. Sed cum Ciceronem, cum bonos alios multum diuque legeris, contriveris, edidiceris, concoxeris et rerum multarum cognitione pectus impleveris, ac iam componere aliquid ipse parabis, tum demum velim quod dicitur sine cortice nates, atque ipse tibi sis aliquando in consilio, sollicitudinemque illam morosam nimis et anxiam deponas effingendi tantummodo Ciceronem tuasque denique vires universas pericliteris. Nam qui tantum ridicula ista quae vocatis liniamenta contemplantur attoniti, nec illa ipsa, mihi crede satis repraesentant, et impetum quodammodo retardant ingenii sui, currentique velut obstant et, ut utar plautino verbo, remoram faciunt. Sed ut bene currere non potest qui pedem ponere studet in alienis tantum vestigiis, ita nec bene scribere qui tamquam de praescripto non audet egredi. Postremo scias infelicis esse ingenii nihil a se promere, semper imitari. Vale (Garin, *Prosatori Latini*, pp. 902-04).

14 I would take issue with the judgment of Ferruccio Ulivi that imitation for Poliziano was a purely hedonistic exercise, a disinterested sipping of nectar "senza troppo preoccuparsi . . . che quell'essenza dei fiori sia, poi, digerita e trasformata," *L'imitazione nella poetica del rinascimento* (Milan: Marzorati, 1959), p. 18. The failure of transformation in this case was not due in my judgment to a failure of absorption.

15 *Nicolai de Cusa Opera Omnia,* ed. L. Baur (Leyden: Meier, 1937), 5:57.

16 Marsilio Ficino, *Platonica Theologia,* ed. and trans. R. Marcel (Paris: Les Belles Lettres, 1964), 2:258.

17 Ibid., 2:256.

18 Andre Chastel comments:

L'âme est donc l'intériorité même de l'univers, qui passe tout entière par l'homme, et évolue selon les décisions de sa liberté. Ficin revient perpétuellement sur cette présence réciproque de l'univers à l'homme et de l'homme à l'univers par l'activité de l'âme, mais en même temps il pose, avec force, comme le veut Platon, l'indépendance de l'esprit par rapport aux déterminations physiques. . . . L'âme peut rejoindre Dieu par cette pointe extrême de la contemplation dont parlent les mystiques; mais par son activité naturelle qui est d'embrasser, d'épurer et d'exprimer le réel sans résidu, elle coincide intégralement avec l'oeuvre divine, elle l'exerce dans toute sa profondeur (*Marsile Ficin et l'art* [Geneva-Lille: Droz, 1954], p. 43).

19 Friedrich Nietzsche, *The Use and Abuse of History*, trans. A. Collins (Indianapolis: Bobbs-Merrill, 1957), p. 7.

20 Garin, *Prosatori Latini*, p. 908.

21 David Quint, trans., *The "Stanze" of Angelo Poliziano* (Amherst: University of Massachusetts Press, 1979), pp. xi–xii.

22 Quotations of Poliziano's Italian poetry are from Agnolo Poliziano, *Stanze per la Giostra. Orfeo. Rime*, ed. B. Maier (Novara: Istituto Geografico de Agostini, 1968). Translations of the *Stanze* are from Quint.

23 *Claudian*, trans. M. Platnauer (London' Heinemann, 1922), 2.345.

24 E in questo preciso modo di assimilazione e di sublimazione della realtà nella letteratura che risiede il segno segreto di tutta l'opera polizianea. Il mondo di Poliziano, il suo universo, è costituito da un organico complesso di unità letterarie, ciascuna delle quali non è l'archetipo o una sorte d'universale dell'oggetto che le pertiene, ma il nodo in cui convergono e si riassommano tutte le espressioni letterarie effettivamente ottenute da quell'oggetto fino al momento in cui l'unità viene utilizzata. E questa sostanza letteraria che costituisce il sema di ciascuna unità: la quale, pertanto, risulta caratterizzata da una sua natura decisamente corposa e, ad un tempo. esclusivamente letteraria (Mario Martelli, "La semantica di Poliziano," *Rinascimento* 13 [1973]: 26–27).

25 Ovid, *Metamorphoses*, trans. F. J. Miller, rev. G. P. Goold (Cambridge, Mass.: Harvard University Press, 1977), vol. 1.

26 Quint comments: "Pacification and erotic subordination merge at the divine level in the union of Venus and Mars, the culminating tableau of Book I." He illuminates this tableau with suggestive references to Lucretius and Ficino, and concludes: "Ficino's mythography neatly expresses the poem's dichotomy between self-centered irascibility and altruistic love. Cupid explicitly compares Julio the hunter to the Mars who loses his belligerence when recumbent in the lap of Venus (II, 11). Simonetta is to Julio as Venus is to Mars. Human history finds its parallel in the mythic, universal order." *The "Stanze,"* p. xx. This homology may well exist within the poem, even if Poliziano's Venus finally appears as more Lucretian than Ficinian, more a goddess of fecundity than of altruism or Neoplatonic sublimation.

27 Images of death and violence recur to trouble the ostensibly idyllic surface of book 1: in the noted absence of death and war during the golden age (stanza 20); in the terror of the hunted animals (30–31), in the centaur simile (32), in the hunters' fear that Giuliano has lost his life (62–66), in the allusions to Philomela of 60 and to Proserpina of 67, in the presence of Cruelty and Despair in Venus's garden (75), in the death of the flower described by stanza 78, in the violence of the beasts in the garden (86–87: see p. 167), in the sculpted castration of Uranus (97–98: see p. 167). These forces, still muted and intermittent in book 1, become dominant in book 2. On this theme throughout Poliziano's canon, see Juliana Hill, "Death and Politian," *Durham University Journal* 46 (1954): 96–105.

28 Del Lungo, pp. 98, 103.

29 By Gian-Paolo Biasin, "Messer Jacopo giù per Arno se ne va . . . ," in *Modern Language*

Notes 79 (1964): 1-13, and by Eugenio Donato, "Death and History in Poliziano's *Stanze*," *Modern Language Notes* 80 (1965): 27-40. My reading of Poliziano is indebted to this latter article.

30 *Stanze per la Giostra. Orfeo. Rime*, ed. Maier, p. 95.

31 Ibid., p. 271.

32 Del Lungo, p. 117.

33 Full Latin text quoted by Ida Maier, *Ange Politien: La Formation d'un poète Humaniste* (Geneva: Droz, 1966), p. 117.

34 The entire poem is given by Ida Maier, pp. 72-77. The passage quoted is lines 213-22.
The myth of Aesculapius had been used as a symbol of humanist restoration by Boccaccio in the preface to his *De genealogia deorum*: "I can quite realize this labor to which I am committed—this vast system of gentile gods and their progeny, torn limb from limb and scattered among the rough and desert places of antiquity and the thorns of hate, wasted away, sunk almost to ashes; and here am I setting forth to collect these fragments, hither and yon, and fit them together, like another Aesculapius restoring Hippolytus" (Charles G. Osgood, *Boccaccio on Poetry* [Princeton: Princeton University Press, 1930], p. 13). Latin text in *Genealogie deorum gentilium Libri*, ed. V. Romano (Bari: Laterza, 1951), 1:9. For other images of humanist restoration of mangled bodies, see Petrarch's letter to Quintilian, *Fam.* 24.7, and Poggio's letter to Guarino of Verona announcing his discovery of the complete manuscript of Quintilian. Poggio writes: "Hitherto ... among us ... Quintilian was to be had only in such a mangled and mutilated state ... that neither the figure nor the face of the man was to be distinguished in him. ... But the greater was our grief and our vexation at the maiming of that man, the greater is our present cause for congratulation. Thanks to our searching, we have restored Quintilian to his original dress and dignity, to his former appearance, and to a condition of sound health" (Quoted and translated by M. E. Cosenza, *Petrarch's Letters to Classical Authors* [Chicago: University of Chicago Press, 1910], pp. 92-93). Latin text in *Poggii Epistolae*, ed. T. Tonelli (Florence: Marchini, 1832), 1.27. For this last reference I am indebted to an unpublished essay by A. B. Giamatti on the Aesculapian myth and images of humanist restoration.

35 Del Lungo, p. 7.

36 Ibid., p. 4.

37 Ibid., p. 15.

38 Edited by A. Perosa (Rome: Storia e Letteratura, 1954). For the passage paraphrased, see lines 104-17.

39 Edgar Wind, *Pagan Mysteries in the Renaissance* (New York: Norton, 1968), p. 133. Quint discusses this passage ("*Stanze*," p. xxi) in a more favorable light to support his interpretation of Vulcan's sculpted panels.

40 Plutarch, "On the *ei* at Delphi," *Moralia* 388F-389A, and Macrobius, *In somnium Scipionis* 1.12.

41 Of these the most useful is N. Sapegno, *Comento alle Rime del Poliziano* (Rome: Ateneo, 1953). However the old edition of Carducci is also still helpful: *Le Stanze, l'Orfeo e le Rime di Messer Angelo Ambrogini Poliziano* (Bologna: Zanichelli, 1912). See as well R. Lo Cascio, *Lettura del Poliziano—le "Stanze per la giostra"* (Palermo: Flaccovio, 1954).

42 Angelo Poliziano, *Miscellaneorum Centuria Seconda*, ed. Vittore Branca and Manlio Pastor Stocchi (Florence: Alinari, 1972), 4:3.

Chapter 9. Sixteenth-Century Quarrels

1   Pico's first letter is dated October 1512. Bembo's reply is dated January 1513, but was published in 1530. Pico's second letter is of uncertain date but was published with the first in 1518. On the subject of this exchange, see Giorgio Santangelo, *Il Bembo critico e il principio d'imitazione* (Florence: Sansoni, 1950); Dante della Terza, "*Imitatio*: Theory and Practice. The Example of Bembo the Poet," *Yearbook of Italian Studies* 1 (1971): 119–41; introduction to Angiolo Gambaro, ed. and trans., *Il Ciceroniano o dello stile migliore*, by Desiderio Erasmo (Brescia: La Scuola Editrice, 1965). See also the secondary literature on Renaissance theory of imitation surveyed in chap. 5, n. 34.

2   Quotations from the three letters are taken from Giorgio Santangelo, *Le epistole "De imitatione" di Giovanfrancesco Pico della Mirandola e di Pietro Bembo* (Florence: Olschki, 1954). This quotation appears on pp. 27–28. Translations of all Latin passages quoted in this chapter, with the exception of those by Erasmus, are by Daniel Kinney.

3   Santangelo, *Le epistole*, pp. 72–73.

4   Ibid., p. 42.

5   Ibid., p. 45.

6   Pietro Bembo, *Prose della volgar lingua*, ed. M. Marti (Padua: Liviana, 1955), p. 15.

7   Baldassare Castiglione, *Il Libro del Cortegiano con una scelta delle Opere minori*, ed. B. Maier (Turin: U.T.E.T., 1964), pp. 145–46. Translation from Charles S. Singleton, trans., *The Book of the Courtier* (Garden City, N.Y.: Doubleday, 1959), pp. 58–59.

8   Castiglione's use of Cicero's rhetorical works, and in particular the *De oratore*, is so visible and frequent that the reference would have been unmistakable for any educated contemporary reader. The opening pages of book 1 virtually translate Cicero, and the opening of book 4 follow him almost as closely. But having pointed to his authenticating model, in his own series of conversations about an ideal public figure Castiglione systematically draws the reader's attention to what diverges from the Roman model. Thus one is led to perceive his courtier as a more urbane and graceful norm, less grave and less responsible than the Roman orator-statesman, but more flexible, more variously accomplished, and possibly more open to spiritual transcendence. An itinerary from *orator* to *cortegiano* is sketched which does a kind of justice to both *termini*, paying an homage to the classical text which is not blind and accepting the specificity of its own historical moment.

9   For the shift toward a regulative criticism, see Ezio Raimondi, "Dalla natura alla regola," in *Rinascimento inquieto* (Palermo: Manfredi, 1965), pp. 7–21.

10 Ralph G. Williams, ed. and trans., *The "De arte poetica" of Marco Girolamo Vida* (New York: Columbia University Press, 1976), book 3.217–20.

11 In his learned and closely argued essay "Imitation and the Renaissance Sense of the Past: The Reception of Erasmus' *Ciceronianus*" *Journal of Medieval and Renaissance Studies* 9 (1979): 157, G. W. Pigman III writes that the treatises on imitation which followed Erasmus's "call into question the extent and significance of [the] Renaissance discovery of the remoteness of the past." Pigman's essay documents admirably the resistance to the awareness of this remoteness in the neoclassicism of the second quarter of the sixteenth century. But his essay does not in my opinion prove that the Renaissance discovery as a whole has been overestimated. In some cases, such as Camillo and Calcagnini, he seems to me to neglect passages that do not support his argument. He himself cites other critics (Ricci, Melanchthon, Vives) who to one degree or another do reflect some awareness of

historical distance. What Pigman does demonstrate irrefutably is the uneasiness with history felt by classical theorists at this period. In this demonstration and in his cogent analysis of the phenomenon, Pigman's essay makes a significant contribution.

12 Giulio Camillo Delminio, "Della imitazione," in Bernard Weinberg, ed., *Trattati di poetica e retorica del Cinquecento*, 4 vols. (Bari: Laterza, 1970-74), 1:169. (Henceforth *Trattati*.)

13 *Trattati*, 1:208.

14 Ibid., 1:444.

15 The two types of imitation are both present and virtually conflated in *L'Aretino ovvero Dialogo della pittura* (1557) by Lodovico Dolce, who writes, speaking of ancient statues: "La mirabil perfezion delle quali chi gusterà e possederà a pieno, potrà sicuramente corregger molti difetti di essa natura, e far le sue pitture riguardevoli e grate a ciascuno: perciocchè le cose antiche contengono tutta la perfezion dell'arte, e possono essere esemplari di tutto il bello." Edited by Carlo Téoli (Milan: Daelli, 1863), pp. 34-35. [Whoever appreciates and fully makes his own their wonderful perfection will be able to correct with assurance many defects of nature, and render his paintings appealing and agreeable to everyone, because ancient works of art contain all the perfection of art, and can be considered to exemplify all beauty.]

16 "In ogni età qualsivoglia lingua nelle parole qualche mutatione riceva.... Se all nostra [riguardiamo], si come il Petrarca, & il Boccaccio la trovarono non poco mutata da quel, che trovato l'aveano Dante, Cino, e Guido Cavalcanti: così hoggi si vede in molte voci da quel, ch'ella fù nella prima, e nella seconda, & in ciascuna altra età cangiata: e vedràssi anchora ne' futuri secoli da se stessa cangiare.... Somigliasi il parlare al denaro, che in diverse regioni, & in diversi tempi cangia uso, e forma." *L'Arte poetica* (reprint Munich: Fink, 1971), p. 447. [In every age any language undergoes some alteration in its words.... If we consider our own language, just as Petrarch and Boccaccio found it changed to no small degree from the language which Dante, Cino, and Guido Cavalcanti had inherited, so today it has visibly changed in many words from what it was in its first and second and each succeeding phase. And it will be seen to change again in future centuries.... Speech is like money, which changes use and form in various places and times.]

17 *Trattati*, 2:527.

18 Ibid., 2:633, 641.

19 Giordano Bruno, *De gl'heroici furori* (Turin: U.T.E.T., 1928), pp. 33-35.

20 For a rewarding discussion of the architectural problem of anachronism and its analogies to the linguistic and literary problem, see the first section of Paolo Portoghesi's *Rome of the Renaissance*, trans. P. Sanders (London: Phaidon, 1972). Note especially p. 30: "In the large-scale subjects handled by Bramante, architectural and figurative elements far removed from the Golden Age are found together with classical ones. Hence arises the contradiction connected with the difficulty of translating into architectural Latin esthetic functions and values which derive from entirely different sources. The forced quality of the translations which were attempted reproduced that paradoxical contamination which was the object of Erasmus's derision."

21 *Il Ciceroniano*, ed. Gambaro, p. 126.

22 Ibid., p. 194.

23 Ibid., pp. 178-80. The (slightly expanded) translations of this and the following passages by Erasmus are taken from Izora Scott, trans., *Ciceronianus, or A Dialogue on*

the Best Style of Speaking, Columbia University Contributions to Education, Teachers College Series, No. 21 (New York: Teachers College, Columbia University, 1908). This passage appears on pp. 81-82.

24 Pigman, "Imitation and the Renaissance sense of the past," argues that this historical decorum is the central concept of the *Ciceronianus* and quotes passages (pp. 159-61) from a number of Erasmus's earlier works, especially his *Life of Jerome* and his correspondence, to show that the historical argument was uppermost in his opposition to Ciceronianism.

25 *Il Ciceroniano*, p. 190. Scott, p. 86.

26 *Il Ciceroniano*, p. 290. Scott, p. 123.

27 *Il Ciceroniano*, p. 164. Scott, pp. 75-76.

28 *Il Ciceroniano*, p. 290.

29 *Il Ciceroniano*, pp. 286-88. Scott, pp. 121-22. Terence Cave's *The Cornucopian Text: Problems of Writing in the French Renaissance* (Oxford: Clarendon Press, 1979) contains the most searching analysis of the *Ciceronianus* I have seen. This is not the place for a discussion of all the issues he raises. One point, however, related to Erasmus's comments on the uniqueness of the inner self, requires a response. Cave refers to Erasmus's lifelong attack on externals and finds this inconsistent with the act of writing. "The movement of his writing towards *autrui*, whether the addressees of his letters or his polemical adversaries, is an act of self-definition which carries a deep ambiguity. For his whole value-system, based as it is on interiority, on *pectus*, on the plenitude of self, is compromised by the public, exterior nature of writing" (p. 47). This seems to me a dubious oversimplification of Erasmus's ethic. The attack on externals in the church as in Latin style was of a piece with the attack on the self-indulgent privacy of monasticism. The valorization of interiority led for Erasmus to a valorization of authentic charity and social responsibility.

30 ". . . Neque vero is imitari Ciceronem dicendum est, qui excerptas ex illo sententias ac versus, quasi Centones consuit, quemadmodum facere nonnullos videmus. Ses *hexin* sibi quisque faciat, ut ultro se Ciceronis verba offerant, quae cum ita coniungimus, ut res nostras explicent, tamen collocatio et series partium debet habere quandam Ciceronis similitudinem." Philip Melanchthon, *Opera*, ed. C. G. Bretschneider, 28 vols. (Halle: Schwetschke, 1846), vol. 13, col. 497. [Nor should we say that a man imitates Cicero if he culls words and lines out of Cicero and stitches them together, one might say, into Centos, as we see that some do. Let each man acquire an inward mastery such that Cicero's words present themselves quite spontaneously; when we join these to express our thoughts, the arrangement and sequence of clauses ought still to bear some likeness of Cicero.]

31 Melanchthon, *Opera*, vol. 13, col. 497.

32 Ibid.

33 Geoffroy Tory, *Champ Fleury*, ed. G. Cohen (Paris: Bosse, 1931), f. 12.

34 Estienne Pasquier, *Choix de lettres*, ed. D. Thickett (Geneva: Droz, 1956), pp. 75-76.

35 Ibid., p. 132.

36 On Le Roy and other theories of linguistic change of the later French Renaissance, see Claude-Gilbert Dubois, *Mythe et langage au seizieme siecle* (Bordeaux: Ducros, 1970), pp. 116-19.

37 In the preface to his *Prieres et oraisons de la Bible* (1542), Dolet wrote: "Telle est l'opinion de tous rhetoriciens, que une des principales parties de l'art oratoire consiste

en imitation. Et non seulement leur opinion est vraye, quant à ceste part: mais il fault tenir asseurement, qu'en toutes choses bonnes, & louables imitation a le premier lieu. Car imitation n'est qu'ung exemple des choses parfaictes, & emerveillables en leur genre." Quoted by E. V. Telle in his edition of *L'Erasmianus sive Ciceronianus d-'Etienne Dolet* (Geneva: Droz, 1974), p. 434. In Dolet's treatise *La maniere de bien traduire d'une langue en aultre* (1540), a perception emerges of the uniqueness of each linguistic world.

38 Jacques Peletier du Mans, *L'Art poëtique départi an deus livres* (Geneva: Slatkine reprints. 1971), pp. 36, 18.

39 Cave comments that Peletier "is in this chapter walking a theoretical tightrope" (*The Cornucopian Text*, p. 58). After quoting the conclusion of the chapter at length, Cave sums up with insight and felicity the humanist dilemma: "The miraculously living, yet alien, language of the ancients offers a model of (almost) perfect discourse which demands emulation; to sever oneself from it is to commit oneself to a fragile and obscure present, but to attempt to repeat it in the vernacular is to incur the risk of falsity and emptiness. If only repetition and plenitude could be combined, if ony the dead substitution of word for word could be replaced by a harmonious mirroring of two texts, perfectly identical and equally authentic, then Cicero, Homer, Virgil, Ovid, would speak again in French" (p. 59).

40 Joachim Du Bellay, *La Deffence et Illustration de la Langue Francoyse*, ed. H. Chamard (Paris: Didier, 1948), p. 12. Future references will indicate the page in this edition within parentheses after each quotation.

41 Henri Chamard, *Histoire de la Pléiade* (Paris: Didier, 1939), 1:177, 190; V. L. Saulnier, *Du Bellay* (Paris: Hatier, 1968), pp. 48–49; Michel Dassonville, "De l'unité de *La Deffence et illustration de la langue françoyse*," *Bibliothèque d'Humanisme et Renaissance* 27 (1965): 96–107; Michel Deguy, *Tombeau de Du Bellay* (Paris: Gallimard, 1973), p. 108; Cave, *The Cornucopian Text*, p. 59.

42 Margaret W. Ferguson, "The Exile's Defense: Du Bellay's *La Deffence et Illustration de la Langue Françoyse*," *PMLA* 93 (1978): 275–89.

43   In reality throughout the whole body of Erasmus's work there coexist two different views of history, each one owing much to his humanist predecessors but fundamentally incompatible with each other. . . . The first was an essentially cyclical conception derived originally from the classical philosophers and historians. The second was a linear interpretation resting ultimately on the implications of the Christian religion. . . .

    This dualism is apparent in his most comprehensive expressions on the subject of historical change and the relation between past and present. He is constantly using the expressions *renovatio, restoratio, instauratio*. . . . What was the nature of these renewals and restorations? We have already seen that in arguing against the Ciceronians Erasmus rejected the concept of a past which could be recaptured and imitated in its entirety. But if the stage was a different one and the play had never been performed before, it was still possible to hope that the characters might express intellectual and moral qualities of a height equal to or greater than those attained in great ages of the past (Myron P. Gilmore, *Humanists and Jurists* [Cambridge, Mass.: Harvard University Press, 1963], pp. 107–09).

44 Cave, *The Cornucopian Text*, pp. 75–76.

45 V. N. Voloshinov, *Marxism and the Philosophy of Language,* trans. L. Matejka and I. R. Tritunik (New York: Seminar Press, 1973), pp. 102–03. Some students of Soviet criticism have come to believe that this book was largely written by Mikhail Bakhtin.

46 Chamard, *Deffence,* p. 104, n. 1. Chamard cites Guillaume des Autelz, who in his *Replique aux furieuses defenses de Louis Meigret* is said to advise Du Bellay to "oser être original en s'enfranchissant des anciens et des Italiens." In fact, des Autelz had objected to imitation as exemplified by Du Bellay's *Olive* and *Vers lyriques,* where he alleges it to be virtually indistinguishable from translation, which is proscribed by the *Deffence.* "Je pense qu'il y ha bien à dire," he continues, "à considerer en quoy gist l'artifice, et la grace d'un bon auteur, pour s'efforcer de l'ensuivre par semblable chemin: & à luy desrober du tout son invention, ses mots, & ses sentences." *Replique* (Lyon: Jean de Tournes, 1551), p. 59. To criticize this extreme degree of imitative proximity is not in itself to advocate total artistic independence. Des Autelz goes on to call for the emergence of a native genre, but the unnamed contemporary poet he singles out for enthusiastic praise must be Maurice Scève, who was of course saturated in Italian culture and anything but *affranchi* in Chamard's sense.

Chapter 10. Imitative Insinuations in the Amours *of Ronsard*

1 All quotations from the love poems are taken from Pierre de Ronsard, *Les Amours,* ed. H. and C. Weber (Paris: Garnier, 1963). References to this edition are indicated by "W" followed by the page number. All other quotations from Ronsard are taken from the *Oeuvres complètes,* ed. P. Laumonier (completed by I. Silver and R. Lebègue), 20 vols. (Paris: Société des Textes Français Modernes, 1914–75). References to this edition are indicated by "L" followed by the volume and page number. The quotation above is from the Laumonier edition, vol. 1, p. 78.

2 Sebillet speaking of the poet: "Encor pourra-il grandement locupléter et l'invention et l'économie [of the poem], de la lecture et intelligence des plus nobles Pöetes Grecz et Latins, esquelz les plus braves pöetes de ce temps, s'ilz en fussent interrogez, avoueroient devoir la bonne part de leur style et éloquence: car, a vray dire, ceuz sont les Cynes, dés ailes desquelz se tirent les plumes dont on escrit proprement." In a later passage: "Je desire pour la perfection de toy Pöete futur, en toy parfaitte congnoissance dés langues Gréque et Latine: car elles sont lés deus forges d'ou nous tirons lés piéces meilleures de notre harnois." Thomas Sebillet, *Art Pöetique Françoys,* ed. F. Gaiffe (Paris: Cornély, 1910), pp. 28, 167.

3 "Let us take care lest, misled by a mistaken view of imitation, we choose the worn out, antiquated, and *recherché* as models." (Vitabimus, ne imitationis errore decepti, desita, antiquata . . . et ab usu remota in exemplum nobis sumamus.) (Paris: Julianus, 1575), f. 49v. Omphalius's work appears to have been composed primarily as a textbook; the greater part is given over to variation charts like those found in Erasmus's *De copia.* The author is vehemently Ciceronian.

4 This duality can be located in two lines of the prefatory "Voeu" opening the first collection of *Amours* and addressed to the Muses:

Si tout ravy des saults de voz carolles
D'un pied nombreux j'ay conduit vostre bal. . . .   [W 3, variant]

"Ravy" alludes to the doctrine of inspirational furies. "Nombreux" implies a precise control of rhythmic cadence appropriate to verse composed for musical settings. Muret's note on "nombreux": "Plein de nombres: c'est à dire, que le pied est absolu et parfait artizan des cadences, mesures & marques requises à la dance."

5 L 8:350, 17:424.

6 Terence Cave, "Ronsard's Mythological Universe," in *Ronsard the Poet*, ed. T. Cave (London: Methuen, 1973), pp. 168–70.

7 R. R. Bolgar, *The Classical Heritage and its Beneficiaries* (Cambridge: Cambridge University Press, 1954), pp. 87–88.

8 H. Weber, *La Création poétique au XVIe siècle en France* (Paris: Nizet, 1956), p. 122.

9 *Canzoniere* 129, 155, 288.

10 For the figure of the nymph in French Renaissance poetry, see Françoise Joukovsky-Micha, *Poésie et mythologie au XVIe siecle* (Paris: Nizet, 1969), pp. 73–120.

11 This same effect of metamorphic reversal occurs in "Le Houx," which tells how a nymph ravished by Pan is transformed into a holly, a bush of which grows by the window of Ronsard's friend Jean Brinon. Brinon in this account becomes a kind of magician whose voice

> A ce hous esmerveillé,
> Comme s'il fust oreillé,
> Fait venir à sa fenestre
> Pour ouyr parler son maistre;
> Et peu s'en faut qu'il ne met
> Dans la chambre son sommet,
> Ses cheveux et ses oreilles,
> Pour ouyr mille merveilles,
> Et pour du tout se laisser
> A son Brinon embrasser.   [L 6:144–45, variant]

The metamorphic direction is doubled, so that the holly acquires ears, hair, and an affection for this new Orpheus.

12 The discussion that follows and in fact the entire chapter is indebted to the essay by Ian McFarlane, "Aspects of Ronsard's Poetic Vision," in *Ronsard the Poet*, ed. Cave. McFarlane points out (p. 18) that Ronsard "is fascinated by the temptation to be absorbed by water."

13 See Guy Demerson, *La Mythologie classique dans l'oeuvre lyrique de la Pléiade* (Geneva: Droz, 1972), pp. 44–45; also L. Hautecoeur, *Les Jardins des dieux et des hommes* (Paris: Hachette, 1959), pp. 107–28.

14 Compare another description of Jupiter making love to Juno.

> Elle, deçà & là eparses
> Enchaine ses mains à son col,
>   Lui, dedans ses mouelles arses
>   Avale un amour tendre & mol,
> Et en baisant ce grand corps, fait renaistre
> Le beau printens saison du premier estre.   [L 1:262–63]

15 This useful term was first employed, to my knowledge, by André Gendre. "Ronsard . . . se trouve progressivement gagné, jusqu'à s'y perdre, par les différents éléments de la nature, grâce à un jeu de reflets multiples. Nous avons donné à cette attitude particulière de Ronsard le nom de symbiose." *Ronsard poète de la conquête amoureuse* (Neuchâtel: Editions de la Baconnière, 1970), pp. 363–64.

16 Demerson, *Mythologie classique*, p. 14.

17 "Ronsard's mythological universe is centered at the threshold of supernatural experience, or conversely at the limits of purely human experience: it expresses a heightened sense of 'reality,' reflecting the world of men yet releasing it from contingency." "Ronsard's Mythological Universe," p. 195.

18 McFarlane, "Aspects of Ronsard's Poetic Vision," p. 39.

19 Weber cites a "source" of the sestet in a sonnet by Lelio Capilupi, but it is noteworthy that the "follastre" undulation of the hair is missing in that poem.

20 Lines 3–4 are based on a Lucretian subtext:

> postremo pereunt imbres, ubi eos pater Aether
> in gremium matris Terrai praecipitavit.   [*De rerum natura*, 1.250–51]
> [Finally the rain disappears when father Ether has poured it into the lap of mother Earth.]

21 "I hope that in speaking this proud word I have hit the mark, like an archer." Pindar, sixth Nemean ode, stanza 2.

22 *Virgil*, trans. H. R. Fairclough, vol. 1 (London: Heinemann, 1920).

23   Inde, ubi prima fides pelago, placataque venti
> Dant maria, et lenis crepitans vocat Auster in altum,
> Deducunt socii naves et litora complent.
> Provehimur portu, terraeque urbesque recedunt.   [*Aeneid* 3.69–72]
> [As soon as we could trust the ocean, when winds offered us smiling seas and the whisper of a breeze invited us onto the deep, my comrades crowded to the beach and launched our ships. We sailed forth from the haven, and the land and its cities sank behind us.]   [trans. W. F. Jackson Knight]

Chapter 11. Du Bellay and the Disinterment of Rome

1 Quotations from *Les Regrets* and *Les Antiquitez de Rome* are taken from Joachim Du Bellay, *Les Regrets et autres oeuvres poètiques*, texte établi par J. Jolliffe, introduit et commenté par M. A. Screech (Geneva: Droz, 1966). Other quotations from Du Bellay are from the *Oeuvres poétiques français de Joachim Du Bellay*, ed. H. Chamard, 6 vols. (Paris: Didier, 1961).

2 On the figure of the antiquary, see Arnaldo Momigliano, "Ancient History and the Antiquarian," in his *Contributo alla storia degli studi classici* (Rome: Storia e Letteratura, 1955). See also the charming essay by Charles Mitchell, "Archaeology and Romance in Renaissance Italy," in *Italian Renaissance Studies*, ed. E. F. Jacob (London: Faber and Faber, 1960), pp. 455–83.

3 Compare the parallelism of the grandiose political, linguistic, and literary future prophesied in the *Deffence*, where the organic imagery, carried over from preceding passages indebted to Speroni, does not altogether obliterate traces of the necromantic

metaphor ("ensevelie," "sortira de terre"). "Monarchie" in the following passage means "universal empire." "Le tens viendra (peut estre), & je l'espere moyennant la bonne destinée Francoyse, que ce noble & puyssant Royaume obtiendra à son tour les resnes de la monarchie, & que nostre Langue (si avecques Francoys n'est tout ensevelie la Langue Francoyse) qui commence encor' à jeter ses racines, sortira de terre, & s'elevera en telle hauteur & grosseur, qu'elle se poura egaler aux mesmes Grecz & Romains, produysant comme eux des Homeres, Demosthenes, Virgiles & Cicerons, aussi bien que la France a quelquefois produit des Pericles, Nicies, Alcibiades, Themistocles, Cesars & Scipions" (Joachim Du Bellay, *La Deffence et Illustration de la Langue Francoyse*, ed. H. Chamard [Paris: Didier, 1948], pp. 27-28).

4 English translations of the *Aeneid* are taken from the translation by W. F. Jackson Knight.

5 Lucan, *Pharsalia*, trans. R. Graves (Baltimore: Penguin, 1956), pp. 29-30. On the presence of Lucan throughout the sequence, see F. M. Chambers, "Lucan in the *Antiquitez de Rome*," *PMLA* 60 (1945): 937-48.

6 Horace, Epode 16:

> Altera iam teritur bellis civilibus aetas
> suis et ipsa Roma viribus ruit.
> Quam . . .
> nec fera caerulea domuit Germania pube
> parentibusque abominatus Hannibal,
> impia perdemus devoti sanguinis aetas.
> [Already a second generation is worn down by civil wars and Rome falls from its own strength. She whom . . . neither barbarous Germany with its blue-eyed youth could overcome, nor Hannibal cursed by parents, we ourselves are impiously bringing down, a generation of damned blood.]

Lucan, *Pharsalia* 1.27-32:

> Rarus et antiquis habitator in urbibus errat,
> horrida quod dumis multosque inarata per annos,
> Hesperia est, desuntque manus poscentibus arvis.
> Poenus erit; nulli penitus descendere ferro
> contigit; alta sedent civilis volnera dextrae.
> [If only a rare inhabitant wanders among the ruins, if the fields lie fallow year after year, bristling with thorns and pleading in vain for the plough—who, pray, is to blame? Not Pyrrhus, not Hannibal! Neither of those proud antagonists succeeded in wounding Rome so deeply as she wounded herself. Only when brothers fall out is the sword driven home.]   [trans. Graves, pp. 25-26]

7 This reading of *Ant.* 21 is supported by the pervasive imagery of voyaging and shipwreck that runs throughout *Les Regrets*, always in reference to the speaker's own experience. Sonnet 26 is especially relevant.

> Si celuy qui s'appreste à faire un long voyage,
>   Doit croire cestuy la qui a ja voyagé,
>   Et qui des flots marins longuement oultragé,
>   Tout moite & degoutant s'est sauvé du naufrage,

Tu me croiras (Ronsard) . . .
  Puis que j'ay devant toy en ceste mer nagé,
  Et que desja ma nef descouvre le rivage.
Donques je t'advertis, que ceste mer Romaine
  De dangereux escueils & de bancs toute pleine
  Cache mille perils. . . .

Gilbert Gadoffre has discussed the theme of voyaging in this collection in *Du Bellay et le sacré* (Paris: Gallimard, 1978), pp. 121ff. Compare the "Elegia ad Janum Morellum," ll. 121–24: "Like the sailor caught by surprise on the Ionian sea, who has saved only the prow of his boat from shipwreck, I have steered as best I could through the waves, without experience of the ocean or maritime skill." The original Latin elegy can be found in Du Bellay, *Poésies*, ed. M. Hervier (Paris: Richelieu, 1954), 5:12–20.

8 Relevant elements of Du Bellay's mythopoeic vision are discussed in John C. Lapp, "Mythological Imagery in Du Bellay," *Studies in Philology* 61 (1964): 109–27. Images and concepts of creation utilized by Du Bellay are discussed by Robert Valentine Merrill, *The Platonism of Joachim Du Bellay* (Chicago: University of Chicago Press, 1925), pp. 19–38.

9 Chamard 1:81, sonnet 64. Compare the account of creation in the "Chant de l'Amour et du Printemps" (Chamard 5:38):

Amour le premier des Dieux
Formant ceste masse ronde,
D'un discord melodieux
Lia les membres du monde.

Le ciel courbe il estendit
Dessus la terre abaissee,
Et la terre en l'air pendit
D'une rondeur balancee.

Compare also sonnet 9 of the "Treize Sonnetz de l'Honneste Amour," "L'aveugle Enfant, le premier né des Dieux" (Chamard 1:145), and the opening of the second "Hymne Chrestien" (5:407).

10 The passage (bk. 1, chap. 11) is based on Speroni but gives ample expression to the architectural metaphor that recurs so frequently in the *Deffence*. The interpolated Aesculapian allusion is already familiar to us.

Mais vous ne serez ja si bons massons (vous, qui estes si grands zelateurs des Langues Greque & Latine) que leur puissiez rendre celle forme que leur donnarent premierement ces bons & excellens architectes: & si vous esperez (comme fist Esculape des membres d'Hippolyte) que par ces fragmentz recuilliz elles puyssent estre resuscitées, vous vous abusez, ne pensant point qu'à la cheute de si superbes edifices conjoint à la ruyne fatale de ces deux puissantes monarchies, une partie devint poudre, & l'autre doit estre en beaucoup de pieces, les queles vouloir reduire en un seroit chose impossible."   [*Deffence*, pp. 79–80]

Other instances of the architectural metaphor in Du Bellay applied to literary composition can be found in sonnet 13 of the "Treize Sonnetz," *Les Regrets* 157 and 158, the

"Evocation . . . de Guynes" (Chamard 6:31–32), and the letter to Morel describing his poem "Tumulus Henrici II" and justifying his adoption there of a "Doric" rather than "Corinthian" style. Of the various poetic temples in Ronsard's poetry, one might cite the temple in honor of "Messeigneurs le Connestable et des Chastillons," Laumonier ed., 6:259.

11 The sonnet, "Avant qu'Amour, du Chaos otieux," is contained in the 1552 collection of the *Amours* (Weber, p. 34). The account of creation in the "Ode de la Paix, Au Roi" appears in lines 37–68, Laumonier ed., 3:5–7. From the preface to the *Franciade*:

> Les Poëtes . . . ne cherchent que le possible, puis . . . d'une petite cassine font un magnifique palais, qu'ils enrichissent, dorent et embellissent par le dehors de marbre, jaspe, et porphire, de guillochis, ovalles, frontispices et piedsdestals, frises et chapiteaux, et le dedans des tableaux, tapisseries eslevées et boffées d'or et d'argent. . . . Apres ils adjoustent vergers et jardins, compartimens et larges allées. [16:340]

Compare the passage in Bembo's *Prose della volgar lingua* likening those who labor to master dead languages but neglect their own to "men endeavoring to erect at great expense magnificent palaces gleaming with marble and wrought gold in some distant and lonely country, but in their own city dwell in miserable houses." (Italian text in Marti edition, p. 8.) Peletier du Mans uses conventional imagery when, in praising the *Aeneid*, he speaks of "tout le batiment si bien devisé, si bien fondé et en si belle assiette, qu'il contente l'oeil en toute la montre." *L'Art poëtique*, ed. A. Boulenger (Paris: Les Belles lettres, 1930). p. 206.

12 Baldassare Castiglione, *Il Libro del Cortegiano con una scelta delle Opere minori*, ed. B. Maier (Turin: U.T.E.T., 1964), p. 617.

13 Italian text in *Scritti d'arte del Cinquecento*, ed. Paola Barocchi (Milan and Naples: Ricciardi, n.d.), 2:1529.

14 "Fu tale questo studio, che rimase il suo ingegno capacissimo di poter vedere nella immaginazione Roma, come ella stava quando non era rovinata." Giorgio Vasari, *Opere*, ed. G. Milanesi (Florence: Sansoni, 1878), 2:338.

15 G. W. Hegel, *Philosophy of History*, trans. J. Sibree (New York: Dover, 1956), pp. 72–73.

16 "Io son per dimonstrar in questo libro la forma, e gli ornamenti di molti Tempii antichi, de'quali ancora si veggono le ruine, e sono da me ridotti in disegno: accioche si possa da ciaschuno conoscere da quel forma debbano, e con quali ornamenti fabricar le Chiese. Et benche d' alcuni di lora se ne vegga picciola parte in piede sopra terra, io nondimeno da quella picciola parte, considerato anco le fondamenta, che si sono potute vedere, sono andato conietturando quali dovessero essere, quando erano intiere." Andrea Palladio, *L'Archittetura* (Venice: Brogiollo, 1642), 4:4. English translation by N. Du Bois.

17 The *Antiquarie Prospettiche romane* is described by André Chastel, *Marsile Ficin et l'art* (Geneva: Droz, 1954), p. 155, n. 56.

18 Jean Lemaire de Belges, *Oeuvres*, ed. J. Stecher (Louvain: Lefever, 1882), 2:292. On the interest of the French Renaissance in ruins, see Françoise Joukovsky, *La Gloire dans la poésie française et néolatine du XVIe siècle* (Geneva: Droz, 1969), pp. 95–96, 150–51, 307ff.

19 The key sentence reads in Latin: "Nam congregare semper ligna, lapides, coementa, stultissimum videri potest, si nihil aedifices ex illis." The Latin text appears in *Il*

Rinascimento italiano, ed. E. Garin (Milan: Istituto per gli Studi di Politica Internazionale, n.d.), pp. 70-71.

20 George Hersey, unpublished paper kindly communicated to the author.

21 Expressed in a letter to Lorenzo de'Medici, quoted in Garin, *Il Rinascimento italiano*, pp. 51-52.

22 The "antre tenebreux" with its Cimmerian darkness is described in lines 37-43 (Chamard 3:5). For the arch, see lines 493-96, p. 25, and for the temple, lines 512-16, p. 26.

23 *Gargantua*, chap. 1.

24 *Paradise Lost*, 1.713-15.

25 Michel de Montaigne, *Journal de voyage en Italie*, in *Oeuvres complètes*, ed. A. Thibaudet and M. Rat (Paris: Pléiade, 1962), pp. 1212-13. In his essay "De la vanité," pp. 975-76, Montaigne pays a more traditional homage to ancient Rome and its ruins. A study of his relation to antiquity would reveal him to be no less *ondoyant* in this matter than in others. In his "Defence de Seneque et de Plutarque," Montaigne wrote that his book was pieced together from fragments of these two authors: "La familiarité que j'ay avec ces personnages icy, et l'assistance qu'ils font à ma vieillesse et à mon livre massonée de leurs despouilles, m'oblige à espouser leur honneur" (p. 699).

For Rome as its own tomb, compare the line in Du Bellay's "Romae Descriptio": "Ipsaque nunc tumulus mortua sui est."

26 Dora and Erwin Panofsky argue that the arresting painting by Jean Cousin, *Eva Prima Pandora*, in the Louvre was originally intended to be a *Roma Prima Pandora*. Part of their argument depends on this sonnet. In the painting, dated by the Panofskys around 1550, Eva/Roma has left open the lid of the red urn containing forms of evil, thus allowing them to prey upon men. This discussion appears in *Pandora's Box* (London: Routledge and Kegan Paul, 1956), pp. 62ff.

Chapter 12. Wyatt: Erosion and Stabilization

1 *Caxton's own Prose*, ed. N. F. Blake (London: Deutsch, 1973), pp. 128-29.

2 Ibid., pp. 78, 80.

3 *Virgil's Aeneid*, translated into Scottish verse by Gavin Douglas, ed. D. F. C. Coldwell (Edinburgh: Blackwood, 1957), vol. 2, bk. 1, ll. 142-43.

4 Coldwell discusses Douglas's anachronisms in the introduction to his *Selections from Gavin Douglas* (Oxford: Clarendon, 1964), pp. vii-viii.

5 These two epigrams have heretofore been regarded as one, and are so printed in the edition of More's Latin epigrams by Bradner and Lynch. Daniel Kinney however argues persuasively that lines 13-26 of epigram 177 in that edition constitute a separate poem. See his article, "More's Epigram on Brixius' Plagiarism: One Poem or Two?" *Moreana*, no. 65 (1981): 37-44.

6 *The Latin Epigrams of Thomas More*, ed. L. Bradner and C. Lynch (Chicago: University of Chicago Press, 1953), epigram 177 ll. 23-26. Translation by Daniel Kinney, "More's Epigram."

7 ". . . purpureos aliorum pannos hinc atque inde insutos illi tuo crassissimo bardocucullo." *The Correspondence of Sir Thomas More*, ed. E. F. Rogers (Princeton: Princeton University Press, 1947), Epistle 86, pp. 130-31. Richard Sylvester comments on this passage: "More's own literary principles emerge quite clearly as he castigates Brixius for lifting phrases from the classics without showing any awareness of the context from

which they came. . . . More's lesson . . . must surely run something like this: we must always ask whether or not the writer who tesselates his work with classical phrases is using them as real echoes that draw upon their original context to reinforce the new passage in which they appear" (R. S. Sylvester, "Thomas More: Humanist in Action," in *Essential Articles for the Study of Thomas More*, ed. R. S. Sylvester and G. P. Marc'hadour [Hamden, Conn.: Archon Books, 1977], p. 468).

8 More writes: "Ego igitur quum in te taxassem alia furto subrepta veteribus, alia perabsurde tractata, omnia denique sic abs te narrata, ut neque in rebus veritas esset, neque in verbis fides." *Correspondence*, Ep. 86, pp. 218–21. (I arraigned some elements in your poem which you snatched like a thief from the ancients, other elements which you handled most absurdly, and all the elements which you narrated in such a way that there was neither truth in the matter nor credibility in the words.) Translation by Daniel Kinney, who comments: "Inattention to *fides rerum*, a discreditable scorn for his own real historical context, has made it inevitable that Brixius' own choice of words should lack *fides*, or 'credit,' in much the same way that his style of retelling the facts does: in denying the historical reality of the gulf between Classical poets and himself, Brixius makes it impossible for himself to achieve enough critical distance from his models to determine just what in their style he should imitate and what he should avoid." ("More's Epigram," p. 42).

9 Quotations from Wyatt's poetry are taken from *Collected Poems of Sir Thomas Wyatt*, ed. K. Muir (Cambridge, Mass.: Harvard University Press, 1950). I have modernized the usage of u, v, i, and j. The number in parenthesis following each quotation refers to the numbering of this edition. The passage here quoted is from 96, "In Spayne," ll. 15–16. We still lack a definitive text for Wyatt and doubtless will never see all the questions pertaining to his canon resolved. The most sensible solution so far to this latter problem seems to me incorporated in the edition of the modernized text by R. A. Rebholz: Sir Thomas Wyatt, *The Complete Poems* (Baltimore: Penguin, 1978).

10 Quoted in *Collected Poems of Sir Thomas Wyatt*, ed. K. Muir and P. Thomson (Liverpool: Liverpool University Press, 1969), p. 436.

11 This distinction holds in my view even if Patricia Thomson is correct in taking Chaucer's "Balade de Bon Conseyl" as a subtext of Wyatt's poem in her article "Wyatt's Boethian Ballade," *Review of English Studies* 15 (1964): 262–67. I argue below that the values expressed in Chaucer's ballade are essential for understanding Wyatt.

12 This poem is discussed and compared to other English versions of the same Senecan chorus by H. A. Mason, *Humanism and Poetry in the Early Tudor Period* (London: Routledge and Kegan Paul, 1959), pp. 181–86.

13 Otto Hietsch, *Die Petrarcaübersetzungen Sir Thomas Wyatts* (Vienna and Stuttgart: Braunmuller, 1960). Among the many other discussions of the Petrarch–Wyatt relationship, the following are particularly full: Sergio Baldi, *La Poesia di Sir Thomas Wyatt* (Florence: Le Monnier, 1953); Patricia Thomson, *Sir Thomas Wyatt and his Background* (Stanford University Press, 1964); D. L. Guss, *John Donne, Petrarchist* (Detroit: Wayne State University Press, 1966). The notes to the relevant poems by Thomson in the Muir-Thomson edition are especially helpful.

14 The fact that Wyatt is here translating a madrigal by Dragonetto Bonifacio makes his song no less characteristic of his own poetic temper. Wyatt chose to English this poem in preference to others.

15 Hietsch, *Die Petrarcaübersetzungen Wyatts*, p. 72.

16 Thomson's note to line 9 accuses Wyatt of missing Petrarch's point. but she seems rather to have missed Wyatt's.

17 Rebholz edition, p. 454. Rebholz's analysis is indebted to Mason's, *Humanism and Poetry*, pp. 206-21.

18 Thomson's note comments on the phrase "in the feld:" "Wyatt's addition is not altogether appropriate, since Love has fled from the battle." I take this phrase to refer not to the battlefield but to military life in the open air, without the protection from the elements of a "residence."

19 For a fuller discussion of this word and an analysis of its importance in another medieval work, see K. A. Burrow, *A Reading of "Sir Gawain and the Green Knight"* (New York: Barnes and Noble, 1966), pp. 42ff.

20 "Truth is as precious a jewel as our dear Lord Himself." Passus I, ll. 85, 87. Holy Church continues to praise this virtue. The excerpts cited below (ll. 88-91, 94-101) are given in the translation of J. F. Goodridge (Baltimore: Penguin, 1959), p. 72.

> He who speaks nothing but the truth, and acts by it, wishing no man ill, is like Christ, a god on earth and in Heaven—those are Saint Luke's words. . . . And kings and nobles should be Truth's champions: they should ride to war and put down criminals throughout their realms, and bind them fast till Truth has reached a final verdict on them. That is clearly the proper profession for a knight—not merely to fast one Friday in a hundred years, but to stand by every man and woman who seeks plain truth, and never desert them for love or money.

21 Kenneth Muir, *The Life and Letters of Sir Thomas Wyatt* (Liverpool: Liverpool University Press, 1963), p. 38. Thomson, *Sir Thomas Wyatt*, p. 37, quotes the poet's father on receiving the news of his son's imprisonment in 1536: "If he be a true man, as I trust he is, his truth will him deliver."

22 Sir Thomas Wyatt, *Collected Poems*, ed. J. Daalder (London: Oxford University Press, 1975), p. 18.

23 In the editions by Muir and by Muir and Thomson, a semicolon is placed after "aggreable." This is removed by Daalder and Rebholz, I think correctly.

24 The commentary and edition of Petrarch's *Canzoniere* by Giovanni Andrea Gesualdo, published in 1533, presents sonnet 190 as the description of an "amorosa caccia." It is uncertain whether Wyatt had seen this edition when he composed "Who so list." Thomson has discussed his relation to the various commentaries on the *Canzoniere* in "Wyatt and the Petrarchan Commentators," *Review of English Studies* 10 (1959): 225-33.

It is perhaps worth noting that the *impresa* of Lucrezia Gonzaga portrayed a white hind under a laurel with the motto "Nessun mi tocchi." See A. Salza, *Luca Contile* (Florence: Carnesecchi, 1903), p. 214.

25 Alastair Fowler writes: "Even if 'Who so list to hunt' belongs to a love-complaint sub-genre with a Petrarchan tradition, Wyatt was free to modify its individual types. He could use or ignore its forms, to make a distinct work in neither obedience nor reaction to Petrarch. What matters is the poetic use to which Wyatt puts his material and his forms, whether Petrarchan or other" (*Conceitful Thought: The Interpretation of English Renaissance Poems* [Edinburgh: Edinburgh University Press, 1975], p. 4). Wyatt was certainly free to modify, but once he chose his subtext, he was not free not to react. He was not committed to obedience, but once he had made an allusion to the

well-known poem by Petrarch a constitutive element of his own, he *was* committed to some form of reaction.

26 Horace, *Satires*, 2.5, 75-76, 93-98.

Chapter 13. Accommodations of Mobility in the Poetry of Ben Jonson

1 One easy way to measure this importance is to consult Vives's name in the index of T. W. Baldwin's survey, *William Shakespere's Small Latine and Lesse Greeke*, 2 vols. (Urbana: University of Illinois Press, 1944).

2 *Joannis Ludovici Vivis Valentini Opera omnia*, 8 vols. (Valencia: Monfort, 1782-90; repr. London: Gregg, 1964), 6:389. The English text is from *Vives: On Education*, trans. Foster Watson (Cambridge: Cambridge University Press, 1913), p. 232. References are to these editions.

3 "No art or discipline was ever conceived at the beginning in such unblemished condition that it did not have a mixture of useless and perishable waste. The powers of human nature never produce something perfect and complete; there is always something missing to the peak of possible perfection" (Quoted by Carlos G. Noreña, *Juan Luis Vives* [The Hague: Nijhoff, 1970], p. 150). Latin text in *Opera omnia*, 6:16.

4 *Ben Jonson*, ed. C. H. Herford, Percy and Evelyn Simpson, 11 vols. (Oxford: Clarendon Press, 1925-51), 8:567. Future quotations from Jonson will be taken from this edition; references will indicate the volume and page.

5 Quoted by Noreña, *Vives*, p. 161. *Opera omnia*, 6:61.

6 Roger Ascham, *The Schoolmaster*, ed. L. V. Ryan (Ithaca, N.Y.: Cornell University Press, 1967), p. 115. In the case of Ascham I have decided to alter my practice of quoting Renaissance authors in the original spelling, since Ascham is not a poet and since sixteenth-century spelling would impose a misleading quaintness on his prose for many modern readers.

7 Ibid., p. 140.

8 Ascham criticizes Ricci's treatise on imitation for stopping short of the detailed, exhaustive comparisons that would really illuminate the art of the imitator. Ricci might have cited a number of episodes in which Virgil follows Homer (Ascham lists them), and other briefer passages: ". . . as similitudes, narrations, messages, descriptions of persons, places, battles, tempests, shipwrecks, and commonplaces for divers purposes, which be as precisely taken out of Homer as ever did painter in London follow the picture of any fair personage. And when these places had been gathered together by this way of diligence, then to have conferred them together by this order of teaching: as, diligently to mark what is kept and used in either author in words, in sentences, in matter; what is added; what is left out; what ordered otherwise, either *praeponendo, interponendo*, or *postponendo*, and what is altered for any respect. . . . If Riccius had done this, he had not only been well liked for his diligence in teaching but also justly commended for his right judgment in right choice of examples for the best imitation" (Ibid., pp. 124-25; see also pp. 117-18).

9 Colet writes that the pupil at Saint Paul's school should "above all besyly lerne and rede good latyn authours of chosen poetes and oratours, and note wysely how they wrote, and spake, and study alway to folowe them, desyring none other rules but their examples." Colet goes on to state that rules and precepts are less useful to the pupil than reading,

listening, and "besy imitacyon with tongue and penne." From the "Accidence for the scholars of Saint Paul's," Appendix B of J. H. Lupton, *A Life of John Colet* (London: George Bell and Sons, 1909), pp. 291-92.

In 1560, Thomas Wilson wrote:

> Now, before we use either to write, or speake eloquently, wee must dedicate our myndes wholy, to followe the most wise and learned men, and seeke to fashion as wel their speache and gesturing, as their witte or endyting. The which when we earnestly mynd to doe, we can not but in time appere somewhat like them. For if they that walke in the Sunne, and thinke not of it, are yet for the most part Sunne burnt, it can not be but that they which wittingly and willingly travayle to counterfet other, must needes take some colour of them, and be like unto them in some one thing or other, according to the Proverbe, by companying with the wise, a man shall learne wisedome (*The Arte of Rhetorique*, ed. G. H. Mair [Oxford: Clarendon Press, 1909], p. 5).

10 On the formulary rhetoric, see Wilbur Samuel Howell, *Logic and Rhetoric in England, 1500-1700* (New York: Russell and Russell, 1961), pp. 138-45.

11 "An Apologie for Poetry," in *Elizabethan Critical Essays*, ed. G. G. Smith, 2 vols. (Oxford: Oxford University Press, 1937), 1:195.

12 Douglas Bush, *English Literature in the Earlier Seventeenth Century* (Oxford: Clarendon Press, 1962), pp. 107-08.

13 Quoted by Walter Ong, *Ramus, Method, and the Decay of Dialogue* (Cambridge, Mass.: Harvard University Press, 1958), p. 264.

14 Ong, *Ramus*, p. 222.

15 See Rosemond Tuve, *Elizabethan and Metaphysical Imagery* (Chicago: University of Chicago Press, 1947).

16 Gabriel Harvey, a convert to Ramism, offers a kind of *confiteor* in his *Ciceronianus*, an inaugural lecture to a course published in 1577: "I valued words more than content, language more than thought. . . . I believed that the bone and sinew of imitation lay in my ability to choose as many brilliant and elegant words as possible, to reduce them into order, and to connect them together in a rhythmical period. In my judgment . . . that was what it meant to be a Ciceronian." To be a true Ciceronian, Harvey said: "Consider not merely the flowering verdure of style, but much rather the ripe fruitage of reason and thought." Cited and translated by Howell, *Logic and Rhetoric*, pp. 251-52. Harvey blames his preceptors for the shortcomings of his literary outlook, and by extension the English educational system of his youth.

17 Morris W. Croll, *Style, Rhetoric, and Rhythm*, ed. J. M. Patrick et al. (Princeton: Princeton University Press, 1966); George Williamson, *The Senecan Amble* (Chicago: University of Chicago Press, 1951) and *Seventeenth Century Contexts* (Chicago: University of Chicago Press, 1961); Wesley Trimpi, *Ben Jonson's Poems: A Study of the Plain Style* (Stanford, Calif.: Stanford University Press, 1962); K. G. Hamilton, *The Two Harmonies* (Oxford: Clarendon Press, 1963).

18 "This kind of expression . . . hath bin deservedly despised and may be set down as a distemper of Learning." Francis Bacon, *De Augmentis Scientiarum*, in *Works*, ed. Spedding, Ellis, and Heath, 14 vols. (London: Longman, 1858-74), 1:452. The English translation was made by Gilbert Wats and published in 1640. Quoted by Croll, *Style, Rhetoric, and Rhythm*, p. 38, n. 40.

19 W. K. Wimsatt and Cleanth Brooks, *Literary Criticism: A Short History* (New York: Vintage Books, 1957), p. 158.

20 Samuel Daniel, *Poems and a Defence of Ryme*, ed. A. D. Sprague (Chicago: University of Chicago Press, 1965), p. 143.

21 In the masque *The Fortunate Isles, and their Union*, 7:719-21.

22 See F. Smith Fussner, *The Historical Revolution: English Historical Writing and Thought, 1580-1640* (New York: Columbia University Press, 1962); F. J. Levy, *Tudor Historical Thought* (San Marino, Calif.: Huntington Library, 1967); and especially Arthur B. Ferguson, *Clio Unbound: Perception of the Social and Cultural Past in Renaissance England*, Duke Monographs in Medieval and Renaissance Studies, no. 2 (Durham, N.C.: Duke University Press, 1979).

23 See my essay "Ben Jonson and the Centered Self," *Studies in English Literature* 10 (1970): 325-48.

24 Jonas Barish, "Jonson and the Loathed Stage," in *A Celebration of Ben Jonson*, ed. William Blissett et al. (Toronto: University of Toronto Press, 1973), pp. 30-31.

25 One can follow the process of substantivizing narrative in the simile elaborated by the *Discoveries* comparing the action of a poem to a house. Jonson begins by stressing the necessary unity of action, then veers away to speak of amplitude and proportion. "As for example; if a man would build a house, he would first appoint a place to build it in, which he would define within certaine bounds: So in the Constitution of a Poeme, the Action is aym'd at by the Poet, which answers Place in a building; and that Action hath his largenesse, compasse, and proportion. . . . So that by this definition wee conclude the fable, to be the imitation of one perfect, and intire Action; as one perfect, and intire place is requir'd to a building" (8:645). The effect of the comparison is to impose a spatial, static form on what might normally be regarded in temporal, sequential terms. This passage would appear to be original with Jonson. A later passage deriving from Heinsius uses the same analogy to make a different point: "For as a house, consisting of diverse materialls, becomes one structure, and one dwelling; so an Action, compos'd of diverse parts, may become one Fable Epicke, or Dramaticke" (8:648).

26 *Volpone* 3.7.211ff.

27 Harris Friedberg discusses Jonson's habitual testing of metaphor and distrust of analogy in "Ben Jonson's Poetry: Pastoral, Georgic, Epigram," *English Literary Renaissance* 4 (1974): 111-36.

28 "Jonson discovers a way of combining the energy of his fantasy-tormented characters with the artistic clarity and neatness of his simpler verse in those poems that exploit the figure of the poetic persona or the dramatic speaker." Arthur F. Marotti, "All about Jonson's Poetry," *English Literary History* 39 (1972): 208-37. Marotti discusses this art of combination on pp. 228-35.

29 Barish, "Loathed Stage," pp. 51-52.

30 Quotations from Martial and translations are taken from his *Epigrams*, trans. W. C. A. Ker, 2 vols. (Cambridge, Mass.: Harvard University Press, 1968). The poem cited is epigram 52 of book 11.

31 The metaphor of life as gift or loan is discussed by David Kay in his essay "The Christian Wisdom of Ben Jonson's 'On My First Sonne,' " *Studies in English Literature* 11 (1971): 125-36.

32 F. R. Leavis, *Revaluation: Tradition and Development in English Poetry* (London: Chatto and Windus, 1959), p. 21.

33 See especially Ian Donaldson, "Jonson's Ode to Sir Lucius Cary and Sir H. Morison," *Studies in the Literary Imagination*, 6, no.1 (April 1973): 139–52, and Richard S. Peterson, *Imitation and Praise in the Poems of Ben Jonson* (New Haven and London: Yale University Press, 1981), chap. 5.

34 Seneca, *Ad Lucilium epistulae morales*, trans. R. M. Gummere, 3 vols. (Cambridge, Mass.: Harvard University Press, 1970), 3:2–5.

35 Several of these exfoliating words are discussed in the fine chapter devoted to this ode by Peterson, *Imitation and Praise*.

36 The originality and importance of Spelman (1564?–1641) are discussed by J. G. A. Pocock, *The Ancient Constitution and the Feudal Law* (Cambridge: Cambridge University Press, 1957), chap. 5, and by Fussner, *Historical Revolution*, pp. 101ff. The following passage from Spelman's essay "Of Parliaments," quoted by Fussner, p. 104, illustrates his historicist outlook. "When States are departed from their original Constitution, and that original by tract of time worn out of memory; the succeeding Ages viewing what is past by the present, conceive the former to have been like to that they live in, and framing thereon erroneous propositions, do likewise make thereon erroneous inferences and Conclusions.... I desire for my understanding's sake to take a view of the beginning and nature of Parliaments; not meddling with them of our time ... but with those of old; which now are like the siege of Troy, matters only of story and discourse." Spelman essentially seeks to write historiography free of anachronistic superstition.

37 Leavis, *Revaluation*, p. 19.

38 "[Lectiones] sunt autem, ut existimo, necessariae, primum ne sim me uno contentus." *Epistulae morales*, 84.

Index

Absorption. *See* Assimilation; Digestive metaphor

Adamite language, in Dante, 4–5, 7, 11, 13, 87

Adult models, in ancient imitative theory, 54–56, 81–82. *See also* Models

Aemulatio. See Emulation

Aeschines, 65

Aesculapius, 165, 169, 235

Aesop, 246

Alamanni, Luigi, 246

Alberti, Leon Battista, 8, 148, 178, 233, 234, 296*n*11

Alcaeus, 69, 70

Alcibiades, 64

Alcuin, 81, 83; imitative theory of, 83–84; *Rhetoric,* 83–84, 309*n*7

Allegory: Christian, 105–06, 109, 110; English tradition of, 20; medieval, 22, 24, 25, 35, 96; in Petrarch, 94, 95, 105–06, 109–10, 127–28; in Ronsard, 210

Allusion, 50; Horatian, 67–72, 73, 74; and intertextuality, 16–19, 49, 50, 136, 138 (*see also* Intertextuality); repetition distinguished from, 49

Alonso, Dámaso, 315*n*7

Amphion theme, in Du Bellay, 229–33, 238

Amyot, Jacques, 32–33

Anachronism, 2, 8, 28–53; ancient theories on, 56, 57; classicistic, sixteenth-century debates on, 171–96; and humanism, 8, 9–10, 30, 33, 34–53, 154–55, 228, 235–36, 265, 292–93; in linguistic historicity, 9–11, 17, 30, 33; medieval, 8, 17, 18, 30, 35–36, 86, 87

Ancient imitation and imitative theory, 54–80, 81–83; adult models in, 54–56, 81–82; on anachronism, 56, 57; of Aristotle, 54, 55, 56, 59; assimilation in, 60–66, 74–76, 151, 154; of Cicero, 55, 60, 62–66, 78, 154; of Dionysius, 57–60, 79; education as model in, 54–56, 62, 81–82; vs. emulation, 58–59, 78, 79; and Greek decline, 56, 57, 66, 72–80; historical awareness in, 56, 57, 64, 66–67, 73, 76–77, 79–80; of Homer, 56; of Horace,

60, 67–72; of Isocrates, 55, 56, 59, 62, 64, 65; and linguistic historicity, 56, 57, 64, 66, 71, 73, 76; of Longinus, 78–79; of Macrobius, 82–83; metaphorization in, 59–60, 62, 67–72, 73–76; originality in, 70, 71; of Philodemus, 56–57; of Quintilian, 54–55, 60, 76–78; rhetorical, 56–57, 58, 60, 61, 62–66, 81; of St. Augustine, 81–82, 108; of Seneca the elder, 72–73, 75; of Seneca the younger, 73–76; of Theophrastus, 55–56; transitivity in, 66–72, 73, 76–78; of Virgil, 82–83. *See also* Antiquity; Greek imitation and imitative theory; Roman imitation and imitative theory

Annius of Viterbo, 236

Antiquity, 54–80; humanist awareness of, 8, 28–53, 57, 80, 88–99, 148, 233–38; and humanism, debates on, *see* Debates and quarrels, sixteenth-century; and humanism, unreliability of texts, 148–49, 156; imitative theories in, *see* Ancient imitation and imitative theory; and Middle Ages, 17, 28–30, 35, 81, 83–88; subreading texts of, 93–100, 131. *See also* Classicism; Greek imitation and imitative theory; Roman imitation and imitative theory; Rome

Apian metaphor, 84, 147; and assimilation, 74, 98–99; Lucretian-Horatian, 73–74; in Petrarch, 98–99, 199; in Ronsard, 199–200; in Seneca the younger, 73–74, 199

Apuleius, 45

Aquinas, St. Thomas, 13

Aquitaine, Guillaume d', 25

Archaeological metaphor, 44–45, 92, 93, 94, 229–38. *See also* Disinterment; Rome

Archilochus, 69, 70, 170

Architecture: Roman, Renaissance attitudes toward, 9, 44, 88–93, 175, 233–38, 240–41; themes on, in Du Bellay, 220–32, 238–41. *See also* Rome

Archpriest of Hita, 144

Arendt, Hannah, 314*n*8

Aretino, Pietro, 246, 251

339

DATE DUE

DEMCO 38-297